Windows Forensics Analyst Field Guide

Engage in proactive cyber defense using digital forensics techniques

Muhiballah Mohammed

<packt>

BIRMINGHAM—MUMBAI

Windows Forensics Analyst Field Guide

Group Product Manager: Pavan Ramchandani
Publishing Product Manager: Khushboo Samkaria
Book Project Manager: Ashwin Dinesh Kharwa
Senior Content Development Editor: Adrija Mitra
Technical Editor: Yash Bhanushali
Copy Editor: Safis Editing
Language Support Editor: Safis Editing
Proofreader: Safis Editing
Indexer: Subalakshmi Govindhan
Production Designer: Prafulla Nikalje
Senior DevRel Marketing Coordinator: Marylou De Mello
DevRel Marketing Coordinator: Shruthi Shetty

First published: October 2023

Production reference: 1290923

Published by Packt Publishing Ltd.
Grosvenor House
11 St Paul's Square
Birmingham
B3 1RB

ISBN 978-1-80324-847-9

www.packtpub.com

In loving memory of my mother, whose love, support, and guidance have shaped me into the person I am today. I dedicate this book to you, Mom. You were my first teacher, my best friend, and my biggest fan. You taught me the importance of hard work, compassion, and kindness. You always believed in me, even when I didn't believe in myself. I miss you every day, but I know that you are always with me in spirit. This book is a small way for me to honor your memory and share your love with the world. I hope that it will inspire others to be the best versions of themselves, just like you taught me to be. Thank you for everything, Mom. I love you, always.

To my dearest wife, this book is dedicated to you, my love. It is a testament to your love, support, and belief in me. I could not have written this book without you. You have been my biggest supporter throughout this journey, from the early days of brainstorming to the final edits. I am so grateful for your love and support. You are my best friend, my partner in crime, and the love of my life.

I love you, always and forever.

Muhiballah Mohammed

Contributors

About the author

Muhiballah Mohammed is a cybersecurity expert and enthusiast, experienced in security operations centers, digital forensics, and incident response. With 10 years of experience, he has worked in a variety of roles in the cybersecurity field, including SOC analyst, consultant, and forensic investigator, and has helped build multiple entities' SOC and DFIR teams. He has experience in investigating a wide range of cyber incidents.

Muhiballah is passionate about providing help to organizations so that they can protect themselves against cyber threats, and he is also a mentor and teacher to new students in the cybersecurity field. He loves sharing his knowledge and experience with others, and he is always looking for new ways to help people learn about cybersecurity.

I want to thank the people who have been close to me and supported me, especially my wife, my family, and my beloved SIC friends.

About the reviewers

Waleed Alanazi has a bachelor's degree in information systems from the Islamic University of Madinah. He has over 5 years of experience in digital forensics, incident response, and malware hunting. He is a former Cisco employee. Waleed was the first-place winner of a 2018 government hackathon and the 2023 DFIR NetWars from the SANS Institute. Waleed's areas of expertise include Windows forensics and incident response. He has had the privilege of working on incidents related to threat actors at the APT level. He can be found on Twitter at @D2Rz_, where he regularly shares his thoughts and insights on digital forensics and security.

I would like to express my sincere gratitude to my family and my friends, specifically, Muhiballah Mohammed, for giving me the opportunity to be a technical reviewer for this book. I hope that my contributions will help to make this book a valuable resource for the security community.

Mohammed El-Haddad is a seasoned cybersecurity professional with over a decade of experience in both cybersecurity and information technology. He possesses more than seven years of pure experience in cybersecurity operations center operations, management, incident response, and threat Intelligence. He is a results-driven leader who has successfully led and managed cross-functional teams of security professionals, ensuring the protection of critical assets and continuous improvement of security postures. Currently, he's employed as a full-time CSOC manager.

I'd like to thank my family, mentors, managers, and colleagues for their support, guidance, and belief in me. I would also like to extend a special thanks to my father, mother, and beloved wife for their boundless love, unwavering support, and selfless sacrifices that have shaped my path in immeasurable ways, and I am forever thankful.

Table of Contents

3

Memory Forensics for the Windows OS   65

4

The Windows Registry   103

5

User Profiling Using the Windows Registry   141

Part 2: Windows OS Additional Artifacts

6

Application Execution Artifacts   167

7

Forensic Analysis of USB Artifacts 189

8

Forensic Analysis of Browser Artifacts 207

9

Exploring Additional Artifacts 225

Preface

In the ever-changing digital world, where information is constantly flowing and our lives are increasingly digitized, the need for strong digital forensics skills is more important than ever. Welcome to *Windows Forensics Analyst Field Guide: Engage in proactive cyber defense using digital forensics techniques*, a comprehensive guide that explores the complex world of Windows digital forensics.

The digital age has changed our lives in many ways. We now can connect with people all over the world, have access to information at our fingertips, and can be more productive than ever before. However, this digital revolution has also created new challenges. Cyber threats and data breaches are on the rise, and it is more important than ever to be able to protect our digital data.

One way to protect our digital data is to understand the digital footprints we leave behind. Every time we use a computer or smartphone, we create a trail of data that can be used to track us, identify us, and even steal our identity. By understanding these digital footprints, we can take steps to protect our privacy and security.

The ability to uncover, analyze, and interpret digital traces is a valuable skill in the digital age. This skill is known as digital forensics, and it is used by law enforcement, businesses, and individuals to investigate cybercrimes, data breaches, and other digital incidents.

Join us as we embark on this compelling journey through the heart of Windows forensics. Together, we will uncover the truth hidden within digital landscapes and uphold the principles of justice, security, and integrity in our digital age.

Who this book is for

This book is for anyone who wants to learn about Windows-based digital forensics. It covers everything from the basics of the Windows operating system to the latest techniques for investigating digital evidence.

The book starts by introducing the Windows architecture, filesystems, and registry. It then discusses how to collect and preserve digital evidence from Windows systems. The book also covers the different types of digital evidence that can be found on Windows systems, such as user activity, application artifacts, and network interactions.

The book is full of practical examples and exercises, so you can learn by doing. It also includes a glossary of terms and a list of resources for further learning.

Whether you are a novice or a seasoned investigator, this book will give you the skills and knowledge you need to conduct successful Windows-based digital forensics investigations.

What this book covers

Chapter 1, Introducing the Windows OS and Filesystems and Getting Prepared for the Labs, covers an introduction to Windows forensics and the Windows operating system. It will also cover the main aspects of the Windows operating system.

Chapter 2, Evidence Acquisition, covers powerful tools utilized in triaging Windows evidence, such as KAPE and FTK Imager. We will learn how to set up a proper evidence acquisition process and use the tools that we have at our disposal to preserve digital evidence.

Chapter 3, Memory Forensics for the Windows OS, discusses how volatile data is considered a gold mine for digital forensics. We will learn how to preserve volatile evidence and deep dive into forensic analysis using volatility.

Chapter 4, The Windows Registry, covers the Windows registry, which is a hierarchal database that holds hardware and software settings, user preferences, and more. We will learn about this amazing artifact and how to analyze it using open source tools.

Chapter 5, User Profiling Using the Windows Registry, covers profiling system details using the Windows registry, which is a fundamental technique in digital forensics and system analysis. Investigators can gain valuable insights into the system's history, configuration, and user activities.

Chapter 6, Application Execution Artifacts, discusses how investigating execution evidence is considered a must in digital forensics and incident response. In this chapter, we dive into artifacts that play a pivotal role in investigations, helping forensic analysts reconstruct timelines, understand user interactions, and detect potential security incidents.

Chapter 7, Forensic Analysis of USB Artifacts, looks at USB devices, which are now essential tools for data storage and transfer. While their convenience is undeniable, their widespread use also poses challenges in the field of digital forensics. We will focus on tracking USB devices using multiple artifacts.

Chapter 8, Forensic Analysis of Browser Artifacts, discusses how as our lives become increasingly digital, web browsers have become the gateways to vast amounts of information, communication, and activity. We will cover multiple browsers and how to properly conduct an investigation.

Chapter 9, Exploring Additional Artifacts, provides an overview of additional artifacts that help forensic examiners to further examine an incident, such as the master file table and event logs. Our objective is to optimize the utilization of these resources.

To get the most out of this book

You will need a basic understanding of Windows operating system usage.

Software/hardware covered in the book	OS requirements
VMware Workstation (latest version)	Windows
FTK Imager	Windows

Each chapter has a *Technical requirements* section that mentions the tools needed along with links to download them.

Conventions used

There are a number of text conventions used throughout this book.

`Code in text`: Indicates code words in text, database table names, folder names, filenames, file extensions, pathnames, dummy URLs, user input, and Twitter handles. Here is an example: "We discussed `NTUSER.DAT`, which is a registry hive containing information about user activity, including the execution of programs and the use of various applications."

A block of code is set as follows:

```
kape.exe --tsource C:\ --tdest C:\ KAPE\output\ --target
!BasicCollection,Symantec_AV_Logs,Chrome,ChromeExtensions,
Edge,Firefox,InternetExplorer,WebBrowsers,ApacheAccessLog,
$Boot,$J,$LogFile,$MFT,Amcache,ApplicationEvents,EventLogs,
EventLogs-RDP,EventTraceLogs,EvidenceOfExecution,FileSystem,
MOF,Prefetch,RDPCache,RDPLogs,RecentFileCache,Recycle,RecycleBin,
RecycleBinContent,RecycleBinMetadata,RegistryHives,
RegistryHivesSystem,RegistryHivesUser,ScheduledTasks,SRUM
```

Any command-line input or output is written as follows:

```
PECmd.exe  -d C:\Windows\Prefetch --csv C:\temp --csvf Prefetch.csv
```

Bold: Indicates a new term, an important word, or words that you see onscreen. For example, words in menus or dialog boxes appear in the text like this. Here is an example: "What we notice here is that the **Values** tab holds data encoded in ROT-13. By clicking on the **UserAssist** tab, we can get the same details in human-readable format; you can also use decoding tools to decode the value as needed if that is required."

> **Tips or important notes**
> Appear like this.

Get in touch

Feedback from our readers is always welcome.

General feedback: If you have questions about any aspect of this book, mention the book title in the subject of your message and email us at customercare@packtpub.com.

Errata: Although we have taken every care to ensure the accuracy of our content, mistakes do happen. If you have found a mistake in this book, we would be grateful if you would report this to us. Please visit www.packtpub.com/support/errata, selecting your book, clicking on the Errata Submission Form link, and entering the details.

Piracy: If you come across any illegal copies of our works in any form on the Internet, we would be grateful if you would provide us with the location address or website name. Please contact us at copyright@packt.com with a link to the material.

If you are interested in becoming an author: If there is a topic that you have expertise in and you are interested in either writing or contributing to a book, please visit authors.packtpub.com.

Reviews

Please leave a review. Once you have read and used this book, why not leave a review on the site that you purchased it from? Potential readers can then see and use your unbiased opinion to make purchase decisions, we at Packt can understand what you think about our products, and our authors can see your feedback on their book. Thank you!

For more information about Packt, please visit packt.com.

Share Your Thoughts

Once you've read *Windows Forensics Analyst Field Guide*, we'd love to hear your thoughts! Scan the QR code below to go straight to the Amazon review page for this book and share your feedback.

https://packt.link/r/1803248475

Your review is important to us and the tech community and will help us make sure we're delivering excellent quality content.

Download a free PDF copy of this book

Thanks for purchasing this book!

Do you like to read on the go but are unable to carry your print books everywhere?

Is your eBook purchase not compatible with the device of your choice?

Don't worry, now with every Packt book you get a DRM-free PDF version of that book at no cost.

Read anywhere, any place, on any device. Search, copy, and paste code from your favorite technical books directly into your application.

The perks don't stop there, you can get exclusive access to discounts, newsletters, and great free content in your inbox daily

Follow these simple steps to get the benefits:

1. Scan the QR code or visit the link below

https://packt.link/free-ebook/9781803248479

2. Submit your proof of purchase
3. That's it! We'll send your free PDF and other benefits to your email directly

Part 1:
Windows OS Forensics and
Lab Preparation

In this part of the book, we will give an overview of the Windows operating system and learn how this amazing operating system works. In addition to this, you will learn the basics of the digital forensics process and how to set up a digital forensics lab environment and start acquiring evidence using open source tools. Also, we will dive into understanding the process of forensic acquisition and carry out a deep-dive analysis of collected artifacts in a forensic manner.

This part contains the following chapters:

- *Chapter 1, Introducing the Windows OS and Filesystems and Getting Prepared for the Labs*
- *Chapter 2, Evidence Acquisition*
- *Chapter 3, Memory Forensics for the Windows OS*
- *Chapter 4, The Windows Registry*
- *Chapter 5, User Profiling Using the Windows Registry*

1
Introducing the Windows OS and Filesystems and Getting Prepared for the Labs

In our work and personal lives, we use multiple **operating systems** (**OSs**) on different devices, including our desktops, laptops, and smartphones, on a daily basis. To understand more about this concept, we will cover in-depth knowledge about what an OS is and then focus on the Windows OS, which is the most popular OS by far for personal and corporate needs.

In the world of technology, Windows has become the leading OS for PCs and other devices. Thus, having a comprehensive understanding of this OS and the insights it can provide during digital forensic investigations is crucial. This chapter aims to provide an overview of the fundamental concepts of digital forensics and incident response in the context of Windows OS. Moreover, the chapter also explores the concept of **Volume Shadow Copy Service** (**VSS**) and its significance in digital forensics. VSS is a crucial feature of Windows OSs that enables the creation of shadow copies of files and folders at a particular point in time. As a result, VSS serves as an essential source of information for forensic investigators, allowing them to reconstruct events and gather evidence from a particular moment in time.

Understanding the basic concept of OSs will significantly aid in gaining knowledge of what we are investigating as forensic examiners and what value we get from these artifacts.

In this chapter, we will cover the following topics:

- What is a Microsoft OS?
- The modern Windows OS and filesystems
- Digital forensics and common terminology
- Windows VSS
- Preparing a lab environment

Technical requirements

In this chapter, we are going to prepare our environment for labs, so we need to be able to install a trial version of **VMware** or **Oracle VirtualBox** and an ISO file for **Windows 10**.

VMware is available here: `https://www.vmware.com/mena/products/workstation-pro/workstation-pro-evaluation.html`.

VirtualBox is available here: `https://www.oracle.com/sa/virtualization/technologies/vm/downloads/virtualbox-downloads.html`.

The Windows OS ISO is available here: `https://www.microsoft.com/en-gb/software-download/windows10`.

> **Important note**
>
> For lab preparation, if you are proceeding with the VMware product, please use the free 30-day trial or a legitimate product key.

What is a Microsoft OS?

As a forensic examiner, understanding the concept of an OS is crucial. Microsoft announced Windows for the first time on November 10, 1983, as a **graphical user interface** (**GUI**) that provided users with a friendly interface and layer to interact with the command-line-based **MS-DOS** code that was released previously. This started a new era for user interfaces and made it easy for people who did not know how to interact with a **disk operating system** (**DOS**) to work and learn with computers.

According to the latest articles and research, a Windows OS is installed on almost 76% of devices across the globe (desktop and laptop). The desktop OS market share is illustrated in *Figure 1.1*:

Market Share OS

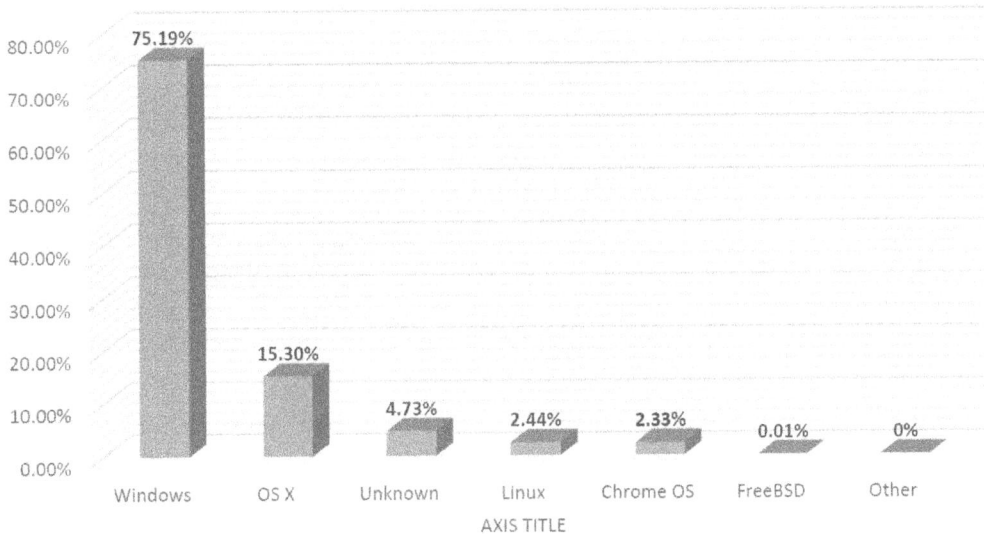

Figure 1.1 – Desktop OS market share

As we can see in the preceding chart, Microsoft OSs dominate the market for desktops and laptops. Microsoft developed multiple versions of the Windows OS including **Windows NT**, **Windows NT 3.1**, and most famously, **Windows XP**, to name a few.

We now know that the Windows OS is one of the most widely used OSs in the world, providing an interface between the user and the computer hardware. The main components of the Windows OS are the kernel, drivers, system utilities, and user-mode components. In this part of the book, we will take a closer look at each of these components and their roles in how the Windows OS functions:

- **Kernel**: The kernel is the core component of a Windows OS. It is responsible for managing the system's resources, such as memory, process scheduling, and input/output operations. The kernel also provides an interface between the user-mode components and the hardware. The Windows OS uses a hybrid kernel that combines the features of a microkernel and a monolithic kernel. The microkernel approach provides a small, secure, and stable kernel that is responsible for managing the basic system resources. The monolithic kernel approach provides a single, large, and complex kernel that is responsible for managing both basic system resources and more advanced features, such as device drivers.

- **Drivers**: Drivers are software components that allow an OS to interact with a computer's hardware. They act as intermediaries between the OS and the hardware, translating the requests from the OS into instructions that the hardware can understand. A Windows OS includes a wide range of drivers, including device drivers, filesystem drivers, and network drivers.

- **System utilities**: System utilities are software components that provide basic functionality to an OS. They are responsible for tasks such as disk defragmentation, disk cleanup, and system backup and restore. Some of the most commonly used system utilities in a Windows OS include Task Manager, Control Panel, and File Explorer.

- **User-mode components**: User-mode components are software components that provide a user interface to an OS. They allow users to interact with the OS and perform tasks such as creating, editing, and deleting files, launching applications, and accessing system settings. Some of the most commonly used user-mode components in the Windows OS include the **Start** menu, the desktop, and the taskbar.

- **Security component**: A Windows OS plays a critical role in protecting a user's data and the system itself from various threats such as viruses, malware, and hacking attacks. There are several security components and functionalities in the Windows OS that work together to provide a secure environment for users, such as the following:

  - **User Account Control (UAC)**: UAC is a feature in Windows OSs that helps prevent users from making unauthorized changes to the system by requiring them to enter their credentials beforehand. This helps prevent malicious software from making unauthorized changes to the system, such as installing malware or modifying system settings.

  - **Windows Defender**: Windows Defender is a built-in antivirus software that provides real-time protection against malware and other threats. It uses a combination of signature-based detection and heuristics-based detection to identify and remove malware, and it also provides regular updates to keep its threat definitions up-to-date.

  - **Windows Firewall**: The Windows Firewall is a network security system that helps protect a system from unauthorized access by controlling incoming and outgoing network traffic. It provides a range of configuration options, including the ability to block incoming traffic, allow outgoing traffic, and create rules to allow or block specific traffic.

  - **BitLocker**: BitLocker is a full-disk encryption feature that helps protect user data by encrypting an entire hard drive. It provides a secure environment for sensitive data and helps prevent unauthorized access to data if a system is lost or stolen. This is one of the challenges we face as forensic investigators; if an acquired image is encrypted, then a decryption key is needed to perform memory forensics.

  - **Security Accounts Manager (SAM)**: SAM is a component of a Windows OS that manages user accounts and security policies. It is responsible for maintaining a database of user accounts and their associated security policies, such as password policies, account lockout policies, and access control lists.

- **Internet Explorer Security**: Internet Explorer is the default web browser in a Windows OS, and it includes several security features to help protect users while browsing the web. These features include security zones, which allow users to specify the level of security for different websites, and **ActiveX** controls, which help prevent malicious software from being installed on the system.

- **SmartScreen Filter**: SmartScreen Filter is a feature in a Windows OS that helps protect users from downloading and running malicious software by analyzing the contents of downloaded files and warning the user if the software is known to be malicious.

- **Windows Management Instrumentation (WMI)**: WMI is a set of tools and technologies that allow you to manage Windows-based computers. WMI can be used to automate administrative tasks, collect data about computers, and monitor computer health.

In addition to these main components, a Windows OS also includes a number of additional features and components such as the **registry**, the **filesystem**, and the **security model**. The registry is a database that stores information about the system configuration and the installed applications. The filesystem is responsible for organizing and managing files and directories on a computer's hard drive. The security model is responsible for enforcing the system's security policies and controlling access to the system's resources.

One of the key strengths of a Windows OS is its compatibility with a wide range of hardware and software. This is achieved through the use of device drivers, which allow the OS to interact with a wide range of hardware devices such as printers, scanners, and digital cameras. The Windows OS also includes support for a wide range of filesystems, including **New Technology File System (NTFS)**, **File Allocation Table (FAT)**, **Extensible File Allocation Table (exFAT)**, and **Resilient File System (ReFS)**, making it easy for users to access their files and data on different types of storage media.

Another important feature of a Windows OS is its user-friendly interface. The OS includes a range of GUI elements such as icons, windows, and menus that make it easy for users to navigate and interact with the system. The **Start** menu provides a central location to access system utilities and installed applications, while the desktop provides a convenient workspace for performing tasks and accessing files and folders.

Understanding the Windows OS and its filesystem is crucial for forensic investigators. With the knowledge gained from this chapter, investigators will be able to effectively collect and analyze digital evidence.

In the next main section, we will delve into the history of the Windows OS, exploring its various versions and features and how they have evolved over time. This knowledge will provide a solid foundation for understanding the inner workings of the OS, which is essential for conducting thorough digital investigations.

The modern Windows OS and filesystems

In this section, we will cover multiple OSs introduced by Microsoft, as previously mentioned.

Windows XP

Windows XP is a widely used and well-known OS developed by Microsoft Corporation. It was first released on August 24, 2001, and was available in both Home and Professional editions. Windows XP was the successor to the popular Windows 98 and Windows 2000 OSs and was the first OS to feature the now-iconic **Windows Start** button and taskbar.

One of the most significant changes in Windows XP was its user interface. The new user interface was designed to be more user friendly and intuitive, making it easier for users to access and use their applications and files. The new interface included a **Start** button and taskbar that allowed users to quickly access their applications and files without having to navigate through complex menus. The **Start** menu was also redesigned to be more efficient and organized, with the ability to be customized by adding and removing items.

A significant additional feature of Windows XP was its improved support for hardware and software. Windows XP was designed to work well with new hardware technologies such as USB devices, digital cameras, and other multimedia devices. It also supported new software technologies such as **.NET Framework**, which allowed developers to create more powerful and sophisticated applications.

One more major change in Windows XP was its *security features*. Windows XP was designed to be more secure than previous versions of Windows, with improved support for firewalls, encryption, and other security features. It also included a built-in antivirus software called Windows Defender that helped protect users from malware and other security threats.

Another key feature of Windows XP was its *networking capabilities*. Windows XP was designed to be a more reliable and efficient network OS, making it easier for users to connect to the internet, networks, and other devices. It also included improved support for wireless networks, allowing users to easily connect to Wi-Fi networks and other wireless devices.

One of the most popular features of Windows XP was its *multimedia capabilities*. Windows XP was designed to be a more multimedia-friendly OS, with improved support for digital music and video, digital cameras, and other multimedia devices. It also included **Windows Media Player**, which allowed users to play music and videos, and **Windows Movie Maker**, which allowed users to create and edit their own videos.

Windows XP was also designed to be a more stable and reliable OS, with improved support for hardware and software. It included a number of performance improvements, such as faster boot times and improved system resource management, which helped make the OS more responsive and efficient.

Despite its many features and improvements, Windows XP was not without its flaws. Some users reported compatibility issues with older hardware and software, and the OS was also criticized for its security vulnerabilities, which were exploited by hackers and malware authors.

Despite these issues, Windows XP remained a popular OS for many years, with millions of users around the world relying on it for their daily computing needs. Microsoft continued to release updates and security patches for Windows XP, helping to address its security vulnerabilities and improve its performance.

We can say that Windows XP was a major milestone in the history of OSs, and its impact on the computing industry is still felt today. Its user friendly interface, improved hardware and software support, and multimedia capabilities helped make it one of the most widely used and well-loved OSs of all time. Although it has since been replaced by newer and more advanced OSs, Windows XP remains an important part of the computing world, and its legacy will continue to influence the future of OSs for years to come.

Windows Vista

Windows Vista, also known as Windows NT 6.0, was an advanced OS developed by Microsoft Corporation and released on January 30, 2007. It aimed to enhance the user experience, support newer hardware and software technologies, improve security and networking capabilities, and provide multimedia-friendly features to users.

One of the major changes in Windows Vista was its visually appealing user interface, which included the new **Aero** style with transparency and other visual effects. Additionally, Windows Vista improved support for new hardware and software technologies such as high-definition displays, multi-core processors, and the .NET Framework.

Moreover, Windows Vista was designed to be more secure than its predecessors, with enhanced support for firewalls, encryption, and security features such as UAC. UAC was a security feature introduced in Windows Vista. It was designed to help prevent unauthorized changes to the system by requiring user approval for any action that could potentially affect the system's configuration or security.

It also boasted efficient networking capabilities, making it easier for users to connect to the internet, networks, and wireless devices.

Furthermore, Windows Vista was a more multimedia-friendly OS, with improved support for digital music, videos, cameras, and other multimedia devices. It included Windows Media Player and Windows Movie Maker, which enabled users to play and edit music and videos.

Despite its many features and improvements, Windows Vista was not without its flaws. Some users reported compatibility issues with older hardware and software, and the OS was also criticized for its performance and resource requirements that were often higher than those of its predecessor, Windows XP.

Despite these issues, Windows Vista remained a popular OS for many years, with millions of users around the world relying on it for their daily computing needs. Microsoft continued to release updates and security patches for Windows Vista, helping to address its performance and security issues.

It was an important milestone in the history of OSs, and its impact on the computing industry is still felt today. Its user friendly interface, improved hardware and software support, and multimedia capabilities helped make it one of the most advanced and sophisticated OSs of its time. Although it has since been replaced by newer and more advanced OSs, Windows Vista remains an important part of the computing world, and its legacy will continue to influence the future of OSs for years to come.

Windows 7, 8 and 8.1

Windows 7 was a widely used OS developed by Microsoft Corporation, and it was released to the public on October 22, 2009. Windows 7 was designed to be an improvement on its predecessor, Windows Vista, with a number of new features and improvements designed to make it easier and more efficient to use.

One of the most significant changes in Windows 7 was its improved performance. Windows 7 was designed to be faster and more responsive than Windows Vista, with a more streamlined and efficient design. This improved performance was achieved through a number of changes, including the use of a new filesystem, improved memory management, better support for hardware and software, and an improved user interface. Windows 7 was designed to be more user friendly and intuitive than Windows Vista, with a more refined and polished look and feel. The new interface included a new taskbar that made it easier to switch between applications and access frequently used files and folders. Moreover, Microsoft enhanced security on Windows 7; it was designed to be more secure than Windows Vista, with improved support for firewalls, encryption, and other security features, which helped protect users from malicious software and other security threats by requiring them to confirm any actions that could potentially harm the system.

One of the most popular features of Windows 7 was its improved networking capabilities. Windows 7 was designed to be a more reliable and efficient network OS, making it easier for users to connect to the internet, networks, and other devices. It also included improved support for wireless networks, allowing users to easily connect to Wi-Fi networks and other wireless devices.

Another key feature of Windows 7 was its multimedia capabilities. Windows 7 was designed to be a more multimedia-friendly OS, with improved support for digital music and video, digital cameras, and other multimedia devices. It also included Windows Media Player, which allowed users to play music and videos, and Windows Movie Maker, which allowed users to create and edit their own videos.

Windows 7 also had important implications for forensic investigations. The OS created various forensic artifacts including registry hives, system files, and event logs, which could be used by forensic investigators to uncover valuable information and evidence. By examining these artifacts, forensic investigators could gain insights into a user's activities, identify any malicious software or security threats, and recover lost or deleted data.

The **Windows 8** and **8.1** versions were released on October 26, 2012, with significant changes, including a **Metro**-designed user interface and optimization of touch-based devices such as tablets, also start screen that display all of the app as titles, and more.

Windows 10

Windows 10 was introduced to users on September 30, 2014. This was one of the best OSs and received positive feedback from end users, and it brought back a desktop-oriented interface. It also introduced multiple system security features such as **multi-factor authentication (MFA)**.

This was a brief and general discussion about Windows OSs. We will not cover all aspects and features of OSs; however, you can check out Microsoft's documentation for further details.

> **Important note**
> In this book, we will focus on Windows 10 artifacts; however, the same analysis steps can be applied to artifacts of previous Windows OS versions.

Figure 1.2 shows the start menu and apps in the GUI of Windows 10.

Figure 1.2 – Windows 10 interface and Start menu

In the upcoming section, we will delve into the world of digital forensics and explore why this field is crucial for investigating and analyzing digital evidence.

Digital forensics and common terminology

In this section, we will delve into the basics of digital forensics by discussing the common terminology, types of investigations, and the overall process involved. This will deepen your understanding of a digital forensics life cycle and offer insights into each stage of the process. We will also take a closer look at how typical casework is carried out.

What is digital forensics?

Digital forensics, also known as computer forensics, is the branch of forensic science that deals with the preservation, collection, examination, and analysis of electronic data to investigate digital-related crimes and incidents. The goal of digital forensics is to uncover and recover evidence from digital devices such as computers, smartphones, and other electronic devices, and use this evidence in criminal and civil investigations.

Digital forensics is a multidisciplinary field that draws on expertise from various areas such as computer science, information technology, and law enforcement. Digital forensics experts use a variety of tools and techniques to perform their investigations including data acquisition, data analysis, and data visualization. They must be familiar with a wide range of OSs, software applications, and file formats, and must be able to navigate the intricacies of digital data storage and retrieval.

Digital forensics is used in a variety of contexts including cybercrime investigations, intellectual property disputes, civil litigation, and other legal proceedings. Digital evidence is often critical to the outcome of these cases, and digital forensics plays a key role in uncovering and preserving this evidence. Digital forensics is also used to determine the cause of security breaches and system failures, and to identify potential vulnerabilities in digital systems. In the modern era of technology, digital forensics is an important part of analyzing suspicious cybercriminal attacks with the objective of identifying them. The mitigation and eradication of threat actors is a critical aspect of the work performed by digital forensics and incident response engineers and consultants.

There are several types of computer forensics, each of which is used for specific purposes and requires different techniques and approaches. Some of the most common types of computer forensics include the following:

- **Criminal forensics**: Criminal forensics is a type of computer forensics that is used in the investigation of criminal activities such as cybercrime, hacking, identity theft, and other digital-related crimes. Criminal forensics focuses on uncovering and preserving evidence that can be used to prosecute the individuals responsible for these crimes.

- **Civil forensics**: Civil forensics is a type of computer forensics that is used in civil litigation such as intellectual property disputes, contract disputes, and other civil proceedings. Civil forensics focuses on uncovering and preserving evidence that can be used to support or refute a party's claims in a legal case.

- **Incident response forensics**: Incident response forensics is a type of computer forensics that is used to investigate and respond to security breaches and other incidents that impact the security and integrity of digital systems. Incident response forensics focuses on identifying the cause of the incident, assessing the extent of the damage, and developing a plan of action to prevent future incidents.

- **Network forensics**: Network forensics is a type of computer forensics that focuses on the examination of network traffic and system logs in order to uncover evidence of security breaches, cyberattacks, and other network-related incidents. Network forensics involves the use of specialized tools and techniques to capture and analyze network traffic, and to identify and track the source of the incident.

- **Mobile forensics**: Mobile forensics is a type of computer forensics that focuses on the preservation, collection, examination, and analysis of data stored on mobile devices such as smartphones and tablets. Mobile forensics is often used in criminal investigations but can also be used in civil and incident response forensics.

- **Live forensics**: Live forensics is a type of computer forensics that involves the collection and analysis of data from a live computer system while it is still running. Live forensics is often used in incident response forensics, and it is considered a critical component of the incident response process because it can provide valuable insight into the state of a system at the time of an incident.

- **Memory forensics**: Memory forensics is the branch of digital forensics that focuses on the examination of a computer's volatile memory, or RAM. The goal of memory forensics is to uncover information that is stored in memory and to use this information to assist in the investigation of digital crimes and incidents. Memory forensics can be used to uncover information about system processes, network connections, and malicious activity, and is considered a critical component of the digital forensics process because it can provide valuable evidence that would otherwise be lost if a system were shut down. Memory forensics requires specialized tools and techniques to capture and analyze data stored in memory, and it is often used in conjunction with other forms of digital forensics to provide a comprehensive understanding of a digital incident.

Regardless of the type of computer forensics, the process typically involves several key phases, including the following:

1. **Preservation**: The preservation phase involves the collection and preservation of evidence in a manner that ensures its authenticity and integrity. This often involves making a forensic image of the evidence and storing it in a secure location.

2. **Collection**: The collection phase involves the acquisition of evidence, which may involve the use of specialized tools and techniques to capture data from the source. The collection phase is critical to the success of the investigation, as it is important to collect as much evidence as possible in order to ensure a comprehensive examination.

3. **Examination**: The examination phase involves the analysis of evidence to uncover relevant information and identify potential sources.

The future of digital forensics is promising. The increasing reliance on digital technology in all aspects of our lives will continue to drive the need for forensics experts who can investigate and resolve digital crimes and incidents.

As technology continues to evolve, digital forensics will also need to adapt to new and emerging technologies. For example, **cloud computing**, the **Internet of Things (IoT)**, and **blockchain** will all present new challenges and opportunities for digital forensics experts.

Artificial intelligence and **machine learning** are also expected to play a major role in the future of digital forensics. These technologies can be used to automate the process of data collection and analysis, making it faster, more efficient, and more effective.

With the increasing number of digital crimes and incidents, the demand for digital forensics experts is expected to continue to grow in the coming years. This provides a bright outlook for those interested in pursuing a career in this field.

A **forensic analyst/examiner** should have a great detailed understanding of the operating system to be able to identify the proper evidence related to incident or case he is working on, and document his finding based on analyzed evidence.

While we are conducting an examination of forensic artifacts, the main goal is to investigate digital crime, which is an illegal activity committed using a digital device such as a PC or mobile device, and extract the evidence via a proper forensic process to present it. Also, the evidence extracted needs to be preserved with integrity; in some cases, the examiner might need to recover evidence such as deleted files to justify an action or point to a suspected criminal.

As a forensic examiner or analyst, it is important to have a comprehensive understanding of various aspects of digital forensics, including the following:

- **Technical knowledge**: A strong understanding of computer systems, software, and hardware is essential for a forensic examiner or analyst. This includes knowledge of OSs, filesystems, data storage, and networking concepts.

- **Legal knowledge**: Forensic examiners need to be familiar with the laws and regulations that govern digital forensics, including privacy laws, data protection laws, and intellectual property laws. They also need to understand how to preserve the chain of custody of digital evidence and how to present evidence in a court of law.

- **Investigative techniques**: Digital forensics is an investigative process, so it is important for forensic examiners to have a thorough understanding of the methods and techniques used in conducting a digital investigation. This includes knowledge of data collection, analysis, and preservation techniques, as well as the use of specialized tools and software.

- **Communication skills**: Digital forensics is a complex and technical field, so it is important for forensic examiners to have strong communication skills in order to effectively explain their findings to others. This includes the ability to translate complex technical information into layman's terms and to present findings clearly and concisely.

- **Professional ethics**: Digital forensics involves access to sensitive and confidential information, so it is important for forensic examiners to understand and adhere to professional ethics and standards. This includes being impartial and unbiased in their analysis, maintaining confidentiality, and protecting the privacy of individuals.

- **Continuing education**: Technology is constantly evolving, so it is important for forensic examiners to stay up-to-date with the latest developments and techniques in the field. This requires a commitment to ongoing learning and professional development.

By developing a deep understanding of these key areas, forensic examiners and analysts can become effective and professional in their work, contributing to the advancement of the field of digital forensics and providing valuable support to law enforcement and organizations in the fight against cybercrime.

> Cybercriminals
>
> Cybercriminals are individuals or groups who engage in illegal activities using digital technology. They use the internet, computer systems, and other digital technologies to carry out a variety of crimes including hacking, identity theft, fraud, extortion, and intellectual property theft. These individuals often operate in secret, making it difficult to detect and prevent their criminal activities. They can target individuals, organizations, and even entire governments, and can cause significant harm by stealing sensitive information, disrupting critical systems, or causing financial losses.

Digital forensic terminology

When working as a forensic examiner, you will, on a daily basis, encounter people talking about certain terms when it comes to investigation. Understanding the terminology helps us as examiners to communicate properly – for example, when we talk about a forensic image, what do we mean? Do we need a full image or a triage image? What are SSD and HDD?

In this section of the book, we will cover most of these terms. The following table lists some useful keywords for a digital forensic analyst:

Keyword	Description
Acquisition	The stage in a computer forensics investigation where the data involved is collected
Allocated space	The logical area on a hard disk or other media assigned to a file by the OS
Bit	The smallest unit of measurement used to quantify digital data
Bit-by-bit copy	A copy of every consecutive sector on a hard disk or other media, without regard to the allocation of data
Chain of custody	A detailed record of the handling and control of digital evidence from the time it is collected until it is presented in court; used to demonstrate the authenticity and integrity of the evidence and to establish the credibility of the investigation
Disk mirroring	When data is copied to another hard disk or another area on the same hard disk in order to have a complete, identical copy of the original
File carving	A process used to recover files and data from unallocated disk space or damaged filesystems; involves identifying and extracting complete files based on their unique file headers and footers
File format	The structure by which data is organized in a file
Forensic image	A forensically sound and complete copy of a hard drive or other digital media
Hash value	The numerical value of a fixed length that uniquely identifies data
Live analysis	The process of performing an on-the-spot analysis of digital media, rather than switching it off and shutting it down
Metadata	Data that is stored in a filesystem or the header of a file, and provides information about the file
Registry hives	Subfiles that make up a Windows registry; individual Windows user settings and some histories of usage are kept in various hives and can be updated as a computer is used
Steganography	Hiding information within a seemingly ordinary message so that only the intended recipient knows of its existence
Unallocated space	The free space on a hard drive that can be used to store data
Write block	Hardware and/or software methods to prevent the modification of content on a media storage unit, such as a CD or thumb drive

Table 1.1 – Terminologies for digital forensics

> **Important note**
> We will cover forensic artifacts of Windows separately in upcoming chapters. Each artifact will be explained and analyzed, so be prepared to be amazed by how rich Windows is when it comes to artifacts.

To become a great digital forensics examiner, you need to have a strong foundation in informatics and computer science. Many people, like me, started their careers on helpdesks, as computer technicians, or in IT security, where they gained familiarity with some of the tools needed to recover data. If you have similar experience, this book will help you prepare for your dream career as a digital forensics investigator.

The process of digital forensics

Like any other science branch, digital forensics has its own processes and procedures to follow. The following is a brief explanation of each step:

1. **Identification**: This is the first step in the digital forensics process and involves identifying the need for a digital forensics investigation. This may be the result of cybercrime, such as hacking or data theft, or it may be part of a larger investigation, such as an internal audit or compliance review.

2. **Preparation and preservation**: Before conducting any type of digital forensics investigation, it is important to prepare and plan for the process. This includes identifying the goals of the investigation, determining the scope of the investigation, and obtaining the necessary resources and equipment. It is also important to preserve evidence in its original form. This includes making copies of data and storing it in a secure and tamper-proof manner.

3. **Collection and evidence seizure**: This is the first step in the actual investigation process. The goal of this phase is to preserve the evidence and prevent any potential modification or destruction of data. This can involve seizing physical devices, such as computers and storage media, or collecting data from a remote source, such as a cloud service.

4. **Examination and analysis**: In this phase, the forensic examiner will examine the collected data in detail in order to identify relevant information and evidence. This may involve the use of various tools and techniques, including file carving, data extraction, and data analysis.

5. **Documentation and presentation**: In some cases, a forensic examiner may be required to present their findings in a court of law or other legal proceedings. This requires clear and concise communication skills and the ability to explain complex technical information in a way that is easily understandable to non-technical audiences.

When conducting an investigation using the aforementioned process, taking detailed notes of each step and action is critical to ensuring that the evidence is not tampered with. Additionally, if another examiner is collaborating with you during the investigation, having detailed notes can facilitate effective communication and ensure that everyone is on the same page.

The five key steps of this process are illustrated in *Figure 1.3*:

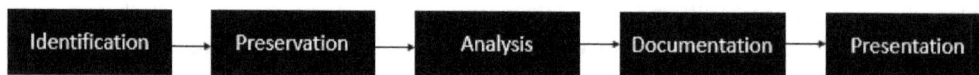

Figure 1.3 – Digital forensics process steps

Digital evidence

Digital evidence can be any form or type of digitalized file or media from an electronic source, including logs, files, social media posts, and much more.

Conducting a forensic examination requires knowledge of the technical concepts of digital evidence, such as computers. You need to know the main components and how they are structured, as well as the type of digital media to handle the evidence. In this book, we will cover some technical theory before jumping into practical analysis for each evidence type.

Some of the digital evidence types are as follows:

- **User activity generated in an endpoint**
- **Documents and text files**
- **Audio and video files**, including CCTV
- **Digitalized images**
- **Security control logs**, such as IDS and PCAP
- **Digital file metadata**

For example, let's take metadata, which is data about data. Most digital files hold valuable information that adds forensic value to an investigation, such as who created a file, owner information, and creation time, as we can see in the following screenshot, which illustrates the use of **ExifTool**, which displays metadata for a file:

```
ExifTool Version Number        : 10.43
File Name                      : gkape.exe
Directory                      : .
File Size                      : 60 MB
File Modification Date/Time    : 2021:11:16 21:10:32+00:00
File Access Date/Time          : 2021:11:16 21:11:32+00:00
File Creation Date/Time        : 2021:11:16 21:09:22+00:00
File Permissions               : rw-rw-rw-
File Type                      : Win32 EXE
File Type Extension            : exe
MIME Type                      : application/octet-stream
Machine Type                   : Intel 386 or later, and compatibles
Time Stamp                     : 2081:06:23 06:50:00+00:00
PE Type                        : PE32
Linker Version                 : 48.0
Code Size                      : 62711808
Initialized Data Size          : 375296
Uninitialized Data Size        : 0
Entry Point                    : 0x3bd070e
OS Version                     : 4.0
Image Version                  : 0.0
Subsystem Version              : 6.0
Subsystem                      : Windows GUI
File Version Number            : 1.1.0.1
Product Version Number         : 1.1.0.1
File Flags Mask                : 0x003f
File Flags                     : (none)
File OS                        : Win32
Object File Type               : Executable application
File Subtype                   : 0
Language Code                  : Neutral
Character Set                  : Unicode
Comments                       : Graphical tool to drive KAPE
```

Figure 1.4 – ExifTool output for an executable Kroll Artifact Parser and Extractor (KAPE)

With the fast growth in technology and types of digital evidence, when dealing with different types of incidents and cases, we need to focus on the most important type of evidence. When collecting digital evidence, an examiner needs to know that they can lose data once a system is shut down – in the case of a computer, for example. When responding to an incident, the most immediate priority should be collecting **volatile data**.

Volatile data refers to information that is stored in temporary memory and lost when a system is powered off. This includes data stored in a system's **random-access memory** (**RAM**) and any data that is being processed or temporarily stored in a cache.

Figure 1.5 – RAM sample image

Volatile data can include active system processes, network connections, and open files and applications. In a digital forensics investigation, capturing volatile data can provide valuable information about the state of a system at a specific point in time.

On the other hand, **non-volatile data** refers to information that is stored on a persistent storage device, such as a hard drive, which remains intact even when a system is powered off. Non-volatile data can include files, documents, images, and system configurations. In a digital forensics investigation, non-volatile data can provide a more comprehensive view of the system's history and activity.

It is important to note that while volatile data can be lost when a system is powered off, it can still be captured and analyzed through a process known as live analysis. This involves collecting data directly from a live system, without first creating a forensic image of the data. Live analysis is typically used in time-sensitive investigations or when it is not possible to obtain a forensic image of the data.

In digital forensics, it is critical to preserve and analyze both volatile and non-volatile data in order to obtain a complete picture of a system's activity and state. Volatile data can provide insight into the current state of the system, while non-volatile data can provide a historical view of the system's activity. By combining these two types of data, forensic examiners can build a more comprehensive and accurate picture of the system's behavior and any potential digital evidence.

In the upcoming chapters, we will talk about the acquisition of a memory image and how to perform analysis of a memory image.

In the next section, we will explore the concept of Windows Shadow Copy and its significance in digital forensics and incident response.

Windows VSS

VSS is a feature of Windows OSs that allows users to take snapshots of the state of their hard drive at a specific point in time. These snapshots, known as **shadow copies**, can be used to restore previous versions of files and directories in the event of data loss or corruption.

From a digital forensics perspective, volume shadow copies can be a valuable source of evidence. They provide a historical record of the state of the hard drive, including deleted and altered files. This information can be used to reconstruct the chain of events that occurred on the system and to identify any suspicious activity.

Volume shadow copies are stored as part of the VSS, which is a component of Windows that provides the functionality to create and manage shadow copies. VSS maintains a list of all shadow copies on a particular volume, allowing a user to select and restore the desired shadow copy.

One of the key benefits of volume shadow copies is that they are created automatically in the background, without the user's intervention. This means that even if a user is unaware of the feature, it can still contain valuable evidence. In addition, the shadow copies are stored in a hidden and protected area of the hard drive, making it difficult for attackers to tamper with or destroy them.

When conducting a digital forensics examination, it is important to capture and preserve shadow copies to ensure that evidence remains intact. This can be done by creating a forensic image of a hard drive, which can then be analyzed for the presence of shadow copies. Once the shadow copies have been identified, the forensic examiner can extract and analyze the contents to identify any relevant information.

By using VSS, we can track changes in an **New Technology File System (NTFS)** filesystem. However, it does not store data every time a user changes a file; instead, it typically stores data once a week or as configured by a user on the machine.

When conducting a digital forensic investigation and searching for any suspicious or malicious activity, such as file deletion, we can utilize the VSS to obtain valuable forensic evidence. By comparing the original content of the hard drive with that stored in VSS, we can determine whether any changes or tampering have occurred.

To check VSS on your local machine, you can run `CMD.exe` with admin privileges and use the following command to list the shadow copies:

```
Vssadmin list shadows
```

The following screenshot shows the output of the preceding command:

```
Administrator: Command Prompt

Microsoft Windows [Version 10.0.19044.2364]
(c) Microsoft Corporation. All rights reserved.

C:\WINDOWS\system32>vssadmin list shadows
vssadmin 1.1 - Volume Shadow Copy Service administrative command-line tool
(C) Copyright 2001-2013 Microsoft Corp.

Contents of shadow copy set ID: {c5ca2ae9-8842-42c9-9b86-b857d48de25c}
    Contained 1 shadow copies at creation time: 12/18/2022 8:35:17 AM
        Shadow Copy ID: {f72aac40-b40a-4357-ba03-d814b3fba6ed}
            Original Volume: (C:)\\?\Volume{f20b9e5c-c631-42f5-8bdd-83d4045e2047}\
            Shadow Copy Volume: \\?\GLOBALROOT\Device\HarddiskVolumeShadowCopy1
            Originating Machine: LAPTOP-SUD025L1
            Service Machine: LAPTOP-SUD025L1
            Provider: 'Microsoft Software Shadow Copy provider 1.0'
            Type: ClientAccessibleWriters
            Attributes: Persistent, Client-accessible, No auto release, Differential, Auto recovered

Contents of shadow copy set ID: {46c1353f-7c9b-41b8-91c6-ac63d6fb3510}
    Contained 1 shadow copies at creation time: 12/20/2022 9:38:05 AM
        Shadow Copy ID: {70bd011e-7754-4ef2-84a8-a0a8a1e83eaf}
            Original Volume: (C:)\\?\Volume{f20b9e5c-c631-42f5-8bdd-83d4045e2047}\
            Shadow Copy Volume: \\?\GLOBALROOT\Device\HarddiskVolumeShadowCopy2
            Originating Machine: LAPTOP-SUD025L1
            Service Machine: LAPTOP-SUD025L1
            Provider: 'Microsoft Software Shadow Copy provider 1.0'
            Type: ClientAccessibleWriters
            Attributes: Persistent, Client-accessible, No auto release, Differential, Auto recovered
```

Figure 1.6 – Vssadmin command output

Another useful trick is mounting a shadow copy using a Windows command line. On a live machine, we can manually mount and browse VSS data using the following `mklink` command, which creates a symbolic link to VSS. To do this, we need to invoke `cmd.exe` to use the `mklink` utility, as `powershell.exe` will not work:

```
mklink /d C:\shadow_copy_test \\?\GLOBALROOT\Device\
HarddiskVolumeShadowCopy1\
```

Create a symbolic link to VSS by using the following command line:

```
C:\Windows\system32>mklink /d C:\shadow_copy_test \\?\GLOBALROOT\Device\HarddiskVolumeShadowCopy1\
symbolic link created for C:\shadow_copy_test <<===>> \\?\GLOBALROOT\Device\HarddiskVolumeShadowCopy1\

C:\Windows\system32>
```

Figure 1.7 – Mounting a volume shadow using mklink

Now, in the C drive, we can see a new symbolic link has been created and linked to the shadow copy, and we can browse it as a normal file:

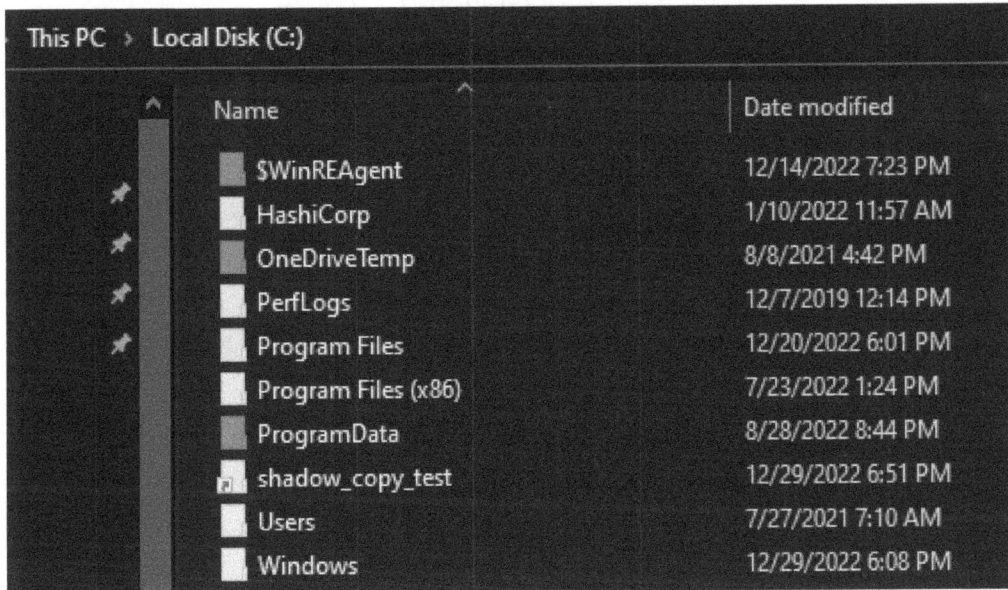

This PC > Local Disk (C:)	
Name	**Date modified**
$WinREAgent	12/14/2022 7:23 PM
HashiCorp	1/10/2022 11:57 AM
OneDriveTemp	8/8/2021 4:42 PM
PerfLogs	12/7/2019 12:14 PM
Program Files	12/20/2022 6:01 PM
Program Files (x86)	7/23/2022 1:24 PM
ProgramData	8/28/2022 8:44 PM
shadow_copy_test	12/29/2022 6:51 PM
Users	7/27/2021 7:10 AM
Windows	12/29/2022 6:08 PM

Figure 1.8 – Mapped shadow copy in the C drive

There are other utilities and tools that help to mount VSS, such as **Arsenal Image Mounter** and **VSCMount**; however, we will leave the option to you to explore more tools and test them within the labs.

In the next section, we will discuss and prepare the lab environment for digital forensic investigations.

Preparing a lab environment

To prepare for this book's exercises, we will work now on deploying a forensics lab with tools that we will utilize during our investigation of each artifact. In this section, we will show you how to install a VMware workstation to deploy our Windows OS (Windows 10).

Note that to prepare labs for this book, I will proceed and deploy a lab virtual machine on a VMware product; if you prefer to use VirtualBox, you can apply the same steps when installing Windows OS.

Let's start with installing **Workstation 17 Pro**:

1. Visit the following link to download the trial version of Workstation 17 Pro for Windows (this is the latest version available as of December 2022):

    `https://www.vmware.com/mena/products/workstation-pro/workstation-pro-evaluation.html`

2. Click on **DOWNLOAD NOW**; it will prompt you to save the executable file, as shown here:

Figure 1.9 – VMware Workstation download page

3. Now, double-click on the executable file and then click **Next**:

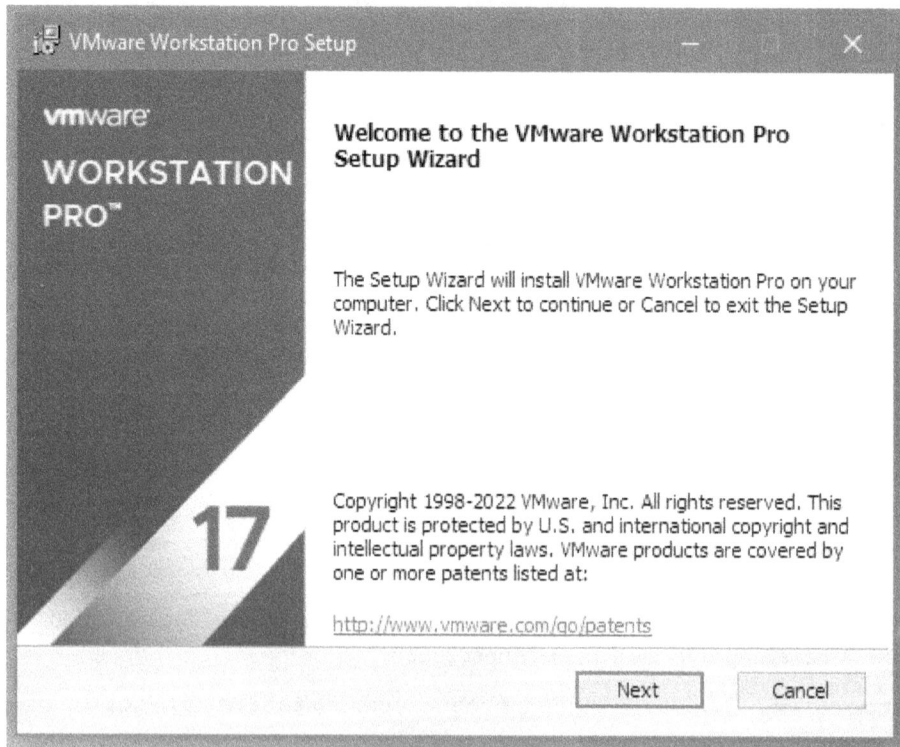

Figure 1.10 – VMware Workstation installation process – part 1

4. Once prompted for an end user license, accept it by checking the *free trial* option and then click **Next**. It will prompt you to select the path to install Workstation 17 Pro; click on **Next** once you have selected it:

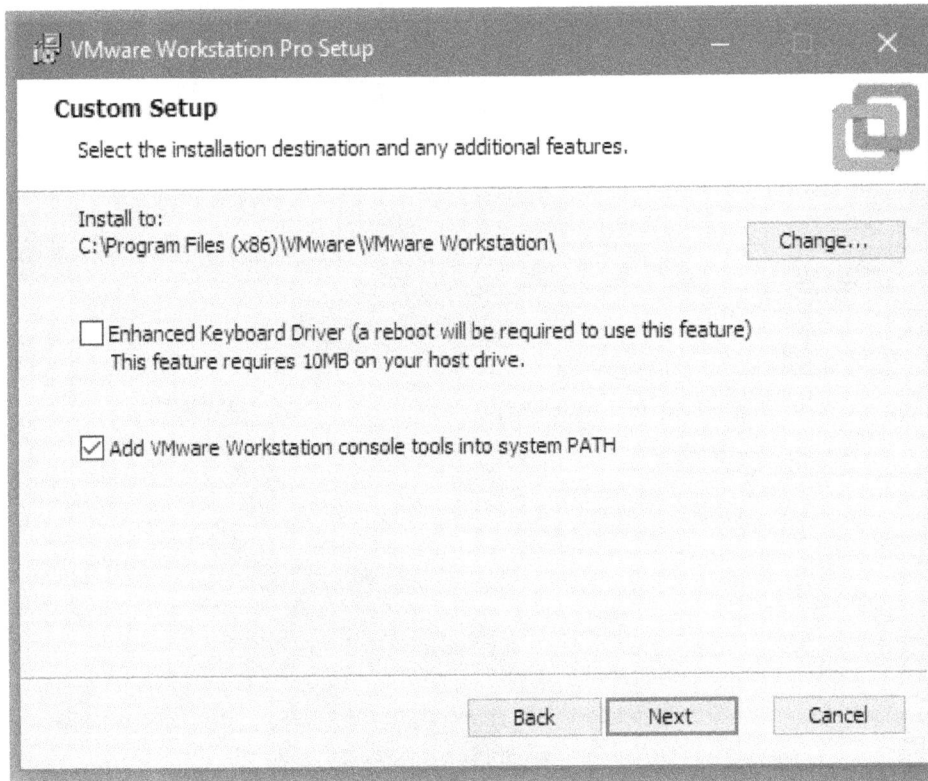

Figure 1.11 – VMware Workstation installation process – part 2

5. Select the **Desktop** and **Start Menu Programs Folder** options to create a shortcut or add a VMware workstation application to the **Start** menu:

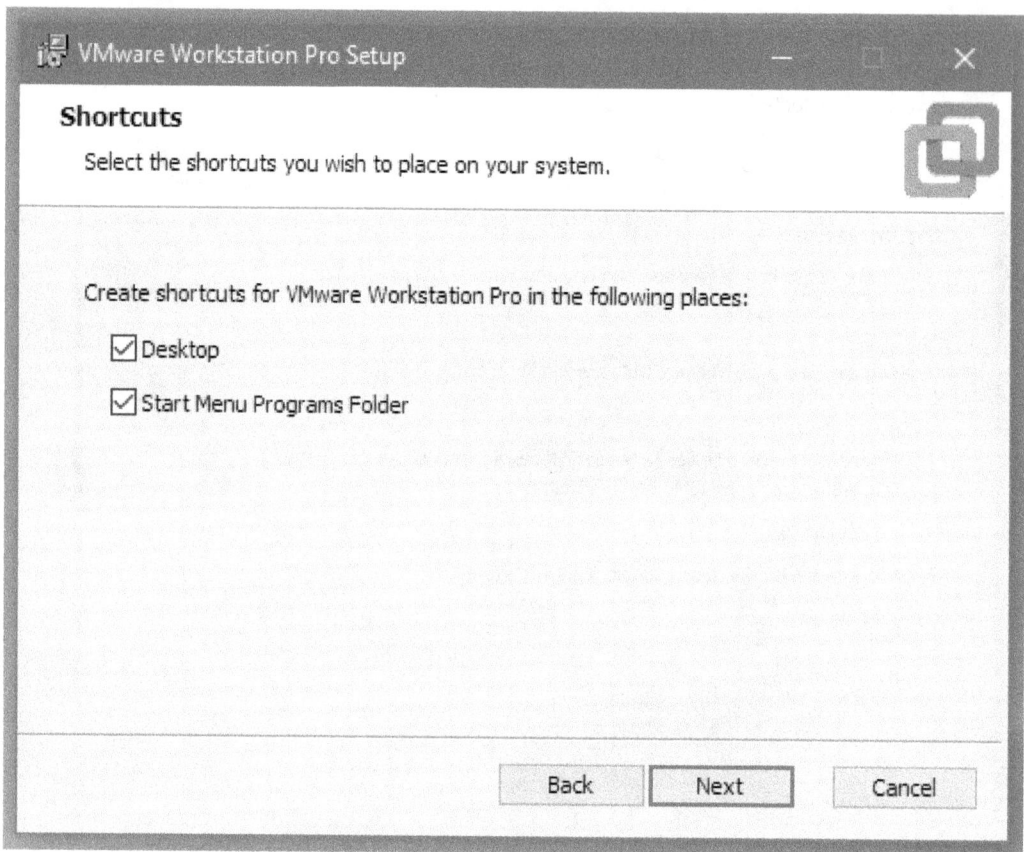

Figure 1.12 – VMware Workstation installation process – part 3

6. Now, once we click on **Next**, it will start installing the application. The process might take a couple of minutes, depending on your system specifications:

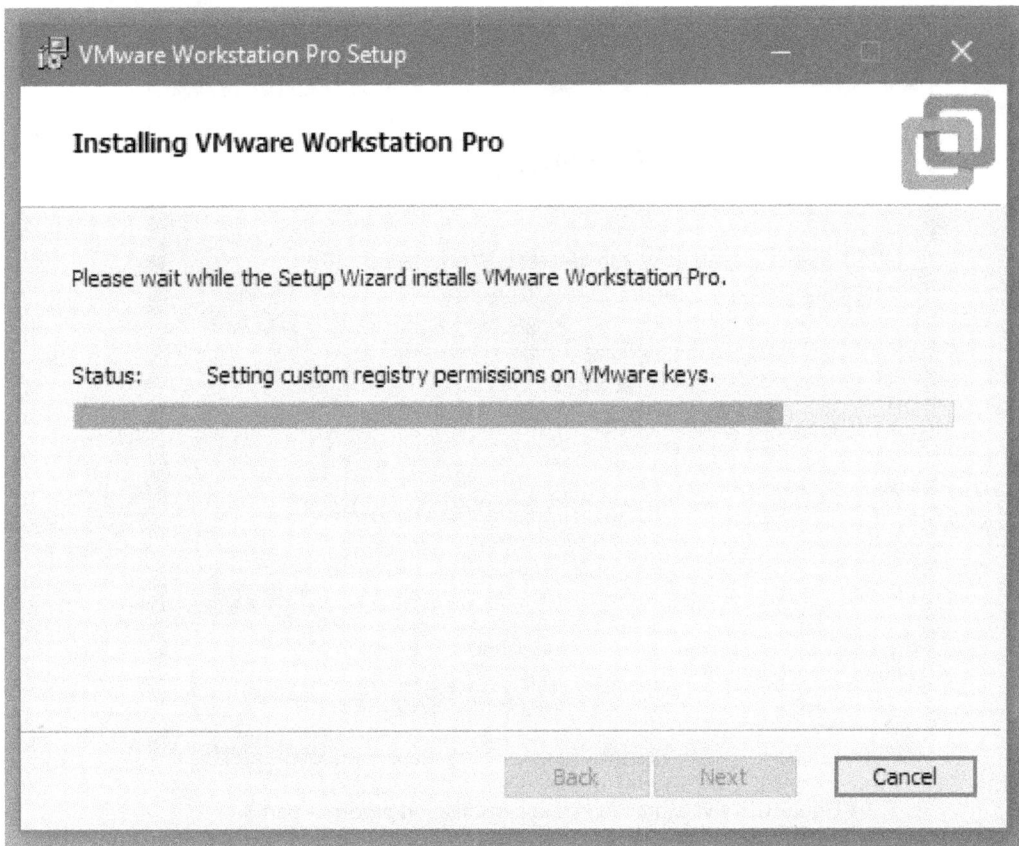

Figure 1.13 – VMware Workstation installation process – part 4

7. The last step for this process is to either select the **I want to try VMware Workstation 17 for 30 days** option or use a legitimate key to activate your product, and then click on **Continue**:

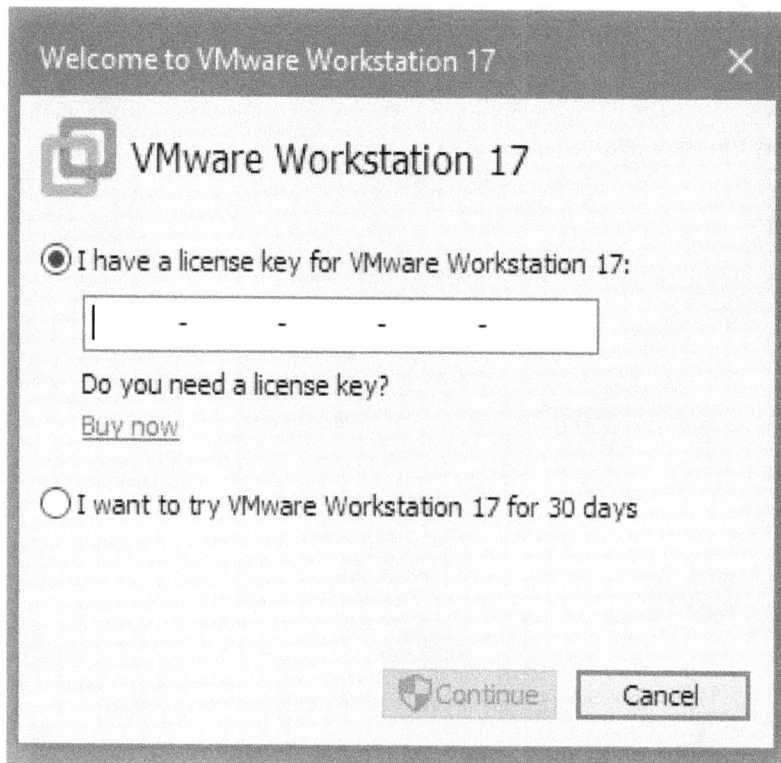

Figure 1.14 – VMware Workstation installation process – part 5

Once Workstation 17 Pro is installed, you can see the **Library** pane and the **Home** tab, which shows your virtual machines:

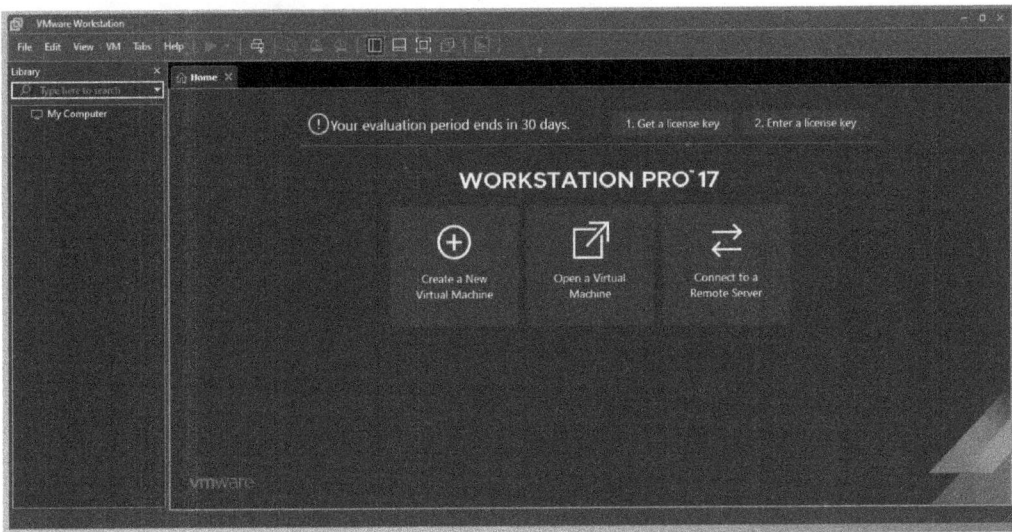

Figure 1.15 – VMware Workstation interface

For the next exercise, let's start making a Windows ISO file to install on a virtual machine:

1. Visit the following link and click on **Download Now**; it will download media creation tools for us to use:

   https://www.microsoft.com/en-us/software-download/windows10

2. Double-click on the Windows 10 Setup executable and accept the license (the tools will take some time to download, depending on your network speed):

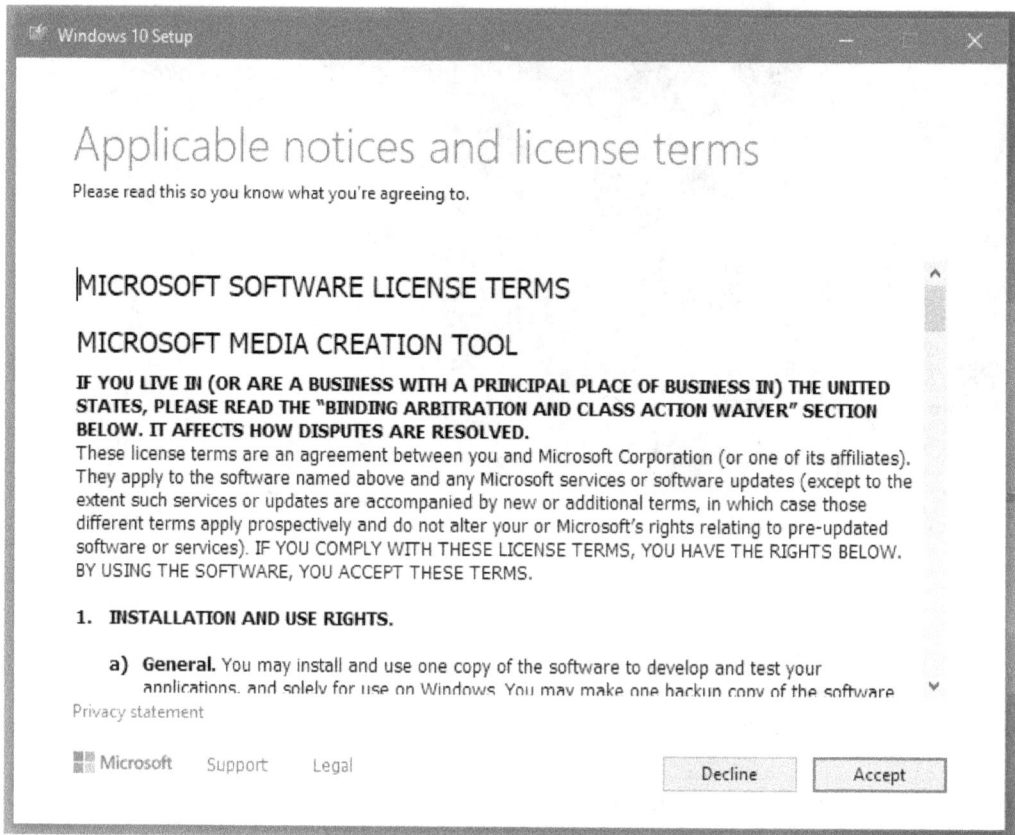

Figure 1.16 – Preparing Windows 10 ISO – part 1

3. Select the **Create installation media (USB flash drive, DVD, or ISO file) for another PC** option:

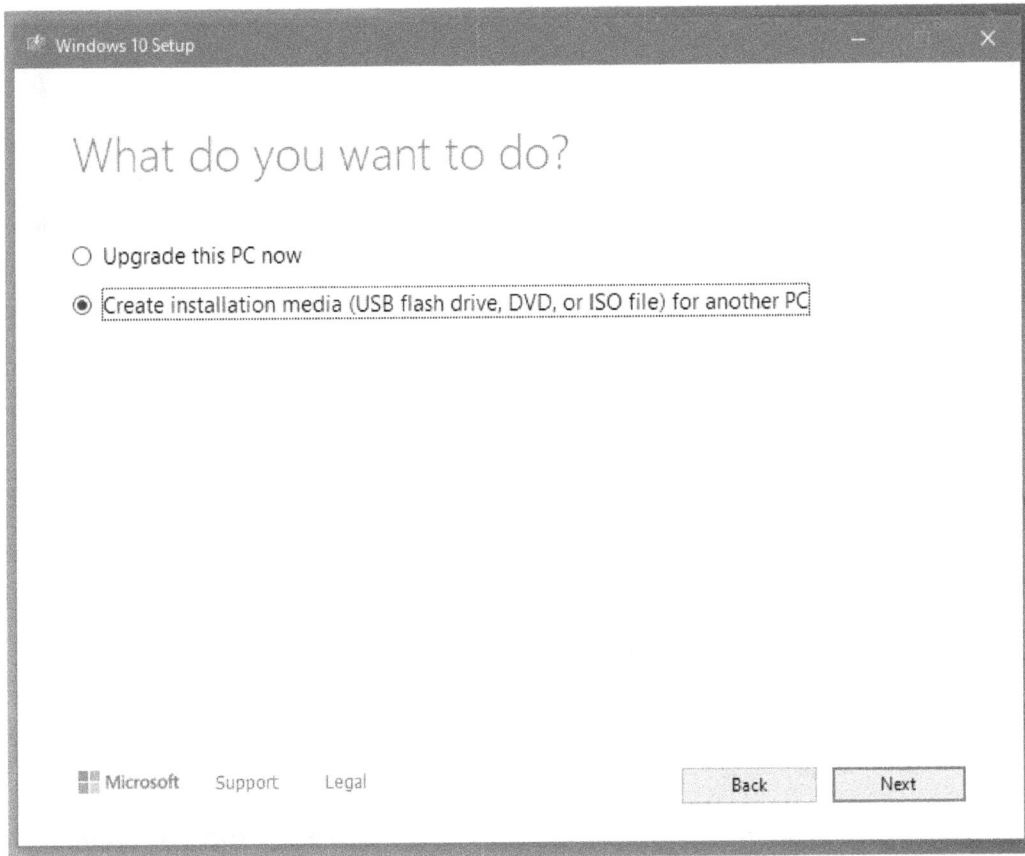

Figure 1.17 – Preparing Windows 10 ISO – part 2

4.   Select the architecture that you want (in our case, we will proceed with **64-bit (x64)**):

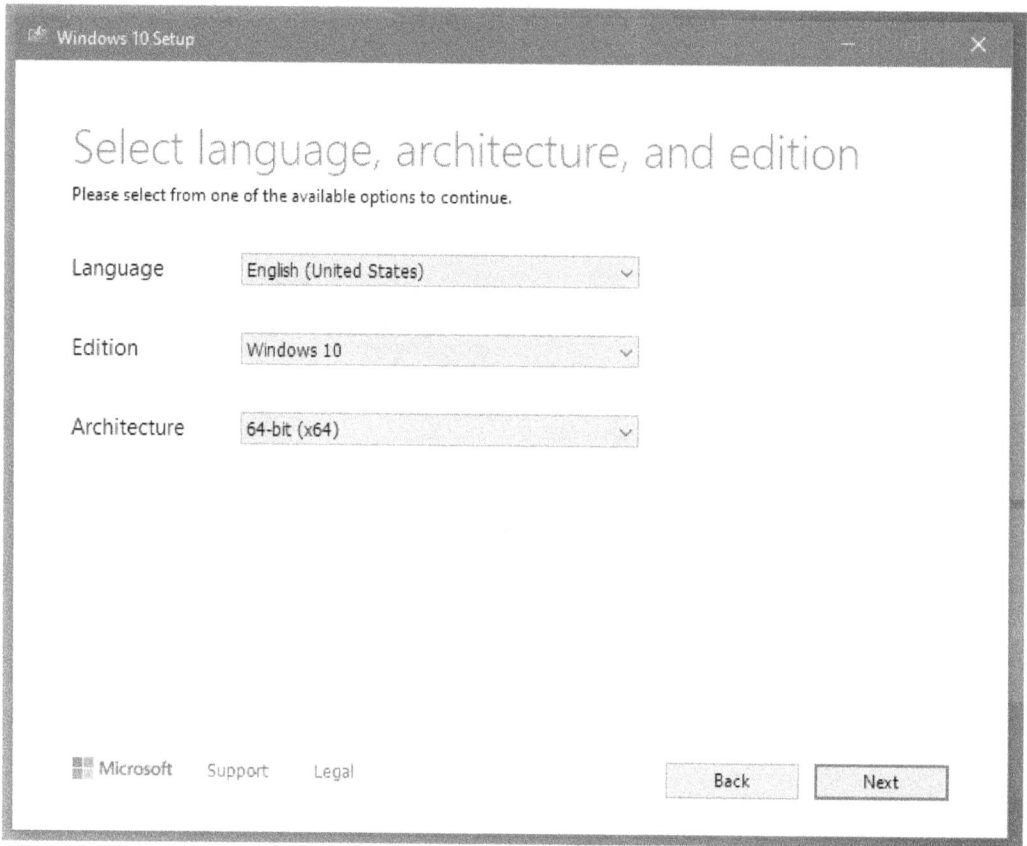

Figure 1.18 – Preparing Windows 10 ISO – part 3

5. Now, we will select the **ISO file** option and the saving path on your local machine to download and create a Windows 10 image:

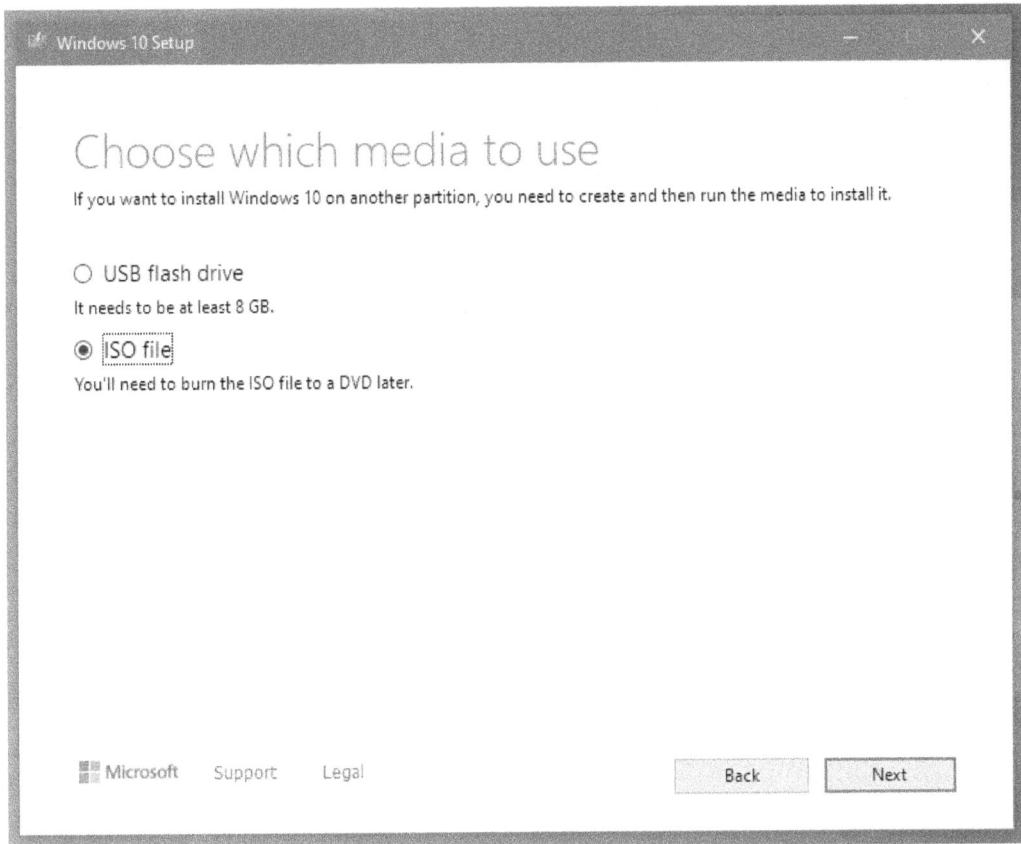

Figure 1.19 – Preparing Windows 10 ISO – part 4

The next exercise is to install Windows 10 as a virtual machine on Workstation 17 Pro:

1. Click on **Click Virtual Machines** > **Create VM** and select the **Typical** installation option:

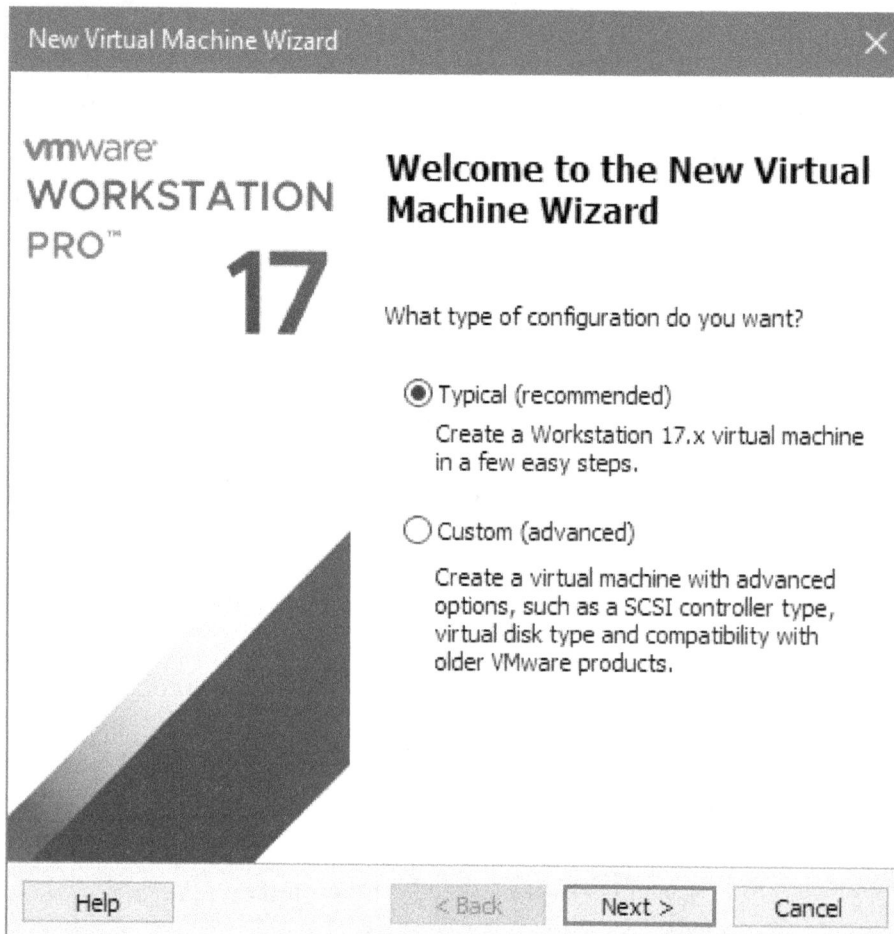

Figure 1.20 – Windows 10 installation process – part 1

2. Click on the **Installer disc image file (iso)** option, as shown in the following screenshot, and select the path for the Windows 10 ISO file:

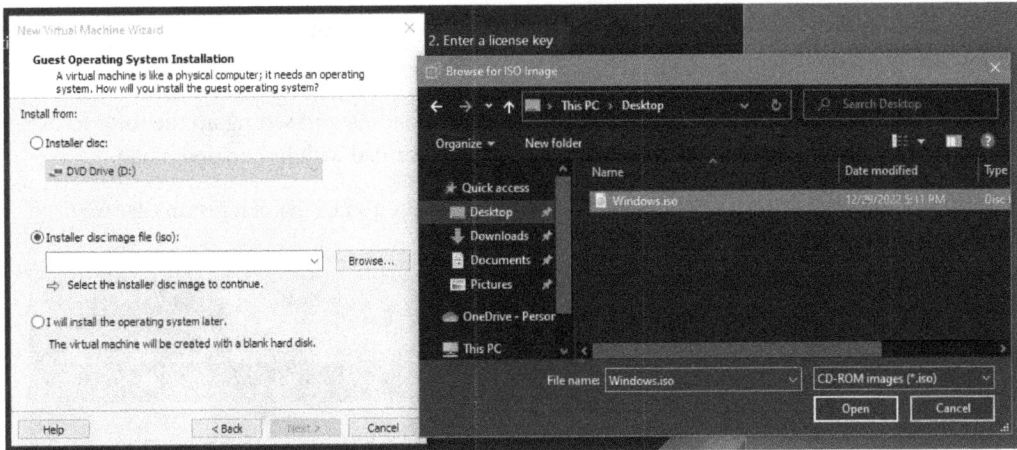

Figure 1.21 – Windows 10 installation process – part 2

3. Click **Next** and name the virtual machine DFIR Labs, assign 60 GB as the virtual HDD, and select a minimum of 4 GB of RAM:

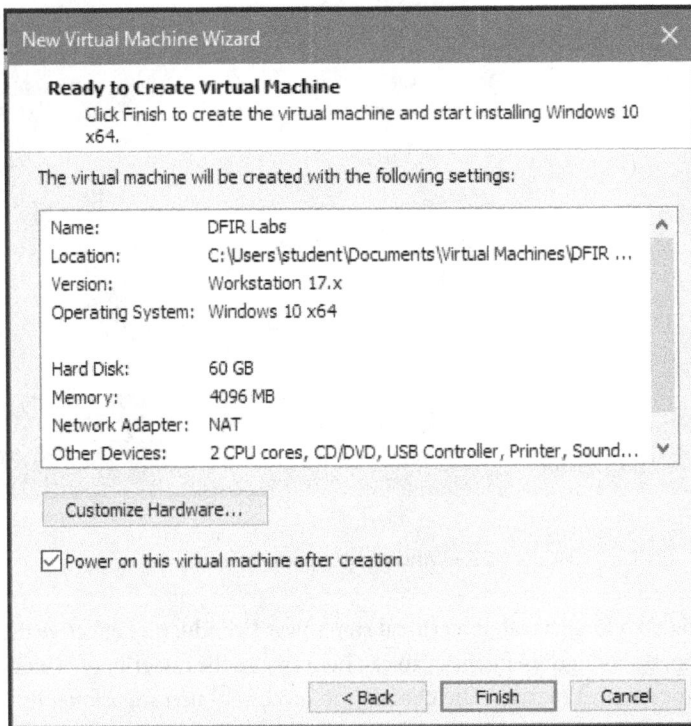

Figure 1.22 – Virtual machine settings

4.   The last step is to follow the Windows installation guide and run the virtual machine, for which we are all set up now.

During the exercises in the next chapters, we will start downloading and setting up the tools to use for our investigation and artifact analysis each tool will be presented with link to download.

Now we have completed setting up our virtual machine. Let's take a snapshot of it just in case we need to revert and avoid re-installing it.

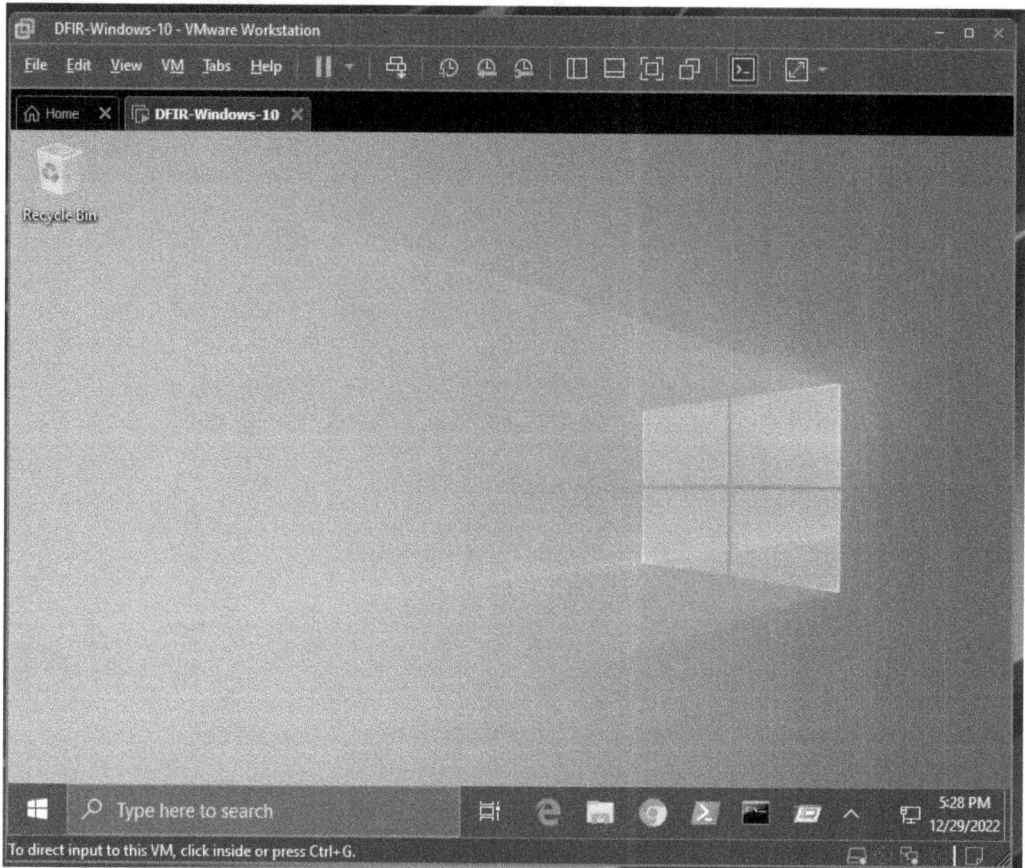

Figure 1.23 – Windows 10 ready for a lab

In conclusion, setting up a forensic lab is a critical step toward conducting effective digital forensics investigations. A properly configured forensic lab can help ensure the integrity of evidence, streamline the investigation process, and increase the chances of successful investigations. By following the guidelines and best practices outlined in this chapter, forensic analysts can establish a reliable and efficient forensic lab that can meet the demands of modern digital investigations.

Summary

In this chapter, we covered the fundamental concepts and principles of digital forensics, including the importance of a chain of custody, the authenticity and reliability of evidence, and the need for a thorough and systematic approach to the examination of digital evidence. We also discussed the ethical considerations involved in digital forensics and the importance of following established legal and professional standards.

We learned how to set up a virtual environment that simulates a real-world scenario. This allows us to safely and securely test and practice digital forensic techniques without risking damage to real systems. We also learned how to take snapshots of virtual machines and revert to previous states, which is an essential tool for creating controlled testing environments and preserving evidence.

This chapter also provided an overview of the tools and techniques used in digital forensics, including forensic imaging, data recovery, and analysis tools. The goal of this fundamental chapter on digital forensics was to provide a comprehensive understanding of the field and its various components, as well as to provide a foundation for further study and specialization.

In the upcoming chapter, we will be covering the important topic of memory forensics and acquisition. We will explore the significance of memory analysis in digital forensics and how it can help in identifying and investigating potential security breaches. Additionally, we will discuss the different methods of acquiring memory images and their importance in conducting effective digital investigations. Stay tuned for an in-depth discussion on this critical aspect of digital forensics.

Questions

Before ending this chapter, I would encourage you to answer the following questions based on your understanding and research:

1. What is operating system forensics?
2. What type of evidence can we collect?
3. Why did digital forensics become an important science?
4. What are the investigative procedures involved in computer forensics?
5. What is VSS?

2

Evidence Acquisition

As we discussed in the previous chapter, digital forensics is a rapidly growing field of computer science that focuses on identifying, collecting, analyzing, preserving, and presenting digital evidence. It is used to investigate cybercrime, identify malicious activity, and recover lost or deleted data. The acquisition of digital evidence from a **Windows operating system** (**Windows OS**) is an important part of the digital forensics process.

As we know, Windows OS is one of the most widely used operating systems in the world. It is used by millions of people for personal and business purposes. As such, it is a prime target for cybercriminals who seek to gain access to sensitive information or disrupt operations.

Acquiring digital evidence from a Windows machine is a complex process that requires specialized knowledge and tools.

In this chapter, we will cover the following main topics:

- An overview of evidence acquisition for Windows OS
- A forensic analyst's jump bag (first responder kit)
- Understanding the order of volatility
- Acquisition tools for Windows OS
- Evidence collection and acquisition exercise

Technical requirements

For this chapter's exercise, we will utilize the **virtual machine** (**VM**) configured previously and install several tools for data acquisition and mounting, as follows:

- KAPE: https://www.kroll.com/en/services/cyber-risk/incident-response-litigation-support/kroll-artifact-parser-extractor-kape
- FTK Imager: https://www.exterro.com/ftk-imager

> **Important note**
>
> For labs, we will use KAPE and FTK Imager to acquire forensic evidence. We will use this evidence for educational purposes; however, the same applies to real-world incidents.

An overview of evidence acquisition for Windows OS

One of the important stages in digital forensics is acquisition. This is the process of collecting digital evidence from a computer system running an operating system. This evidence can be used to investigate and prosecute criminal activities, as well as to provide information for civil litigation. Digital forensics acquisition involves the collection of data from a variety of sources, including hard drives, removable media, network connections, and other digital devices.

Here is a brief overview of the steps that are performed during digital forensics acquisition:

1. The first step in digital forensics acquisition is to identify the source of the evidence. This includes determining what type of device or system is being examined and what type of data is stored on it.

2. Once this has been established, the next step is to create an image or copy of the data on the device or system. This image will be used as a reference point for further analysis and investigation.

3. The next step in digital forensics acquisition is to analyze the image or copy created in order to identify any potential evidence that may be present. This includes examining filesystems, registry entries, application logs, and other areas where data may be stored. Once any potential evidence has been identified, it must then be extracted from the image or copied to preserve its integrity and authenticity.

4. Once all relevant evidence has been extracted from the image or a copy has been created during digital forensics acquisition, it must then be analyzed further in order to determine its relevance and value as evidence. This analysis typically involves examining file headers and footers, analyzing metadata associated with files, examining application logs for suspicious activity, and other techniques designed to uncover hidden information or patterns that may indicate criminal activity.

Several types of digital forensics acquisitions can be performed on Windows operating systems, as follows:

- **Physical acquisitions** (also known as **dead acquisitions**): Physical acquisitions involve collecting data directly from a physical device such as a hard drive or USB drive

- **Logical acquisitions** (also known as **live acquisitions**): Logical acquisitions involve collecting data from logical sources such as files stored on a computer

- **Virtual acquisitions** (also known as **VM acquisitions**): Virtual acquisitions involve collecting data from VMs such as those used by cloud computing services such as **Amazon Web Services** (**AWS**)

Each type of acquisition requires different tools and techniques in order to properly collect all relevant evidence without compromising its integrity or authenticity.

In addition to these three types of digital forensics acquisition for Windows operating systems, there are also several specialized tools available that can help investigators quickly identify potential sources of evidence on a computer system running Windows OS. These tools include forensic imaging tools that can create an exact replica of an entire hard drive, registry analysis software that can examine registry entries for suspicious activity, malware analysis tools that can detect malicious code, network monitoring tools that can detect unauthorized access attempts, and file carving software that can recover deleted files from unallocated space on a hard drive.

In the following screenshot, we can see a driver cloning device:

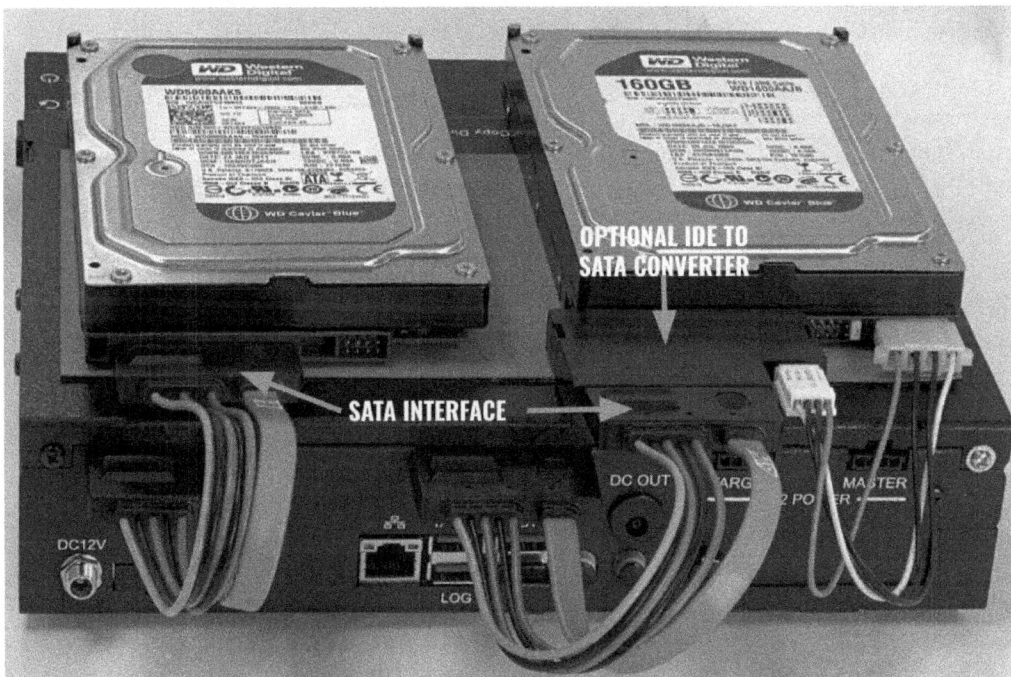

Figure 2.1 – FX2260 Forensic & IT Multi-Interface Drive Cloning Appliance by Storage Heaven
(`https://www.storageheaven.com/FX2042-HDD-Duplicator-p/y-2042.htm`)

As we've covered the concept of a write blocker, let's now move into another set of tools that forensic examiners mostly use—jump bags.

A forensic analyst's jump bag (first responder kit)

A digital forensic examiner's jump bag is a collection of tools and equipment used by digital forensics analysts to collect, analyze, and report on digital evidence. It is an essential part of any digital forensics investigation and can be used to quickly respond to a crime scene or other incident. The contents of a jump bag vary depending on the type of investigation being conducted but typically include items such as hard drives, flash drives, memory cards, cables, adapters, and other hardware. Additionally, the analyst may also carry software such as forensic imaging tools and analysis programs.

The purpose of a jump bag is to provide the analyst with all the required tools and equipment for a successful investigation. This includes items that are required for data collection, such as hard drives and memory cards, as well as items that are required for analysis, such as forensic imaging software. Having all these items in one place allows the analyst to quickly respond to an incident without having to search for individual pieces of equipment or software. Additionally, it allows them to easily transport their equipment from one location to another if needed.

When creating a jump bag for a digital forensics investigation, all items must be organized in an efficient manner so that they can be easily accessed when needed. This includes labeling each item clearly so that they can be identified quickly during an investigation. Additionally, it is important that all items are securely stored in order to protect them from damage or theft while in transit or at a crime scene.

In addition to hardware and software tools, other items should be included in a digital forensics analyst's jump bag, such as protective clothing (for example, gloves), evidence bags/containers (for example, plastic bags), evidence markers (for example, numbered tags), documentation forms (for example, **chain-of-custody (CoC)** forms), and reference materials (for example, cheat sheets). These additional items help ensure that the analyst has everything they need when responding to an incident or conducting an investigation. By organizing their jump bag efficiently and including additional items such as protective clothing and reference materials, analysts can ensure they have everything they need when responding to incidents or conducting investigations. Here is a list of examples of jump bag contents:

- **USB flash drives and external storage devices**: USB drives are used to transfer data from one computer to another. They should be securely encrypted and labeled with the investigator's name and contact information. They are also used to collect volatile data and live forensic evidence.

- **Digital camera**: A digital camera is used to take pictures of the scene of a crime or incident for documentation purposes.

- **Laptop computer and cables and adapters**: Cables and adapters are needed to connect devices such as computers, cameras, and external hard drives for data transfer purposes.

- **Forensic software**: Forensic software is used by investigators to analyze digital evidence on-site. Examples include EnCase, FTK Imager, Autopsy, and X-Ways Forensics. Another set of tools are the ones we will use to collect and preserve volatile data such as memory.

- **Evidence bags/containers**: Evidence bags/containers are used to store physical items such as cell phones or computers that may contain digital evidence for further analysis in a lab setting.

The following screenshot shows an example of a jump bag's contents:

Figure 2.2 – Digital forensics analyst's jump bag

In the next section, we will understand the importance of the order of volatility.

Understanding the order of volatility

When it comes to digital forensics, understanding the **order of volatility** is essential. This concept is especially important when dealing with Windows forensic evidence. The order of volatility refers to the order in which data is lost from a computer system when it is powered off or shut down. It is important to understand this concept to properly analyze and interpret Windows forensic evidence.

The order of volatility can be broken down into two categories, as follows:

- **Volatile data**: Volatile data is the most ephemeral and will be lost first when a system is powered off or shut down. This includes data stored in RAM, such as running processes, open files, and network connections.

- **Non-volatile data**: Non-volatile data includes information stored on hard drives or other storage media that may remain intact after a system has been powered off or shut down. This includes information such as filesystem metadata, registry entries, user profiles, deleted files, and unallocated space on hard drives. Non-volatile data includes information that will remain intact even after a system has been powered off or shut down for an extended period of time. This includes information such as deleted files and unallocated space on hard drives.

When analyzing Windows forensic evidence, it is important to understand the order of volatility to properly interpret the evidence. For example, if an investigator needs to determine which processes were running on a computer at the time it was powered off or shut down, they should focus on volatile data first since this type of information will be lost first when the system is powered off or shut down. On the other hand, if an investigator needs to determine which files were deleted from a computer prior to it being powered off or shut down, they should focus on non-volatile data since this type of information will remain intact even after a system has been powered off for an extended period of time.

In addition to understanding which types of data are more likely to be lost when a computer system is powered off or reset, investigators should also understand how different types of storage media affect the order of volatility in Windows forensics. For example, hard drives are generally considered less volatile than **random access memory** (**RAM**) as they retain their contents even when the computer system is powered off or reset. However, certain types of hard drives such as **solid-state drives** (**SSDs**) are more volatile than traditional hard drives and may require special handling by investigators in order to ensure that all relevant evidence can be recovered successfully.

Here, you can see a screenshot comparing an SSD and a **hard disk drive** (**HDD**):

Figure 2.3 – SSD versus HDD

Once investigators understand which types of data are stored on a computer system and how it is stored, they can then begin to prioritize their efforts when collecting and analyzing evidence based on the order of volatility. For example, if an investigator knows that certain types of data are more likely to remain intact than others, they can focus their efforts on those types first before moving on to less volatile types later. Additionally, if an investigator knows that certain types of data will be overwritten or destroyed quickly, they can take steps to collect those pieces before they disappear forever.

Now that we have learned about forensics concepts, let's dive into acquisition tools.

Acquisition tools for Windows OS

The process of evidence acquisition involves gathering digital evidence from devices to be analyzed and presented. It is imperative that this evidence is collected in a forensically sound manner using tools that preserve its integrity. In this section, we will explore various tools for acquisition and triage.

One of the most common methods of acquiring digital evidence is disk imaging. Disk imaging involves making an exact copy of all data stored on a hard drive or another storage device. This copy can then be analyzed by forensic investigators without altering the original data on the drive. **Disk imaging** can also be used to create backups of important data, which can then be used if the original data is lost or corrupted. When performing disk imaging for Windows forensics, several steps must be taken to ensure that all relevant data is captured and preserved properly.

The first step is to identify which drives need to be imaged and what type of image should be created (for example, full disk image, logical image, and so on). Once this has been determined, the investigator will need to acquire write blockers and other hardware devices required for creating an image without altering any existing data on the drive(s). Next, software tools such as FTK Imager or EnCase can be used to create an exact copy of all data stored on the drive(s).

Finally, once the image has been created, it should be verified using **checksums/hashing**, which are used to verify the integrity of digital evidence. A checksum is a unique value generated by a mathematical algorithm based on the data contained in a file. By comparing the checksum of an original file to that of a copy, investigators can determine if the copy has been altered or tampered with. Checksums are crucial in detecting evidence tampering and ensuring that evidence is admissible in court to ensure its accuracy and integrity before being stored for further analysis. Let's dive into FTK Imager now and start creating our first forensic image.

> **Important note**
> All of the acquisition and analysis steps will be done using the previously configured Windows VM. Please refer back to *Chapter 1,* if the VM is not ready.

Using FTK Imager

Before jumping into the steps on how to acquire a Windows image, we will install FTK Imager from the previously shared link in the *Technical requirements* section. Once the binary has downloaded on your VM, click **Next**. As usual, it will take a couple of steps to download and install FTK Imager. Once installed, this is what the **graphical user interface (GUI)** will look like:

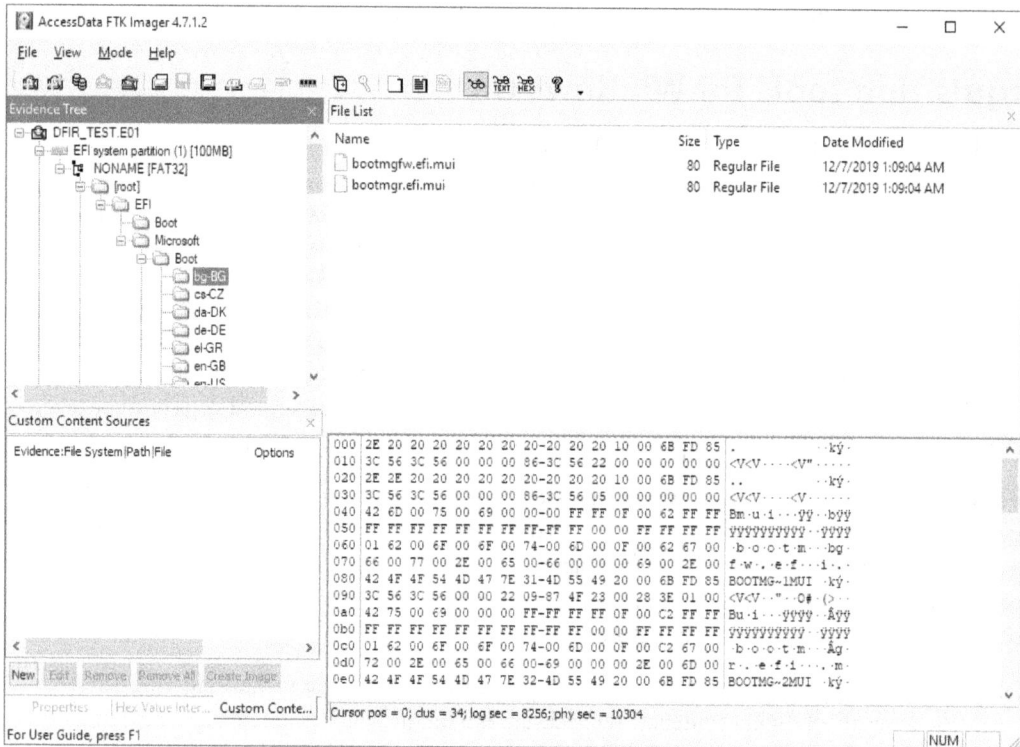

Figure 2.4 – FTK Imager GUI

FTK Imager is a powerful forensic imaging tool used by law enforcement and corporate investigators to acquire data from computers and other digital devices. It is a free, open source tool developed by AccessData, a leading provider of digital forensics solutions that has since been acquired by Exterro. FTK Imager allows users to quickly and easily create an exact image or clone of any storage device, including hard drives, USB flash drives, CDs/DVDs, and memory cards.

It is designed to be easy to use while still providing powerful features. It has a simple GUI that allows users to quickly select the source device they want to image and the destination where the image will be stored. The software also supports multiple imaging formats such as **EnCase (E01)**, **raw (DD)**, **Advanced Forensic Format (AFF)**, and **Secure Multi-Access Recovery Technology (SMART)**. Additionally, FTK Imager can create images that are encrypted with **Advanced Encryption Standard (AES)** 256-bit encryption for added security, and it includes several advanced features that make it an invaluable tool for digital forensics investigations. For example, it has the ability to search for specific keywords within an image file or across multiple images at once. It can also carve out files from unallocated space on a drive or partition, which can be useful in recovering deleted files or providing evidence of malicious activity on a system. Additionally, it has the ability to create hashes of images that can be used to verify their integrity during an investigation.

Let's start creating our first forensic image, as follows:

1. Click on the FTK Imager icon on the desktop. It will present the GUI shown here:

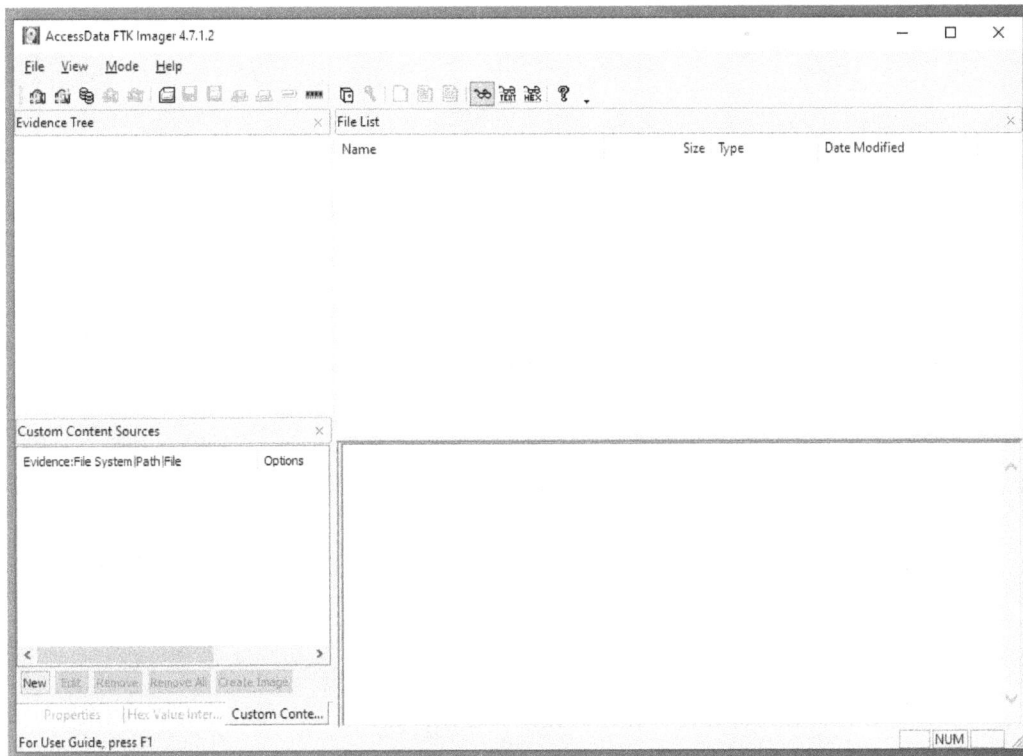

Figure 2.5 – FTK Imager GUI

2. Click on the **File** option, select **Create Disk Image…**, and then select **Physical Drive**, as shown in the next two screenshots:

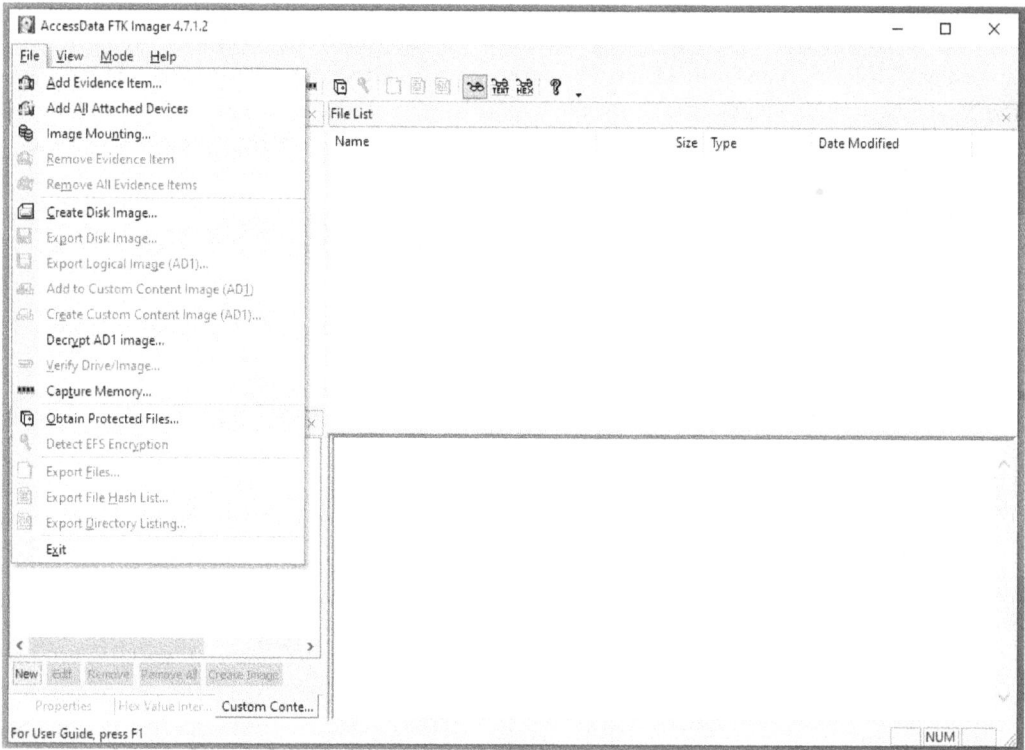

Figure 2.6 – FTK Imager: Creating a disk image (step 1)

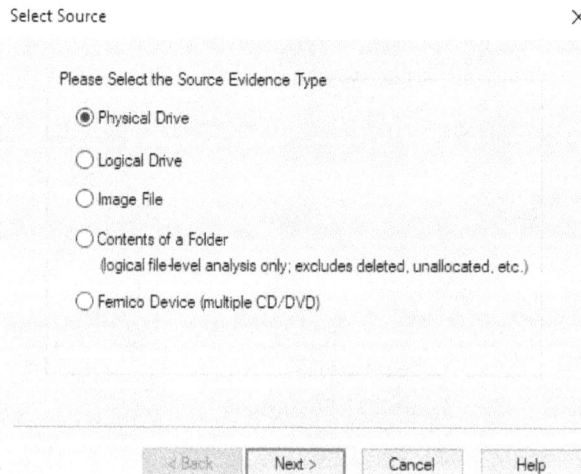

Figure 2.7 – FTK Imager: Creating a disk image (step 2)

3. Once we select **Physical Drive**, it will prompt us to select a drive from the list of available drives. Click **Finish**:

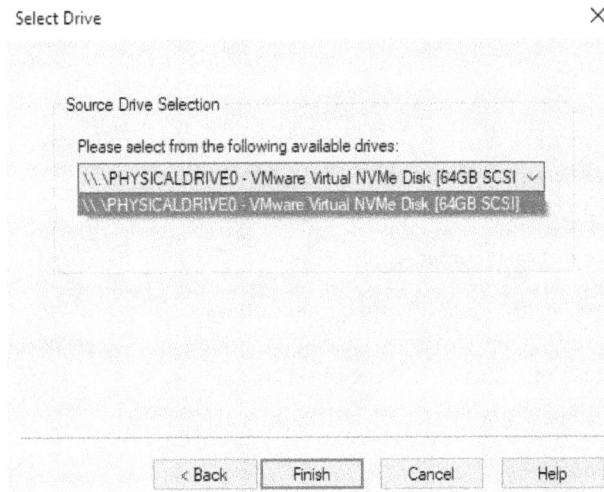

Figure 2.8 – FTK Imager: Creating a disk image (step 3)

Figure 2.9 – Clicking Add FTK imager will show the options for image creation

4. In this step, we need to select the settings for image destination and file type. We will select the **E01** format; however, you can select any type from the list. The differences between each type are listed here:

- **Raw (dd)**: This is common among forensic analysis tools. This format does not contain any metadata, headers, or even magic values.

- **AFF**: In this format, the disk image created does not lock the user into a proprietary format, which prevents them from being able to properly analyze it.

- **SMART**: This file format is good for Linux filesystems since it keeps the images as pure bit-streams with optional compression.

- **E01**: This format compresses the image file. Images in this format will start with case information in the header and footer, which has a **Message Digest Method 5 (MD5)** hash of the entire bit stream. This case information contains the date and time of acquisition, the investigator's name, special notes, and an optional password:

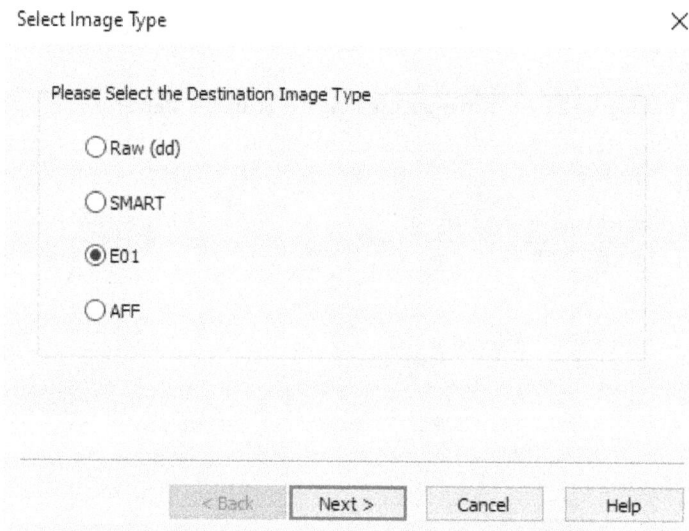

Select Image Type   ✕

Please Select the Destination Image Type

    ○ Raw (dd)

    ○ SMART

    ◉ E01

    ○ AFF

    < Back   Next >   Cancel   Help

Figure 2.10 – FTK Imager: Selecting an image type

5.   Now, we need to fill in evidence information related to our case. This information will be vital for identifying evidence found in the image and relating it with other types of evidence that are available for that specific case:

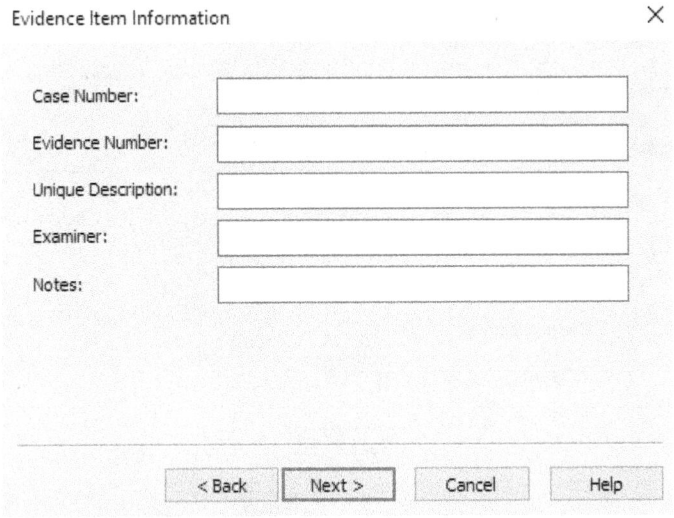

Evidence Item Information   ✕

Case Number:

Evidence Number:

Unique Description:

Examiner:

Notes:

< Back   Next >   Cancel   Help

Figure 2.11 – FTK Imager: Creating case information

6.   In this step, we will select the destination path for evidence. This is where we want to place our image file and other related files after the acquisition. Once the destination path is selected, click on **Finish**, and it will start creating the image:

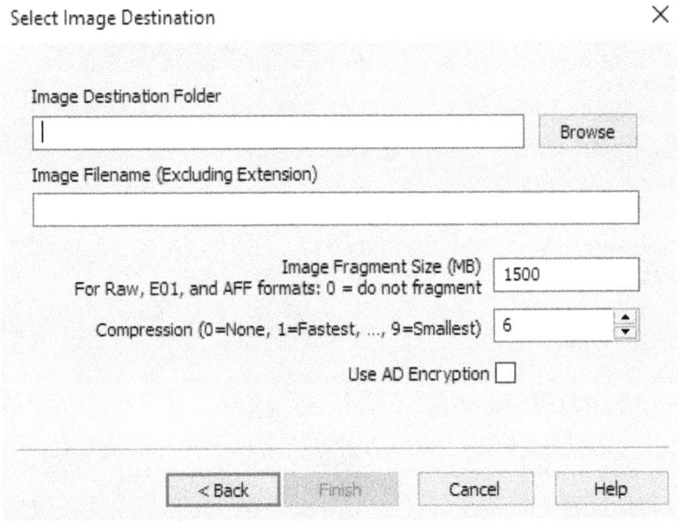

Select Image Destination   ✕

Image Destination Folder

| Browse

Image Filename (Excluding Extension)

Image Fragment Size (MB)   1500
For Raw, E01, and AFF formats: 0 = do not fragment

Compression (0=None, 1=Fastest, ..., 9=Smallest)   6

Use AD Encryption ☐

< Back   Finish   Cancel   Help

Figure 2.12 – FTK Imager: Selecting a destination path

The following screenshot shows that the image creation process has started. It will take some time. Grab a cup of coffee and watch the newest episode of the *One Piece* anime:

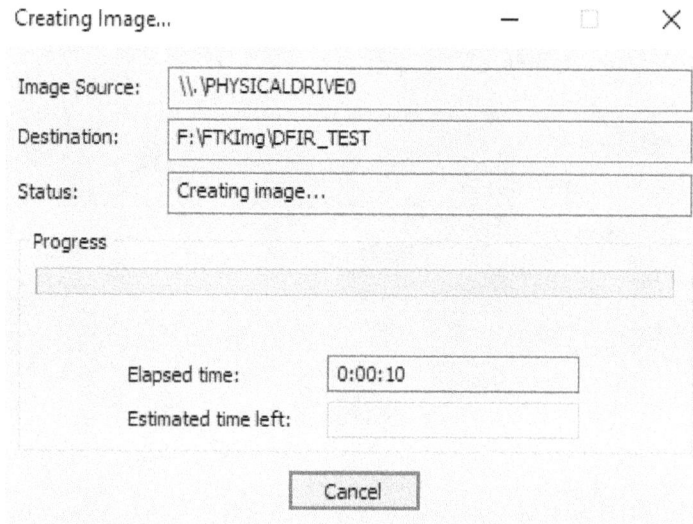

Figure 2.13 – FTK Imager image creation process

Once the process has been completed, it will show us the **Drive/Image Verify Results** window, which holds the hash and other details about the image:

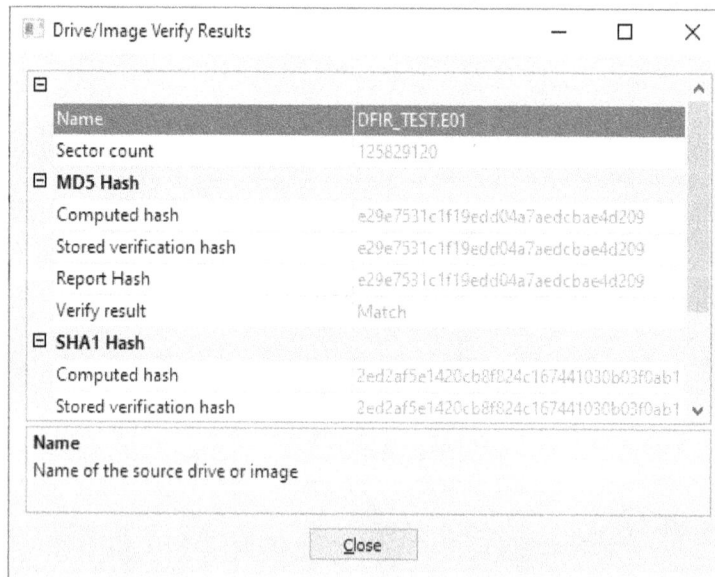

Figure 2.14 – Drive/Image Verify Results window

Now that our image is ready, we can move on to collecting triage images using KAPE.

Using KAPE

KAPE is a valuable forensic tool designed to expedite the triage process by swiftly identifying and parsing the most pertinent artifacts from a target device or storage location. With its rapid execution, KAPE enables investigators to quickly pinpoint and prioritize critical systems relevant to their cases. Furthermore, KAPE can be employed to gather essential artifacts prior to initiating the imaging process. Once the imaging phase is underway, the data extracted by KAPE can be examined for potential leads and utilized to construct timelines, and so on.

KAPE is designed to be used in the early stages of an investigation when time is of the essence. It can quickly scan a triage image for artifacts such as deleted files, registry entries, user accounts, system information, and more. This allows forensic examiners to quickly identify potential evidence that may be relevant to their investigation. KAPE can be used to collect the most critical artifacts at the start of the traditional imaging process.

KAPE serves two primary functions, as outlined here:

- Artifact and file collection
- Processing collected artifacts with a forensic analyzer

On its own, KAPE does not do anything in relation to either of these functions; rather, they are achieved by reading configuration files on the fly and, based on the contents of those files, collecting and processing them. This makes KAPE very extensible in adding or extending functionality.

KAPE divides its functionality into two main parts, as follows:

- **Targets**: Targets are files that define which artifacts and information are to be collected. Basically, they are configurations that hold details such as file paths and so on. They are written in YAML and are easy to read and understand; examples are LNK files and Jump List files, which we will explore in more depth later in *Chapter 9*.

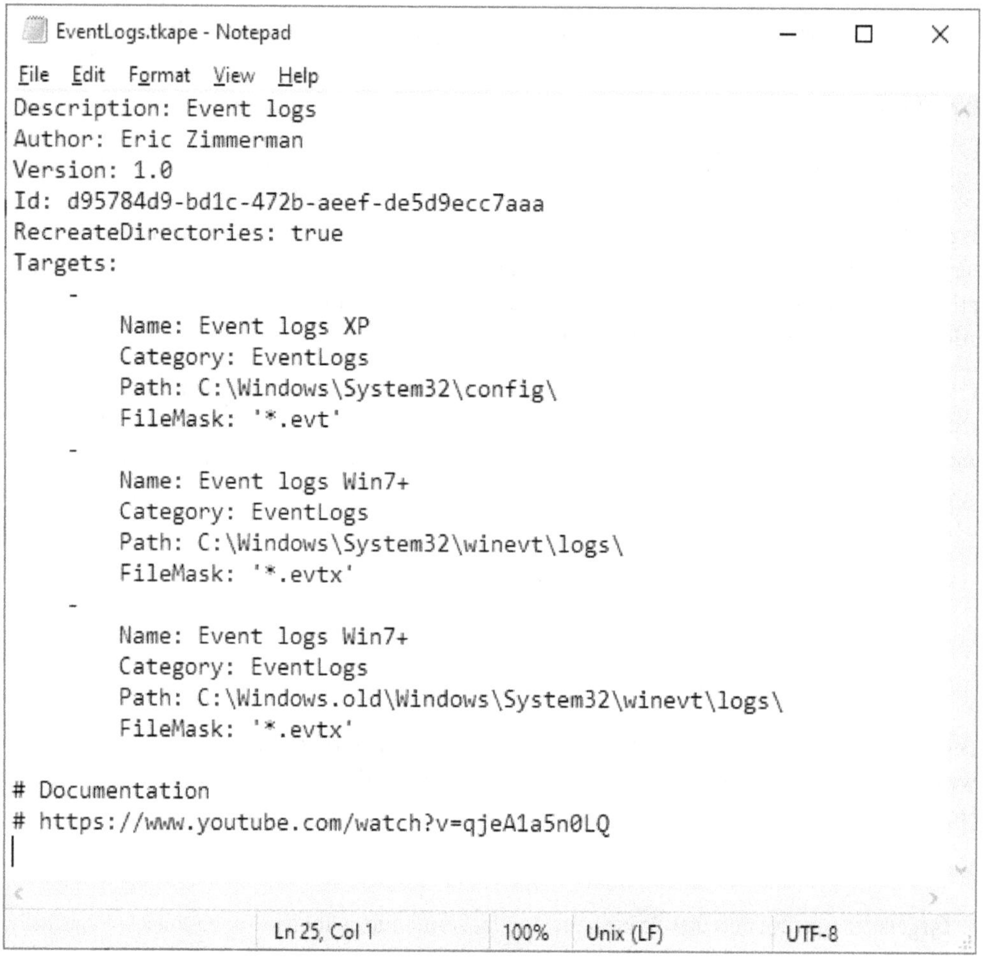

```
Description: Event logs
Author: Eric Zimmerman
Version: 1.0
Id: d95784d9-bd1c-472b-aeef-de5d9ecc7aaa
RecreateDirectories: true
Targets:
    -
        Name: Event logs XP
        Category: EventLogs
        Path: C:\Windows\System32\config\
        FileMask: '*.evt'
    -
        Name: Event logs Win7+
        Category: EventLogs
        Path: C:\Windows\System32\winevt\logs\
        FileMask: '*.evtx'
    -
        Name: Event logs Win7+
        Category: EventLogs
        Path: C:\Windows.old\Windows\System32\winevt\logs\
        FileMask: '*.evtx'

# Documentation
# https://www.youtube.com/watch?v=qjeA1a5n0LQ
```


Figure 2.15 – KAPE target for Event Logs

- **Modules**: Modules are like targets; however, they are used to run a forensic parser and analyze artifacts. They process files and define the processing tools (scripts or applications) and options that will be run against the source data, as we can see in *Figure 2.16*, we can see `EvtxCMD.exe` with a command line for parsing event logs.

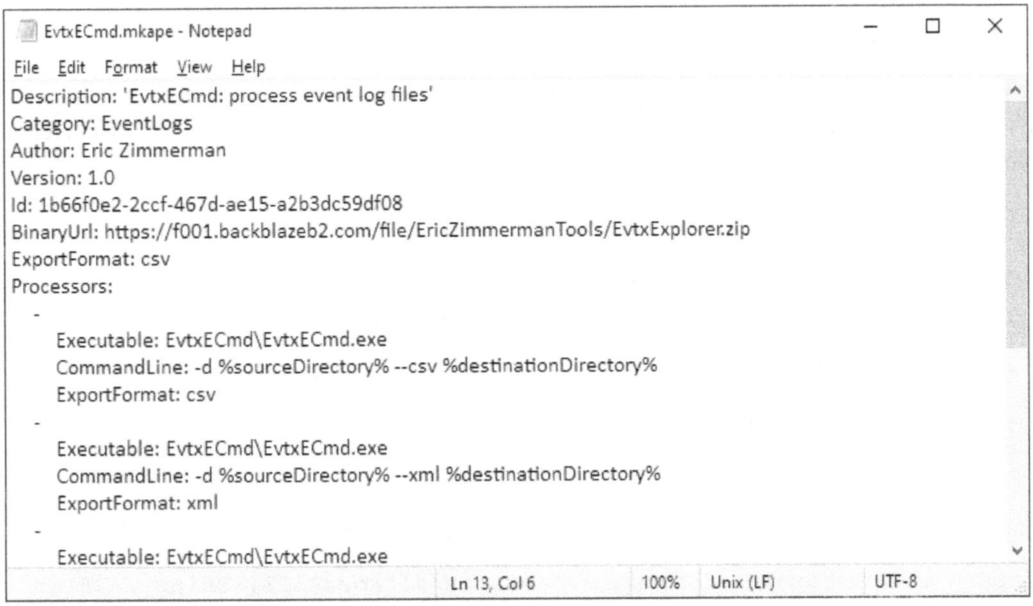

Figure 2.16 – KAPE EvtxCmd module

To install KAPE, we will directly download it from the GitHub repository or by using the link provided at the beginning of this chapter in the *Technical requirements* section. We have two modes of KAPE: GUI and command line. If you proceed to download it using the command line, invoke the `Get-ZimmermanTools.ps1` script as an admin using PowerShell. It will download all required programs within the specified folder path, as illustrated in the following screenshot:

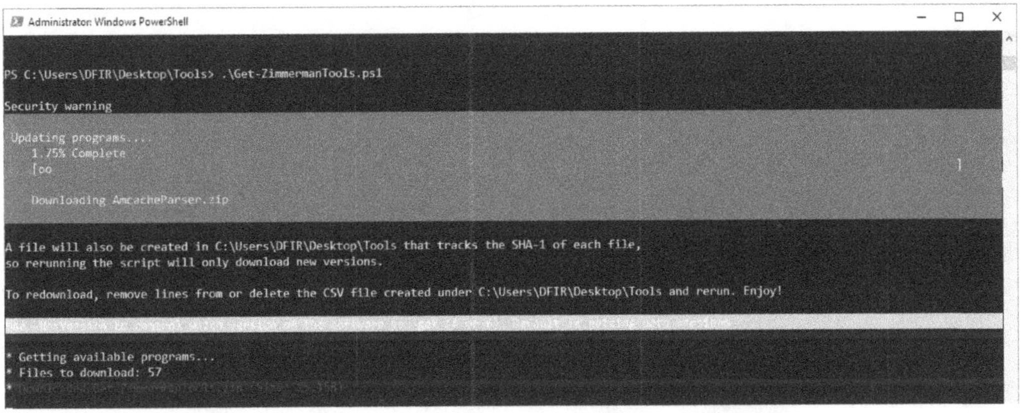

Figure 2.17 – Downloading KAPE using a PowerShell script

Creating a triage image using KAPE

We will use the GUI version as it provides an easy way to build and construct a triage image. For now, we will select multiple target sources and will deep dive into analysis at a later stage of this book for each artifact.

To explain what each switch represents in KAPE, we will give a brief explanation here:

- `tsource`: This is the source in which we select the drive letter—it is required
- `target`: This is the path for target configuration without an extension
- `tdest`: This is the path at which we want to save a copy of the triage data
- `tlist`: This displays available targets with descriptions
- `tflush`: When `true`, delete the directory specified by `-  -  tdest` before searching

For more details regarding switches, you can refer back to Eric Zimmerman's guide on KAPE:

`https://ericzimmerman.github.io/KapeDocs/#!Pages%5C3.-Using-KAPE.md`

Let's now have a look at the KAPE GUI and start collecting defined forensic artifacts:

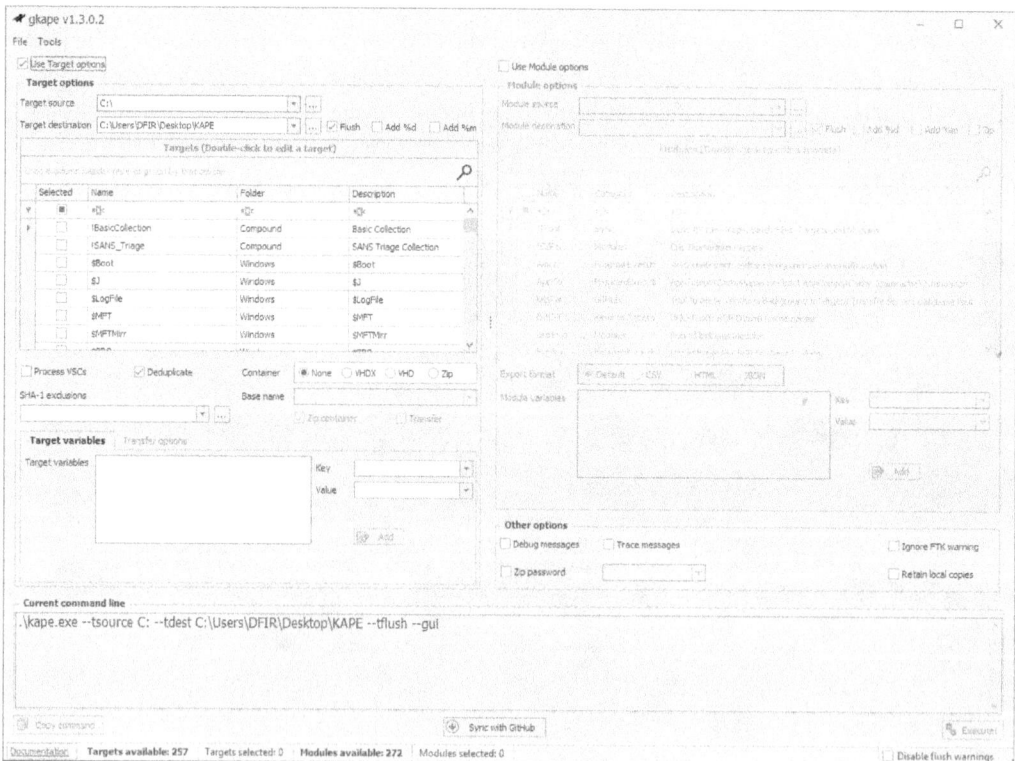

Figure 2.18 – KAPE GUI

In the highlighted **Target source** and **Target destination** parts, we will select where we want to collect triage data from and where we want to save the output file.

> **Important note**
>
> Before starting the acquisition process using KAPE, please verify that all targets were downloaded into the `target` folder. If not, then invoke the `Get-KAPEUpdate.ps1` script.

Let's start to collect our first triage data, as follows:

1.   Open the KAPE GUI; you will see multiple options there:

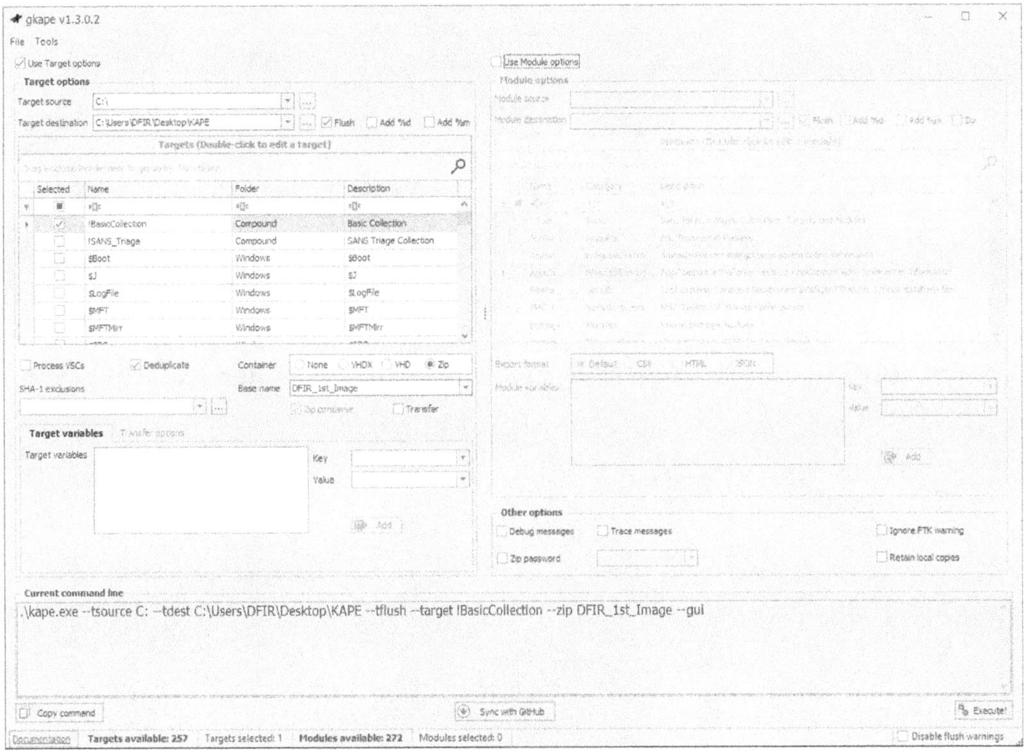

Figure 2.19 – Options in the KAPE GUI

2. Click on **Target source** and select a source for triage collection:

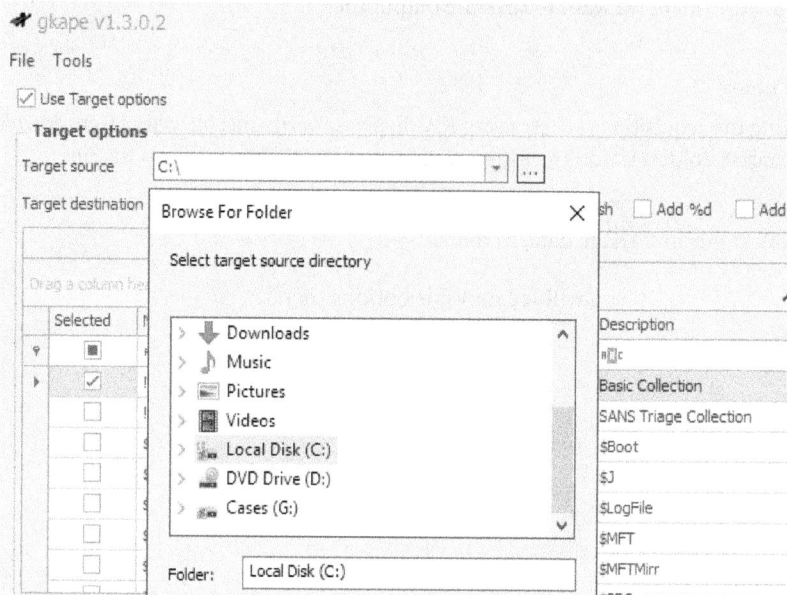

Figure 2.20 – KAPE target selection

3. Then, make a selection for **Target destination** to save the output of the collected triage to a specific path:

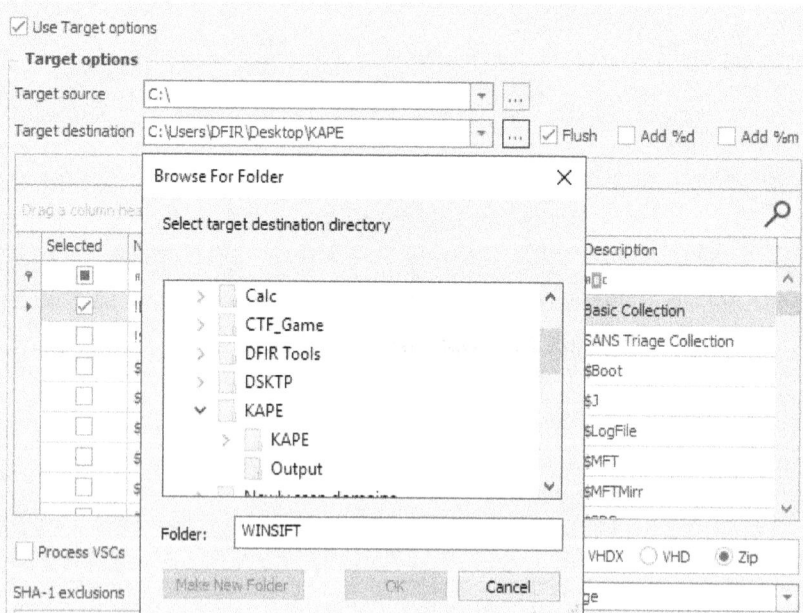

Figure 2.21 – KAPE target output selection

4. For the next step, select the target file that you want to use to collect the artifacts. We will use the `!BasicCollection` target file. This will collect event logs, evidence of execution, and other artifacts mentioned within the target file:

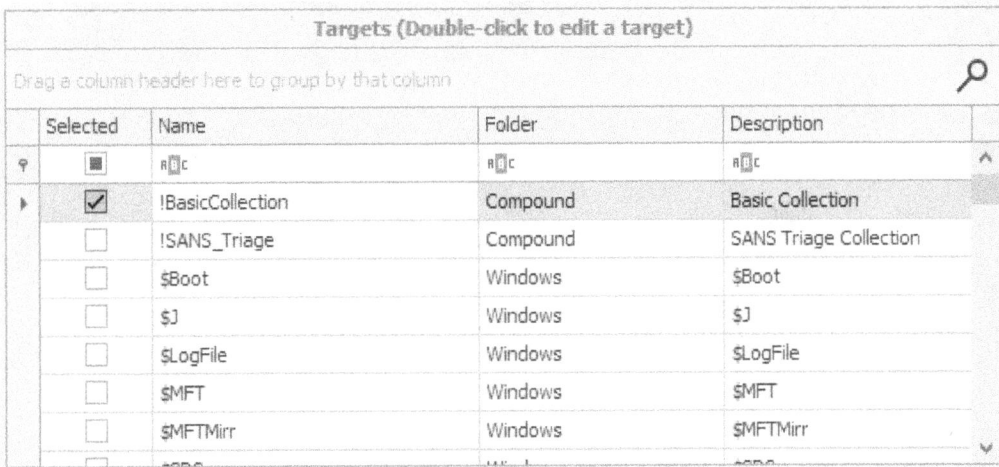

Figure 2.22 – Target file selection

5. Now, for this step, the examiner will select the format of the output if they want to export the collected triage data. We will use Zip format here:

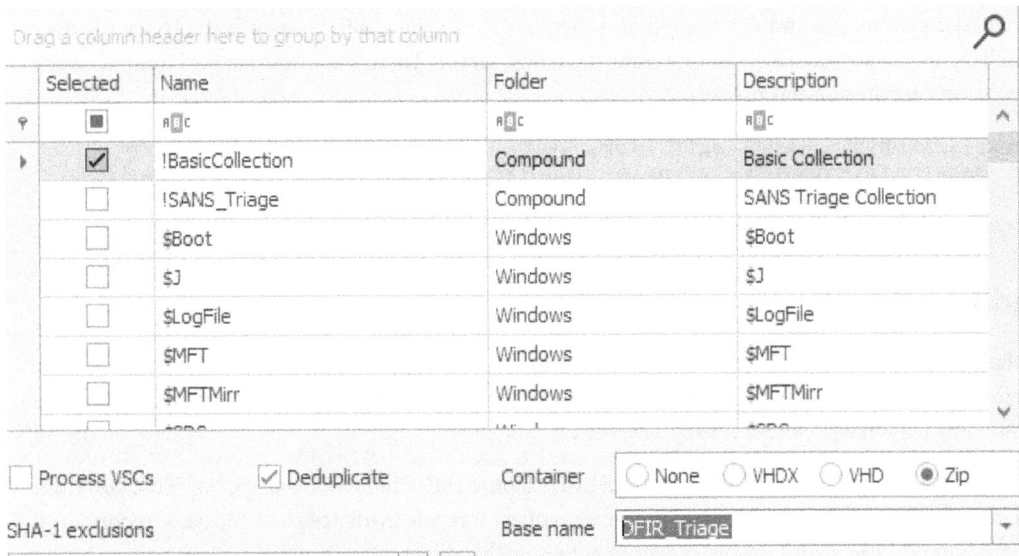

Figure 2.23 – KAPE container selection

6. We are all set to go now. Click on **Execute!**, and it will open a new window with details. Once the collection is done, we will navigate to the Output folder and check the output files. We will find a log file and a Zip file. From here, we can extract the evidence and analyze it:

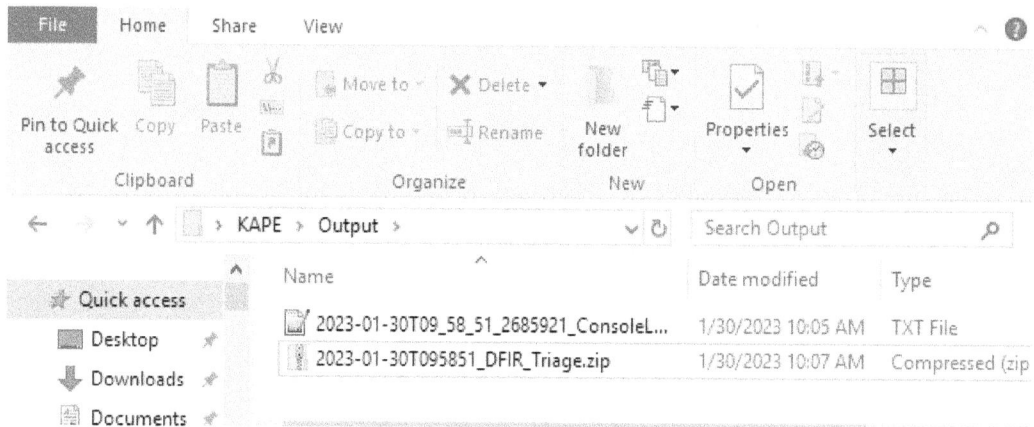

Figure 2.24 – KAPE Output folder

In cases where we do not have the luxury of using the KAPE GUI, we can initiate the triage process using the command line. This is helpful in cases where the examiner will pull the logs remotely and have at their disposal **endpoint detection and response** (EDR) access with a live response.

We will define a source and destination and then use KAPE capabilities to push the triage file over a publicly hosted server. This will represent the triage server. Then, the examiner will jump into the server and start the analysis process:

```
C:\Users\DFIR\Desktop\KAPE\KAPE>kape.exe  --tsource C:\ --tdest C:\
Windows\DFIR\KAPE\%d%m --target !BasicCollection --zip kapetriage
--scc KAPECollection --zip kapetriage --scs 10.10.10.10  --scp 22
--scu USER --scpw "P@SSWrD"
```

Additional tools

We have covered FTK Imager and KAPE, which are the most commonly used tools when it comes to a forensic examiner's day-to-day tasks. However, we have other tools that we can use based on the situation or personal preference, such as **CyLR**.

Let's dive into using CyLR. CyLR is a powerful live response collection tool developed by Alan Orlikoski and Jason Yegge. It is designed to help examiners collect forensic evidence from the **New Technology File System** (NTFS). CyLR enables examiners to quickly collect triage images.

CyLR helps in collecting raw files as it does not use or interact with Windows APIs. Also, it uses memory optimization for collected artifacts and uses **Secure File Transfer Protocol** (**SFTP**) to push the triage over a network.

CyLR covers acquisition from multiple operating systems, such as Linux and macOS. Let's see how to acquire an image using CyLR, as follows:

1. Download CyLR using the official GitHub repository at `https://github.com/orlikoski/CyLR/releases` and extract it.

2. Use the config file to modify the artifacts collection. In this step, we will add the evidence we need to acquire by providing the full path, as shown in the following screenshot. Note that we need to replace `<USERNAME>` with the username that we need to pull evidence from:

```
 1   E:\$MFT
 2   E:\Windows\inf\setupapi.dev.log
 3   E:\Windows\Appcompat\Programs
 4   E:\Windows\System32\winevt\logs
 5   E:\Windows\Tasks
 6   E:\Windows\Prefetch
 7   E:\Windows\System32\config\SAM
 8   E:\Windows\System32\config\SYSTEM
 9   E:\Windows\System32\config\SOFTWARE
10   E:\Windows\System32\config\SECURITY
11   E:\Windows\System32\config\SAM.LOG1
12   E:\Windows\System32\config\SYSTEM.LOG1
13   E:\Windows\System32\config\SOFTWARE.LOG1
14   E:\Windows\System32\config\SECURITY.LOG1
15   E:\Windows\System32\config\SAM.LOG2
16   E:\Windows\System32\config\SYSTEM.LOG2
17   E:\Windows\System32\config\SOFTWARE.LOG2
18   E:\Windows\System32\config\SECURITY.LOG2
19   E:\ProgramData\Microsoft\Search\Data\Applications\Windows
20   E:\Users\<USERNAME>\AppData\Roaming\Microsoft\Windows\Recent
21   E:\Users\<USERNAME>\NTUSER.DAT
22   E:\Users\<USERNAME>\NTUSER.DAT.LOG1
23   E:\Users\<USERNAME>\NTUSER.DAT.LOG2
24   E:\Users\<USERNAME>\AppData\Local\Microsoft\Windows\Explorer
```

Figure 2.25 – CyLR config file

3. For CyLR usage, we can check the parameter to use by running `CyLR -h`. This is the output:

```
Usage: CyLR [Options]... [Files]...

The CyLR tool collects forensic artifacts from hosts with NTFS file systems
quickly, securely and minimizes impact to the host.

The available options are:
-od
        Defines the directory that the zip archive will be created in.
        Defaults to current working directory.
        Usage: -od <directory path>
-of
        Defines the name of the zip archive will be created. Defaults to
        host machine's name.
        Usage: -of <archive name>
-c
        Optional argument to provide custom list of artifact files and
        directories (one entry per line). NOTE: Please see
        CUSTOM_PATH_TEMPLATE.txt for sample.
        Usage: -c <path to config file>
-d
        Same as '-c' but will collect default paths included in CyLR in
        addition to those specified in the provided config file.
        Usage: -d <path to config file>
-u
        SFTP username
        Usage: -u <sftp-username>
-p
        SFTP password
        Usage: -p <password>
-s
        SFTP Server resolvable hostname or IP address and port. If no port
        is given then 22 is used by default.  Format is <server name>:<port>
        Usage: -s <ip>:<port>
-os
        Defines the output directory on the SFTP server, as it may be a
        different location than the ZIP generate on disk. Can be full or
        relative path.
        Usage: -os <directory path>
```

Figure 2.26 – CyLR -h output

5. Then run cmd as administrator, change directory to the `CyLR` folder, and execute the following command:

```
CyLR.exe -c Config.txt
```

The following screenshot shows the output of the previous command:

```
Collecting File: C:\Windows\System32\winevt\logs\Windows PowerShell.evt
Collecting File: C:\Windows\Prefetch\ReadyBoot\Trace1.fx
Collecting File: C:\Windows\Prefetch\ReadyBoot\Trace2.fx
Collecting File: C:\Windows\Prefetch\ReadyBoot\Trace3.fx
Collecting File: C:\Windows\Prefetch\ReadyBoot\Trace4.fx
Collecting File: C:\Windows\Prefetch\ReadyBoot\Trace5.fx
Collecting File: C:\Windows\Prefetch\AgAppLaunch.db
Collecting File: C:\Windows\Prefetch\AgCx_SC4.db
Collecting File: C:\Windows\Prefetch\AgGlFaultHistory.db
Collecting File: C:\Windows\Prefetch\AgGlFgAppHistory.db
Collecting File: C:\Windows\Prefetch\AgGlGlobalHistory.db
Collecting File: C:\Windows\Prefetch\AgGlUAD_P_S-1-5-21-1302835572-1852
Collecting File: C:\Windows\Prefetch\AgGlUAD_S-1-5-21-1302835572-185288
Collecting File: C:\Windows\Prefetch\AgRobust.db
Collecting File: C:\Windows\Prefetch\Layout.ini
Collecting File: C:\Windows\Prefetch\PfSvPerfStats.bin
Collecting File: C:\Windows\Tasks\SCHEDLGU.TXT
Collecting File: C:\$MFT
Extraction complete. 0:01:00.9176216 elapsed

C:\Users\faisal\Desktop>CyLR.exe -u skadi -p skadi -s 192.168.106.141
```

Figure 2.27 – CyLR output

We are now capable of collecting triage data using multiple tools. In conclusion, KAPE and CyLR are both valuable tools for digital forensics investigators. KAPE is a rapid and configurable tool that can be used to identify and process relevant artifacts from image files. This can help investigators to quickly focus on critical systems and build timelines. CyLR, on the other hand, is a straightforward and efficient tool that can be used to collect system and event logs from live systems. This can be helpful for investigators who need to collect evidence from systems that are still in use.

Evidence collection and acquisition exercise

In this section, we will apply what we have learned so far. Proceed as follows:

1. Using KAPE, collect the prefetch file by using the command line.
2. Collect registry hives using the KAPE GUI.
3. Perform image acquisition using FTK Imager and name the image `Forensic_Image_01`.
4. Configure CyLR to collect only $MFT and execute it.

Summary

In this chapter, we discussed the tools and techniques used to acquire and collect digital forensic evidence. We learned about the effective use of tools such as KAPE and FTK Imager, which can help us to properly acquire evidence and ensure its integrity. By familiarizing ourselves with these tools, we can better navigate the complexities of forensic investigations and preserve the CoC for the evidence we collect.

By understanding this chapter, you will be able to collect and preserve digital evidence using various tools.

In the next chapter, we will explore the field of memory forensics. Memory forensics is the process of analyzing a computer's volatile memory, which can provide valuable insights into active processes, network connections, and potential malicious activity. We will discuss prominent tools and methodologies used in memory forensics, and we will learn how to use these tools to uncover advanced threats and expose intricate attack vectors.

I hope you are excited to join us on this journey into the fascinating world of memory forensics, which will be our topic for the next chapter!

3

Memory Forensics for the Windows OS

Memory forensics is a branch of digital forensics that focuses on the analysis of computer memory (RAM) to extract valuable information about a system's state at a specific point in time. Unlike other forms of digital evidence, memory provides a live view of what happened on a computer at a given moment, including running processes, network connections, and system information. This makes memory forensics an important tool in incident response and cybercrime investigations, as it can provide valuable insights into the inner workings of a computer and reveal information that might not be available from other sources.

Memory forensics is a complex field that requires a deep understanding of computer systems, memory management, and the behavior of operating systems and applications. However, the insights gained from memory forensics can be invaluable in incident response, criminal investigations, and security assessments. By providing a comprehensive view of the state of a computer's memory at a specific point in time, memory forensics can help organizations identify and respond to security incidents, improve their overall security posture, and protect against future attacks. Acquiring digital evidence from a Windows machine is a complex process that requires specialized knowledge and tools. To understand this process and gain insights into the tools, we will cover the following topics in this chapter:

- Memory forensic concepts and techniques
- Memory acquisition tools
- Using Volatility to analyze memory dumps and plugins
- Windows hibernation files and crash dumps
- A memory forensics analysis exercise

Technical requirements

In this chapter, we will work with memory acquisition and analysis tools. Using the following links, you can access and download them, and installation is fairly straightforward:

- **FTK Imager**: `https://www.exterro.com/ftk-imager`
- **Volatility:** `https://www.volatilityfoundation.org/releases`
- **WinPmen**: `https://github.com/Velocidex/WinPmem`
- **DumpIt**: `https://zeltser.com/memory-acquisition-with-dumpit-for-dfir-2/`
- **Belkasoft RAM Capturer**: `https://belkasoft.com/ram-capturer`
- **MAGNET RAM Capture**: `https://support.magnetforensics.com/s/software-and-downloads?productTag=free-tools`

Understanding memory forensics concepts and techniques

By delving into the realm of memory forensics, investigators gain profound insights into the inner workings of a system, thereby enabling the identification of critical evidence and a thorough understanding of digital incidents.

The process of memory forensics typically involves acquiring a memory dump, which is a snapshot of the contents of a computer's RAM, and analyzing it using specialized tools, such as **Volatility** or **Rekall**.

These tools provide the ability to examine data stored in memory, extract relevant information, and perform an in-depth analysis of various aspects of a system, such as running processes, network connections, and system information.

One of the key advantages of memory forensics is the ability to investigate an incident in real time or near real time. When combined with live system analysis, memory forensics can provide a complete picture of an incident, allowing an investigator to quickly identify its root cause and take steps to mitigate the damage done. This may be particularly important in cases in which the attacker is still active or a rapid response is required.

Memory forensics can be used to investigate a wide range of incidents, including malware infections, data breaches, and other security incidents. By analyzing the contents of a computer's memory, investigators can identify running processes, network connections, and other indicators of compromise that can help to identify the source of the attack and the extent of the damage.

One of the challenges in memory forensics is the complex and dynamic nature of computer memory. Memory is constantly being allocated and deallocated, making it difficult to capture a complete snapshot of a system's state at a specific point in time. In addition, many modern operating systems use techniques such as virtual memory and paging, which can complicate the analysis of memory dumps.

Some techniques to overcome the challenges

To overcome these challenges, memory forensics tools use a range of techniques to identify and analyze relevant information in the memory dump. Some of these techniques include the following:

- **Signature scanning**: This involves searching for known signatures or patterns of data in a memory dump. For example, the memory dump might contain the signature of a specific type of malware, which can be used to identify the presence of that malware on the system.

- **Process enumeration**: This involves identifying the running processes on the system and analyzing the data associated with those processes, such as open files, network connections, and memory usage. By analyzing the data associated with each process, investigators can identify suspicious activity and determine the root cause of an incident.

- **Network analysis**: This involves analyzing the network connections established by a system and the data transmitted over those connections. By analyzing the network traffic, investigators can identify the source and destination of the traffic, the type of data being transmitted, and other key details.

- **File carving**: This involves extracting files and other data from the memory dump. By analyzing the extracted data, investigators can identify the source of the data, the type of data, and other key details.

Now is an ideal time to let you know about an awesome book on memory forensics – *Practical Memory Forensics*, written by *Svetlana Ostrovskaya* and *Oleg Skulkin*. However, since this book is not fully dedicated to memory forensics, we will only cover the fundamentals in order to understand the overall concepts.

The following figure shows memory types.

Figure 3.1: A memory types sample

Why memory forensics is important

Memory forensics is an important subfield of digital forensics because it provides a unique and valuable source of information to analyze and investigate security incidents on computer systems. Here are some reasons why memory forensics is important for digital forensics:

- **Volatile nature of memory**: Computer memory is a volatile resource, which means that its contents are lost when a system is shut down or restarted. However, when a system is running, the memory contains a wealth of information about the processes, applications, and network activity occurring on the system. Memory forensics provides a way to capture and analyze this information, even after the system has been shut down.

- **Detecting evasion techniques**: During incident response, attackers often use sophisticated techniques to hide their activities on a compromised system, such as using rootkits or other forms of malware that are designed to evade traditional detection methods. Memory forensics can be used to identify and analyze these techniques, providing valuable insights into attackers' methods and motives.

- **Identification of malware**: Malware can be difficult to detect and analyze using traditional methods, especially if it is designed to be stealthy or polymorphic. Memory forensics provides a way to identify and analyze malware that may be hidden or encrypted on a system, allowing investigators to better understand the nature and behavior of the malware.

Moreover, we can utilize memory images in cases such as internal threats and profile user activities, which involves analyzing a user's behavior and activities on a computer system to identify patterns, anomalies, and evidence of malicious activity. Memory analysis can provide a unique source of information to build user profiles, including details about running processes, network activity, and user activity, such as process trees, network connections, and the malicious activities performed.

To understand the structures and artifacts that we can gather by examining memory dump, first, we need to learn about windows components and forensic artifacts.

Exploring the main components of Windows

Windows is an operating system that is widely used on desktops, laptops, and servers. It comprises various components that work together to provide a seamless user experience. Here, we will discuss the main components of the Windows operating system in detail.

The kernel

The **kernel** is the central component of the Windows operating system. It is responsible for managing system resources and providing a communication bridge between the software and hardware components. The kernel has various sub-components, including memory management, process management, input/output management, and security management.

Windows processes

Processes are the programs that are currently running on a Windows system. Each process has its own memory space, and the kernel provides the necessary resources and protection to ensure that processes can execute without interfering with each other.

Windows processes are fundamental components of the Windows operating system. A process is a unit of work that is executed by the operating system. Each process has its own virtual memory space, containing the data and code that the process requires to execute. Windows processes are responsible for executing applications, services, and system components. Processes provide an essential foundation for the operation of the Windows operating system, and their behavior can provide valuable insights into the operation of a system.

Every process in Windows is identified by a unique **process ID (PID)**. This PID is used by the operating system to manage the process, and it can be used by forensic investigators to track the behavior of the process. Each process is also associated with a set of threads. A thread is a unit of execution that operates within a process. Threads share the same memory space as the process in which they run, and they are scheduled by the operating system to execute the code that the process contains.

Processes can be started by a variety of mechanisms, including user interaction, system startup, and the initiation of services. Once a process is running, it can execute code, allocate and deallocate memory, read and write files, and interact with other processes. Processes can also create **child processes**, which inherit the characteristics of the parent process. Child processes can then go on to execute their own code and create further child processes.

A process can consist of multiple threads, each serving the purpose of allocating processor time. In systems with a single processor, multiple threads can be allocated, but only one thread can execute at any given time. Threads have short execution durations before passing control to the next thread, creating the perception of concurrent activities. This illusion gives users the impression that multiple tasks happen simultaneously. In systems with multiple processors, true multithreading occurs, allowing threads from the same process to execute concurrently on different processors. This enables parallel execution and enhances overall system performance.

Controlling the processes

Windows processes can be managed and controlled by a variety of mechanisms. **Task Manager** is a tool that can be used to view and manage the processes running on a Windows system. It is a **graphical user interface (GUI)** that can be used to view and control running processes. Task Manager provides information on each process, including its name, PID, status, and resource usage. Task Manager also provides a mechanism to terminate or suspend processes.

Interacting with the processes

In addition to Task Manager, Windows provides a number of command-line utilities that can be used to interact with processes. For example, the `tasklist` utility can be used to display a list of running processes, along with their PIDs and other information. The `tasklist` utility can be used to terminate a running process.

Windows processes are a critical component of the Windows operating system, and their behavior can provide valuable insights into the operation of a system. Forensic investigators can use tools such as process monitors and process dumps to capture information on running processes. This information can be used to identify malicious activity, such as the execution of malware or the theft of sensitive data. By analyzing the behavior of processes, forensic investigators can gain a deep understanding of the operation of a system and identify the root causes of security incidents.

Exploring some important processes in Windows

We will look mostly at investigating process trees or child and parent process behavior to identify abnormal and suspicious execution patterns. Let's check some of the processes in a Windows environment:

- `Svchost.exe`: This is a generic host process that is used to host several Windows services. It is an essential process and should not be terminated.

- `Explorer.exe`: This process is responsible for the Windows desktop and file explorer. It manages the **user interface (UI)** and allows a user to interact with files and folders.

- `Lsass.exe`: This process is responsible for local security and login policies. It is used to authenticate users and ensure the security of the operating system.

- `Winlogon.exe`: This process is responsible for managing user logon and logout processes. It ensures that the user is authenticated and authorized to use the system.

- `Services.exe`: This process is responsible for starting, stopping, and managing system services. It is a critical process and should not be terminated.

- `Taskmgr.exe`: This is the Windows Task Manager process. It allows users to view and manage running processes, monitor system performance, and adjust system settings.

- `Spoolsv.exe`: This process manages the printing subsystem in Windows. It is responsible for sending print jobs to printers and managing the print queue.

- `Smss.exe`: This is the session manager responsible for creating a new session.

- `Csrss.exe`: A client/server-run subsystem process, this is responsible for managing processes and threads and the Windows API, along with other functions such as mapping driver letters.

- `Wininit.exe`: This is a Windows initialization process, which is responsible for launching `services.exe` and `lsass.exe`.

Windows services

Windows services are programs that run in the background, providing various system-level functions. Services are started automatically when a system boots and continues to run until the system is shut down. Examples of services include *network services*, *printing services*, and *security services*.

On the windows operating system, a service is a program that runs in the background and performs specific tasks without user interaction. Services are started automatically at system startup and can be controlled and managed through the **Services console** or via **command-line tools**.

Windows services have several characteristics that distinguish them from regular applications. For example, they do not have a UI and are designed to run continuously in the background, even when no user is logged on to the system. Services can also run under a specified user account, which may have different privileges from the currently logged-on user.

Services can be categorized into two types:

- **System services**: System services are required for the operating system to function properly and are managed by the **Service Control Manager** (**SCM**)

- **User services**: User services, on the other hand, are started by the user and typically run in the context of the logged-on user's account

Each service has a unique name, a display name, a description, and a status (running, stopped, or paused). In addition, services can be configured to start automatically, manually, or **Disabled**, and they can also have dependencies on other services.

Windows services play a critical role in the operating system, and any issues with them or vulnerabilities can have serious consequences. Malware and other types of attacks often target services to gain persistence on a system or escalate privileges.

Forensic investigators can use memory forensics to analyze system memory and identify any suspicious or malicious services running on a system. By analyzing the service details, dependencies, and execution history, investigators can determine whether a service is related to a security incident or has been tampered with by an attacker.

Device drivers

Device drivers are software components that enable communication between the operating system and hardware devices, such as printers, disk drives, and graphics cards. Device drivers are loaded into memory by the kernel when a hardware device is detected. A faulty device driver can cause crashes, instability, or performance issues on a Windows system.

Device drivers are loaded into the Windows kernel, which is the core of the operating system. Kernel drivers have high-level privileges and can access and control system resources. Because of this, malicious actors often target device drivers to gain access to system resources and escalate their privileges.

Memory forensic examiners can use memory analysis tools such as Volatility to analyze the system's memory and identify any suspicious or malicious device drivers. Examiners can extract information about loaded device drivers, including the driver's name, file path, version, and hardware device information. They can also look for signs of rootkits or other types of malware that may use device drivers to hide their presence on the system.

DLLs

Dynamic Link Libraries (**DLLs**) are a type of shared library that contains code and data that can be used by multiple programs simultaneously. DLLs allow for efficient code reuse and help to reduce the memory footprint of running programs. However, a malicious DLL can be used to compromise a Windows system by executing arbitrary code or taking control of the system.

In Windows, a DLL is a shared library that contains code and data that can be used by multiple programs at the same time. A DLL is loaded into memory when a program needs to use the code or data within it. This helps to reduce the memory footprint of running applications and makes it easier to update or fix code without having to recompile the entire application.

DLLs can be used to provide a wide range of functionality to programs, including the following:

- UI elements such as dialog boxes, buttons, and menus

- Filesystem access and manipulation

- Networking and communication capabilities

- Hardware access and control

- Cryptography and security functionality

- Database access and manipulation

DLLs can be loaded into memory in several ways, including through the use of the `LoadLibrary()` function, which can be called from within an application, or the use of the `rundll32.exe` program to load a DLL from the command line.

While DLLs can provide many benefits to Windows applications, they can also be a source of security vulnerabilities. Attackers can use DLL injection techniques to load their own malicious DLLs into legitimate processes, allowing them to execute their code with the privileges of the targeted process. For this reason, forensic examiners need to be able to identify and analyze DLLs during an investigation to determine their potential impact on the security of a system.

The registry

The **Windows registry** is a hierarchical database that stores configuration settings and options for the operating system and installed programs. The registry is accessed and manipulated by the kernel, device drivers, and applications. A corrupted or malicious entry in the registry can cause system instability, crashes, or other issues.

The Windows registry is a hierarchical database that stores the configuration settings and options for the operating system, installed applications, and hardware components. It contains settings and preferences for user accounts, system configuration, installed software, and hardware devices.

The registry is divided into several main branches, including the following:

- `HKEY_CLASSES_ROOT`: Contains information about registered file types and associated applications
- `HKEY_CURRENT_USER`: Contains settings specific to the currently logged-in user
- `HKEY_LOCAL_MACHINE`: Contains settings for the hardware, operating system, and installed software
- `HKEY_USERS`: Contains settings for each user profile on the computer
- `HKEY_CURRENT_CONFIG`: Contains settings that are dynamically generated based on the current system configuration

Each branch is divided into keys, which can contain subkeys and values. Keys are identified by their names, which can be alphanumeric and separated by backslashes. Values can contain data that is used by the operating system or installed applications.

The Windows registry is essential for the proper functioning of the operating system and applications, but it can also be a valuable source of forensic evidence. Forensic analysts can use various tools to extract and analyze registry data to identify user activity, system configurations, and potentially malicious activity.

However, it is important to note that modifying or deleting registry entries can have severe consequences for the stability and security of a system, so it should only be done with caution and proper knowledge of the potential risks.

We will cover the registry in greater depth in *Chapter 4*.

The filesystem

The filesystem is responsible for organizing and managing files and directories on storage devices. Windows supports various filesystems, including the **New Technology File System** (**NTFS**) and the **File Allocation Table** (**FAT**). The filesystem provides functions for file creation, deletion, read/write operations, and file security.

```
C:\Users\PC>tasklist /m /fi "pid eq 11960"

Image Name                        PID Modules
=========================== ======== =======================================
firefox.exe                     11960 ntdll.dll, KERNEL32.DLL, KERNELBASE.dll,
                                      ucrtbase.dll, mozglue.dll, CRYPT32.dll,
                                      MSVCP140.dll, VCRUNTIME140.dll,
                                      VCRUNTIME140_1.dll, cryptbase.dll,
                                      nss3.dll, ADVAPI32.dll, msvcrt.dll,
                                      sechost.dll, RPCRT4.dll, WS2_32.dll,
                                      WSOCK32.dll, lgpllibs.dll, xul.dll,
                                      bcrypt.dll, WINTRUST.dll, ktmw32.dll,
                                      PROPSYS.dll, combase.dll, VERSION.dll,
                                      MSASN1.dll, bcryptprimitives.dll,
                                      kernel.appcore.dll, ntmarta.dll,
                                      OLEAUT32.dll, msvcp_win.dll, WINMM.dll,
                                      webauthn.dll, winsta.dll, dwrite.dll,
                                      softokn3.dll, freebl3.dll
```

Figure 3.2: A list of DLLs loaded by a Firefox process

Investigation methodology

One of the things we need to understand is that when it comes to memory forensics, what we need to do differs depending on the case that we face. Suppose that you are tasked to investigate an internal threat. What types of artifacts will you examine? Can you get all the information you need from the disk artifacts, or do you need to cross-reference them with the memory artifacts? What are the artifacts that you will focus on? Can you get a complete picture of the incident by analyzing the disk artifacts alone, or do you need to look at the memory artifacts as well?

For example, let's say a company has experienced issues with its network and systems for a few months. They want to identify the source of the problem. As forensic investigators, we have to do a deep-dive investigation, and we discover that there has been a series of data breaches that have occurred from within the company's own network.

Further investigation reveals that the breaches have been caused by an employee who has been deliberately stealing sensitive data and selling it to a competitor. The employee has used their knowledge of the company's network and systems to gain access to the data and cover their tracks.

As the investigator, we use memory forensics to examine the employee's computer and discover evidence of their activity, such as the use of various tools for data exfiltration and obfuscation, as well as evidence of attempts to cover up their tracks. By reporting the findings to the company, they are able to take action to terminate the employee's employment and secure their systems to prevent similar incidents from occurring in the future. The evidence collected during the investigation is also used in legal proceedings against the employee and the competitor who purchased the stolen data.

Another scenario would be the misuse of privilege. In the case of a Windows forensic investigator, misuse of privilege can occur when an authorized user oversteps their boundaries or when an unauthorized user gains access to privileged accounts. For example, a member of the IT department with elevated privileges may intentionally or unintentionally tamper with evidence to cover up their involvement in a security breach.

Understanding Windows architecture

Understanding the technical depth of the main components of Windows is particularly relevant in the context of memory forensics. It provides forensic analysts with a comprehensive understanding of the Windows operating system's underlying architecture, enabling them to effectively analyze memory dumps and extract valuable information for incident response, malware analysis, and digital investigations.

The Windows system architecture consists of several components that work together to provide a stable and secure computing environment. The following are the main components of the Windows system architecture:

- **The Hardware Abstraction Layer** (**HAL**): This is responsible for abstracting the hardware components of a system, including the processor, memory, and input/output devices. The HAL is the layer between the hardware and the OS, which enables the same OS to work with different hardware configurations.

- **The kernel**: The kernel is the core component of the Windows OS. It is responsible for managing system resources, including memory, CPU, and **input/output** (**I/O**) devices. The kernel is loaded into memory during the boot process and runs in privileged mode, allowing it to perform critical system functions.

- **Executive services**: The executive services are a set of functions that run in kernel mode and provide essential operating system services, such as process and thread management, memory management, and I/O management.

- **User mode**: The user mode is a non-privileged mode of the OS to run user applications. User applications access system resources through system calls to the kernel. User mode applies to user applications, system services, and GUIs.

- **Device drivers**: Device drivers are software components that allow the operating system to communicate with hardware devices, such as printers, keyboards, and network cards. They are loaded into memory during the boot process and run in kernel mode.

- **Services**: Services are applications that run in the background and provide specific functionality to an OS, such as remote access, networking, and security. Services run in their own process and can be started, stopped, and managed through the SCM.

- **The registry**: The registry is a hierarchical database that stores configuration settings and options for the operating system, device drivers, services, and applications. The registry is used by the operating system and other software components to store and retrieve system configuration data.

Since this is not a dedicated memory forensics course, we will not cover all aspects of memory architecture and CPU architecture. Once again, *Practical Memory Forensics* by *Svetlana Ostrovskaya* and *Oleg Skulkin* is recommended as one of the best books available to learn about memory forensics for both Windows and Linux.

We have covered multiple aspects of Windows architecture and components, before exploring acquisition and analysis. Now, let's move on and take a deep dive into dumping a memory image.

Looking at the memory acquisition tools

Memory acquisition is a critical component of digital forensics, allowing examiners to capture and analyze the contents of a computer's RAM, including running processes, the system state, and data that may have been deleted or otherwise hidden. The process of memory acquisition typically involves several steps, which may vary depending on the specific tools and techniques used.

The first step in memory acquisition is to identify the target system and determine the appropriate acquisition method. This may involve connecting to the target system remotely, booting from a separate device or media, or using a specialized hardware tool to capture the contents of the system's RAM.

Once the acquisition method has been established, the next step is to select an appropriate tool to capture the memory image. Popular tools for Windows memory acquisition include **FTK Imager**, **DumpIt**, and **WinPmem**, each with its own advantages and limitations. The tool selected will depend on factors such as the size of the target system's RAM, the available storage space for the memory image, and the required level of analysis.

The memory acquisition process itself typically involves copying the contents of the target system's RAM to a storage device, which may be connected directly to the target system or accessed remotely. Depending on the size of the memory image and the available storage space, the acquisition can take anywhere from a few minutes to several hours.

Once the memory image has been acquired, it can be analyzed using specialized tools and techniques to identify running processes, the system state, and other data of interest. This may involve using Volatility plugins, custom scripts, or other analysis tools to identify patterns and anomalies in the data. Finally, once the image has been created, it should be verified, using checksums or other methods to ensure its accuracy and integrity, before being stored for further analysis.

Let's dive into FTK Imager now and start creating our first forensic image.

Using FTK Imager to capture memory

FTK Imager is a powerful digital forensics tool that can be used for memory acquisition in Windows. The process of using FTK Imager to dump memory involves the following steps:

1. **Launch FTK Imager**: First, launch the FTK Imager application on your Windows machine.

2. **Choose Capture Memory…**: In the FTK Imager interface, select the **Capture Memory…** option from the **File** menu. This will open the **Memory Capture** dialog box:

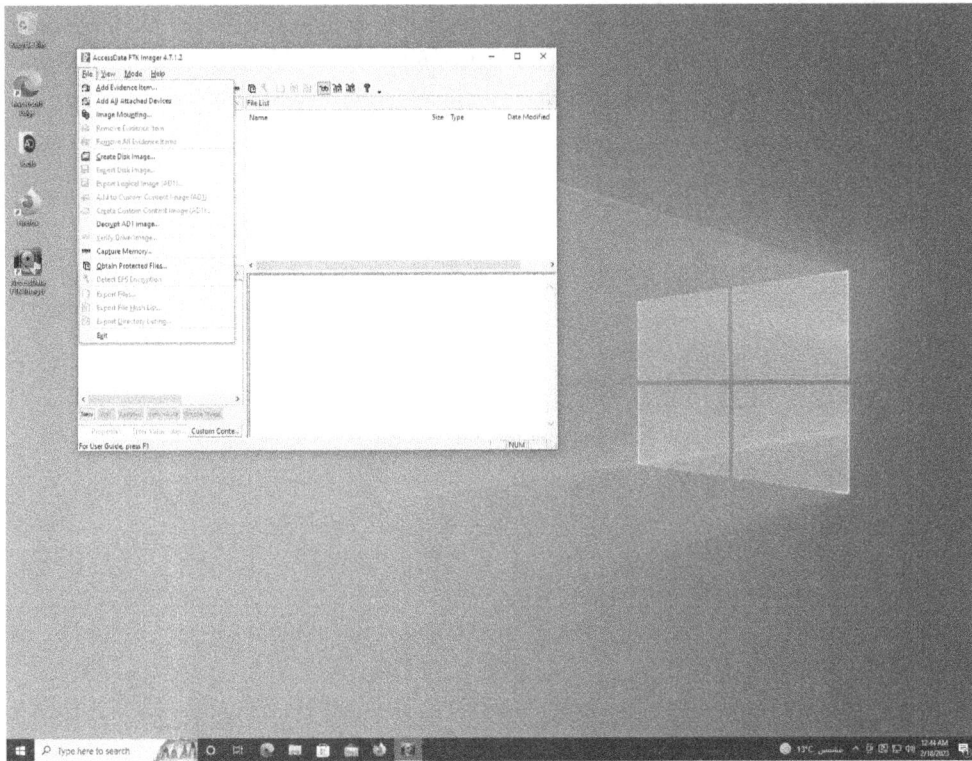

Figure 3.3: FTK Imager | Capture Memory…

3. **Configure the memory dump settings**: In the **Memory Capture** dialog box, you can configure various settings related to memory acquisition, such as the destination path to save to and the filename. Click on the **Capture Memory** button to begin the process.

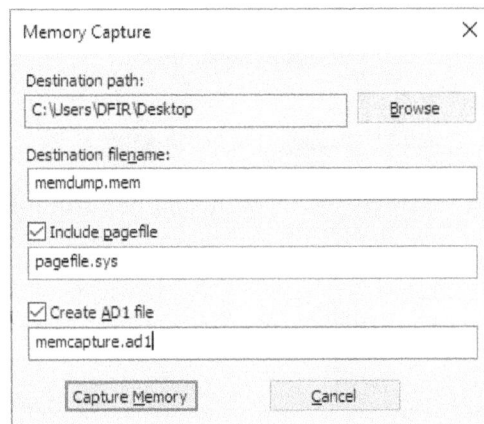

Figure 3.4: FTK Imager | Capture Memory

4. **Wait for the process to complete**: The memory acquisition process may take some time, depending on the size of the memory and the configuration settings. You can monitor the progress of the acquisition in the **Status** area of the **Memory Progress** dialog box.

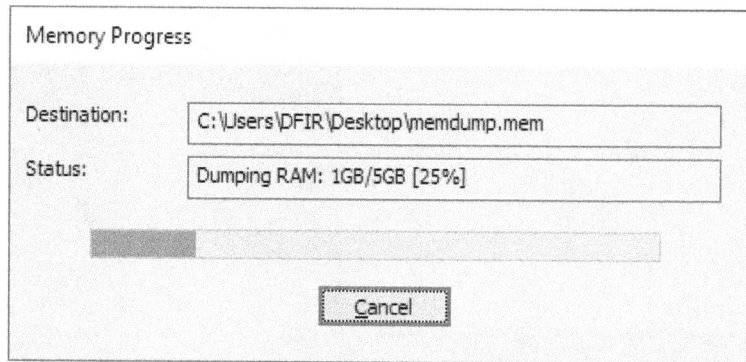

Figure 3.5 – Memory Progress

5. Once the memory acquisition process is complete, you can explore the memory dump file in the saved desired location. The memory dump file will be saved in the format specified in the configuration settings.

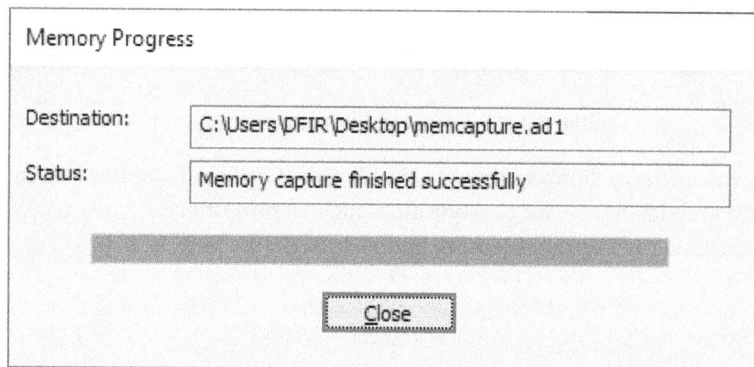

Figure 3.6: Memory capture completed

We can see the output files and the extension under the saved file path.

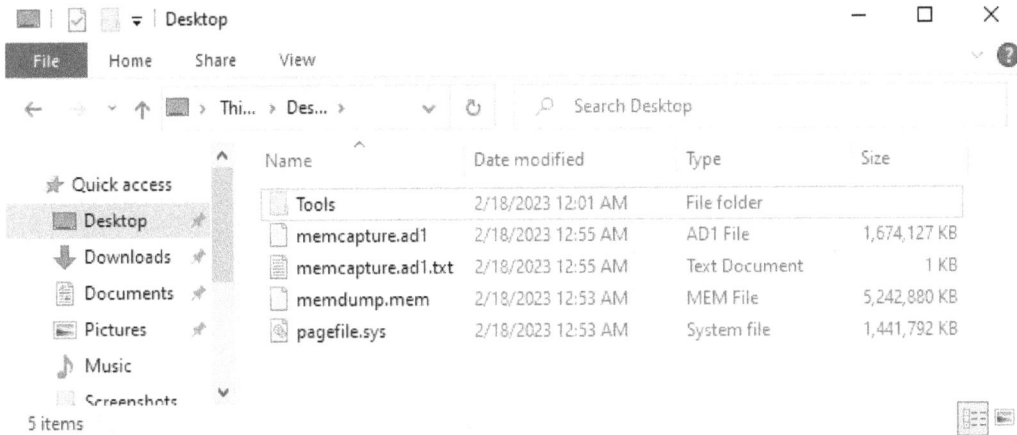

Figure 3.7: FTK Imager output

6. The next step will depend on the situation; either we move the output by using a USB flash drive, or we can push it over to a collection server over the network by using the **Secure Copy Protocol (SCP)**.

FTK Imager is a powerful tool that can be used to acquire volatile memory from a computer. The memory acquisition process is relatively straightforward. By following the guidelines in this section, you can ensure that you acquire a valid and reliable memory image that can be used for forensic analysis.

WinPmem

WinPmem is a memory acquisition tool designed for the Windows operating system that captures the contents of the physical memory (RAM) and saves it in a raw memory dump file. This tool is commonly used by digital forensic examiners for incident response and forensic investigations. The captured memory can be analyzed for forensic evidence, such as open network connections, running processes, registry keys, and other volatile data.

WinPmem is an open source tool and is developed by a community of digital forensic experts. It is designed to be lightweight, efficient, and compatible with a wide range of Windows systems, with support for WinXP and Win10 x86 or x64. The WDK 7600 can be used to include WinXP support. By default, the provided WinPmem executables will be compiled with WDK10, supporting Win7–Win10 and featuring more modern code.

By visiting the GitHub repository by following `https://github.com/Velocidex/WinPmem`, we can access the WinPmem binary using the **Releases** link shown here:

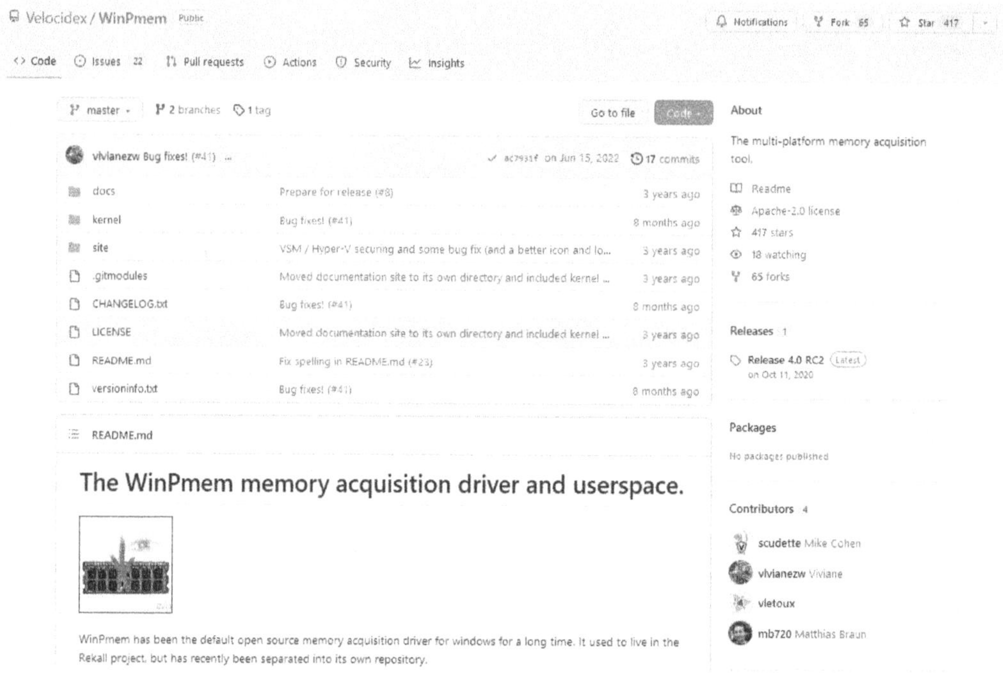

Figure 3.8: The WinPmem GitHub repository

Once we click on **Releases**, we can see a list of binaries for Windows. For the use case in this chapter, proceed to download `winpmem_mini_x64_rc2.exe`:

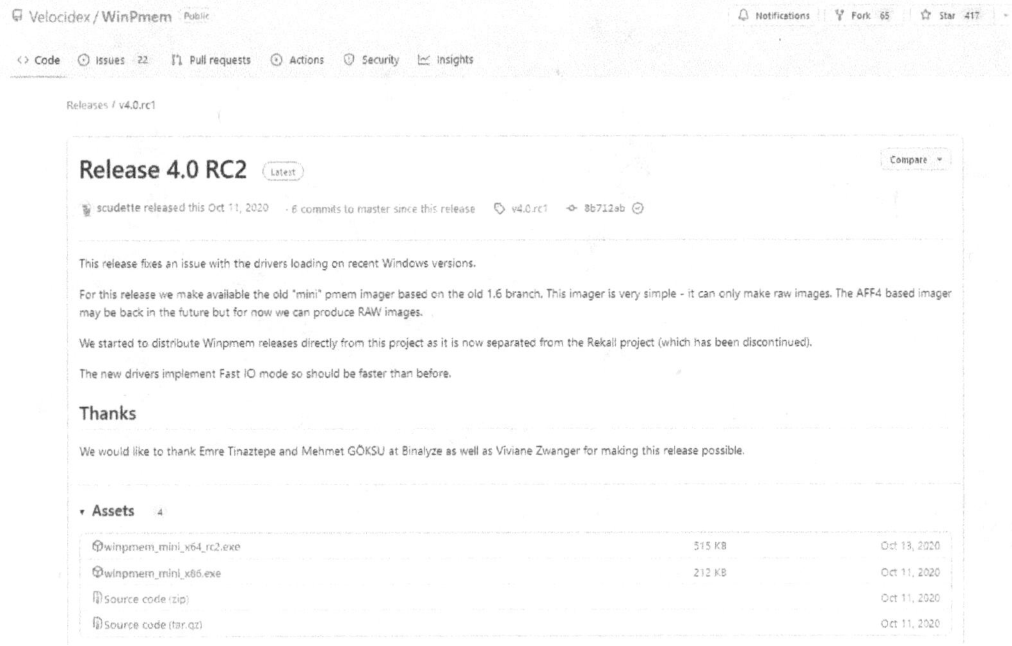

Figure 3.9: The WinPmem Releases page

Let's start the acquisition process using WinPmem:

1. Open Windows Command Prompt (cmd.exe) with administrator privileges and navigate to the WinPmem saved location.

2. By executing the binary with the -h parameter, we see the help list:

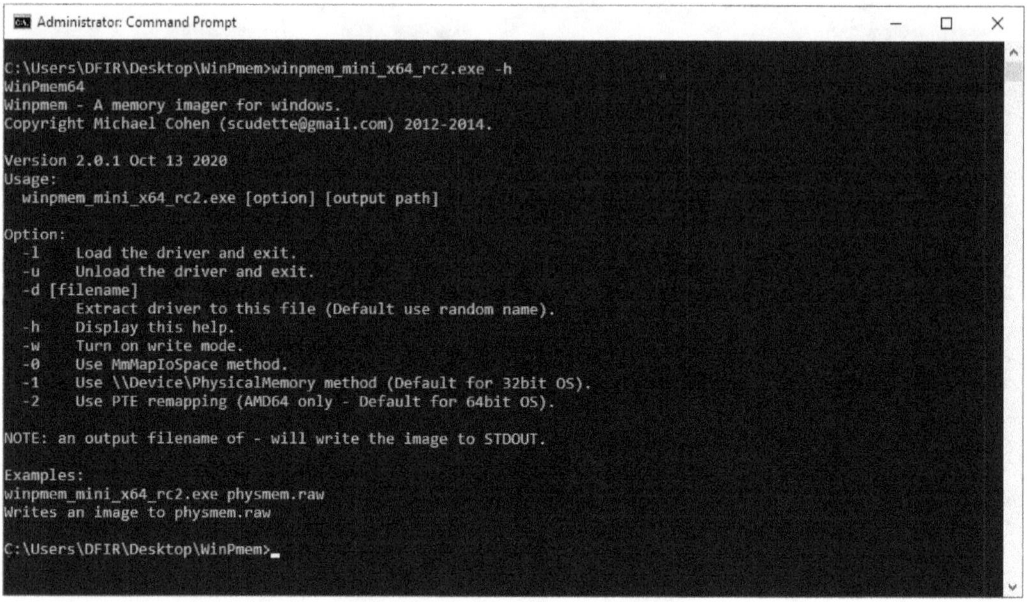

Figure 3.10: The WinPmem help list

3. Run the following command to start the acquisition process:
    `C:\Users\DFIR\Desktop\WinPmem>winpmem_mini_x64_rc2.exe Mem_Winpmem.raw`

    Once the process starts, it will show information within the terminal on the progress of the process:

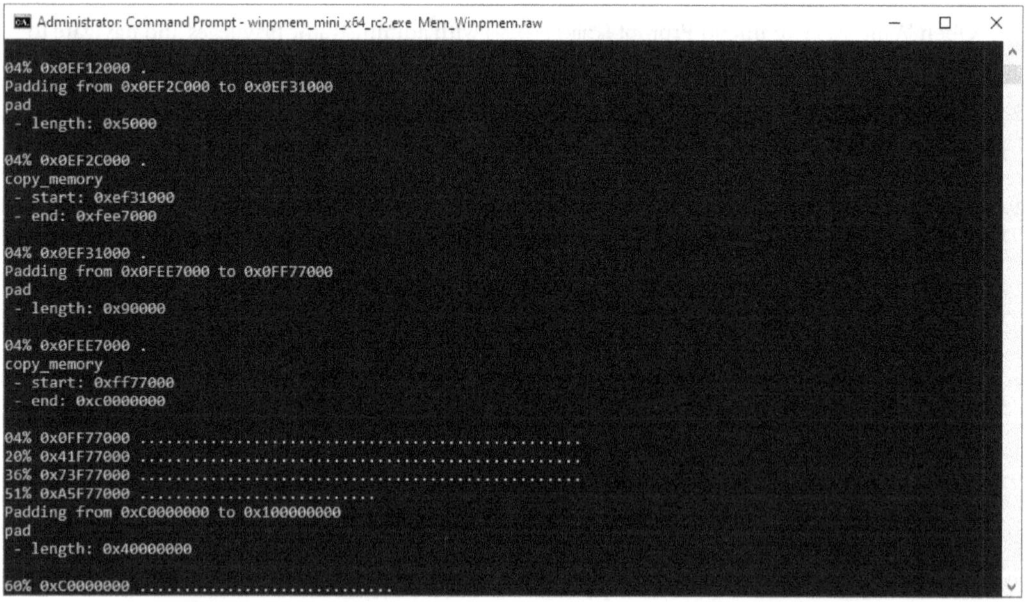

Figure 3.11: WinPmem progress

4. Once the process has been completed, we can navigate to the selected path to save the dump and explore the results.

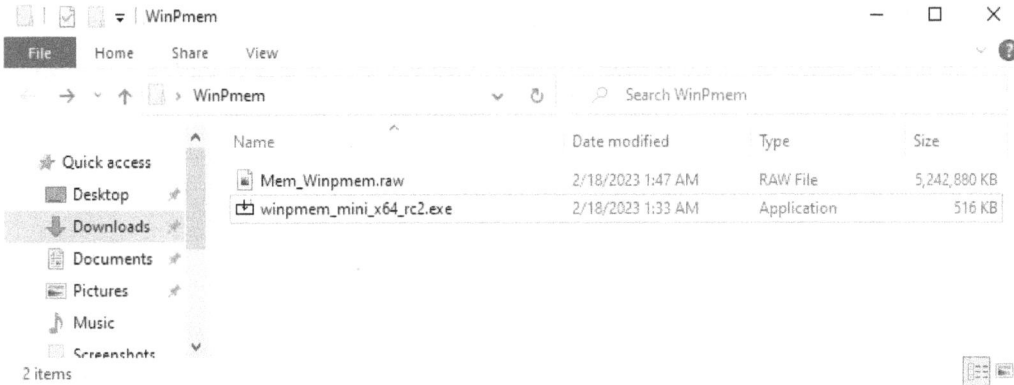

Figure 3.12: The WinPmem output result

WinPmem is a free and open source memory acquisition tool that can be used to dump memory from a Windows system. With a valid and reliable memory image, forensic analysts can gain valuable insights into a suspected incident.

DumpIt

DumpIt is a tool used in digital forensics to acquire memory images from Windows systems. It is designed to be a lightweight, simple-to-use program that can be quickly deployed on a live system or used on a forensic image.

The DumpIt tool is distributed as a standalone executable file that is executed from the command line. It can be run on Windows systems with 32-bit or 64-bit architecture, and it does not require any installation.

The process of using DumpIt to acquire a memory image is straightforward. The tool is downloaded and copied to a USB drive or other storage device. Then, the investigator boots the target system, using a forensic live CD or USB drive, and runs the DumpIt tool. DumpIt then acquires the memory image and saves it to the same storage device that contains the executable.

One advantage of DumpIt is that it is a small, single-purpose tool that can be used quickly and easily. However, this simplicity also means that it has fewer options and features compared to other more complex memory acquisition tools. Additionally, DumpIt does not have the ability to acquire the page file, hibernation file, or unallocated space.

Let's start acquiring a memory image using DumpIt:

1. **Download the DumpIt tool**: The tool can be downloaded from the internet and is available in the form of an executable file. Once downloaded, save the file to a location of your choice.

2. **Launch DumpIt**: To start the memory acquisition process, double-click on the `DumpIt.exe` file to launch the tool.

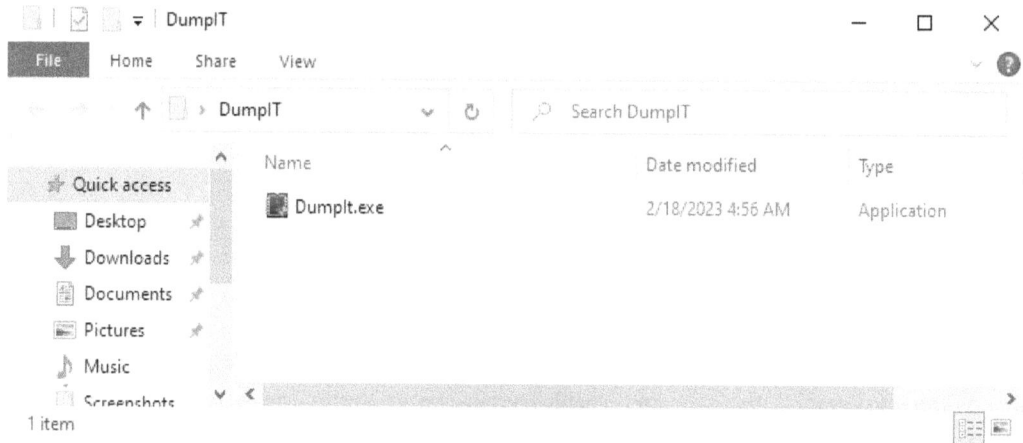

Figure 3.13: The DumpIt executable

As we can see here, once a dump is executed, it will display a very simple yes or no when asking whether you want to continue dumping the memory image.

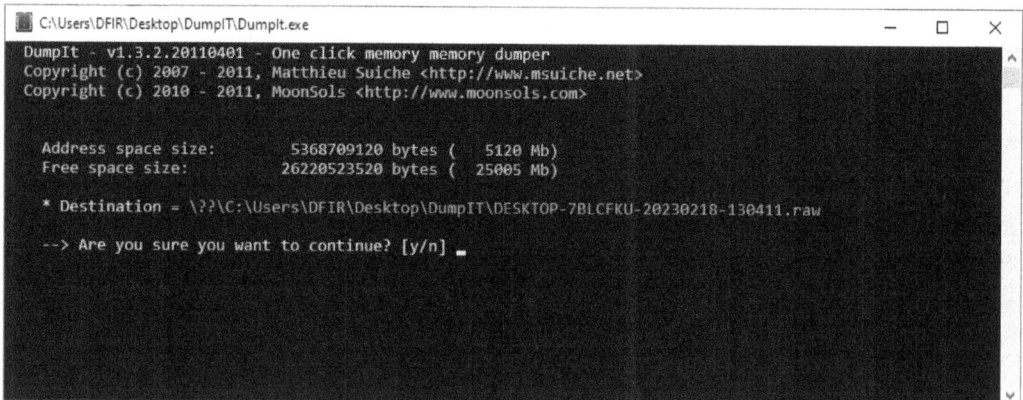

Figure 3.14: The DumpIt binary execution

3. **Begin the acquisition process**: Once you have selected the target location, press the *Y* key from your keyboard to start the acquisition process. The tool will then start to capture the live memory of the system and save it to the target location.

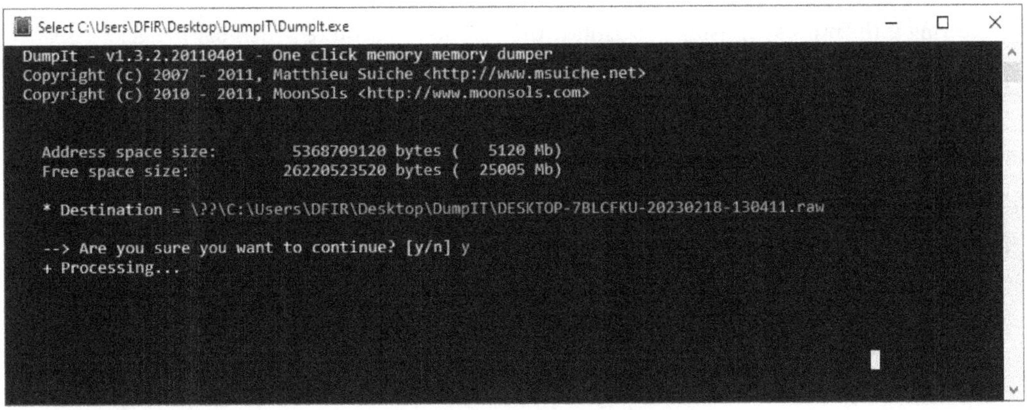

Figure 3.15: DumpIt processing

4. **Wait for the process to complete**: The acquisition process may take some time, depending on the size of a system's memory. It is recommended to wait until the process is complete before closing the tool. Once it's complete, check the directory in which DumpIt was executed. As you can see here, the raw image was saved.

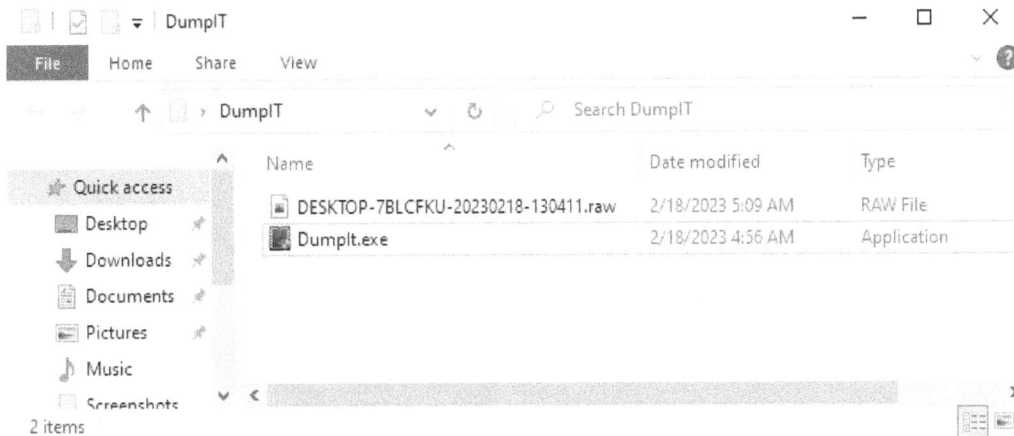

Figure 3.16: The DumpIt output result

Belkasoft RAM Capturer

Belkasoft RAM Capturer is a tool designed for the acquisition of volatile memory, also known as RAM, from a live Windows system. It is used in digital forensics and incident response investigations to collect evidence from a running system, as the information in volatile memory is lost when the system is powered off.

The following is the process of using Belkasoft RAM Capturer to acquire a memory image:

1. Download and install Belkasoft RAM Capturer on the target system.

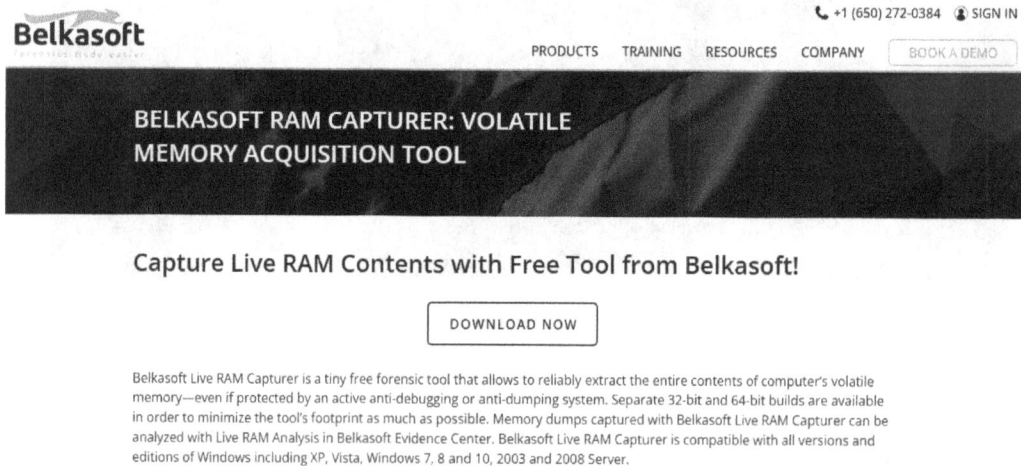

Figure 3.17: Belkasoft RAM Capturer

2. Open Belkasoft RAM Capturer and select the destination folder where you want to store the memory dump.

3. Choose the file format for the memory dump. Belkasoft RAM Capturer supports different file formats, such as raw files, hibernation files, and crash dumps.

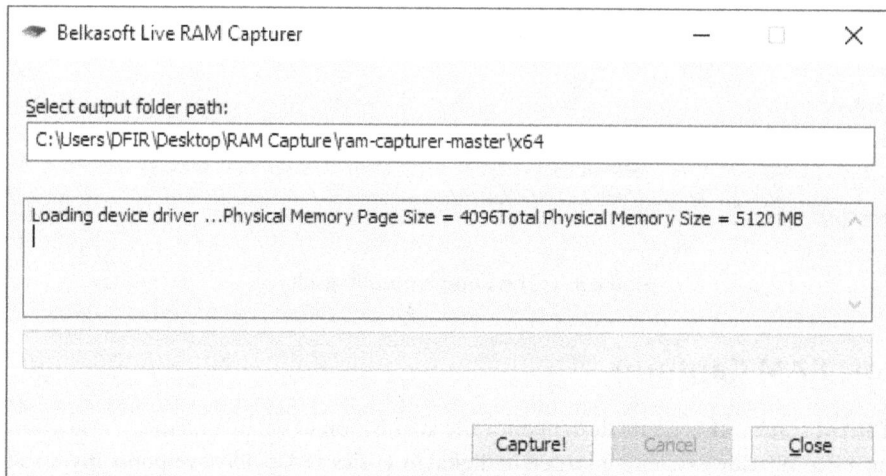

Figure 3.18: Belksoft Live RAM Capturer

4. Start the memory acquisition process by clicking on **Capture!**. Belkasoft RAM Capturer will start to collect the memory image from the system.

5. Wait for the acquisition process to finish. Depending on the size of the memory image and the speed of the system, the process can take from a few seconds to several minutes.

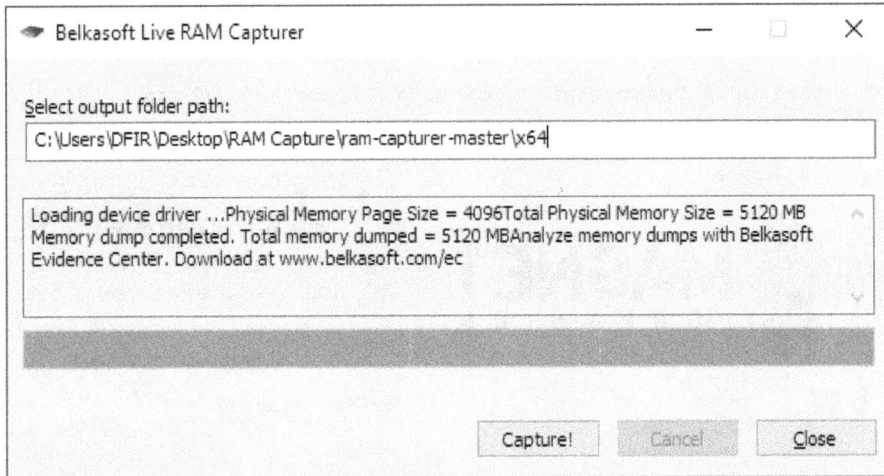

Figure 3.19: The RAM capture completed

Once the RAM capture is complete, as shown here, we can navigate to the output folder and check the result.

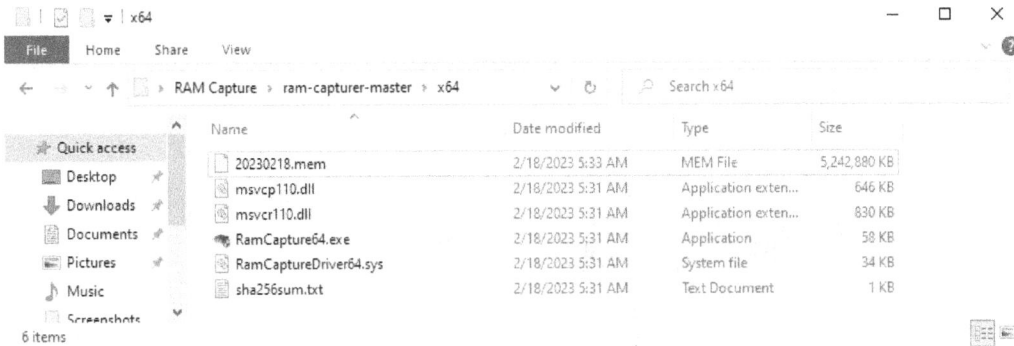

Figure 3.20: The RAM Capture .mem output

MAGNET RAM Capture

MAGNET RAM Capture is a tool used to acquire the memory of a live Windows system. It is a command-line tool designed for forensic investigators to capture volatile data from a running system, which can be analyzed offline to identify potential malicious activity. The tool captures the RAM in a raw format and saves it to a file, which can be analyzed using forensic tools such as Volatility.

To use MAGNET RAM Capture, do the following:

1. Download and install the MAGNET RAM Capture tool on the system being investigated.

2. Open Command Prompt with elevated privileges as an admin, and navigate to the directory where MAGNET RAM Capture is installed.

3. Execute the following command to capture the memory:

```
C:\Users\DFIR\Desktop\WinPmem> MRCv120.exe --filename
<filename>.raw
```

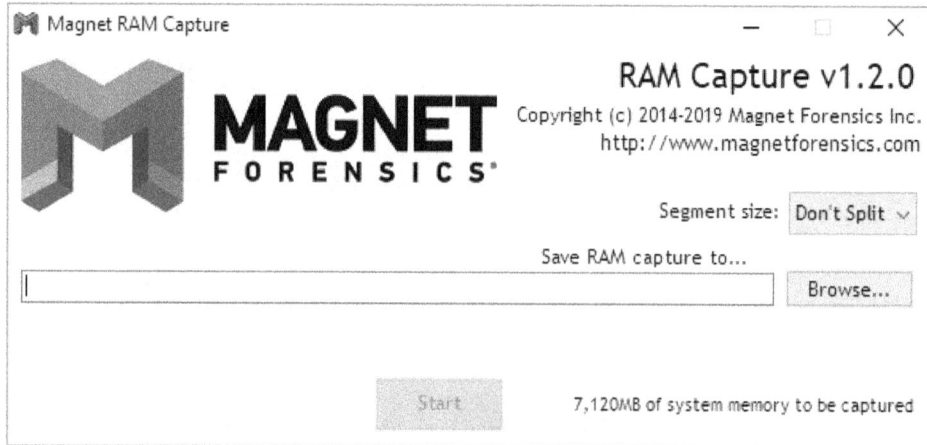

Figure 3.21: The RAM Capture interface

4. Find the destination path by clicking on **Browse…**, and then initiate the capture process by clicking on **Start**.

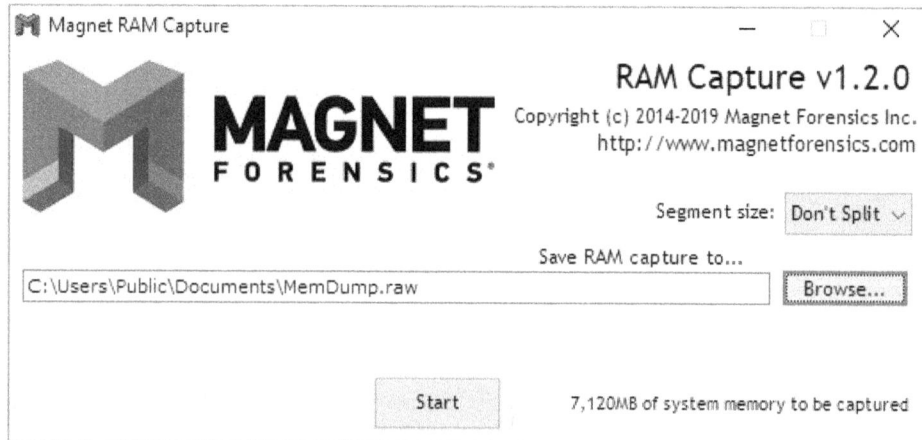

Figure 3.22: RAM Capture selecting the output location

5. Once started, we can see the progress of memory capture; it might take some time, depending on the size of the memory.

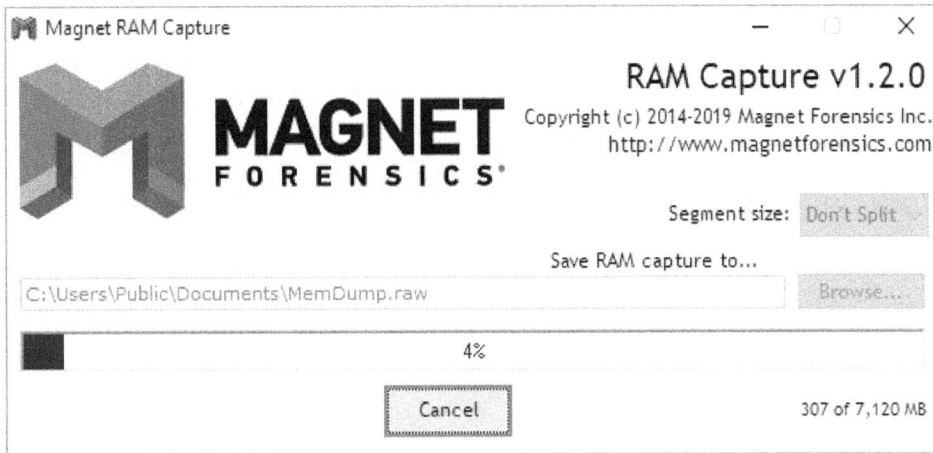

Figure 3.23: RAM Capture processing

Memory acquisition tools are a critical first step in any forensic investigation. By acquiring a valid and reliable memory image, analysts can gain valuable insights into an incident and start to piece together what happened. Now, we will cover a memory analysis tool and how to use it.

Using Volatility to analyze memory dumps and plugins

Volatility is an open source memory forensics framework used to analyze the contents of volatile memory. It provides digital forensic investigators with the ability to extract artifacts from memory dumps, such as running processes, open files, and network connections. The tool is widely used by incident response teams and forensic investigators to collect and analyze volatile memory for evidence in investigations.

Memory forensics is a critical component of modern digital forensics, and the ability to analyze volatile memory is essential in detecting advanced threats, such as rootkits and file-less malware. The volatility framework provides a robust set of features and capabilities to analyze volatile memory and is considered a leading tool in the field of memory forensics.

The Volatility framework supports various operating systems, including Windows, Linux, and macOS. In this section, we will focus on the use of Volatility in Windows memory forensics.

Volatility architecture

The Volatility framework comprises three layers – the core layer, the interface layer, and the plugin layer. The core layer provides the main functionality of the framework, such as memory mapping, parsing data structures, and data extraction. The interface layer provides a unified interface to interact with memory images, while the plugin layer provides functionality for specific operating systems and forensic scenarios.

Volatility plugins

The Volatility framework includes a vast collection of plugins that are designed to extract specific artifacts from volatile memory. The plugins are organized into categories, such as process, network, and filesystem, making it easy to identify and use the required plugin. Each plugin provides a set of commands that can be executed from the command-line interface to extract the desired artifact.

Volatility commands

The Volatility framework provides a command-line interface that can be used to execute the plugins and extract artifacts from volatile memory. The command-line interface is simple to use, and it allows forensic investigators to execute multiple commands and plugins in a single session. The output of the command-line interface is displayed in a human-readable format, making it easy to interpret the results.

Volatility 2 is a memory forensics framework that is used to analyze the memory of Windows, Linux, and macOS systems. It is a powerful tool that can be used to extract a variety of information from memory, including the following:

- **Running processes**: Volatility can be used to list all of the processes that are currently running on a system
- **Open files**: Volatility can be used to list all of the files that are currently open on a system
- **Network connections**: Volatility can be used to list all of the network connections that are currently active on a system
- **Password hashes**: Volatility can be used to extract the password hashes from a system
- **Malware**: Volatility can be used to identify and analyze malware that is present in the memory

To download this version of Volatility, visit `https://github.com/volatilityfoundation/volatility` and click on **Release**. Then, select the required version; we will use `2.6.1` for the sake of this demonstration.

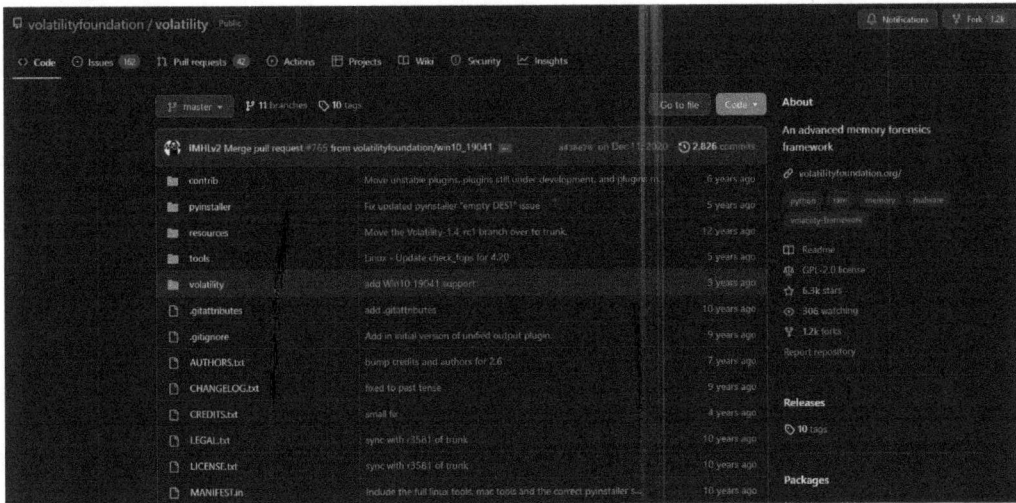

Figure 3.24: Volatility 2.6.1

Usually, we use Volatility in an Ubuntu or Linux environment; however, if you want to use it within the Windows operating system, then make sure to download the prerequisite Python libraries as per the instructions at `https://github.com/volatilityfoundation/volatility/wiki/Installation`.

For this use case, we will use Volatility on Ubuntu.

Since we covered memory acquisition using open source tools, we can now move on to an analysis of acquired memory. We will only briefly touch on the analysis, as this is not a dedicated memory forensics book. Instead, we will explore and focus on the most important plugins from volatility to get a clear idea on how to properly use the Volatility framework.

In the following examples, we used the same memory captured during our labs using the Dump It tool; feel free to apply the same to your memory image.

Before jumping into specific plugins and their usage, we can list the info using the following command:

```
Vol.py –info
```

```
root@siftworkstation: /home/dfir/Desktop
# vol.py --info
Volatility Foundation Volatility Framework 2.6


Profiles
--------
VistaSP0x64             - A Profile for Windows Vista SP0 x64
VistaSP0x86             - A Profile for Windows Vista SP0 x86
VistaSP1x64             - A Profile for Windows Vista SP1 x64
VistaSP1x86             - A Profile for Windows Vista SP1 x86
VistaSP2x64             - A Profile for Windows Vista SP2 x64
VistaSP2x86             - A Profile for Windows Vista SP2 x86
Win10x64                - A Profile for Windows 10 x64
Win10x64_10240_17770    - A Profile for Windows 10 x64 (10.0.10240.17770 / 2018-02-10)
Win10x64_10586          - A Profile for Windows 10 x64 (10.0.10586.306 / 2016-04-23)
Win10x64_14393          - A Profile for Windows 10 x64 (10.0.14393.0 / 2016-07-16)
Win10x64_15063          - A Profile for Windows 10 x64 (10.0.15063.0 / 2017-04-04)
Win10x64_16299          - A Profile for Windows 10 x64 (10.0.16299.0 / 2017-09-22)
Win10x64_17134          - A Profile for Windows 10 x64 (10.0.17134.1 / 2018-04-11)
Win10x86                - A Profile for Windows 10 x86
Win10x86_10240_17770    - A Profile for Windows 10 x86 (10.0.10240.17770 / 2018-02-10)
Win10x86_10586          - A Profile for Windows 10 x86 (10.0.10586.420 / 2016-05-28)
Win10x86_14393          - A Profile for Windows 10 x86 (10.0.14393.0 / 2016-07-16)
```

Figure 3.25: The vol.py --info list of profiles supported

As we can see in the preceding screenshot, this contains some of the profiles that are supported by Volatility.

```
Plugins
-------
agtidconfig             - Parse the Agtid configuration
amcache                 - Print AmCache information
antianalysis            - No docs
apifinder               - No docs
apihooks                - Detect API hooks in process and kernel memory
apihooksdeep            - Detect API hooks in process and kernel memory, with ssdeep for whitel
isting
apt17scan               - Detect processes infected with APT17 malware
atoms                   - Print session and window station atom tables
atomscan                - Pool scanner for atom tables
attributeht             - Find Hacking Team implants and attempt to attribute them using a wate
rmark.
auditpol                - Prints out the Audit Policies from HKLM\SECURITY\Policy\PolAdtEv
autoruns                - Searches the registry and memory space for applications running at sy
stem startup and maps them to running processes
bigpools                - Dump the big page pools using BigPagePoolScanner
bioskbd                 - Reads the keyboard buffer from Real Mode memory
bitlocker               - Extract Bitlocker FVEK. Supports Windows 7 - 10.
cachedump               - Dumps cached domain hashes from memory
callbacks               - Print system-wide notification routines
```

Figure 3.26: A brief list of plugins

Identifying the profile

Identifying the memory dump profile is a critical step in memory forensics with Volatility. The profile specifies the operating system, version, architecture, and service pack level of the memory dump, allowing Volatility to correctly interpret and extract data from the dump.

The imageinfo plugin

To get a high-level overview of the memory sample you are analyzing, use the `imageinfo` command. This command is most commonly used to identify the operating system, service pack, and hardware architecture (32-bit or 64-bit), but it also provides other useful information, such as the **Directory Table Base** (**DTB**) address and the time the sample was collected.

The `imageinfo` command provides a suggested profile that you can use with other plugins in Volatility. This profile is based on the operating system, service pack, and hardware architecture of the memory sample. If there are multiple closely related profiles, the `imageinfo` command will list all of them.

For example, if the memory sample is from a Windows 7 64-bit machine, the `imageinfo` command might suggest the following profiles:

- Win7SP1x64
- Win7SP0x64
- Win7x64

You can then use the suggested profile with other plugins in Volatility. For example, if you want to use the `pslist` plugin to list the processes in the memory sample, you would pass the suggested profile as the parameter to the `-profile=PROFILE` option.

For example, in the following screenshot, we use `vol.py -f MemDump.dp imageinfo`, and we can determine that the matching profile for the memory image is as follows:

```
root@siftworkstation: /home/dfirlab/Desktop/MemDump
# vol.py -f MemDump.raw imageinfo
Volatility Foundation Volatility Framework 2.6
INFO    : volatility.debug    : Determining profile based on KDBG search...
        Suggested Profile(s) : Win7SP1x64, Win7SP0x64, Win2008R2SP0x64, Win2008R2SP1x64_
24000, Win2008R2SP1x64_23418, Win2008R2SP1x64, Win7SP1x64_24000, Win7SP1x64_23418
                  AS Layer1 : WindowsAMD64PagedMemory (Kernel AS)
                  AS Layer2 : FileAddressSpace (/home/dfirlab/Desktop/MemDump/MemDump.r
aw)
                  PAE type : No PAE
                       DTB : 0x187000L
                      KDBG : 0xf800028100a0L
        Number of Processors : 1
  Image Type (Service Pack) : 1
           KPCR for CPU 0 : 0xfffff80002811d00L
       KUSER_SHARED_DATA : 0xfffff78000000000L
        Image date and time : 2019-12-11 14:38:00 UTC+0000
  Image local date and time : 2019-12-11 20:08:00 +0530
```

Figure 3.27: The imageinfo output

The process list and tree

To retrieve a comprehensive list of processes in a system, the `pslist` command can be utilized. This command traverses the doubly linked list (each item have a pointer to next item and previous item listed in memory) indicated by `PsActiveProcessHead` and provides essential details, such as the process offset, name, process ID, parent process ID, number of threads, number of handles, and timestamps indicating when the process started and exited. Starting from version 2.1, it also includes additional information, such as the session ID and whether the process is a `Wow64` process, which indicates the usage of a 32-bit address space on a 64-bit kernel.

By running the following command, we can get a list of processes using the `pslist` plugin:

```
vol.py -f MemDump.raw --profile=Win7SP1x64 pslist
```

Figure 3.28: The pslist plugin output

To visualize the process listing in a hierarchical tree structure, the `pstree` command can be utilized. This command employs a similar technique as `pslist` to enumerate processes, meaning it will not display hidden or unlinked processes. Child processes are denoted by indentation and periods, providing a clear representation of the process hierarchy.

```
root@siftworkstation: /home/dfirlab/Desktop/MemDump
# vol.py -f MemDump.raw --profile=Win7SP1x64 pstree
Volatility Foundation Volatility Framework 2.6
Name                                      Pid    PPid    Thds    Hnds Time
--------------------------------------    ----   ----    ----    ---- ----
 0xfffffa8000f4c670:explorer.exe          2504   3000     34      825 2019-12-11 14:37:14 UTC+0000
 . 0xfffffa8000f9a4e0:VBoxTray.exe         2304   2504     14      144 2019-12-11 14:37:14 UTC+0000
 . 0xfffffa8001010b30:WinRAR.exe           1512   2504      6      207 2019-12-11 14:37:23 UTC+0000
 0xfffffa8001c5f630:wininit.exe            424     312      3       75 2019-12-11 13:41:34 UTC+0000
 . 0xfffffa8001c98530:services.exe         484     424     13      219 2019-12-11 13:41:35 UTC+0000
 .. 0xfffffa8002170630:wmpnetwk.exe        1856    484     16      451 2019-12-11 14:16:08 UTC+0000
 .. 0xfffffa8001f91b30:TCPSVCS.EXE         1416    484      4       97 2019-12-11 13:41:55 UTC+0000
 .. 0xfffffa8001da96c0:svchost.exe         876     484     32      941 2019-12-11 13:41:43 UTC+0000
 .. 0xfffffa8001d327c0:VBoxService.ex      652     484     13      137 2019-12-11 13:41:40 UTC+0000
 .. 0xfffffa8000eac770:svchost.exe         2660    484      6      100 2019-12-11 14:35:14 UTC+0000
 .. 0xfffffa8002199e0:svchost.exe          2368    484      9      365 2019-12-11 14:32:51 UTC+0000
 .. 0xfffffa8001e50b30:svchost.exe         1044    484     14      366 2019-12-11 13:41:48 UTC+0000
 .. 0xfffffa8001d8c420:svchost.exe         816     484     23      569 2019-12-11 13:41:42 UTC+0000
 ... 0xfffffa80021da060:audiodg.exe        2064    816      6      131 2019-12-11 14:32:37 UTC+0000
 .. 0xfffffa8001c38580:svchost.exe         948     484     13      322 2019-12-11 14:16:07 UTC+0000
 .. 0xfffffa8001eba230:spoolsv.exe         1208    484     13      282 2019-12-11 13:41:51 UTC+0000
 .. 0xfffffa8001d376f0:SearchIndexer.      480     484     14      701 2019-12-11 14:16:09 UTC+0000
 ... 0xfffffa8000fff630:SearchProtocol     2524    480      7      226 2019-12-11 14:37:21 UTC+0000
 ... 0xfffffa8001020b30:SearchProtocol     2868    480      8      279 2019-12-11 14:37:23 UTC+0000
 ... 0xfffffa8000ecea60:SearchFilterHo     1720    480      5       90 2019-12-11 14:37:21 UTC+0000
 .. 0xfffffa8000f3aab0:taskhost.exe        2908    484      9      158 2019-12-11 14:37:13 UTC+0000
 .. 0xfffffa8001cf4b30:svchost.exe         588     484     11      358 2019-12-11 13:41:39 UTC+0000
 .. 0xfffffa8001d49b30:svchost.exe         720     484      8      279 2019-12-11 13:41:41 UTC+0000
 .. 0xfffffa8001da5b30:svchost.exe         852     484     28      542 2019-12-11 13:41:43 UTC+0000
 ... 0xfffffa8000f4db30:dwm.exe            3004    852      5       72 2019-12-11 14:37:14 UTC+0000
 ... 0xfffffa8001dfa910:dwm.exe            1988    852      5       72 2019-12-11 14:32:25 UTC+0000
 .. 0xfffffa8001e1bb30:svchost.exe         472     484     19      476 2019-12-11 13:41:47 UTC+0000
 .. 0xfffffa8000d3c400:sppsvc.exe          1508    484      4      141 2019-12-11 14:16:06 UTC+0000
 .. 0xfffffa8001f58890:svchost.exe         1372    484     22      295 2019-12-11 13:41:54 UTC+0000
 .. 0xfffffa8001eda060:svchost.exe         1248    484     19      313 2019-12-11 13:41:52 UTC+0000
 .. 0xfffffa8001eb47f0:taskhost.exe        296     484      8      151 2019-12-11 14:32:24 UTC+0000
 . 0xfffffa8001ca0580:lsass.exe            492     424      9      764 2019-12-11 13:41:35 UTC+0000
 . 0xfffffa8001ca4b30:lsm.exe              500     424     11      185 2019-12-11 13:41:35 UTC+0000
 0xfffffa800154f740:csrss.exe              320     312      9      457 2019-12-11 13:41:32 UTC+0000
```

Figure 3.29: The pstree plugin output

The netscan plugin

You can utilize the netscan command to analyze network artifacts in memory dumps of 32-bit and 64-bit Windows Vista, Windows Server 2008, and Windows 7. This command helps identify TCP endpoints, TCP listeners, UDP endpoints, and UDP listeners. It differentiates between IPv4 and IPv6 addresses, displaying the local and remote IP (if applicable), local and remote port (if applicable), the timestamp of socket binding or connection establishment, and the current state of the network connection.

```
root@siftworkstation: /home/dfirlab/Desktop/MemDump
# vol.py -f MemDump.raw --profile=Win7SP1x64 netscan
Volatility Foundation Volatility Framework 2.6
Offset(P)          Proto    Local Address                Foreign Address      State          Pid      Owner
0x3e80b840         UDPv4    0.0.0.0:3702                 *:*                                 472      svchost.exe
0x3e80b840         UDPv6    :::3702                      *:*                                 472      svchost.exe
0x3e80bbb0         UDPv4    0.0.0.0:3702                 *:*                                 472      svchost.exe
0x3e80bbb0         UDPv6    :::3702                      *:*                                 472      svchost.exe
0x3e820ec0         UDPv4    0.0.0.0:0                    *:*                                 2368     svchost.exe
0x3e820ec0         UDPv6    :::0                         *:*                                 2368     svchost.exe
0x3e825ec0         UDPv4    0.0.0.0:0                    *:*                                 2368     svchost.exe
0x3e825ec0         UDPv6    :::0                         *:*                                 2368     svchost.exe
0x3e86c5a0         UDPv4    0.0.0.0:0                    *:*                                 2368     svchost.exe
0x3e86c5a0         UDPv6    :::0                         *:*                                 2368     svchost.exe
0x3e8acba0         UDPv4    0.0.0.0:59438                *:*                                 472      svchost.exe
0x3e8acba0         UDPv6    :::59438                     *:*                                 472      svchost.exe
0x3e8ae9c0         UDPv4    0.0.0.0:59437                *:*                                 472      svchost.exe
0x3ea062d0         UDPv4    0.0.0.0:19                   *:*                                 1416     TCPSVCS.EXE
0x3ea062d0         UDPv6    :::19                        *:*                                 1416     TCPSVCS.EXE
0x3ea06a40         UDPv4    0.0.0.0:19                   *:*                                 1416     TCPSVCS.EXE
0x3ea10200         UDPv4    0.0.0.0:17                   *:*                                 1416     TCPSVCS.EXE
0x3ea10200         UDPv6    :::17                        *:*                                 1416     TCPSVCS.EXE
0x3ea10970         UDPv4    0.0.0.0:17                   *:*                                 1416     TCPSVCS.EXE
0x3ea39190         UDPv4    0.0.0.0:49194                *:*                                 1372     svchost.exe
0x3ea3c940         UDPv4    0.0.0.0:49195                *:*                                 1372     svchost.exe
0x3ea3c940         UDPv6    :::49195                     *:*                                 1372     svchost.exe
0x3ea5d010         UDPv4    0.0.0.0:0                    *:*                                 1044     svchost.exe
0x3ea5d010         UDPv6    :::0                         *:*                                 1044     svchost.exe
0x3eaab540         UDPv4    0.0.0.0:5355                 *:*                                 1044     svchost.exe
0x3eaab540         UDPv6    :::5355                      *:*                                 1044     svchost.exe
0x3eaaece0         UDPv4    10.0.2.15:137                *:*                                 4        System
0x3ebfe300         UDPv4    0.0.0.0:3702                 *:*                                 472      svchost.exe
0x3ebfeb00         UDPv4    0.0.0.0:59435                *:*                                 472      svchost.exe
0x3ebff1a0         UDPv4    0.0.0.0:3702                 *:*                                 472      svchost.exe
0x3ebff9b0         UDPv4    0.0.0.0:59436                *:*                                 472      svchost.exe
0x3ebff9b0         UDPv6    :::59436                     *:*                                 472      svchost.exe
0x3ec1e6b0         UDPv4    0.0.0.0:5004                 *:*                                 1856     wmpnetwk.exe
0x3ec1ebb0         UDPv4    0.0.0.0:5004                 *:*                                 1856     wmpnetwk.exe
0x3ec1ebb0         UDPv6    :::5004                      *:*                                 1856     wmpnetwk.exe
0x3ec1f7c0         UDPv4    0.0.0.0:5005                 *:*                                 1856     wmpnetwk.exe
```

Figure 3.30: The netscan plugin output

The hivescan and hivelist plugins

If you need to locate the physical addresses of CMHIVEs (registry hives) within memory, you can employ the `hivescan` command:

```
root@siftworkstation: /home/dfirlab/Desktop/MemDump
# vol.py -f MemDump.raw --profile=Win7SP1x64 hivescan
Volatility Foundation Volatility Framework 2.6
Offset(P)
------------------
0x000000000b296010
0x00000000123d0010
0x000000001c9a4010
0x000000001cd57410
0x000000001d7ed010
0x000000001df34010
0x000000002199c300
0x00000000252b4010
0x0000000025d61010
0x00000000276a4010
0x00000000276ce010
0x000000002783f010
0x0000000036d9b010
0x0000000037113010
```

Figure 3.31: The hivescan plugin output

In order to identify the virtual addresses of registry hives present in memory, as well as the complete paths leading to the corresponding hives on disk, the `hivelist` command can be utilized. Running this command beforehand allows you to view the addresses of the hives, enabling you to subsequently extract values from a specific hive.

```
root@siftworkstation: /home/dfirlab/Desktop/MemDump
# vol.py -f MemDump.raw --profile=Win7SP1x64 hivelist
Volatility Foundation Volatility Framework 2.6
Virtual            Physical            Name
------------------ ------------------  ----
0xfffff8a00000d010 0x000000002783f010 [no name]
0xfffff8a000024010 0x00000000276a4010 \REGISTRY\MACHINE\SYSTEM
0xfffff8a00004e010 0x00000000276ce010 \REGISTRY\MACHINE\HARDWARE
0xfffff8a0000b9010 0x0000000037113010 \??\C:\Users\SmartNet\AppData\Local\Microsoft\Windows\UsrClass.dat
0xfffff8a0000c1010 0x0000000036d9b010 \??\C:\Users\SmartNet\ntuser.dat
0xfffff8a000264010 0x000000025d61010 \Device\HarddiskVolume1\Boot\BCD
0xfffff8a001032010 0x00000000252b4010 \SystemRoot\System32\Config\SOFTWARE
0xfffff8a0012ff300 0x000000002199c300 \SystemRoot\System32\Config\DEFAULT
0xfffff8a001491010 0x00000001df34010 \SystemRoot\System32\Config\SECURITY
0xfffff8a0014e9010 0x00000001d7ed010 \SystemRoot\System32\Config\SAM
0xfffff8a0015ab410 0x00000001cd57410 \??\C:\Windows\ServiceProfiles\NetworkService\NTUSER.DAT
0xfffff8a001626010 0x000000001c9a4010 \??\C:\Windows\ServiceProfiles\LocalService\NTUSER.DAT
0xfffff8a00227a010 0x00000000123d0010 \??\C:\Users\Alissa Simpson\ntuser.dat
0xfffff8a0022dc010 0x000000000b296010 \??\C:\Users\Alissa Simpson\AppData\Local\Microsoft\Windows\UsrClass.dat
```

Figure 3.32: The hivelist plugin output

If you need to view the subkeys, values, data, and data types stored within a specific registry key, the `printkey` command can be employed. By default, the `printkey` command will search across all hives and display the key information (if found) for the requested key. This means that if the key is present in multiple hives, the information for the location of the key will be printed for each individual hive.

```
root@siftworkstation: /home/dfirlab/Desktop/MemDump
# vol.py -f MemDump.raw --profile=Win7SP1x64 printkey -K "Microsoft\Security Center\Svc"
Volatility Foundation Volatility Framework 2.6
Legend: (S) = Stable    (V) = Volatile

--------------------------------------
Registry: \SystemRoot\System32\Config\SOFTWARE
Key name: Svc (S)
Last updated: 2019-12-11 14:16:09 UTC+0000

Subkeys:
  (V) Vol

Values:
REG_QWORD       VistaSp1        : (S) 128920218544262440
REG_DWORD       AntiVirusOverride : (S) 0
REG_DWORD       AntiSpywareOverride : (S) 0
REG_DWORD       FirewallOverride : (S) 0
```

Figure 3.33: The printkey plugin output

Another useful plugin is `hivedump`, which is clearly used to dump hives from memory, If you want to obtain a comprehensive list of all subkeys within a hive, you can utilize the `hivedump` command and provide the virtual address of the specific hive as a parameter. This command will recursively display all subkeys contained within the given hive.

```
root@siftworkstation: /home/dfirlab/Desktop/MemDump
# vol.py -f MemDump.raw --profile=Win7SP1x64 hivedump -o 0xfffff8a00227a010
Volatility Foundation Volatility Framework 2.6
Last Written          Key
2019-12-11 14:37:13 UTC+0000  \CMI-CreateHive{D43B12B8-09B5-40DB-B4F6-F6DFEB78DAEC}
2019-12-11 09:11:29 UTC+0000  \CMI-CreateHive{D43B12B8-09B5-40DB-B4F6-F6DFEB78DAEC}\AppEvents
2019-12-11 09:12:08 UTC+0000  \CMI-CreateHive{D43B12B8-09B5-40DB-B4F6-F6DFEB78DAEC}\AppEvents\EventLabels
2019-12-11 09:11:29 UTC+0000  \CMI-CreateHive{D43B12B8-09B5-40DB-B4F6-F6DFEB78DAEC}\AppEvents\EventLabels\.Default
2019-12-11 09:11:29 UTC+0000  \CMI-CreateHive{D43B12B8-09B5-40DB-B4F6-F6DFEB78DAEC}\AppEvents\EventLabels\ActivatingDocument
2019-12-11 09:11:29 UTC+0000  \CMI-CreateHive{D43B12B8-09B5-40DB-B4F6-F6DFEB78DAEC}\AppEvents\EventLabels\AppGPFault
2019-12-11 09:11:29 UTC+0000  \CMI-CreateHive{D43B12B8-09B5-40DB-B4F6-F6DFEB78DAEC}\AppEvents\EventLabels\BlockedPopup
2019-12-11 09:11:29 UTC+0000  \CMI-CreateHive{D43B12B8-09B5-40DB-B4F6-F6DFEB78DAEC}\AppEvents\EventLabels\CCSelect
2019-12-11 09:11:29 UTC+0000  \CMI-CreateHive{D43B12B8-09B5-40DB-B4F6-F6DFEB78DAEC}\AppEvents\EventLabels\ChangeTheme
2019-12-11 09:11:29 UTC+0000  \CMI-CreateHive{D43B12B8-09B5-40DB-B4F6-F6DFEB78DAEC}\AppEvents\EventLabels\Close
2019-12-11 09:11:29 UTC+0000  \CMI-CreateHive{D43B12B8-09B5-40DB-B4F6-F6DFEB78DAEC}\AppEvents\EventLabels\CriticalBatteryAlarm
2019-12-11 09:11:29 UTC+0000  \CMI-CreateHive{D43B12B8-09B5-40DB-B4F6-F6DFEB78DAEC}\AppEvents\EventLabels\DeviceConnect
2019-12-11 09:11:29 UTC+0000  \CMI-CreateHive{D43B12B8-09B5-40DB-B4F6-F6DFEB78DAEC}\AppEvents\EventLabels\DeviceDisconnect
2019-12-11 09:11:29 UTC+0000  \CMI-CreateHive{D43B12B8-09B5-40DB-B4F6-F6DFEB78DAEC}\AppEvents\EventLabels\DeviceFail
2019-12-11 09:11:29 UTC+0000  \CMI-CreateHive{D43B12B8-09B5-40DB-B4F6-F6DFEB78DAEC}\AppEvents\EventLabels\DisNumbersSound
2019-12-11 09:11:29 UTC+0000  \CMI-CreateHive{D43B12B8-09B5-40DB-B4F6-F6DFEB78DAEC}\AppEvents\EventLabels\EmptyRecycleBin
2019-12-11 09:11:29 UTC+0000  \CMI-CreateHive{D43B12B8-09B5-40DB-B4F6-F6DFEB78DAEC}\AppEvents\EventLabels\FaxBeep
2019-12-11 09:12:08 UTC+0000  \CMI-CreateHive{D43B12B8-09B5-40DB-B4F6-F6DFEB78DAEC}\AppEvents\EventLabels\FaxError
2019-12-11 09:12:08 UTC+0000  \CMI-CreateHive{D43B12B8-09B5-40DB-B4F6-F6DFEB78DAEC}\AppEvents\EventLabels\FaxLineRings
2019-12-11 09:12:08 UTC+0000  \CMI-CreateHive{D43B12B8-09B5-40DB-B4F6-F6DFEB78DAEC}\AppEvents\EventLabels\FaxSent
2019-12-11 09:11:29 UTC+0000  \CMI-CreateHive{D43B12B8-09B5-40DB-B4F6-F6DFEB78DAEC}\AppEvents\EventLabels\FeedDiscovered
2019-12-11 09:11:29 UTC+0000  \CMI-CreateHive{D43B12B8-09B5-40DB-B4F6-F6DFEB78DAEC}\AppEvents\EventLabels\HubOffSound
2019-12-11 09:11:29 UTC+0000  \CMI-CreateHive{D43B12B8-09B5-40DB-B4F6-F6DFEB78DAEC}\AppEvents\EventLabels\HubOnSound
2019-12-11 09:11:29 UTC+0000  \CMI-CreateHive{D43B12B8-09B5-40DB-B4F6-F6DFEB78DAEC}\AppEvents\EventLabels\HubSleepSound
2019-12-11 09:11:29 UTC+0000  \CMI-CreateHive{D43B12B8-09B5-40DB-B4F6-F6DFEB78DAEC}\AppEvents\EventLabels\LowBatteryAlarm
2019-12-11 09:11:29 UTC+0000  \CMI-CreateHive{D43B12B8-09B5-40DB-B4F6-F6DFEB78DAEC}\AppEvents\EventLabels\MailBeep
2019-12-11 09:11:29 UTC+0000  \CMI-CreateHive{D43B12B8-09B5-40DB-B4F6-F6DFEB78DAEC}\AppEvents\EventLabels\Maximize
2019-12-11 09:11:29 UTC+0000  \CMI-CreateHive{D43B12B8-09B5-40DB-B4F6-F6DFEB78DAEC}\AppEvents\EventLabels\MenuCommand
2019-12-11 09:11:29 UTC+0000  \CMI-CreateHive{D43B12B8-09B5-40DB-B4F6-F6DFEB78DAEC}\AppEvents\EventLabels\MenuPopup
2019-12-11 09:11:29 UTC+0000  \CMI-CreateHive{D43B12B8-09B5-40DB-B4F6-F6DFEB78DAEC}\AppEvents\EventLabels\Minimize
2019-12-11 09:11:29 UTC+0000  \CMI-CreateHive{D43B12B8-09B5-40DB-B4F6-F6DFEB78DAEC}\AppEvents\EventLabels\MisrecoSound
2019-12-11 09:11:29 UTC+0000  \CMI-CreateHive{D43B12B8-09B5-40DB-B4F6-F6DFEB78DAEC}\AppEvents\EventLabels\MoveMenuItem
```

Figure 3.34: The hivedump plugin output

To explore more plugins, you can review the Volatility command reference page at `https://github.com/volatilityfoundation/volatility/wiki/Command-Reference`.

A brief overview of Volatility 3

As we observed in the previous section of the book, Volatility stands out as a robust and valuable tool for memory forensics. Notably, a more recent iteration of Volatility, known as Volatility 3, has been introduced. This updated version has significantly enhanced the capabilities of the tool, making the analysis and investigation processes considerably more streamlined and accessible. We will look into the common usage of Volatility 3 in this section.

To download it, please visit this link: `https://www.volatilityfoundation.org/3`.

When we use Volatility 2, we run a command by identifying the profile, using the `imageinfo` plugin. In Volatility 3, however, providing a profile is no longer a requirement because Volatility now automatically identifies it. With Volatility 3, the use of profiles has been discontinued; instead, it comes with an extensive library of symbol tables and can generate new ones for most Windows memory images, based on the memory image itself. However, if we need to identify the image, we can use `window.info`, as shown in the following screenshot. Automatic detection of 32-bit and 64-bit systems, as well as major/minor version information of the Windows operating system, is done during the initial analysis. It takes considerable time to perform the analysis for the first time, as it involves downloading necessary information from the Microsoft website and analyzing the memory layers:

```
command: vol.py -f Memory.raw window.info
```

If we run the preceding command, we can see a lot of important information:

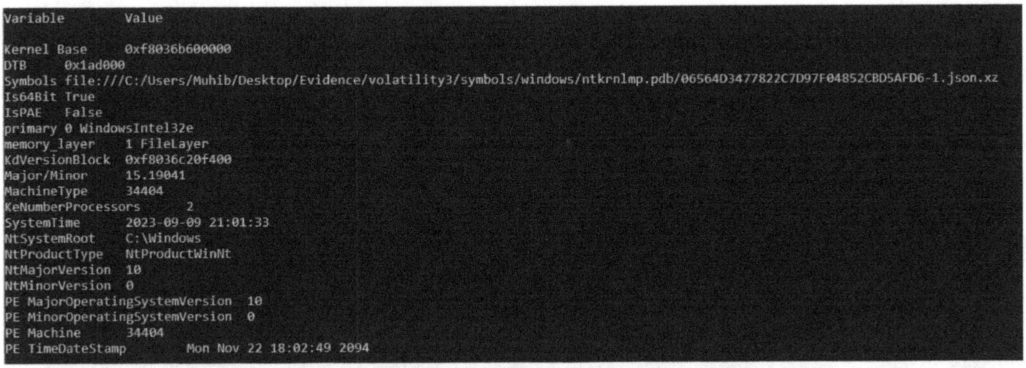

Figure 3.35: Volatility 3's window.info output

Let's focus now on some of the important plugins utilized during the investigation while using Volatility 3.

To list the processes that are present in the captured Windows image, we will utilize the `windows.pslist` plugin, as shown in *Figure 3.36*.

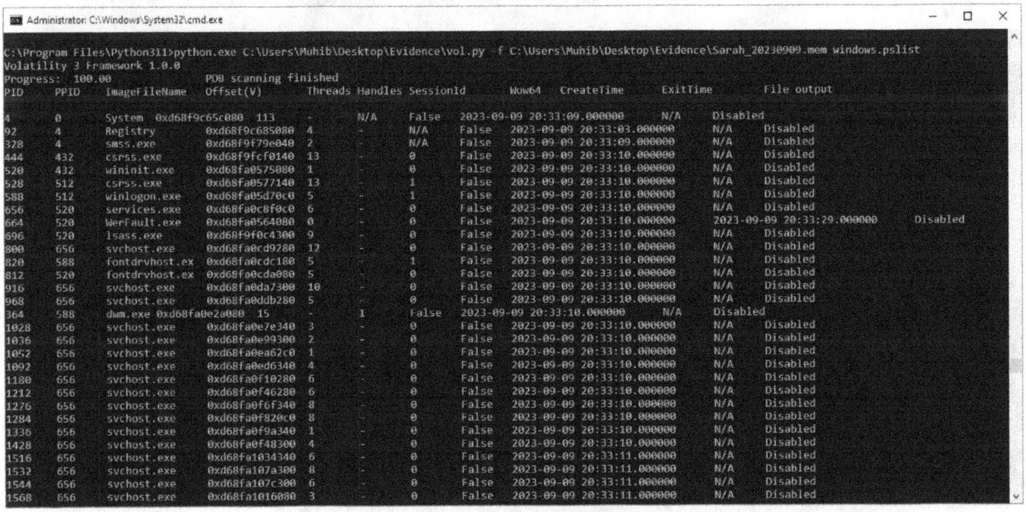

Figure 3.36: Volatility 3's windows.pslist plugin

To scan for processes present in the captured image, we will use the `windows.psscan` plugin, but before jumping in and running the process, we need to differentiate between the `psscan` and `pslist` plugins in Volatility. For the sake of simplicity, we can say that `pslist` uses a similar concept as a Task Manager process or a `tasklist` command that you would run on a live host. The EPROCESS data structure is employed by the Windows kernel to provide a description of each active process.

Within the EPROCESS structure lies information crucial for the operating system to ascertain the location of code and process address space in memory, as well as to identify the threads connected to the given process. The `psscan` module operates without relying on the integrity of the linked list of processes. Instead, it employs heuristic methods to scan memory and identify EPROCESS structures that represent processes. Consequently, it compiles a comprehensive list of processes, even those hidden by rootkits, which may remain undetected by the `pslist` command in Volatility or the `tasklist` command in Windows.

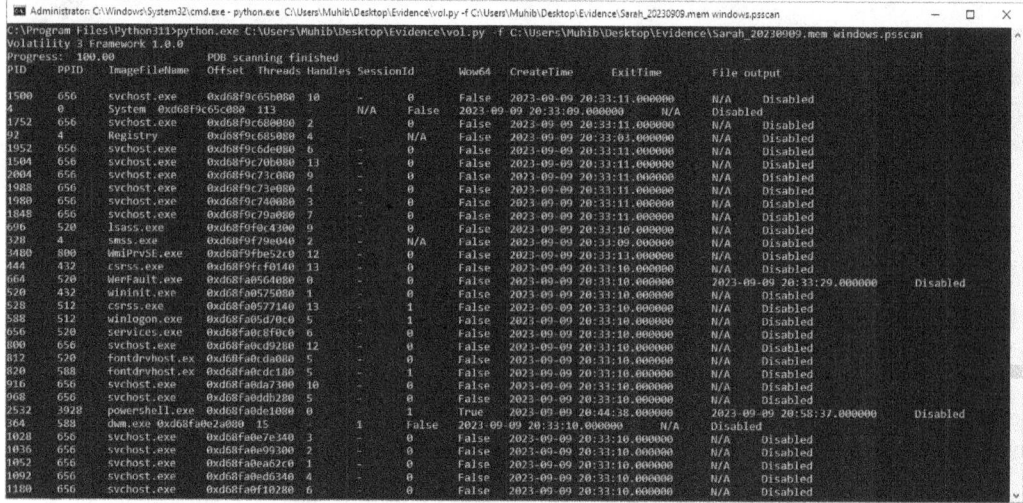

Figure 3.37: The Windows.psscan output

The following screenshot shows the plugin to list processes in a tree based on their parent process ID.

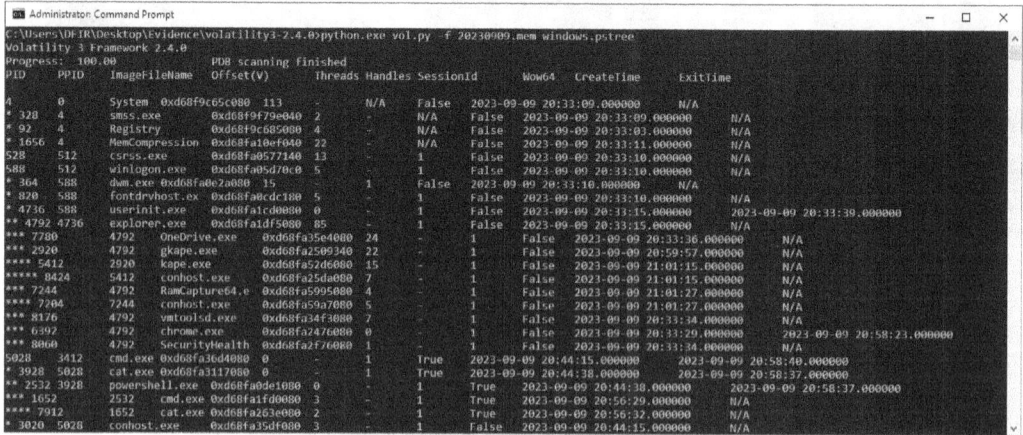

Figure 3.38: The windows.pstree output

The following list represents some of the common plugins in Volatility 3; feel free to test them:

- `windows.bigpools.BigPools,`
- `windows.cmdline.CmdLine,`
- `windows.dlllist.DllList,`
- `windows.driverirp.DriverIrp,`
- `windows.driverscan.DriverScan,`
- `windows.envars.Envars,`
- `windows.filescan.FileScan,`
- `windows.info.Info,`
- `windows.malfind.Malfind,`
- `windows.memmap.Memmap,`
- `windows.modscan.ModScan,`
- `windows.modules.Modules,`
- `windows.mutantscan.MutantScan,`
- `windows.netscan.NetScan,`
- `windows.poolscanner.PoolScanner,`
- `windows.pslist.PsList,`
- `windows.psscan.PsScan,`
- `windows.pstree.PsTree,`
- `windows.registry.certificates.Certificates,`
- `windows.registry.hivelist.HiveList,`
- `windows.registry.hivescan.HiveScan,`
- `windows.registry.printkey.PrintKey,`
- `windows.registry.userassist.UserAssist,`

Now that we have covered Volatility 2 and got an overview of Volatility 3, you can utilize and explore it more in your work.

Evidence collection and acquisition exercise

1. Using the Dump It tool, acquire your own system memory.

2. Identify an acquired memory profile using the Volatility framework.

3. Explore a process list using Volatility, and identify an `smss.exe` process ID.

Summary

In this chapter, we discussed the importance of volatile memory in digital investigations. We emphasized the significance of analyzing volatile memory, as it contains valuable evidence. We also explained how to acquire volatile memory from live systems. Finally, we discussed the volatility framework, a powerful tool for analyzing memory artifacts.

In the next chapter, we will dive deeper and explore Windows Registry.

4
The Windows Registry

As technology continues to advance, digital devices have become increasingly important in our daily lives. These devices—including computers, smartphones, and tablets—store a significant amount of data that can be crucial in investigations related to criminal activities, civil disputes, and corporate investigations. Digital forensic examiners play a vital role in investigating these cases by analyzing digital devices and the data stored on them.

One important aspect of digital forensics is **Windows Registry analysis**. The Windows Registry is a hierarchical database that contains configuration settings and information on the operating system, software applications, and user profiles on a Windows computer. The registry is an essential component of the Windows operating system and is often used by forensic examiners to uncover important information about a system's usage and history.

Windows Registry analysis is an essential skill for digital forensic examiners, and it requires a deep understanding of the Windows operating system and the registry database. Forensic examiners must be familiar with the structure of the registry, the different types of information stored within it, and the methods used to access and analyze that information. In addition, forensic examiners must be aware of the potential risks associated with accessing and manipulating the registry, as any changes made to the database could have unintended consequences on the system.

In this chapter, we will cover the following concepts:

- Windows Registry fundamentals
- Windows Registry hives
- Windows Registry data types
- User registry hives
- Windows Registry acquisition and analysis
- Windows Registry analysis tools

We will conclude the chapter with a short section of exercises.

As you progress through this comprehensive chapter, you will develop a deep familiarity with the Windows Registry and its contents from the perspective of a forensic analyst. The Windows Registry is a critical resource that stores a wealth of valuable information about a Windows operating system, user activity, application settings, and system configurations. As a forensic analyst, understanding the registry's structure and contents is essential, as it holds a treasure trove of digital evidence that can be pivotal in investigations.

Technical requirements

Windows Registry analysis requires certain technical requirements to ensure that the process is executed efficiently and effectively. The following are links to the tools that we will use in this chapter:

- **Registry Explorer**: `https://ericzimmerman.github.io/#!index.md`

- **RegRipper**: `https://github.com/keydet89/RegRipper3.0`

- **Registry Viewer**: `https://www.exterro.com/ftk-product-downloads/registry-viewer-2-0-0`

- **RECmd**: `https://ericzimmerman.github.io/#!index.md`

Windows Registry fundamentals

The Windows Registry is a hierarchical database that stores system configuration information and settings for the Windows operating system. It is a fundamental component of Windows that is used by the operating system to configure and control the operation of the system. The registry consists of a collection of files located in the `C:\Windows\System32\Config` directory, and it is organized into a hierarchical structure consisting of keys, subkeys, and values.

The registry is used by various system processes and applications to store configuration information. It is also a valuable source of information for digital forensics and system administration. Understanding the structure and components of the registry is essential for anyone working with the Windows operating system. The registry can be edited using various tools, but it is important to be cautious when making changes, as incorrect modifications can cause system errors or even system failure. Each key in the registry can contain subkeys and values, and the values in the registry can be of various data types, including string, binary, `DWORD` (32-bit integer), `QWORD` (64-bit integer), and others.

Why do we care about the Windows Registry?

The Windows Registry is a crucial component of the Windows operating system and plays a vital role in maintaining system stability and performance. Here are some of the reasons why the Windows Registry is so important:

- **System configuration**: The Windows Registry contains configuration information for hardware devices, system settings, and software applications. It stores information such as which applications are set to run at startup, which hardware devices are installed on the system, and which system services are running.

- **User preferences**: The Windows Registry also stores user-specific information, such as desktop settings, user profile information, and other user preferences. This allows users to customize their experience on the Windows operating system and provides a consistent environment across different sessions.

- **Troubleshooting**: The Windows Registry can be a valuable tool for troubleshooting system errors and problems. By examining the registry, system administrators and support personnel can determine which settings are causing issues and make changes to resolve the problem.

- **Digital forensics**: The Windows Registry is also an important source of information for digital forensics. It can contain evidence of system and user activity, such as application usage, file access, and network activity. When investigating a computer system, digital forensic examiners often rely on the registry to recover crucial data that can help them identify the source of an incident, determine the scope of an attack, and collect evidence for legal proceedings. This data spans the following areas:

  - **User activity**: The Windows Registry can contain valuable information about user activity on a computer system, such as applications that have been installed, files that have been accessed, and user settings that have been modified. This information can provide important clues for investigators trying to determine which activities took place on the system and who may have been responsible.

  - **Malware analysis**: Malware often leaves traces in the Windows Registry, which can be used to identify the type of malware, how it was installed, and what actions it has taken on the system. Forensic examiners can analyze registry entries to detect and track the behavior of malware, which can help with developing effective remediation strategies.

  - **Timestamps**: The Windows Registry contains time-stamped information about when various events occurred on the system, such as when a user was created, when an application was installed or uninstalled, and when system settings were changed. This information can help investigators establish a timeline of events and reconstruct the sequence of actions that took place on the system.

  - **Evidence preservation**: The Windows Registry can be an important source of evidence in legal proceedings. By preserving registry entries, forensic examiners can provide a verifiable record of system activity that can be used in court to support their findings and testimony.

- **System maintenance**: Regular maintenance of the Windows Registry can help to improve system performance and stability. By removing unnecessary or outdated entries from the registry, users can free up system resources and reduce the risk of system errors and crashes.

As forensic analysts, we can see the value of the Windows Registry when investigating cases such as **computer intrusion**. When investigating computer intrusion, forensic analysts can use the Windows

Registry to identify when the intrusion occurred, which user accounts were compromised, and which applications and systems were accessed. They can also use registry data to determine the type of malware used and how it was installed on the system. In cases of **intellectual property (IP)** theft, forensic analysts can use the Windows Registry to determine which files were accessed and when they were accessed. They can also use registry data to identify which applications were used to access the files and whether they were copied or transferred to other devices. This data could be related to internal threats such as employee misconduct or fraud/harassment cases, for example.

Components of the Windows Registry

We will now delve into the fundamental building blocks of the Windows Registry and explore the distinct components that collectively form this crucial database in the Windows operating system, which holds several key components, each playing a unique role in storing and managing system configurations, user preferences, and application data. Let's take a closer look:

- **Hives**

  The Windows Registry is organized into a series of top-level keys called hives. There are five main hives in the registry, as follows:

  - `HKEY_CLASSES_ROOT` (HKCR): This hive contains information about file types and associations, such as which application should be used to open a specific file type

  - `HKEY_CURRENT_USER` (HKCU): This hive contains information about the current user's desktop settings, environment variables, and other user-specific settings

  - `HKEY_LOCAL_MACHINE` (HKLM): This hive contains information about the hardware and software configuration of the system, including device drivers, system services, and installed software

  - `HKEY_USERS` (HKU): This hive contains information about all user profiles on the system

  - `HKEY_CURRENT_CONFIG` (HKCC): This hive contains information about the current hardware profile of the system

- **Keys and subkeys**

  Each hive in the registry contains keys, which are used to organize and group related settings. Keys can contain subkeys, which are used to further organize and group related settings. For example, the `HKLM\SOFTWARE` key contains subkeys for different software vendors, such as Microsoft, Adobe, and others.

- **Values**

  Values are used to store specific configuration data in the registry. Each value in the registry is associated with a key, and it can be of various data types, including string, binary, `DWORD` (32-bit integer), `QWORD` (64-bit integer), and others. Values are used to store information such as system configuration settings, user preferences, and application settings.

- **Data types**

  Values in the registry can be of various data types, including the following:

  - **String**: This data type is used to store text data

  - **Binary**: This data type is used to store binary data, such as images, audio, and other multimedia files

  - DWORD: This data type is used to store 32-bit integer values

  - QWORD: This data type is used to store 64-bit integer values

  - **Expandable string**: This data type is used to store text data that contains environment variables, which are automatically expanded by the operating system

  - **Multi-string**: This data type is used to store multiple text strings in a single value

Windows Registry hierarchy

The Windows Registry contains keys and values, as previously mentioned. To understand better how to analyze the hives, let's first work on the details of what we see once we open regedit.exe on the Windows OS:

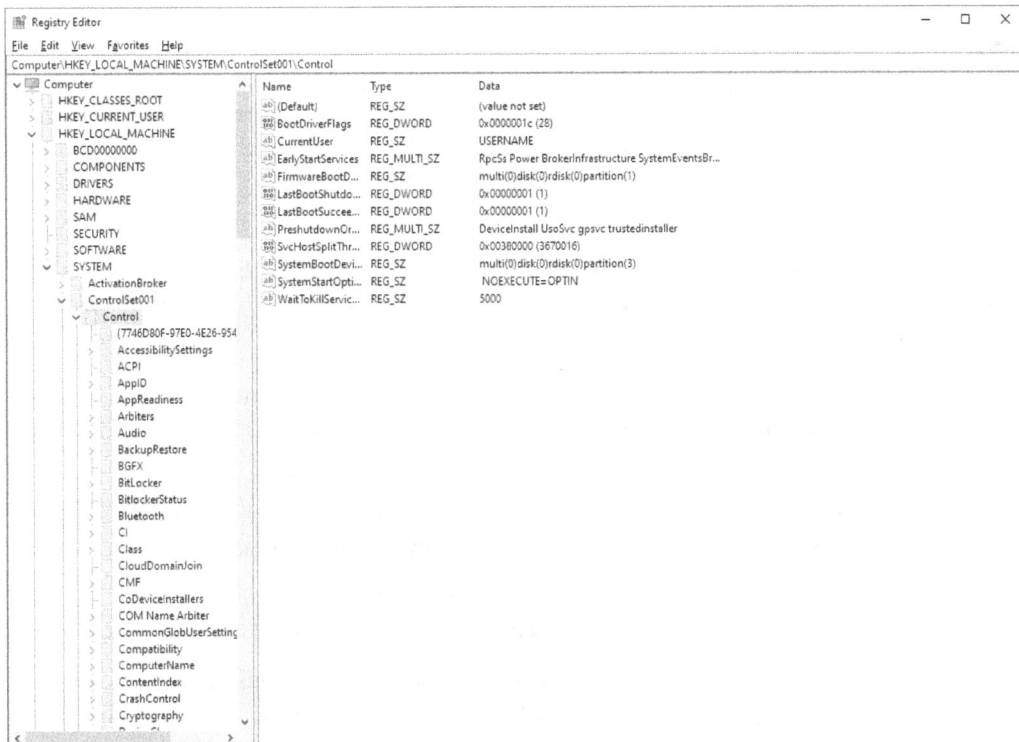

Figure 4.1 – regedit.exe GUI

Let's take a closer look at the numbered items in the screenshot, as follows:

1. **The tree**: The root folder that houses the entire registry.

2. **Subtrees**: Each tree contains subtrees with a specific purpose.

3. **Keys**: These are similar to folders and files in a filesystem that contain subkeys and values, as shown in the preceding screenshot.

4. **Subkeys**: Each subkey is uniquely named in relation to its immediate parent key in the registry hierarchy.

5. **Values**: These are used to define various properties of a key, which we can modify within the registry:

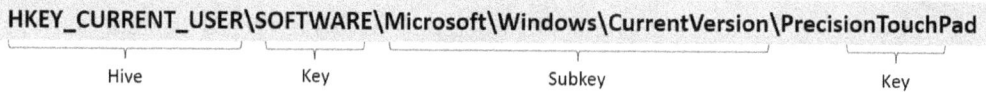

HKEY_CURRENT_USER\SOFTWARE\Microsoft\Windows\CurrentVersion\PrecisionTouchPad

Hive	Key	Subkey	Key

Figure 4.2 – Registry keys

Since we covered the main aspect of Windows Registry components, let's dive into each registry hive and learn the value we get from investigating each one.

Windows Registry hives

The Windows Registry is an essential component of the Microsoft Windows operating system. It stores configuration information for the operating system, hardware devices, and installed applications. The registry is organized into subtrees, which are similar to directories in a filesystem. These subtrees contain keys and values, which hold the configuration data.

The registry is divided into five subtrees: HKCR, HKCU, HKLM, HKU, and HKCC. Each subtree contains keys and values that hold configuration data related to different aspects of the operating system, software, and hardware, as follows:

- HKCR contains information about registered file types, **Object Linking and Embedding** (**OLE**) controls, and **Component Object Model** (**COM**) objects. This subtree is used by Windows to determine how to open files based on their file type.

- HKCU contains configuration data for the current user. This subtree stores user-specific settings such as desktop settings, application preferences, and environment variables.

- HKLM contains configuration data for the local machine. This subtree stores hardware-related information such as device drivers, system settings, and software installation information.

- HKU contains configuration data for all user accounts on the system. This subtree stores user-specific settings such as desktop settings, application preferences, and environment variables.

- HKCC contains configuration data for the current hardware configuration of the system. This subtree is a subset of HKLM and is used by Windows to determine which hardware devices are currently installed on the system.

The registry is a critical component of the Windows operating system, and it is essential to maintain its integrity. Any modification to the registry can affect the stability and performance of the system. Therefore, it is important to be careful when modifying the registry, and it is recommended to take a backup of the registry before making any changes:

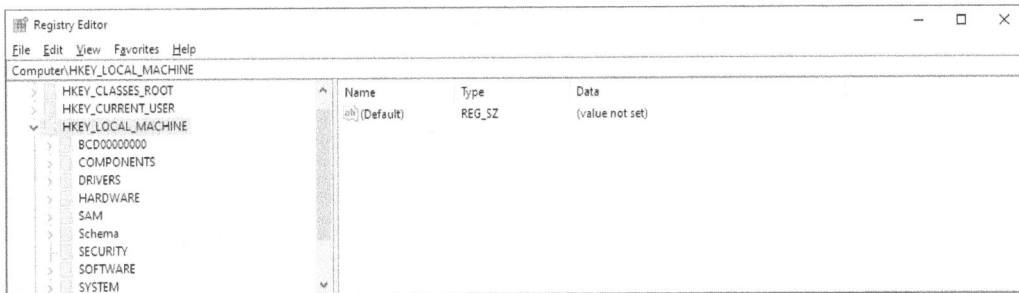

Figure 4.3 – regedit.exe keys

Let's dive into each subtree.

HKLM

HKLM is one of the five subtrees of the Windows Registry, which contains configuration data related to the local machine. This subtree stores system-wide information about the hardware, software, and operating system configuration. The HKLM subtree is a critical component of the Windows operating system, and any changes to its keys and values can affect the stability and performance of the system.

HKLM is organized into subkeys that contain configuration information related to different aspects of the system, such as hardware, software, and security. The subkeys include the following:

- HARDWARE: This subkey contains configuration data related to hardware devices, including device drivers, plug-and-play devices, and system resource allocation

- SOFTWARE: This subkey contains configuration data related to installed software on the system, including application settings, startup programs, and software installation information

- SECURITY: This subkey contains configuration data related to system security, including user account settings, password policies, and security policies

- SAM: This subkey contains the **Security Account Manager (SAM)** database, which stores user account information, including usernames, passwords, and group memberships

- `SYSTEM`: This subkey contains configuration data related to the operating system, including system startup and shutdown settings, system services, and system settings

- `Default`: The default settings for the system variable

In the following table, we have listed each hive with its specific location on the Windows host:

Hive	File Location
SAM	C:\Windows\System32\Config
Security	C:\Windows\System32\Config
System	C:\Windows\System32\Config
Software	C:\Windows\System32\Config

Figure 4.4 – HKLM registry hive location

HKCU

HKCU is a subtree of the Windows Registry that stores user-specific settings and configurations for the user that is currently logged on to the system. This subtree is stored in the user's NTUSER.DAT file, which is located in the user's profile folder. In addition to the NTUSER.DAT file, HKCU is associated with several other hives and files that are important for its proper functioning.

One important file associated with HKCU is the UsrClass.dat file, which contains settings and configuration information for the user's applications and settings. This file is located in the user's profile folder and is loaded into memory when the user logs in. The UsrClass.dat file is responsible for storing user-specific application settings, such as preferences, recent documents, and other user-specific data.

Another important file associated with HKCU is the NTUSER.DAT.LOG file, which is used to keep track of changes made to the HKCU subtree. This file is created when changes are made to the HKCU subtree and is used to recover the registry in case of a system crash or other problems.

The HKCU subtree is divided into several subkeys, each containing specific settings and configurations for the user's profile. Some of the important subkeys in the HKCU subtree are set out as follows:

- `Control Panel`: This subkey contains settings related to the user's control panel, such as the display, mouse, keyboard, and sound settings.

- `Environment`: This subkey contains environment variables that are specific to the user's profile, such as the user's name, home directory, and system path.

- `SOFTWARE`: This subkey contains information about software applications that are installed on the user's computer. Each installed application has its own subkey within this subkey.

- `Microsoft`: This subkey contains settings for Microsoft applications, including Office and Internet Explorer.

- `Windows`: This subkey contains settings for the user's desktop, including the wallpaper, screensaver, and taskbar settings.

- `Printers`: This subkey contains settings for the user's printers, including the default printer and printer preferences.

- `Network`: This subkey contains settings for the user's network connections, including the user's network shares and network printer connections:

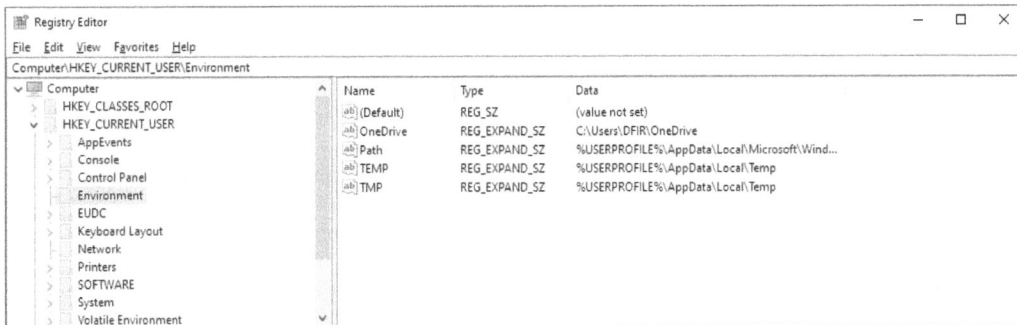

Figure 4.5 – HKCU registry hive

The HKU registry hive is another important section of the Windows Registry and stores configuration data for all user profiles that have logged on to the system. Each user profile is given a unique **security identifier (SID)** number, which is used to identify the user in the registry.

The HKU hive is stored in the `NTUSER.DAT` file located in each user's profile folder under the `C:\ Users` directory. The hive contains configuration settings for the user, including desktop settings, file associations, and application preferences. The file is loaded into the registry when the user logs on and unloaded when the user logs off.

The HKU hive is divided into several subkeys, each corresponding to a specific user profile identified by their SID. The subkeys are named with the user's SID, followed by `_Classes` if the user has any associated file-type associations.

Here are the main subkeys found under HKU:

- `.DEFAULT`: This subkey contains settings that apply to all new user profiles created on the system

- `S-1-5-18`: This subkey contains configuration data for the local system account

- `S-1-5-19`: This subkey contains configuration data for the LocalService account

- `S-1-5-20`: This subkey contains configuration data for the Network Service account

- `S-1-5-21-xxxxxxxxxx-xxxxxxxxxx-xxxxxxxxxx-xxxx`: This subkey contains configuration data for a specific user profile identified by their SID

Each of these subkeys contains similar subkeys to the HKCU hive, such as for the Control Panel, printers, and software, and stores user-specific configuration data for these areas.

It's important to note that the HKU hive is only accessible to the current user or an administrator, as each user's NTUSER.DAT file is only readable by that user or an administrator:

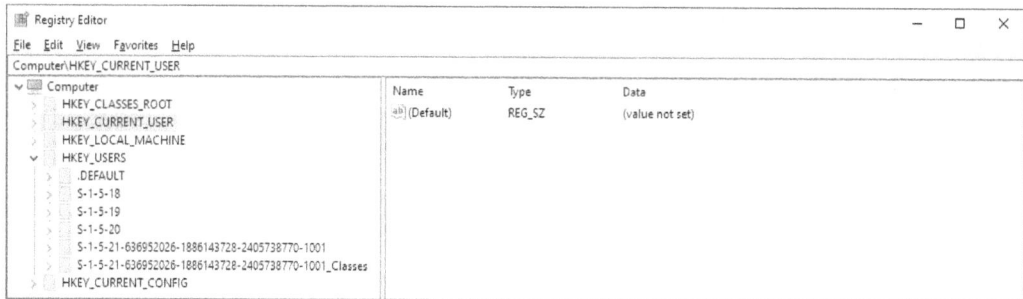

Figure 4.6 – HKU registry hive

HKCR

HKCR is a Windows Registry hive that contains information about file associations, ActiveX controls, and COM objects. It is a merged view of two other registry hives: HKEY_LOCAL_MACHINE\ Software\Classes and HKEY_CURRENT_USER\Software\Classes. Any changes made to the HKCR hive are reflected in both of these hives.

The HKCR hive is organized into a series of keys, each of which contains subkeys and values that store information about specific file types and associated applications. These keys are named after file extensions, **Multipurpose Internet Mail Extensions** (**MIME**) types, or the names of registered file types.

The following are some of the key subkeys of HKCR and their associated values:

- `.exe`: This key stores information about executable files. It contains subkeys for different versions of Windows and associated values such as `DefaultIcon` and `shell`.

- `.docx`: This key stores information about Microsoft Word documents. It contains subkeys for different versions of Word and associated values such as `DefaultIcon` and `shell`.

- `CLSID`: This key contains subkeys for each registered COM object on the system. These subkeys contain values such as `InprocServer32` and `ProgID`.

- `Interface`: This key contains subkeys for each registered COM interface on the system. These subkeys contain values such as `IID` and `TypeLib`.

- `ProgID`: This key stores information about COM objects and their associated programs. It contains subkeys for each registered program and associated values such as `CLSID` and `CurVer`.

The HKCR hive is also associated with several important registry files, including `Classes.dat` and `UserClasses.dat`. The former file contains information about registered file types and their associated applications, while the latter contains user-specific information about file types and applications:

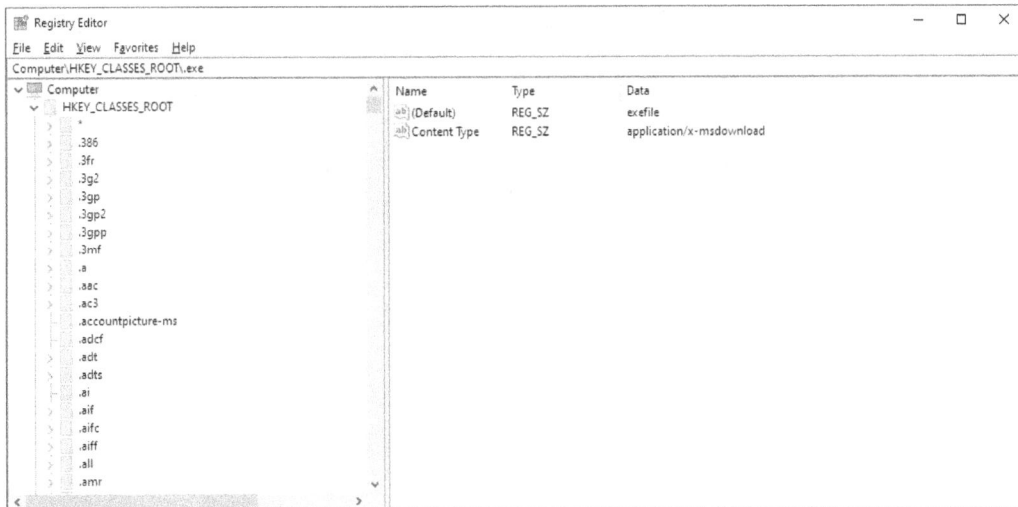

Figure 4.7 – HKCR registry hive

The HKCC registry hive is a subset of the HKLM hive, and it contains information about the current hardware configuration of the computer system. It is used by the Windows operating system to determine the hardware configuration at boot time and to make hardware-related decisions during system operation.

The HKCC hive contains information that is dynamically created by the system during boot time and is stored in the SYSTEM hive of the HKLM hive. This information includes hardware profiles, device drivers, and other configuration data related to the system hardware. The HKCC hive acts as a pointer to the current hardware configuration stored in the HKLM hive.

The HKCC hive consists of several keys that store configuration information for different hardware devices and components. These keys include the following:

- `System`: This key contains information about the current hardware profile, including device drivers and configuration settings.

- `Hardware Profiles`: This key contains information about the different hardware profiles that are configured on the system. Each profile has a **unique ID** (**UID**) and contains configuration settings for the devices that are associated with that profile.

- `Enum`: This key contains information about devices that are installed on the system and their associated drivers.

- `Video`: This key contains information about the video adapter installed on the system, including its configuration settings and driver information.

- `Monitor`: This key contains information about the monitor installed on the system, including its configuration settings and driver information.

- `Network`: This key contains information about network devices installed on the system, including their configuration settings and driver information:

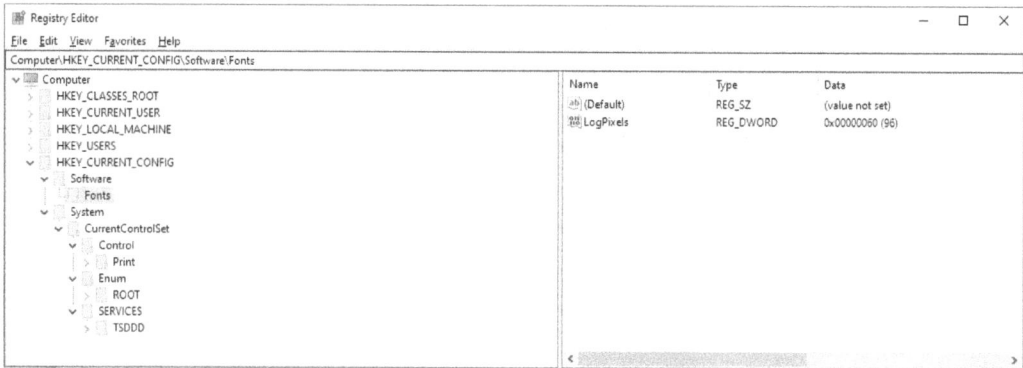

Figure 4.8 – HKCC registry hive

In the next section, we will get to know the data types for each registry entry and understand more about this amazing artifact.

Windows Registry data types

Each entry in the registry is assigned a data type that defines the specific kind of data that the entry can hold. While the registry supports nine different data types, in practical scenarios, you are likely to encounter only a few specific types while managing registry entries. There are several data types in the Windows Registry, including the following:

- `REG_SZ`: A string value that can contain a maximum of 4,096 characters

- `REG_MULTI_SZ`: A string value that can contain multiple strings separated by `null` characters

- `REG_EXPAND_SZ`: A string value that can contain variables that are expanded when the value is retrieved

- `REG_DWORD`: A 32-bit integer value that can be represented in decimal or hexadecimal format

- `REG_QWORD`: A 64-bit integer value that can be represented in decimal or hexadecimal format

- `REG_BINARY`: A binary value that can contain any type of data

- `REG_LINK`: A symbolic link to another registry key

Each data type has its own format and use cases. For example, `REG_SZ` is commonly used to store text-based information such as program paths or user preferences, while `REG_BINARY` is often used to store executable code or other binary data.

When performing forensic analysis, understanding the data types in the Windows Registry is crucial for identifying and interpreting registry keys and values. Forensic analysts must be able to recognize the data types and understand how they affect the behavior of the system or application.

In addition to the basic data types, the Windows Registry also supports several data structures that can contain multiple values. These include the following:

- `REG_RESOURCE_LIST`: A list of hardware resources used by a device or driver

- `REG_FULL_RESOURCE_DESCRIPTOR`: A detailed description of the hardware resources used by a device or driver

- `REG_RESOURCE_REQUIREMENTS_LIST`: A list of resource requirements for a device or driver

- `REG_LINK`: A symbolic link to another registry key

Understanding these data structures is also important for forensic analysis, as they can provide valuable information about the hardware and software configuration of the system.

In the next section, we will dive into two essential elements of the Windows Registry: the `NTDUSER.DAT` file, which houses critical system data, and the user registry hives, containing personalized settings and configurations specific to individual user accounts.

User registry hives

In the Windows Registry, user hives are specific to each user profile and contain settings and configurations for the user's environment. When a user logs on to a Windows system, the operating system loads the user's hive into the system registry. This hive contains a variety of data related to the user's specific settings and preferences, including desktop backgrounds, display settings, login credentials, application settings, and more.

There are two main user hives in the Windows Registry: `HKCU` and `HKU`. The `HKCU` hive contains information specific to the currently logged-in user, while the `HKU` hive contains information for all user profiles on the system.

The `HKU` hive contains subkeys for each user profile on the system, identified by a SID. These subkeys contain user-specific settings and configurations, including the same subkeys found in the `HKCU` hive.

Let's explore these additional system hives, which contain a tremendous amount of useful data.

NTUSER.DAT

The NTUSER.DAT hive is a user-specific hive in the Windows Registry that contains configuration information for the user who is currently logged on. This hive is located in the user's profile folder, typically in the C:\Users<username>\NTUSER.dat directory in Windows 7 and later versions.

The NTUSER.DAT hive stores various settings related to the user's preferences, desktop settings, installed applications, network settings, and more. This hive is loaded into the system's memory when the user logs on to the system and is unloaded when the user logs off. Any changes made to the user's settings during the session are stored in the NTUSER.DAT hive.

The NTUSER.DAT hive is a critical component of the Windows operating system and is frequently analyzed in forensic investigations. Digital forensic analysts can use the NTUSER.DAT hive to gather information about the user's activities on the system, including recently opened documents, user-specific network settings, and other user-specific configuration data. Additionally, the NTUSER.DAT hive can provide evidence of the user's actions in the event of an incident or attack on the system. As an example, let's suppose an organization has reported a security incident where a user's account was compromised and sensitive information was leaked. The forensic analyst is tasked with investigating the incident and identifying any suspicious activities that may have occurred on the compromised user's system.

The analyst can start by acquiring the NTUSER.DAT hive from the user's system and analyzing it. By examining the hive, the analyst can look for any evidence of malicious activity, such as the installation of unauthorized software or modifications to system settings.

One area of interest in the NTUSER.DAT hive is the user's recent activity. The hive contains information on the user's recently accessed files, folders, and programs. By analyzing this data, the analyst can identify any suspicious activity that may have occurred on the system leading up to the security incident.

Additionally, the analyst can examine the user's registry keys and values to identify any changes or modifications made to the system. For example, the analyst can check the Run and RunOnce keys to see whether any suspicious programs or scripts were executed at startup:

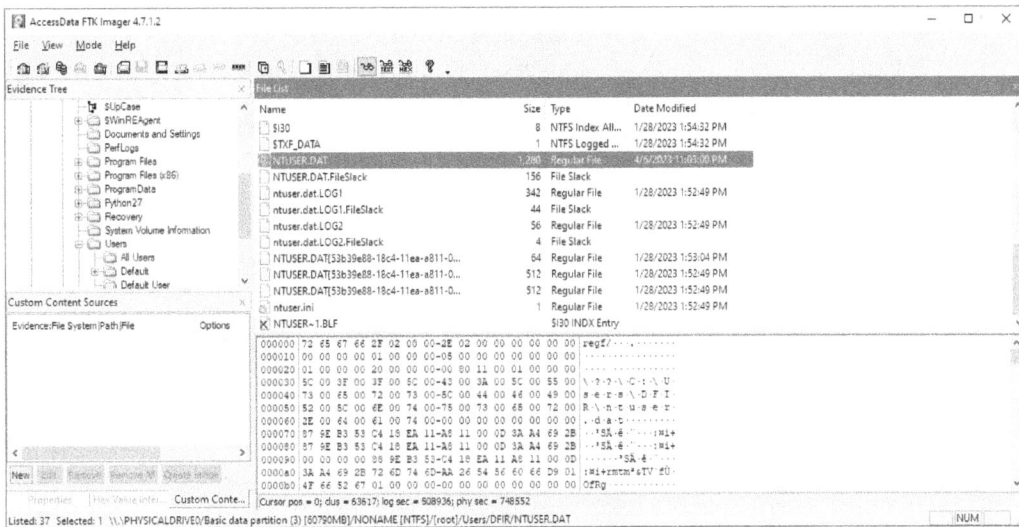

Figure 4.9 – NTUSER.DAT

UsrClass.dat

In Windows, the UsrClass.dat file is a registry hive that stores user-specific information related to the Explorer shell, such as file associations, icons, and COM objects. It is located in the %USERPROFILE%\AppData\Local\Microsoft\Windows folder and is created when a user logs in to their account.

The UsrClass.dat hive is loaded into the HKCU registry key when a user logs in. It contains settings that are specific to the user's profile, such as their desktop settings, sound scheme, and wallpaper. The hive is unloaded when the user logs out or the system shuts down.

Forensic analysts can use the UsrClass.dat hive in investigations to gather information about a user's activities on a system. Some of the information that can be obtained includes the following:

- **File associations**: The UsrClass.dat hive contains information about the file associations specific to a user, which can be useful in determining which applications they were using and what types of files they were working with.

- **Explorer settings**: The hive stores information about the user's Explorer settings, such as the display options for the taskbar, **Start** menu, and folder options. This information can be used to reconstruct the user's desktop environment and determine how they were using the system.

- **Shellbag information**: The UsrClass.dat hive also contains shellbag information, which is a record of the user's folder and file access. This information can be used to reconstruct the user's file and folder access patterns and determine which files they accessed, when they accessed them, and how frequently they did so.

- **Recent documents**: The hive stores information about the user's recent documents, which can provide insight into which files the user was working with and which applications they were using.

It is important to note that the `UsrClass.dat` hive is only accessible when the user is logged in, and a forensic analyst may need to use specialized tools to access and analyze the hive outside of the user's session. Additionally, the information stored in the hive may be encrypted or obfuscated, so further analysis may be required to fully understand its contents:

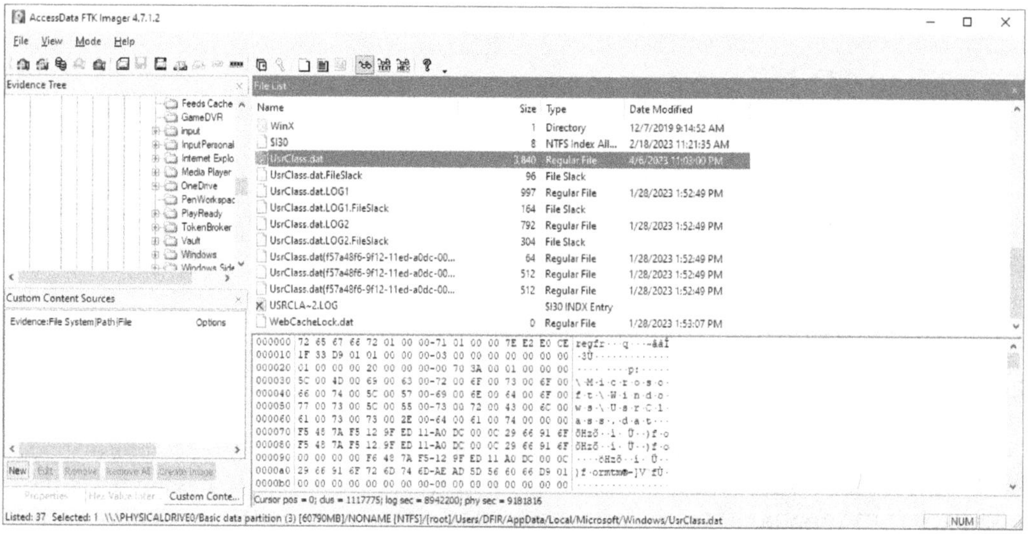

Figure 4.10 – UsrClass.dat

Now that we understand Windows Registry hives and the value that they present to forensic investigations, let's have a look at how to acquire the Windows Registry and start analyzing.

Windows Registry acquisition and analysis

As we covered in previous chapters on how to acquire Windows artifacts and how important such operations are, acquiring the Windows Registry is a crucial step in any forensic investigation, as it contains a wealth of information about the system and its users. There are several methods for acquiring the registry, and the choice of method may depend on the nature of the investigation, the resources available, and the type of system being examined.

One common method for acquiring the registry is through the use of forensic imaging tools, such as EnCase, FTK Imager, or dd. These tools allow for a bit-by-bit copy of the registry hive files to be created, which can then be analyzed in a forensically sound manner. It is important to ensure that the imaging tool used is compatible with the operating system version being examined and that it creates a verified and authenticated copy of the hive files.

Another method for acquiring the registry is to use live forensic techniques, where the registry is acquired while the system is still running. This can be done using specialized tools such as RegRipper, FTK Imager's Live View feature, or **Kroll Artifact Parser and Extractor (KAPE)**. The advantage of this approach is that it can capture volatile registry data that may be lost during shutdown or reboot.

In some cases, it may be necessary to acquire the registry remotely. This can be done using network-based forensic tools, such as FTK Network Acquisition or EnCase Enterprise, or using an EDR solution such as Carbon Black. Utilizing the remote feature, which is called Live Response, and then executing KAPE for collection allows for remote acquisition of the registry hive files over a network connection.

Regardless of the method used, it is important to document the acquisition process thoroughly and maintain a **chain of custody (CoC)** to ensure the integrity of the evidence. It may also be necessary to acquire multiple copies of the registry for backup and redundancy purposes.

We will demonstrate a couple of ways to acquire Windows Registry hives using different tools. We will check first how to acquire them using KAPE, and then we will dive into the usage of FTK Imager, but first, let's see how we can interact with a registry hive on Windows using built-in tools.

regedit.exe and reg.exe

regedit.exe and reg.exe are two different tools available in Windows for working with the registry.

regedit.exe is a graphical tool that allows users to browse and edit the Windows Registry. It provides a user-friendly interface to navigate through the registry keys and values. Users can add, delete, and modify registry keys and values by using regedit.exe. It also provides advanced features such as importing and exporting registry files, searching for specific keys and values, and creating bookmarks for frequently accessed keys.

On the other hand, reg.exe is a command-line tool that provides a way to interact with the registry using scripts and command-line interfaces. It allows users to add, delete, and modify registry keys and values from Command Prompt. reg.exe also provides advanced features such as exporting and importing registry files, querying the registry for specific keys and values, and setting registry permissions.

While regedit.exe is more user-friendly and suitable for interactive use, reg.exe is more suitable for automation and scripting purposes. With reg.exe, it is possible to create batch files or scripts, which can automate repetitive tasks, making it a useful tool for system administrators and forensic analysts:

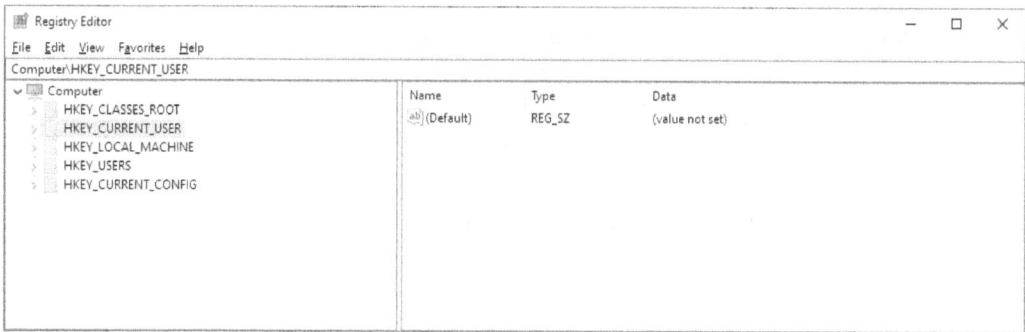

Figure 4.11 – regedit.exe GUI

Here is an example output from the reg.exe help menu:

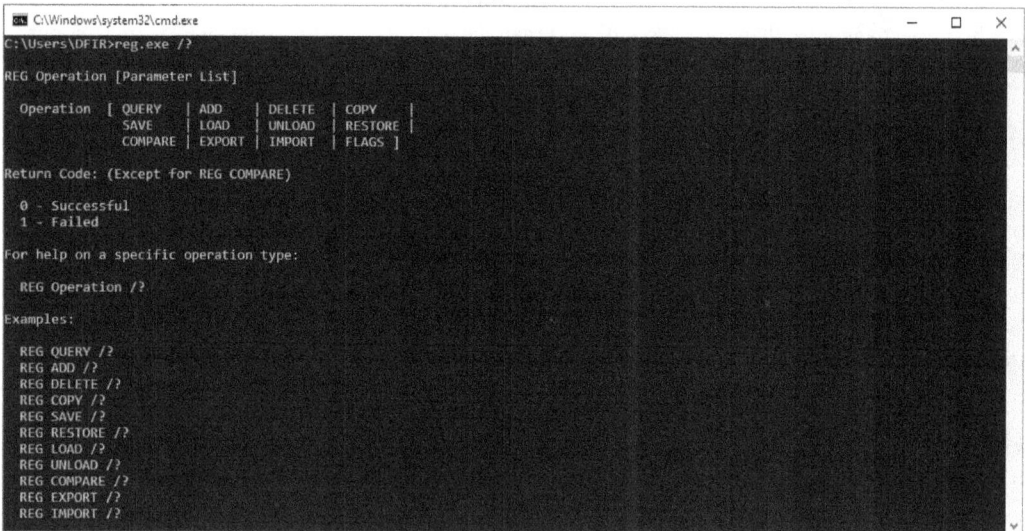

Figure 4.12 – reg.exe command-line options

For example, to view a list of subkeys under the HKEY_LOCAL_MACHINE\SOFTWARE\Microsoft\Windows\CurrentVersion registry key, you would enter the following command:

```
reg query HKEY_LOCAL_MACHINE\SOFTWARE\Microsoft\Windows\CurrentVersion
```

As we can see here, we have queried the Currentversion subkey using reg.exe:

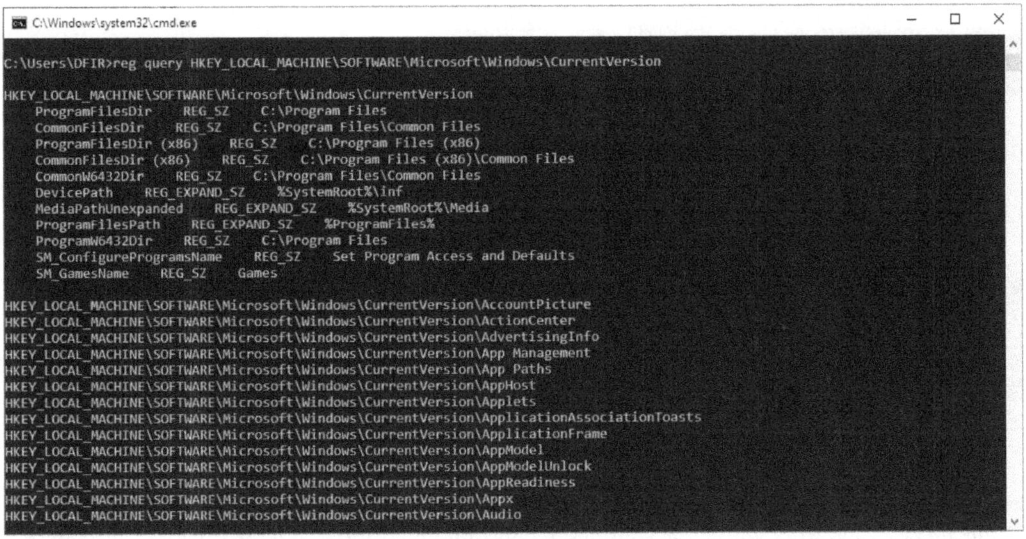

Figure 4.13 – reg query output

powershell.exe

PowerShell is a command-line interface that allows forensic analysts to interact with the Windows Registry. It offers a powerful and flexible way to automate and streamline many aspects of the forensic analysis process. Here are some examples of how PowerShell can be used to interact with the Windows Registry.

The Get-Item cmdlet in PowerShell can be used to read registry keys. The following command can be used to read the value of the DefaultUserName key in the HKLM\Software\Microsoft\ Windows NT\CurrentVersion\Winlogon subkey:

```
Get-ItemProperty -Path "HKLM:\Software\Microsoft\Windows NT\
CurrentVersion\Winlogon" -Name "DefaultUserName"
```

By running the preceding query, we can list needed information as an output using PowerShell:

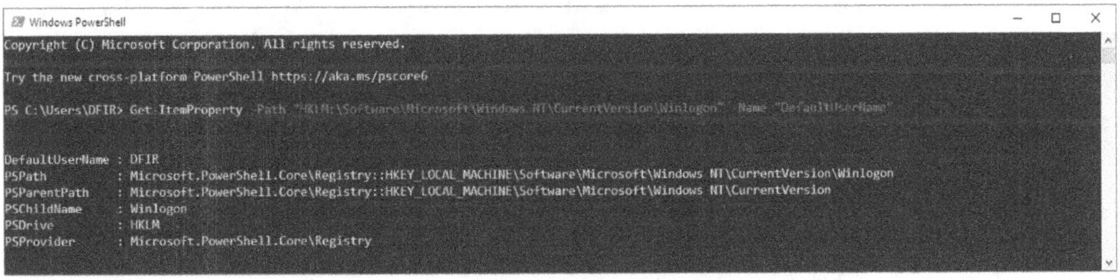

Figure 4.14 – PowerShell usage 1

Another example is to use `Get-ChildItem`, as follows:

```
Get ChildItem HKLM: Software Microsoft PowerShell 1 ShellIDs
```

Another example is to use PowerShell to display child items for a registry key, as we can see here:

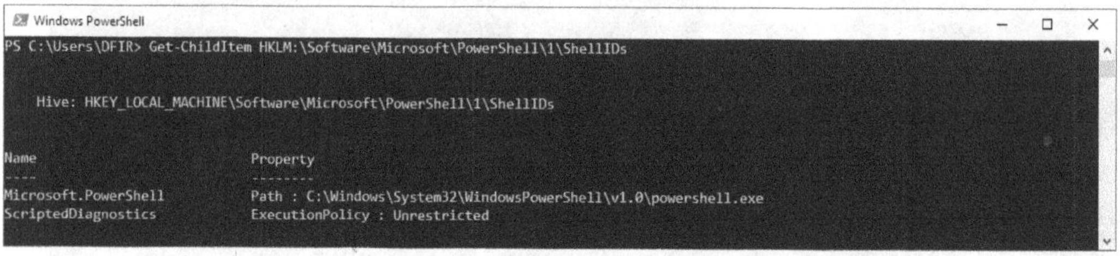

Figure 4.15 – PowerShell usage 2

PowerShell offers a flexible and powerful way to interact with the Windows Registry. With its ability to automate tasks and work with large volumes of data, it is an essential tool for any forensic analyst working with the Windows operating system. The previous example is only one example of how we can interact with it.

Now we have learned how to interact with the registry using various built-in tools within Windows, let's dive into forensic acquisition tools that we can use to acquire the registry.

Windows Registry acquisition

To facilitate our exploration of the Windows Registry, we will employ two powerful tools for acquisition: **KAPE**, a versatile and efficient digital evidence collection tool, and **FTK Imager**, trusted forensic imaging software. These tools will enable us to extract the necessary registry data for in-depth analysis and investigation.

KAPE

KAPE is a free and open source tool used for digital forensics and **incident response** (**IR**). It was developed by the Kroll cyber team to automate the process of collecting and analyzing digital artifacts.

One of the features of KAPE is the ability to parse and extract artifacts from Windows Registry hives. KAPE uses a number of plugins to parse the data in the registry and extract relevant information. These plugins can be customized to fit the specific needs of an investigation.

To acquire the Windows Registry using KAPE, the following steps can be taken:

1. Download and install KAPE from the official website: `https://github.com/EricZimmerman/KapeFiles`.

2. Identify the registry hive(s) that need to be acquired; for us, we will use `RegistryHives`.

3. Run KAPE using the target file to acquire the specified registry hives. You should then see an output similar to this:

Figure 4.16 – KAPE output

Let's break down the command line shown in the preceding screenshot. As we can see in the following snippet, we have multiple parameters within the command:

```
kape.exe --tsource C: --target RegistryHives --tdest "c:\temp\
RegistryOnly"
```

Let's look at these in more detail, as follows:

- kape.exe is the executable file for the KAPE tool that needs to be run in Command Prompt.

- --tsource C: specifies the source of the data that KAPE will acquire, which is the C: drive in this case. t in --tsource stands for "target," which means that KAPE will acquire data from the target source.

- --target RegistryHives specifies the target data that KAPE will acquire, which is the registry hives. This tells KAPE to focus on acquiring the registry hives only.

- --tdest "c:\temp\RegistryOnly" specifies the destination location where KAPE will store the acquired data. t in --tdest stands for "target," which means that KAPE will store the data in the target destination. In this case, KAPE will store the acquired registry hives in the "c:\temp\RegistryOnly" directory.

To explore more regarding target files, KAPE contains target files with the `tkape` extension, which contains specific criteria to collect desired artifacts. By reviewing `RegistryHives`, we can see that it includes both `System` and `User` register hive collections:

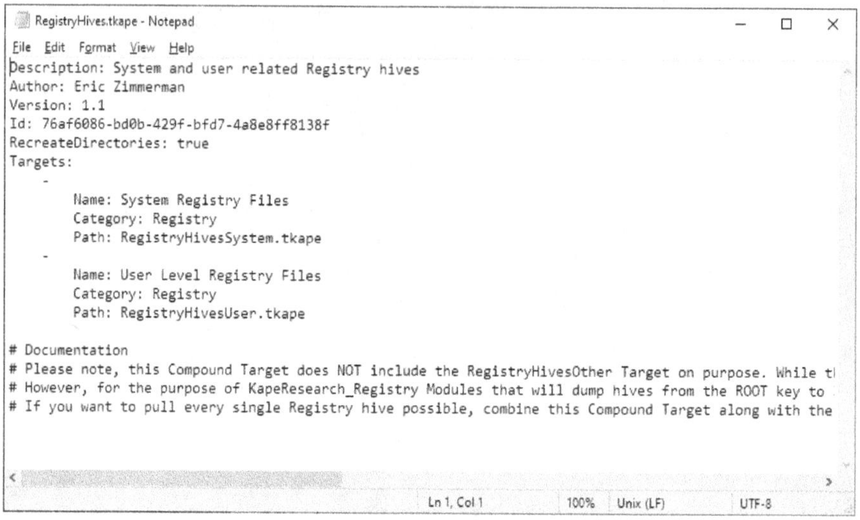

```
RegistryHives.tkape - Notepad
File Edit Format View Help
Description: System and user related Registry hives
Author: Eric Zimmerman
Version: 1.1
Id: 76af6086-bd0b-429f-bfd7-4a8e8ff8138f
RecreateDirectories: true
Targets:
    -
        Name: System Registry Files
        Category: Registry
        Path: RegistryHivesSystem.tkape
    -
        Name: User Level Registry Files
        Category: Registry
        Path: RegistryHivesUser.tkape

# Documentation
# Please note, this Compound Target does NOT include the RegistryHivesOther Target on purpose. While tl
# However, for the purpose of KapeResearch_Registry Modules that will dump hives from the ROOT key to
# If you want to pull every single Registry hive possible, combine this Compound Target along with the
Ln 1, Col 1    100%    Unix (LF)    UTF-8
```

Figure 4.17 – RegistryHives.tkape target file

In the following screenshot, we can see the `RegistryHivesSystem.tkape` file, which contains each registry with the location to acquire using KAPE:

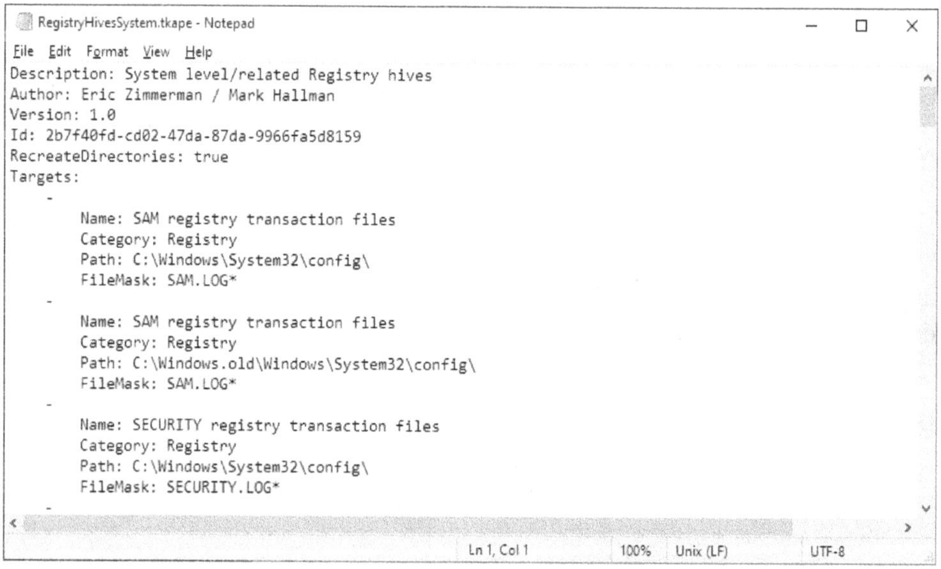

```
RegistryHivesSystem.tkape - Notepad
File Edit Format View Help
Description: System level/related Registry hives
Author: Eric Zimmerman / Mark Hallman
Version: 1.0
Id: 2b7f40fd-cd02-47da-87da-9966fa5d8159
RecreateDirectories: true
Targets:
    -
        Name: SAM registry transaction files
        Category: Registry
        Path: C:\Windows\System32\config\
        FileMask: SAM.LOG*
    -
        Name: SAM registry transaction files
        Category: Registry
        Path: C:\Windows.old\Windows\System32\config\
        FileMask: SAM.LOG*
    -
        Name: SECURITY registry transaction files
        Category: Registry
        Path: C:\Windows\System32\config\
        FileMask: SECURITY.LOG*
    -
Ln 1, Col 1    100%    Unix (LF)    UTF-8
```

Figure 4.18 – RegistryHivesSystem.tkape

FTK Imager

Another tool we discussed previously is FTK Imager. FTK Imager is a popular forensic imaging and analysis tool used by many professionals in the field. It also provides a feature to export Windows Registry hives. This process can be used only to extract the registry from the machine you are working on. The process for exporting the Windows Registry using FTK Imager is set out here:

1. Open FTK Imager and click on the **Add Evidence Item…** option in the **File** menu:

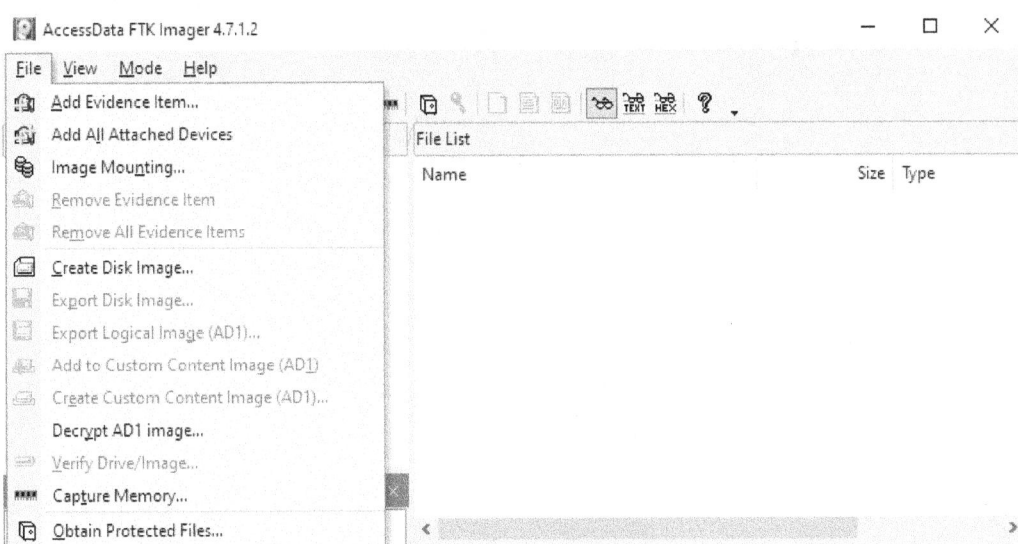

Figure 4.19 – FTK Imager: Add Evidence Item… option

2. Once mounted, navigate to the Windows Registry hive's location.

3. Choose the appropriate hive you want to export. You can choose from five different hives, including SAM, SYSTEM, and so on:

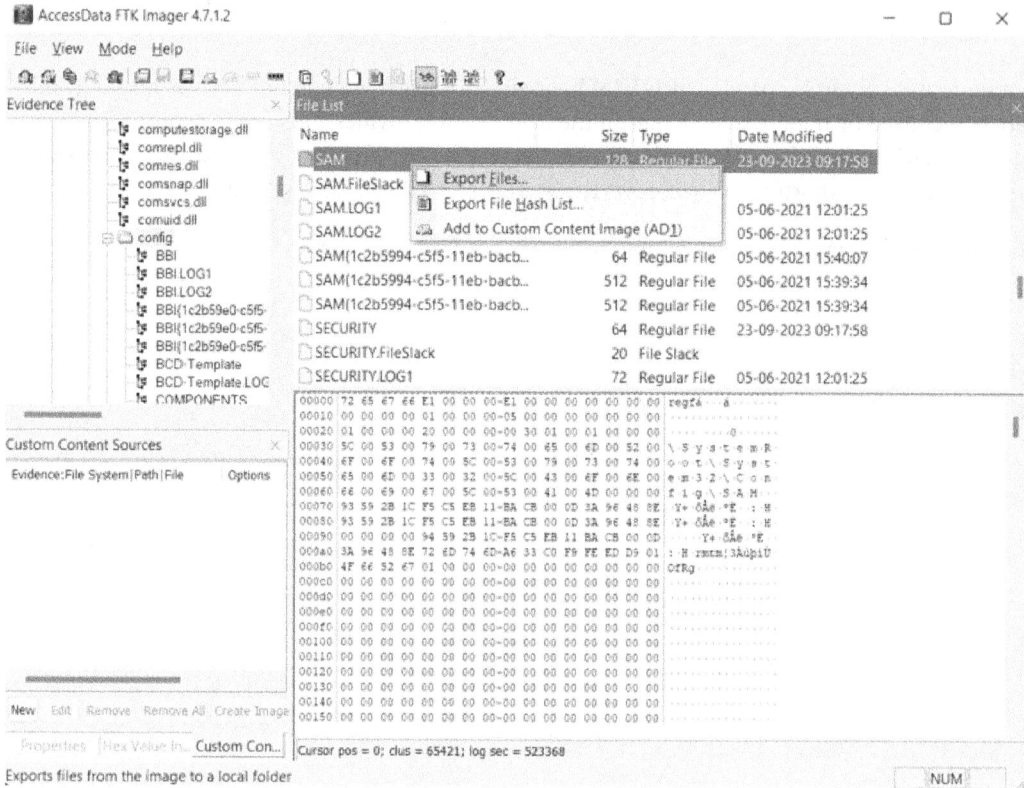

Figure 4.20 – FTK Imager

4.   Right-click and select **Export Files…** and select the destination file.

5.   Give the exported hive a name and click on **Save**.

Once the hive is exported, you can use tools such as `regedit.exe` or third-party tools to analyze it. Exporting a hive can be useful in a forensic investigation when you want to analyze the registry offline. It allows you to view the registry on a different system and analyze it without making any changes to the original registry.

Now we've acquired the registry hives, let's get into the analysis part of this chapter.

Windows Registry analysis tools

When performing Windows Registry analysis, one of the key considerations is whether to perform live or offline analysis. Each approach has its advantages and disadvantages, as outlined here:

- **Live analysis** involves examining the registry hives in their current state while the system is running. The primary benefit of live analysis is that it can provide real-time information about the system's current state. This is useful when analyzing malware or investigating a system that is suspected to have been compromised. However, live analysis can be risky as it can potentially alter the state of the system or result in the loss of volatile data.

- **Offline analysis**, on the other hand, involves analyzing registry hives that have been copied from the target system while it is not running. This can be done by imaging the hard drive or using a forensic tool to extract the hives. The primary benefit of offline analysis is that it eliminates the risk of altering the system state or losing volatile data. It also allows for a more comprehensive analysis of the registry, as all hives are included and there is no interference from the running system.

There are several factors to consider when deciding which approach to use, including the nature of the investigation, the level of volatility in the system, and the availability of tools and resources. In some cases, it may be necessary to use both live and offline analysis in order to obtain a complete picture of the system.

Some tools that can be used for live analysis include Sysinternals Process Monitor and Autoruns, which can provide real-time information about processes and startup programs. For offline analysis, tools such as Registry Viewer and Registry Explorer can be used to analyze exported hives.

Let's start with Registry Explorer.

Registry Explorer

Registry Explorer is a forensic tool designed for analyzing the Windows Registry. It allows users to examine registry hives, view and edit registry keys and values, and search for specific information within the registry.

One of the primary features of Registry Explorer is the ability to mount registry hives as virtual drives. This allows users to analyze the registry without modifying the actual system. By mounting a hive as a virtual drive, users can browse and analyze the hive just as with any other drive on the system. This can be especially useful for performing offline analysis of a system or for analyzing a registry hive from a different system.

Registry Explorer also includes a variety of search and filtering options. Users can search for specific strings within the registry and filter results by key, value, data, and modification date. This can be a powerful tool for quickly locating relevant information within a large registry.

Another useful feature of Registry Explorer is the ability to export registry keys and values to a variety of formats, including text files, XML, and CSV. This can be helpful for documenting findings or for sharing information with other analysts.

To load a registry hive using Registry Explorer, follow these steps:

1. Open Registry Explorer.

2. Click on the **File** menu and select **Load hive**:

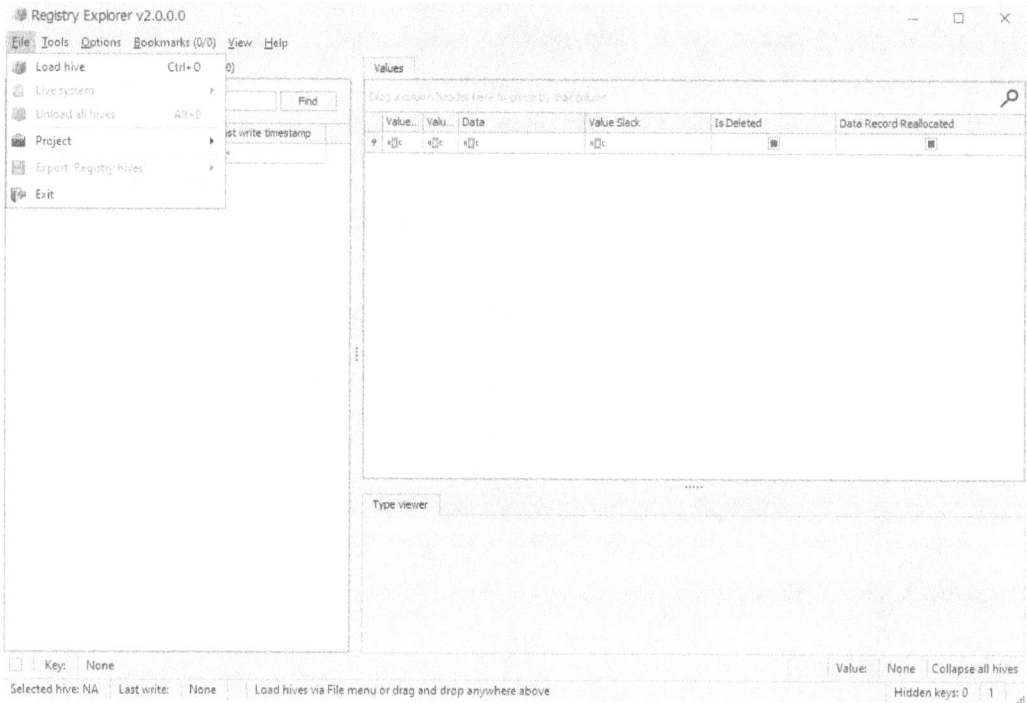

Figure 4.21 – Registry Explorer GUI

3. Browse to the location of the hive file you want to load and select it.

4. Choose a name for the hive, which will be used to identify it within Registry Explorer.

5. Click **OK** to load the hive.

6. You should now see the hive displayed in the left pane of Registry Explorer, under the **Hives** section. You can expand the hive to view its keys and values and perform analysis as needed:

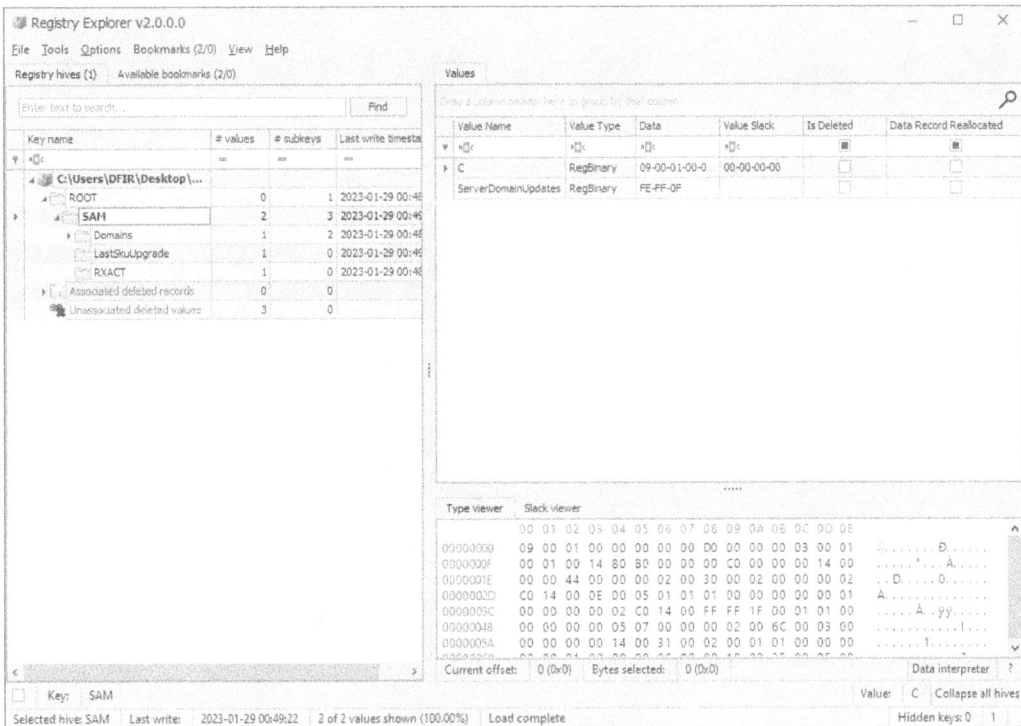

Figure 4.22 – Loaded hive in Registry Explorer

To explain the GUI for Registry Explorer, you can see in the preceding screenshot that we have three highlighted parts, as follows:

1. **Registry hives**: This part holds and displays loaded registry keys.

2. **Values**: The **Values** grid displays all the values present in the key that is currently selected in the **Registry hives** tab. By clicking on a value, a context menu appears, which can be accessed by right-clicking on the value.

3. **Available bookmarks**: The bookmarks menu in Registry Explorer consists of both pre-defined bookmarks (provided with the tool) and user-created bookmarks for quickly accessing frequently visited registry keys. Users can create a bookmark for any registry key or use pre-defined bookmarks, which are displayed under the **Common** menu, while user-created bookmarks are displayed under the **User-created** menu:

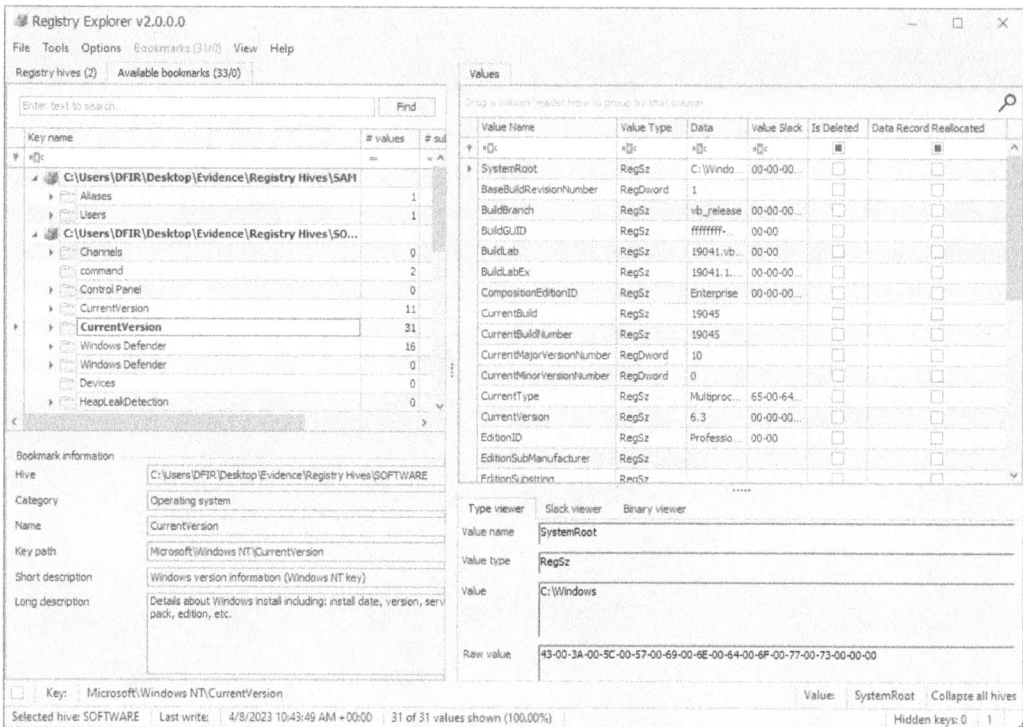

Figure 4.23 – Registry Explorer bookmarks

Registry Explorer is a valuable tool for any forensic analyst working with Windows systems. Its ability to mount registry hives as virtual drives and its powerful search and filtering capabilities make it an essential tool for analyzing the Windows Registry; we will cover it in more depth when analyzing system registry keys.

RegRipper

RegRipper is a popular tool used by forensic analysts for examining and analyzing the contents of Windows Registry hives. It is a command-line tool that works by parsing through hive files and extracting key information. This information is then organized into a report, making it easier for the forensic analyst to analyze and understand.

To use RegRipper, a forensic analyst first needs to obtain the relevant registry hive file from the target system. This can be done using a variety of methods, such as acquiring a forensic image of the system, extracting the hive file manually, or using a tool such as KAPE, as mentioned in the previous section of this chapter.

Once the hive file has been obtained, the analyst can then use RegRipper to parse the contents and extract key information. This is done by running a specific set of plugins, which are designed to extract specific types of data. For example, there are plugins for extracting information about user accounts, installed software, network settings, and much more:

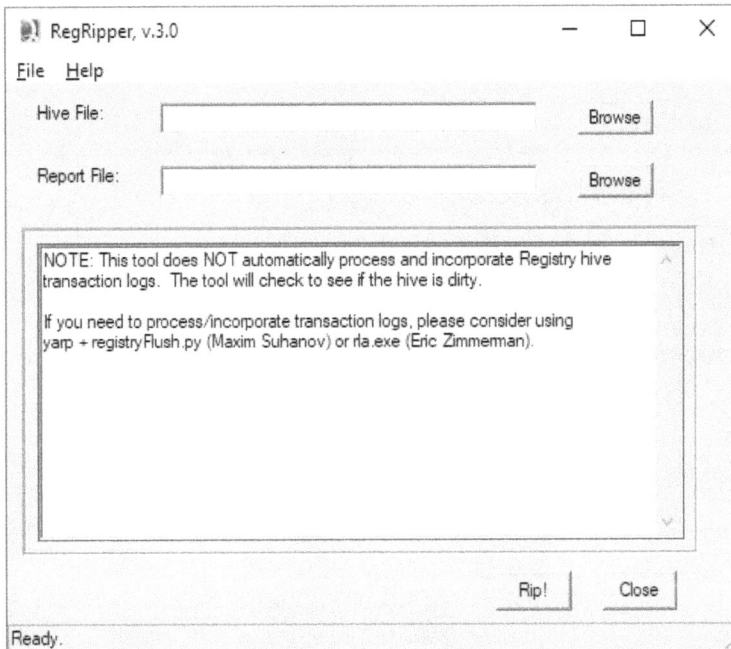

Figure 4.24 – RegRipper.exe GUI

Using RegRipper is quite simple; to load a hive, select **Browse** for the **Hive File** option, then select the **Report File** option, and name the report. Once this step is done, click on **Rip!** and it will start processing.

Once it is done, you can navigate to the desired location of the report and start exploring it:

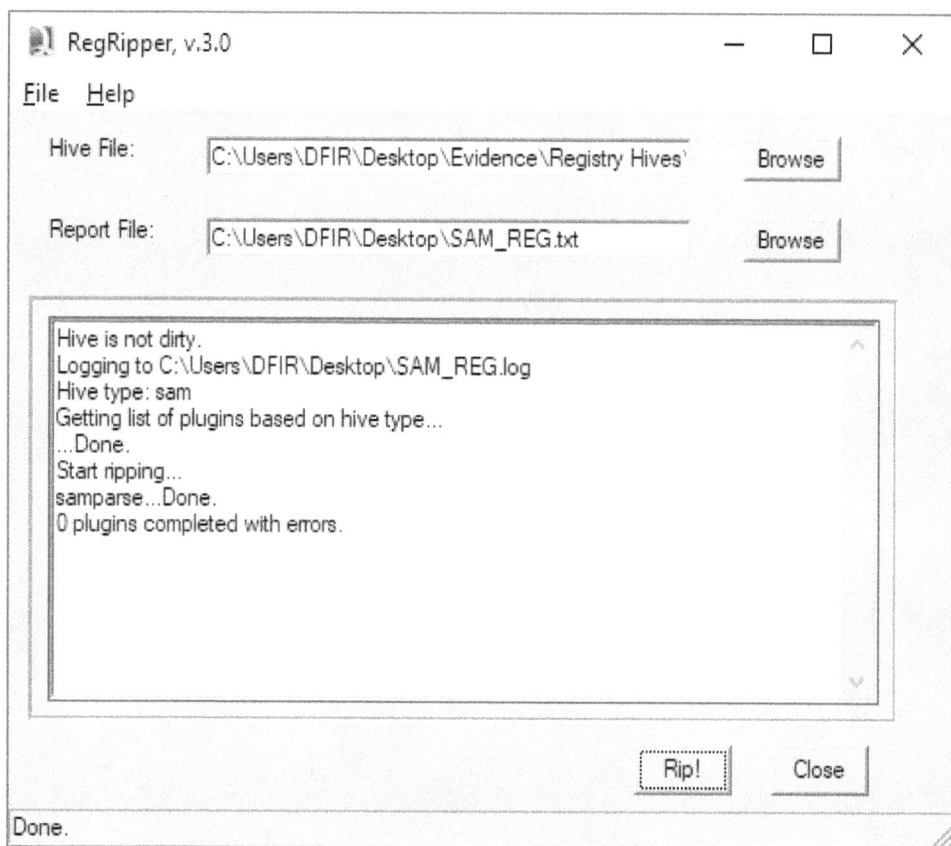

Figure 4.25 – RegRipper.exe GUI process

We can see here the output of the RegRipper tool:

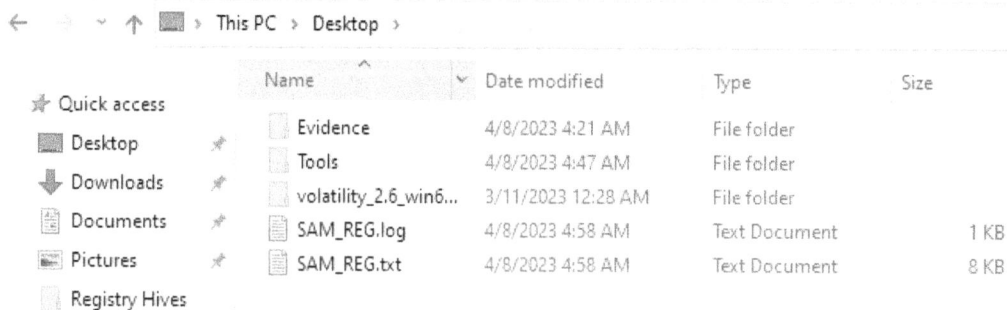

Figure 4.26 – RegRipper output files

By browsing `SAM_REG.txt` in our example, we can see that RegRipper analyzed the details we need to start looking for in our investigation. In this example, we analyzed the SAM registry hive:

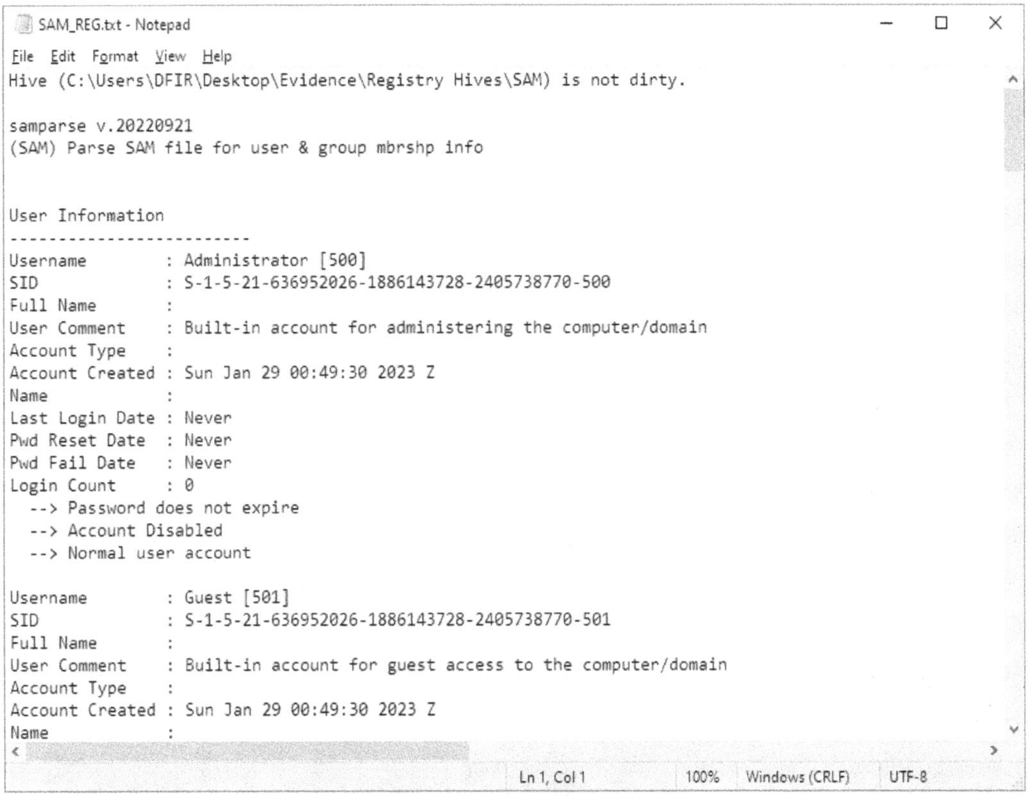

```
SAM_REG.txt - Notepad                                                    —   □   ×
File  Edit  Format  View  Help
Hive (C:\Users\DFIR\Desktop\Evidence\Registry Hives\SAM) is not dirty.

samparse v.20220921
(SAM) Parse SAM file for user & group mbrshp info


User Information
------------------------
Username         : Administrator [500]
SID              : S-1-5-21-636952026-1886143728-2405738770-500
Full Name        :
User Comment     : Built-in account for administering the computer/domain
Account Type     :
Account Created : Sun Jan 29 00:49:30 2023 Z
Name             :
Last Login Date : Never
Pwd Reset Date   : Never
Pwd Fail Date    : Never
Login Count      : 0
  --> Password does not expire
  --> Account Disabled
  --> Normal user account

Username         : Guest [501]
SID              : S-1-5-21-636952026-1886143728-2405738770-501
Full Name        :
User Comment     : Built-in account for guest access to the computer/domain
Account Type     :
Account Created : Sun Jan 29 00:49:30 2023 Z
Name             :

                              Ln 1, Col 1        100%   Windows (CRLF)    UTF-8
```

Figure 4.27 – RegRipper SAM registry details

Another option is to run the tool using the command line. For this, we will use the `rip.exe` file using the Windows command-line terminal:

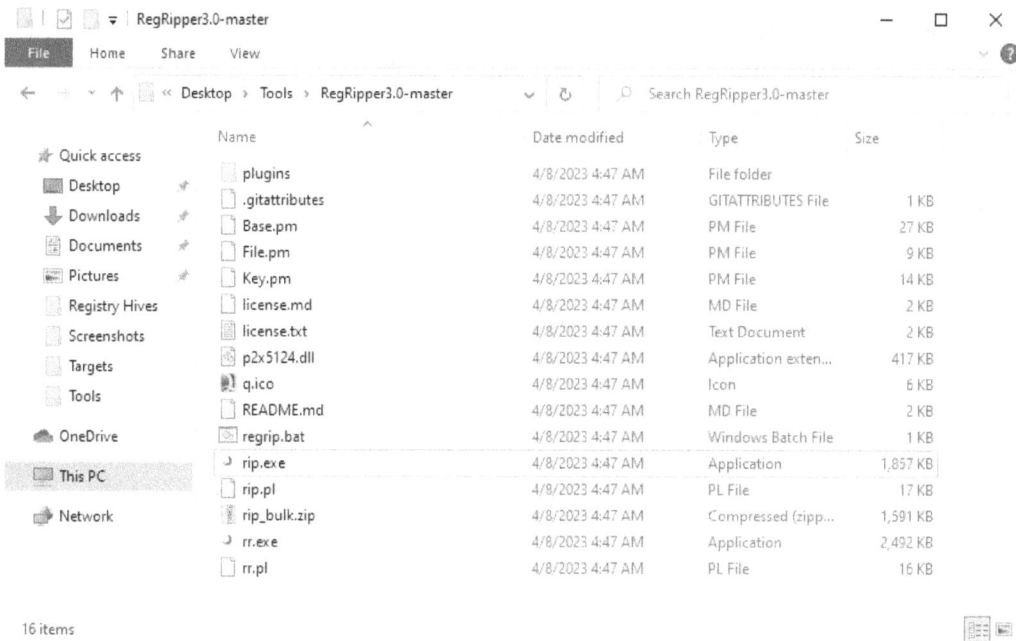

Figure 4.28 – RegRipper SAM registry details (2)

By running `rip.exe` with `-h`, we can list the help option:

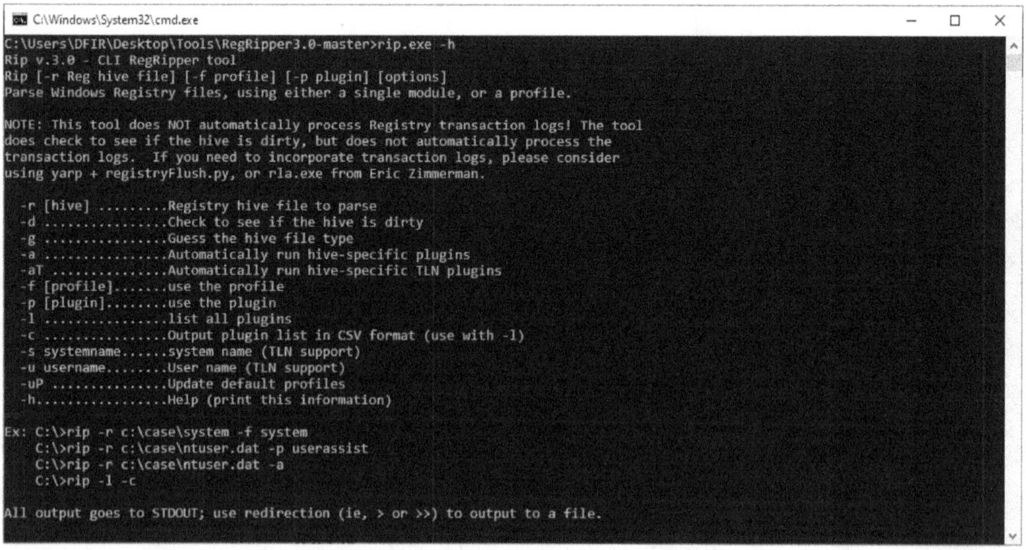

Figure 4.29 – RegRipper help option

As we can see in the preceding screenshot, -r is used to supply the registry hive. Let's run the following command and analyze the same SAM hive as we did using the GUI version. One thing to point out is that we need to redirect the output into a file using >>; otherwise, it will show the output on the screen directly:

```
rip.exe -r "C:\Users\DFIR\Desktop\Evidence\Registry Hives\SAM" -f SAM
>> "C:\Users\DFIR\Desktop\Evidence\Reg_SAM_CMD.txt
```

In the preceding command, we are running rip.exe to parse SAM's registry. The output is shown here:

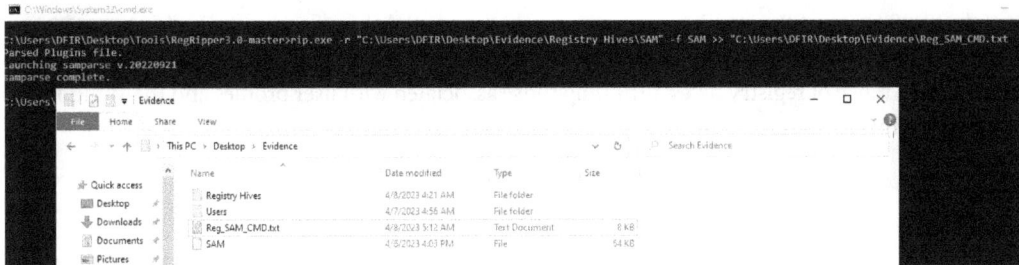

Figure 4.30 – RegRipper output file

As we can see here, the process is completed, and now we can explore the output file, which is Reg_SAM_CMD.txt in our case, as we will get the details for the SAM registry hive:

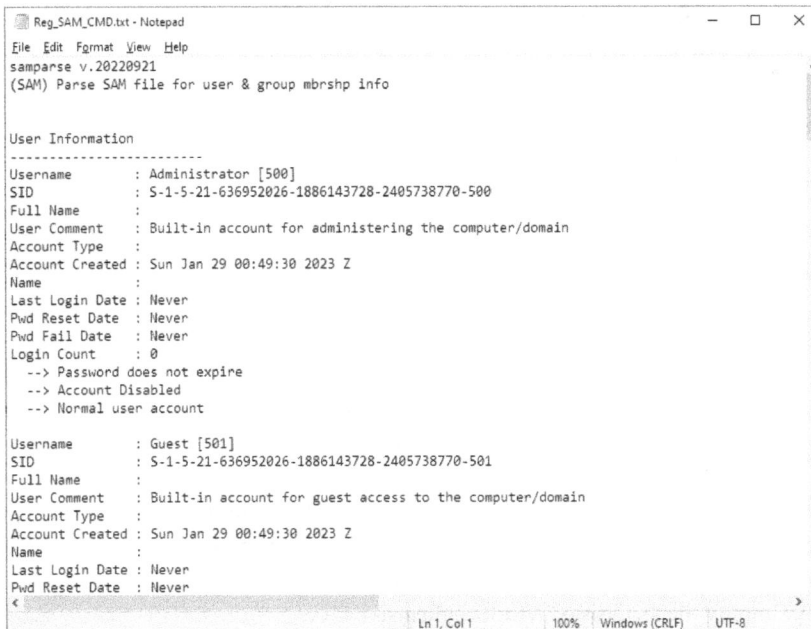

Figure 4.31 – SAM registry hive: RegRipper

Registry Viewer

Registry Viewer is a powerful tool for Windows forensic analysts, allowing them to examine Windows Registry hives in a user-friendly manner. The tool is especially useful for examining hives that have been acquired from a suspect system during a forensic investigation.

With Registry Viewer, analysts can browse through registry keys and subkeys, view and edit values, and search for specific data. The tool also supports the ability to bookmark frequently accessed keys and export data in a variety of formats.

One of the key features of Registry Viewer is its support for multiple hive formats, including NTUSER. DAT, SYSTEM, SAM, SECURITY, SOFTWARE, and UsrClass.Dat. This allows analysts to examine a wide range of registry hives, including those associated with user profiles and the Windows operating system:

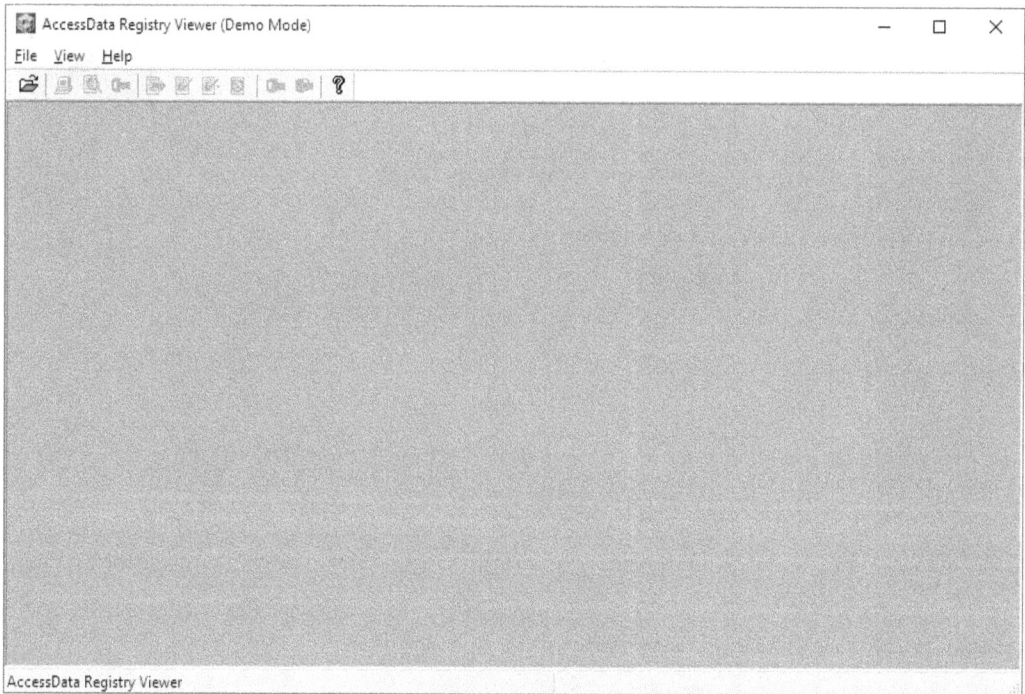

Figure 4.32 – Registry Viewer GUI

In addition to its standard features, Registry Viewer also includes a number of advanced features for experienced analysts, including the ability to compare two hives side by side and view the differences between them. Overall, Registry Viewer is a versatile and powerful tool for Windows forensic analysts that can greatly simplify the analysis of Windows Registry hives.

To load a registry hive into Registry Viewer for analysis, follow these steps:

1. Open Registry Viewer by launching the application.

2. Click on the **File** menu, and then select **Open**. Alternatively, you can press the *Ctrl + O* key combination.

3. Browse to the location where the registry hive is stored on your system, and then select the hive file.

4. Click on the **OK** button to load the registry hive into Registry Viewer.

5. Once the hive is loaded, you can browse through the registry keys and values by expanding the tree structure in the left pane of the application.

6. To view the properties of a particular registry key or value, simply click on it in the left pane. The properties will be displayed in the right pane.

7. You can also search for specific keys or values using the search box located in the upper-right corner of the application:

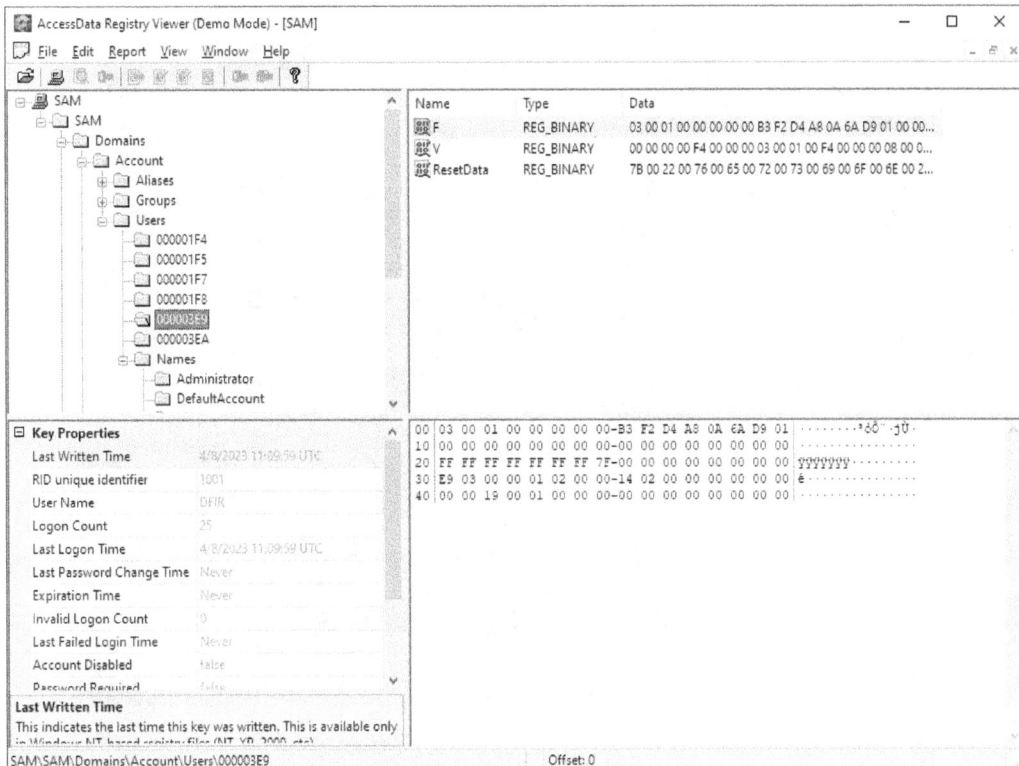

Figure 4.33 – SAM hive in the Registry Viewer GUI

RECmd.exe

`RECmd.exe` is a command-line tool that comes with Registry Explorer, a popular tool used by Windows forensic analysts to examine the Windows Registry. `RECmd.exe` is a powerful tool that allows analysts to automate registry analysis tasks and perform command-line operations on the Windows Registry.

`RECmd.exe` can be used to perform various operations on the registry, such as exporting or importing keys, searching for specific values or keys, and generating reports.

To display the help options, we can run the `RECmd.exe` binary without any parameters:

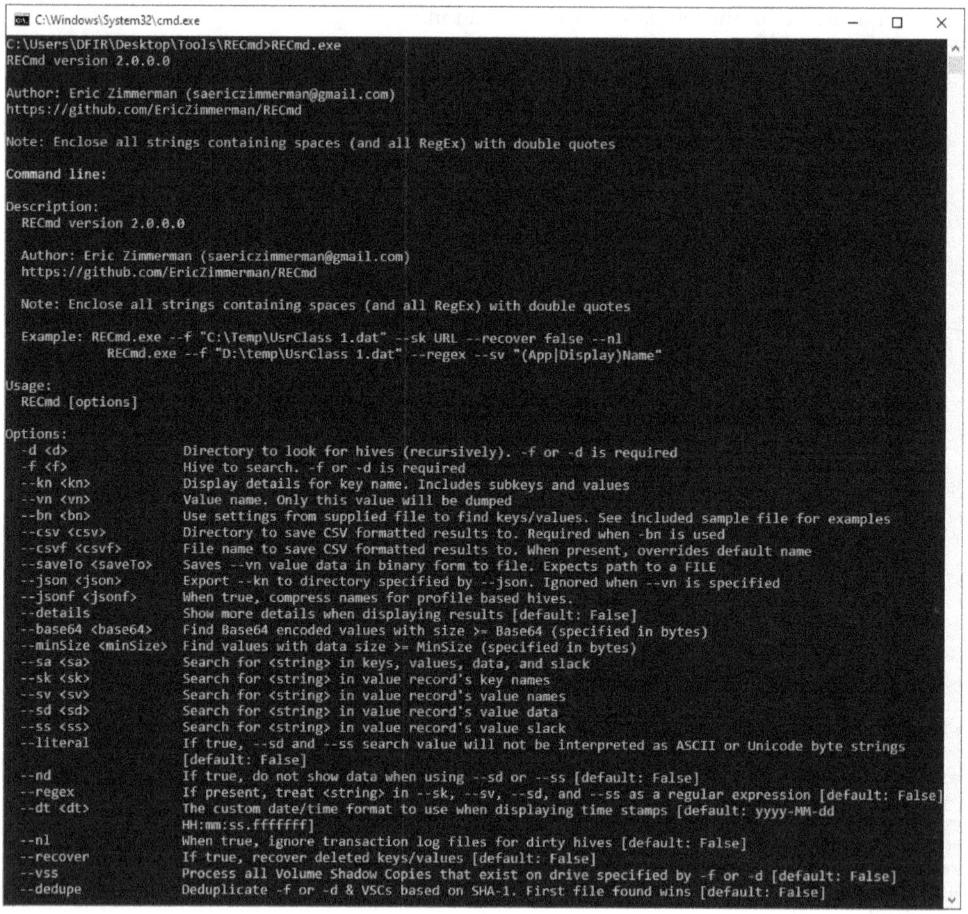

```
C:\Windows\System32\cmd.exe
C:\Users\DFIR\Desktop\Tools\RECmd>RECmd.exe
RECmd version 2.0.0.0

Author: Eric Zimmerman (saericzimmerman@gmail.com)
https://github.com/EricZimmerman/RECmd

Note: Enclose all strings containing spaces (and all RegEx) with double quotes

Command line:

Description:
  RECmd version 2.0.0.0

  Author: Eric Zimmerman (saericzimmerman@gmail.com)
  https://github.com/EricZimmerman/RECmd

  Note: Enclose all strings containing spaces (and all RegEx) with double quotes

  Example: RECmd.exe --f "C:\Temp\UsrClass 1.dat" --sk URL --recover false --nl
           RECmd.exe --f "D:\temp\UsrClass 1.dat" --regex --sv "(App|Display)Name"

Usage:
  RECmd [options]

Options:
  -d <d>                  Directory to look for hives (recursively). -f or -d is required
  -f <f>                  Hive to search. -f or -d is required
  --kn <kn>               Display details for key name. Includes subkeys and values
  --vn <vn>               Value name. Only this value will be dumped
  --bn <bn>               Use settings from supplied file to find keys/values. See included sample file for examples
  --csv <csv>             Directory to save CSV formatted results to. Required when -bn is used
  --csvf <csvf>           File name to save CSV formatted results to. When present, overrides default name
  --saveTo <saveTo>       Saves --vn value data in binary form to file. Expects path to a FILE
  --json <json>           Export --kn to directory specified by --json. Ignored when --vn is specified
  --jsonf <jsonf>         When true, compress names for profile based hives.
  --details               Show more details when displaying results [default: False]
  --base64 <base64>       Find Base64 encoded values with size >= Base64 (specified in bytes)
  --minSize <minSize>     Find values with data size >= MinSize (specified in bytes)
  --sa <sa>               Search for <string> in keys, values, data, and slack
  --sk <sk>               Search for <string> in value record's key names
  --sv <sv>               Search for <string> in value record's value names
  --sd <sd>               Search for <string> in value record's value data
  --ss <ss>               Search for <string> in value record's value slack
  --literal               If true, --sd and --ss search value will not be interpreted as ASCII or Unicode byte strings
                          [default: False]
  --nd                    If true, do not show data when using --sd or --ss [default: False]
  --regex                 If present, treat <string> in --sk, --sv, --sd, and --ss as a regular expression [default: False]
  --dt <dt>               The custom date/time format to use when displaying time stamps [default: yyyy-MM-dd
                          HH:mm:ss.fffffff]
  --nl                    When true, ignore transaction log files for dirty hives [default: False]
  --recover               If true, recover deleted keys/values [default: False]
  --vss                   Process all Volume Shadow Copies that exist on drive specified by -f or -d [default: False]
  --dedupe                Deduplicate -f or -d & VSCs based on SHA-1. First file found wins [default: False]
```

Figure 4.34 – RECmd.exe

Now, since we want to analyze the `SAM` hive in our example, if we want to search for the string of a registry key, we will use `--sk` to search for the key value, as follows:

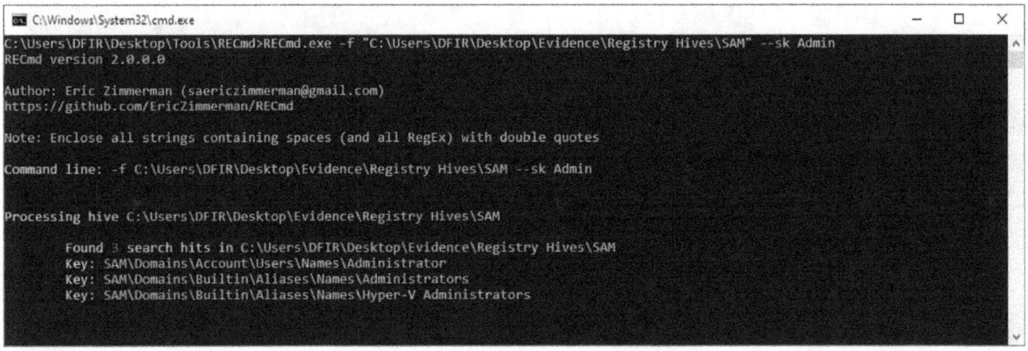

Figure 4.35 – RECmd.exe output

RECmd.exe uses batch scripts to run and search for registry keys. It comes with pre-written batch scripts under the BatchExample folder. For this example, we will use Kroll_Batch.reb.

By running the following command, we can save the output of the analyzed hive in the destination folder:

```
RECmd.exe -f "C:\Users\DFIR\Desktop\Evidence\Registry Hives\SAM" --bn
C:\Users\DFIR\Desktop\Tools\RECmd\BatchExamples\Kroll_Batch.reb --csv
C:\Users\DFIR\Desktop\Evidence\RE_Output.csv
```

By running the preceding command, using RECmd.exe, we can output the registry into a CSV file to analyze it using different tools, as we will see later in this book:

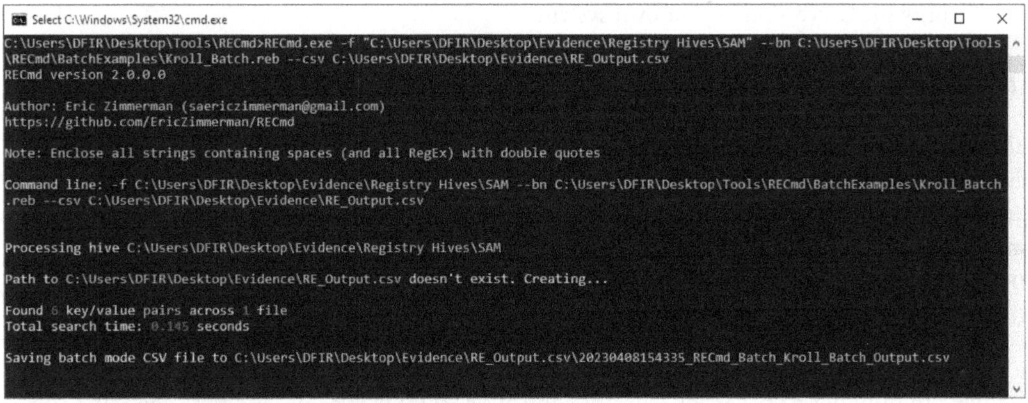

Figure 4.36 – RECmd.exe output

So, as we can see in the following screenshot, the output will contain all the data to analyze. This is only a test for the tool; using it in a real-world scenario would be a much better option, so take your time and explore it more. Eric Zimmerman did a fantastic job of explaining this tool in his GitHub repository:

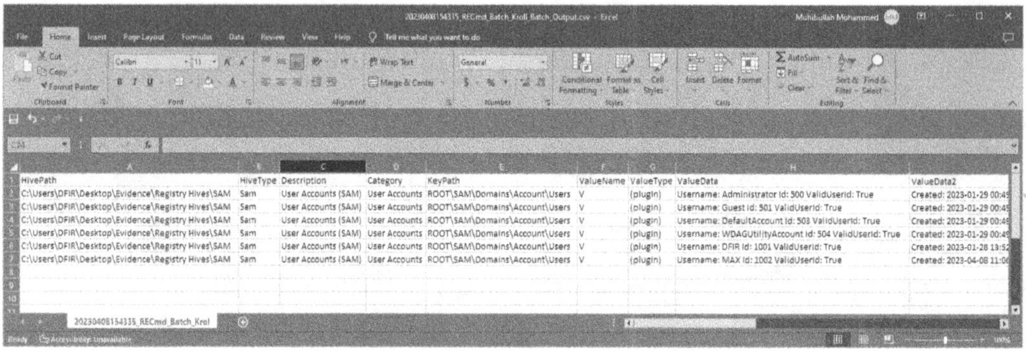

Figure 4.37 – Output file of RECmd.exe

RECmd.exe is a versatile tool that can help automate and streamline Windows Registry analysis tasks for forensic analysts. With its wide range of capabilities and command-line interface, RECmd.exe can be a valuable addition to any forensic analyst's toolkit.

Windows Registry forensic analysis exercises

In this section, we will apply what we have learned so far. Try to work on the following exercises:

1. Using Registry Explorer, analyze the SAM registry hive and identify your own user SID.
2. Using the RegRipper tool, perform analysis on the SAM registry hive.
3. Identify the OS version of your own system.

Summary

In this chapter, we covered the importance of the Windows Registry in forensic analysis and how to utilize it to extract critical information during an investigation. The Windows Registry is a crucial repository of system- and user-level data that provides a timeline of the activities performed on a system. We discussed several Windows Registry hives, including SAM, SECURITY, SYSTEM, and SOFTWARE, which provide a wealth of information related to user activity, system configurations, and network connections.

We explained the importance of profiling system details using the Windows Registry, such as identifying the Windows OS version, current control set, computer name, and time zone. We also covered investigating installed applications, network interfaces, historical network connections, user activities, shutdown information, and more.

We explored how to analyze Windows Registry data using tools such as Registry Explorer. By analyzing the Windows Registry, forensic analysts can determine system and user activity, identify potential security breaches, and create a timeline of events that can be used as evidence in legal proceedings.

In the next chapter, we will be using what we learned from this chapter to profile user activity.

5

User Profiling Using the Windows Registry

In this chapter, we will be using the knowledge of the Windows Registry from the previous chapter to profile user activity.

As forensic examiners, we face cases in which we need to investigate user activity and profile it based on available evidence. In this chapter, we will learn more about initiating investigations and gathering information related to users by diving into the Windows Registry.

We will cover the following main topics in this chapter:

- Profiling system details
- Profiling user activities

We will conclude the chapter with a short section of exercises.

Profiling system details

Forensic profiling refers to the process of identifying and analyzing information that can help to create a detailed profile of a specific individual or group. In the context of digital forensics, forensic profiling involves using various methods and tools to gather information about the system or device under investigation. This can include information about the hardware and software configurations, system settings, installed applications, network settings, user accounts, and other relevant data.

Forensic profiling is important for digital forensic analysts because it can help to establish a baseline of normal system behavior and identify any anomalies or suspicious activities. By understanding the system's profile, analysts can also identify potential sources of evidence and determine which areas of the system to focus on during an investigation.

It is important for forensic analysts to profile system details using the Windows Registry because the registry stores a wealth of information about a system's configuration, settings, installed software, user activity, and other important data. By examining the registry, analysts can gain insights into the history of a system, identify security issues and malware infections, and reconstruct a timeline of events, which can be used to support an investigation or a legal case.

Some specific system details that can be extracted from the registry include information about user accounts and passwords, network settings, system performance and resource usage, installed hardware and software, installed updates and patches, file associations, and recent user activity. This information can be crucial for identifying evidence of unauthorized access, data exfiltration, or other suspicious activity on a system.

Furthermore, profiling system details using the Windows Registry can also aid in **incident response (IR)**, system hardening, and vulnerability assessments. By identifying vulnerabilities, security weaknesses, and system misconfigurations through registry analysis, analysts can recommend and implement measures to enhance system security and prevent future incidents.

We will divide this task into multiple chunks to identify system information related to the OS version, network profiles, and more.

We will demonstrate how to use the Registry Explorer tool for this; however, you can utilize the same concept and apply it using different tools as required.

> **Important note**
>
> In this book, the registry key will be referred to as `HKEY_LOCAL_MACHINE\SOFTWARE\Microsoft\Windows NT\CurrentVersion`. For example, however, when analyzing using Registry Explorer, we use an exported `SOFTWARE` hive, load it, and then navigate to the remainder of the path of the registry: `SOFTWARE\Microsoft\Windows NT\CurrentVersion`.

Let's start by first identifying the OS version.

Identifying the OS version

Identifying the version of the Windows operating system is a critical task for forensic analysts as it provides important information that can help in further analysis of the system. The Windows Registry is a valuable source of information for identifying the OS version as it contains a number of keys that store this information.

One of the most straightforward ways to identify the Windows OS version is by looking at the `HKEY_LOCAL_MACHINE\SOFTWARE\Microsoft\Windows NT\CurrentVersion` registry key. This key contains a number of different values that provide important information about the Windows version, including the current build, the edition of Windows, and the service pack installed, as illustrated in the following screenshot:

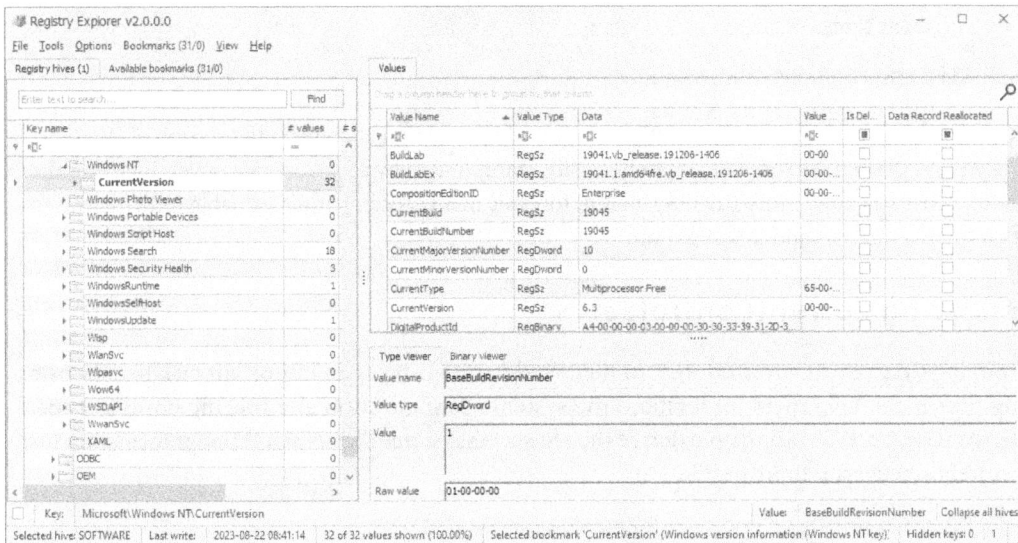

Figure 5.1 – OS build info

Here are some of the values that can be used to identify the version of Windows:

- `CurrentBuild`: This value contains the build number of the current version of Windows

- `CurrentVersion`: This value contains the version number of the current version of Windows

- `ProductName`: This value contains the name of the Windows product that is installed on the system

- `EditionID`: This value contains the edition of Windows that is installed on the system, such as Professional or Home

For example, a system with Windows 10 Professional installed may have the following values:

- `CurrentBuild`: `19045`

- `CurrentVersion`: `6.3`

- ProductName: Windows 10 Pro
- EditionID: Professional

Forensic analysts should always use multiple sources of information to confirm the version of Windows installed on a system, as some keys can be easily manipulated by attackers. However, by using the Windows Registry to identify the OS version, forensic analysts can gather valuable information to help in further analysis and investigation.

Identifying CurrentControlSet

Identifying CurrentControlSet in the Windows Registry is an important task for forensic analysts as it can help them understand the system's configuration at a specific point in time. CurrentControlSet is the portion of the registry that stores the configuration information for the currently active hardware profile.

To identify CurrentControlSet, follow these steps:

1. Open Registry Editor (regedit.exe).

2. Navigate to the following key: HKEY_LOCAL_MACHINE\System\Select.

3. In the right-hand pane, you will see a value called **Current**. This value will have a data type of REG_DWORD.

4. In the **Data** field, you will see a number (typically **1**, **2**, or **3**). This number corresponds to the ControlSet that is currently in use by the system. For example, if the value data is **1**, then **ControlSet001** is currently active:

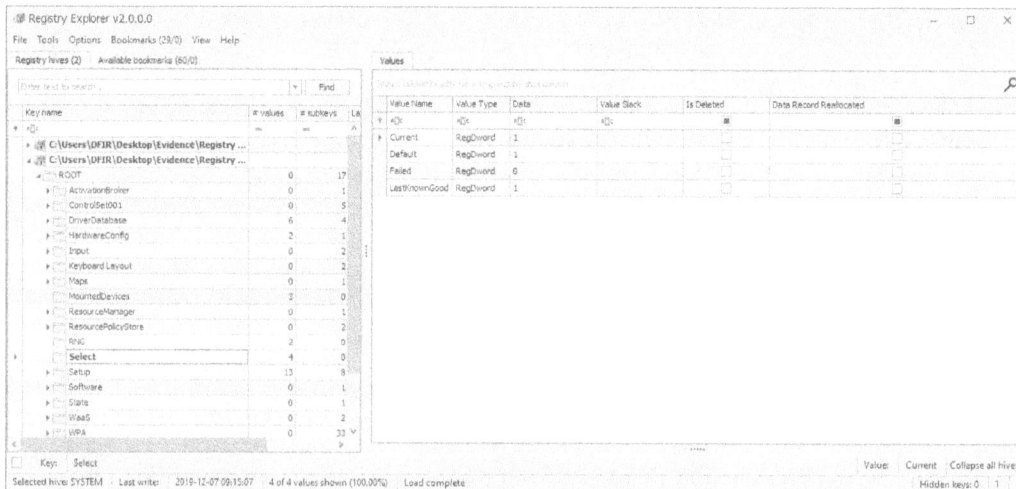

Figure 5.2 – CurrentControlSet

Once you have identified the active `ControlSet`, you can navigate to the corresponding `ControlSet` in the registry to view the configuration information for that hardware profile. This information can be used by forensic analysts to determine the system's configuration, including installed hardware, drivers, and software at the time of the incident being investigated.

Validating the computer name

In Windows, the computer name is stored in the registry and can be accessed using Registry Editor or other tools designed for Windows forensic analysis.

To use Registry Explorer to identify a computer name from the registry, follow these steps:

1. Open Registry Explorer and load the `SYSTEM` hive from the target machine's registry.

2. Navigate to the following key: `HKEY_LOCAL_MACHINE\SYSTEM\CurrentControlSet\Control\ComputerName\ComputerName`.

3. Look at the data associated with the `ComputerName` value. This will provide the computer name associated with the system.

4. Alternatively, you can search the registry for the computer name using the **Find** feature in Registry Explorer. Select the root key (`HKEY_LOCAL_MACHINE`) and click the **Find** button. Enter the computer name in the search box, and Registry Explorer will locate any values or keys containing that string.

5. Otherwise, you can utilize the bookmark feature of Registry Explorer to directly jump to the `ComputerName` registry key.

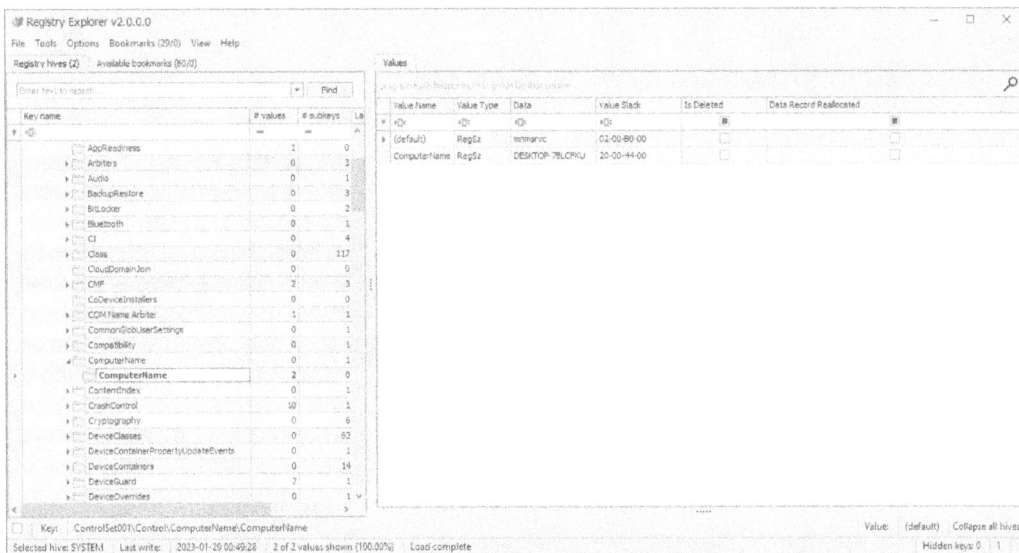

Figure 5.3 – The ComputerName registry key

As we can see, by exploring the `ComputerName` registry key, we can see the result with the hostname, as shown in the following screenshot:

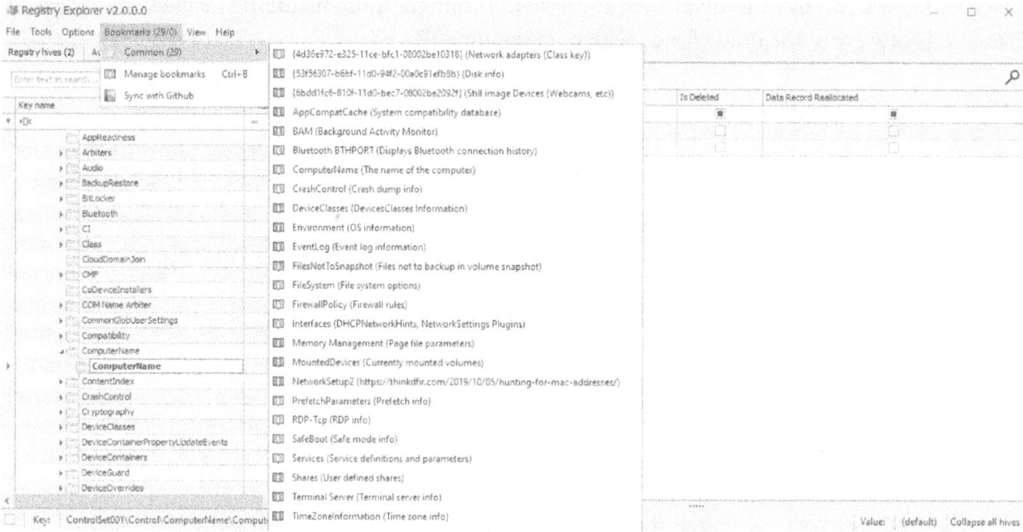

Figure 5.4 – The bookmark feature of Registry Explorer

Identifying the computer name using registry hives is important for forensic analysts because it provides them with vital information about the system being analyzed. The computer name is a **unique identifier (UID)** for the system, and it can help analysts correlate information gathered from various sources during the investigation.

For example, a forensic analyst may come across network traffic logs that contain the computer name of a system involved in a security incident. By cross-referencing this information with the computer name obtained from the registry hives, the analyst can confirm that the system is indeed the same one that was involved in the incident.

Moreover, the computer name can also provide additional context for the investigation. For instance, if a system has a naming convention that indicates its location or function, such as `NYC-Web-01`, this can help the analyst understand the role of the system in the network and its potential impact on the incident.

Identifying time zones

Identifying the time zone that applies to the Windows Registry can be important for forensic analysts because it can provide insight into the geographical location and, potentially, the jurisdiction of the system. The time-zone information is stored in the registry and can be used to determine the local time on the system at the time of an event. This information can be critical in investigations where the timing of events is important, such as in digital forensics investigations or IR. It can also be useful in determining whether the system was being used in the expected location or time zone.

To identify the time zone using Registry Explorer, you need to navigate to the following registry key:

`HKEY_LOCAL_MACHINE\SYSTEM\CurrentControlSet\Control\TimeZoneInformation`

In the following screenshot, we can see the `TimeZoneKeyName` value name presented:

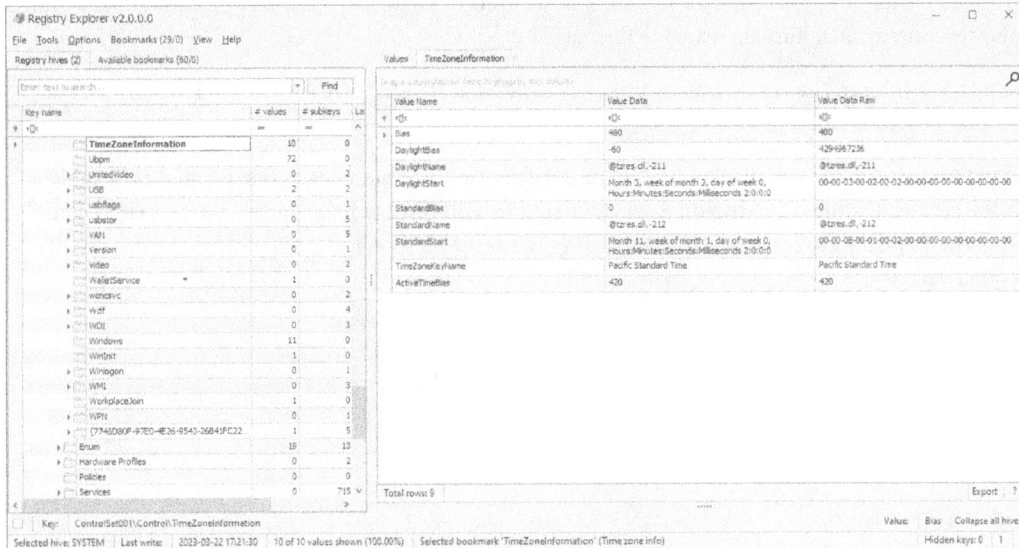

Figure 5.5 – Time-zone information

Once you've selected the `TimeZoneInformation` key, the **Values** grid will display a list of values associated with the key. Look for a value named `StandardName`. The data associated with this value will be the name of the time zone.

For example, if `StandardName`'s data is **Eastern Standard Time (EST)**, this indicates that the time zone is set to Eastern Standard Time.

You can also look for other values in the same key to get additional information about the time zone, such as its **Universal Time Coordinated (UTC)** offset and whether it observes daylight saving time.

Identifying services

The `Services` subkey in the Windows Registry hive contains configuration information about the services running on a system. Each service has a subkey containing settings such as the service's display name, description, start type, the path to the executable, and dependencies on other services.

Analyzing the `Services` subkey can be useful for forensic analysts in several ways. For example, it can help identify which services were running on a system at a given time, including third-party services that may have been installed by an attacker. It can also provide information on the startup type of each service, which can help identify services that were set to automatically start at boot time and may have been used in a persistence mechanism.

To analyze the `Services` subkey, one approach is to use a Windows Registry analysis tool such as Registry Explorer or RegRipper. These tools can be used to navigate to the `Services` subkey and display its contents in a human-readable format.

In Registry Explorer, the `Services` subkey is located at `HKEY_LOCAL_MACHINE\System\CurrentControlSet\Services`.

Clicking on this subkey will display a list of all services on the system, each represented by a subkey with the service's name. Clicking on a service's subkey will display its properties in the right-hand pane of the Registry Explorer window, including the service's start type, the path to the executable, and other settings:

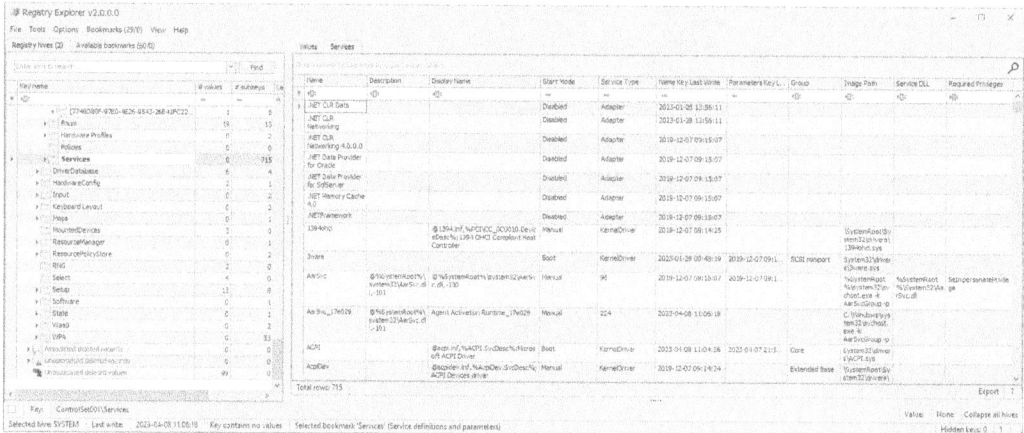

Figure 5.6 – The Services subkey

As we can see, using the `Services` subkey, we can identify the start mode and image path, including the command line.

Figure 5.7 – Services subkey details

One way to investigate is to drill down into the parameters and identify loaded **DLLs** (short for **dynamic link libraries**). In the following screenshot, we took the **AppInfo** service as an example to explore:

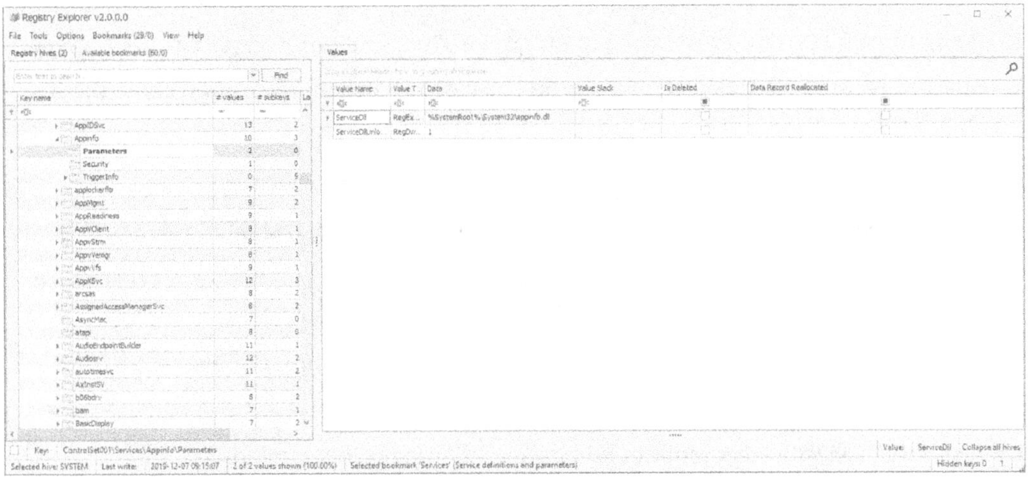

Figure 5.8 – AppInfo service parameters

Analyzing the `Services` subkey in the Windows Registry can provide valuable information for forensic analysts to better understand the system's configuration and identify potential **indicators of compromise (IoCs)**.

Installed applications

In Windows, the registry contains information about all the applications installed on a system. As a forensic analyst, this information can be valuable when investigating a system. In order to investigate installed applications on a Windows system, forensic analysts can use the Software registry. The Software Registry is a subkey located in the Windows Registry that contains information about installed software on a system. It is located at `HKEY_LOCAL_MACHINE\Software` and contains subkeys for each software vendor.

One approach to investigate installed applications using the Software Registry is to search for specific keywords related to software. For example, forensic analysts can search for the name of a particular software application or the name of the vendor. This can be done using the search functionality of the analysis tool being used.

Another approach is to look for specific registry keys that contain information about the installed software. For example, the `uninstall` subkey contains information about installed software, which can be used to track software usage, identify vulnerabilities, and check for any malicious software that may have been installed.

Forensic analysts can also analyze the Software Registry to identify software that has been recently installed or uninstalled. This can be done by checking the timestamps of the registry keys related to installed software. This can provide valuable information about the timeline of events on the system.

To analyze an installed application, do the following:

1. Navigate to the `SOFTWARE\Microsoft\Windows\CurrentVersion\Uninstall` subkey.

2. Analyze the subkeys and values within `uninstall`. Further information about these is listed here:

    - Each subkey within `uninstall` represents an installed application

    - The subkey name is usually the application's **global UID (GUID)** or a UID

    - The values within each subkey provide information about the application, such as the display name, version, publisher, installation date, and `uninstall` command

    - Some applications may have additional subkeys within `uninstall` that provide more detailed information

3. Compare them with other artifacts, keeping the following points in mind:

    - It's important to compare the installed application's information in the Software Registry with other artifacts, such as program files and event logs, to verify the installed applications and their activity

    - Some applications may not leave a clear footprint in the Software Registry, so it's important to consider other artifacts as well

The following screenshot shows an example of installed applications on a system:

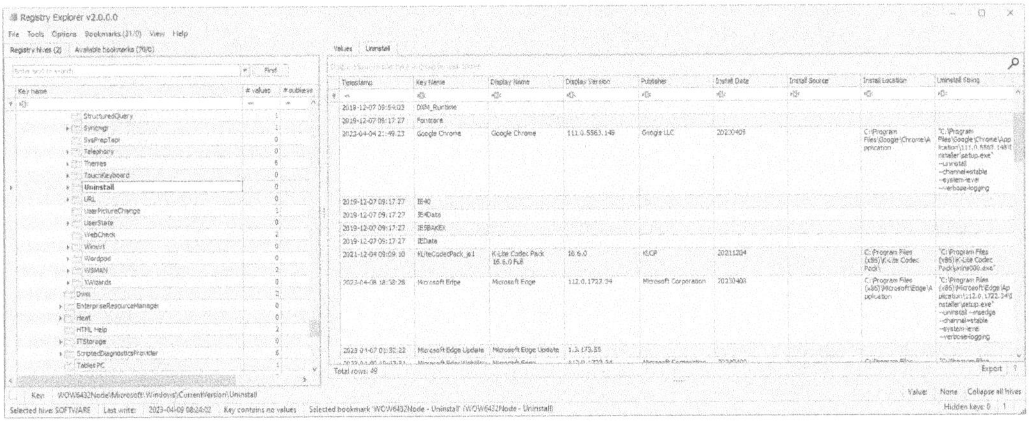

Figure 5.9 – Installed applications

The PrefetchParameters subkey

The PrefetchParameters registry subkey is a part of the Windows operating system that is used to store configuration settings for the Prefetch feature. The Prefetch feature in Windows is used to speed up the loading of frequently used applications by caching data and metadata about the application on the hard drive. The PrefetchParameters subkey is located in the HKEY_LOCAL_MACHINE\ SYSTEM\CurrentControlSet\Control\Session Manager\Memory Management\ PrefetchParameters registry path.

It contains a number of values that control how the Prefetch feature operates, including the following:

- EnablePrefetcher: Determines whether Prefetch is enabled. A value of 0 disables Prefetch, while a value of 1 enables it, and it has two other possible values:

  - 0 = Prefetch disabled

  - 1 = Prefetch enabled on application launch

  - 2 = Boot-enabled Prefetch setting

  - 3 = Prefetch enabled on boot and application launch

- EnableSuperfetch: Determines whether Superfetch is enabled. Superfetch is an enhancement of the Prefetch feature that preloads commonly used applications into memory. A value of 0 disables Superfetch, while a value of 1 enables it.

- TracesProcessed: This indicates the number of application traces that have been processed by the Prefetch feature.

You can see an overview of the Prefetch settings here:

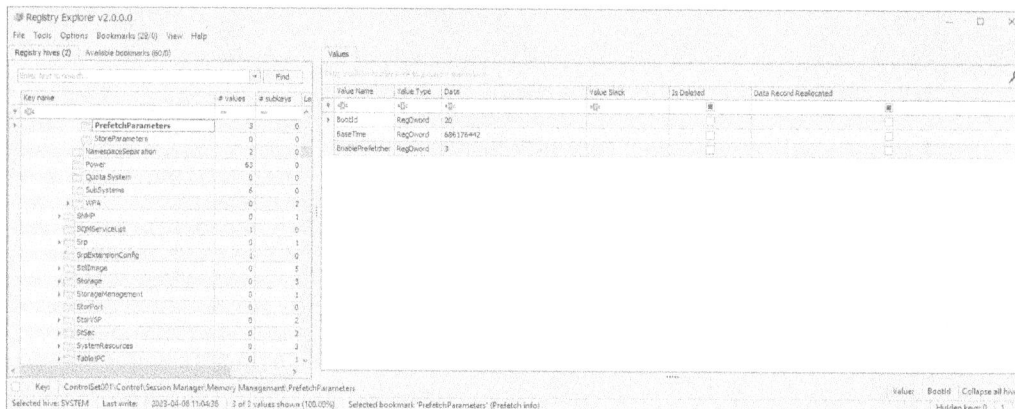

Figure 5.10 – Prefetch settings

We will explore the Prefetch artifact in an upcoming chapter when we discover how to analyze evidence of executed binaries.

Network activities

The Windows Registry contains information about **network interfaces** that are currently installed and configured on the system. This information is stored in several different subkeys within the registry.

The network interface configuration information is stored in the following registry subkeys:

- `HKEY_LOCAL_MACHINE\SYSTEM\CurrentControlSet\Services\Tcpip\Parameters\Interfaces`

- `HKEY_LOCAL_MACHINE\SYSTEM\CurrentControlSet\Services\NetBT\Parameters\Interfaces`

The first subkey contains **Transmission Control Protocol/Internet Protocol** (**TCP/IP**) configuration information for each network interface. Each network interface has a subkey under this key, which is named using a UID known as the interface's GUID. The interface GUID can be used to associate the configuration information with a particular network interface.

The second subkey contains **NetBIOS over TCP/IP** (**NetBT**) configuration information for each network interface. Each interface has a subkey under this key, which is also named using the interface's GUID:

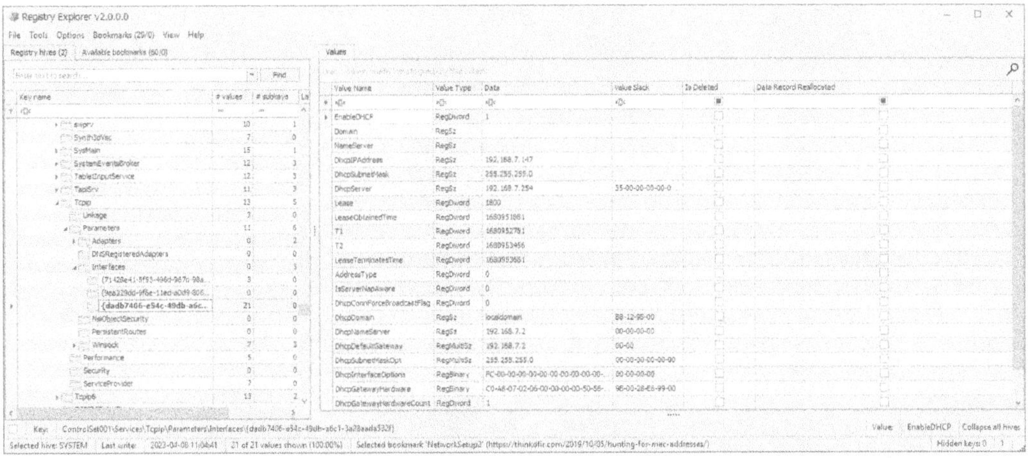

Figure 5.11 – Network interface information

Another option is to investigate historical connections by using the `Software\Microsoft\Windows NT\CurrentVersion\NetworkList\Signatures\Managed` and `Software\Microsoft\Windows NT\CurrentVersion\NetworkList\Signatures\Unmanaged` registry keys, which contain information about network connections that have been made from a Windows computer.

The `Managed` subkey contains information about network connections that are made from managed networks such as domains, which are networks that have been identified by Windows as being trusted, such as corporate networks. The `Unmanaged` subkey contains information about network connections that are made from unmanaged networks, which could be wireless connections and so on, which are networks that have not been identified by Windows as being trusted.

Within each of these subkeys, there are subkeys for each network interface that has been used to make a network connection. The name of each subkey is a UID for the network interface. Each network interface subkey contains values that describe the properties of the network interface, such as the adapter name, the IP address, the subnet mask, the gateway address, and the DNS server address.

Under each network interface subkey, there are subkeys that contain information about network connections that have been made using that network interface. The names of these subkeys are GUIDs that are generated by Windows for each connection. Each connection subkey contains values that describe the properties of the connection, such as the name of the network to which the computer is connected, the type of network, the security mode of the network, the authentication method that was used to connect to the network, and the date and time of the last connection:

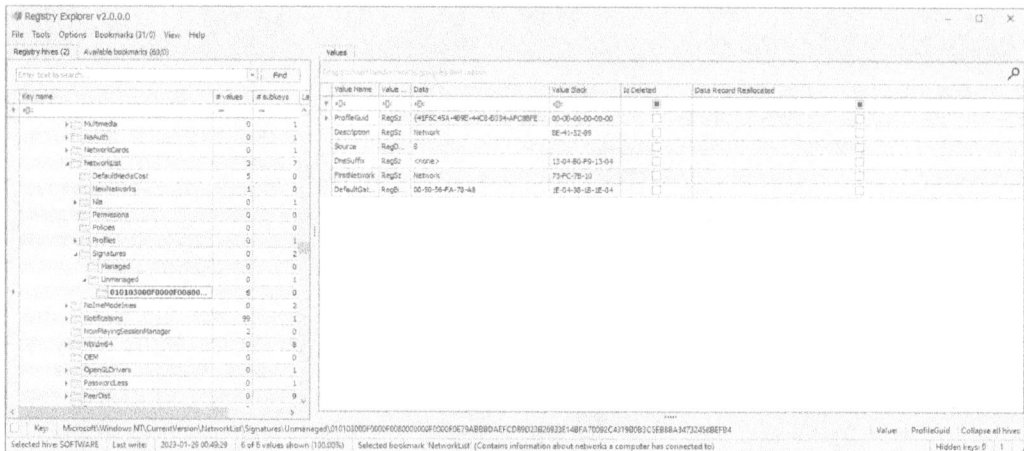

Figure 5.12 – The Unmanaged subkey

Autostart registry keys

The boot autostart location in the Windows Registry refers to entries that control programs and processes that run automatically during the boot process. Analyzing these entries is an essential part of forensic investigations, as malware will often add entries here to ensure that it is launched during system startup. Mostly, this is used as a persistence mechanism by malicious actors. The locations of boot autostart entries in the Windows Registry are as follows:

- `HKEY_LOCAL_MACHINE\SOFTWARE\Microsoft\Windows\CurrentVersion\Run`

- `HKEY_LOCAL_MACHINE\SOFTWARE\Microsoft\Windows\CurrentVersion\RunOnce`

- `HKEY_CURRENT_USER\SOFTWARE\Microsoft\Windows\CurrentVersion\Run`

- `HKEY_CURRENT_USER\SOFTWARE\Microsoft\Windows\CurrentVersion\RunOnce`

- `HKEY_CURRENT_USER\Software\Microsoft\Windows\CurrentVersion\Explorer\User Shell Folders`

- `HKEY_CURRENT_USER\Software\Microsoft\Windows\CurrentVersion\Explorer\Shell Folders`

Some specific examples of suspicious entries that forensic analysts should look out for include entries that include `RunOnce` or `Run`, which indicate that the program will only run once, possibly as part of an installation process. Another example is entries that use command-line parameters, as these may be used to hide the true purpose of the program.

The following screenshot shows an example of the Run subkey:

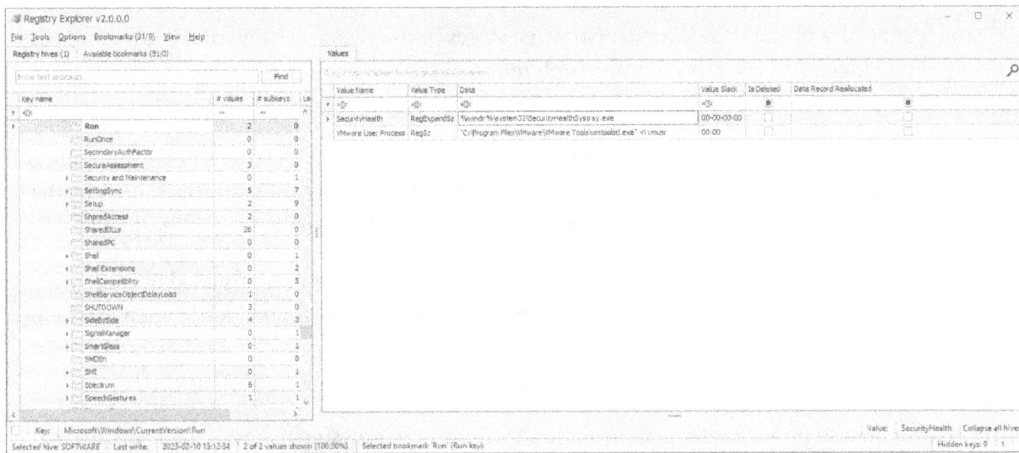

Figure 5.13 – The Run subkey

Please note since we are showing a demo on a virtual machine we created, this registry key usually holds more information in a real-world scenario. It is also important to note that not all entries in the boot autostart location are malicious, and some may be legitimate system processes or user-installed programs. Therefore, it is crucial to use multiple sources of information and employ a thorough analysis process when investigating these entries, as we can see in *Figure 5.14*; in the Everything tab, OneDrive has been added to the run registry keys:

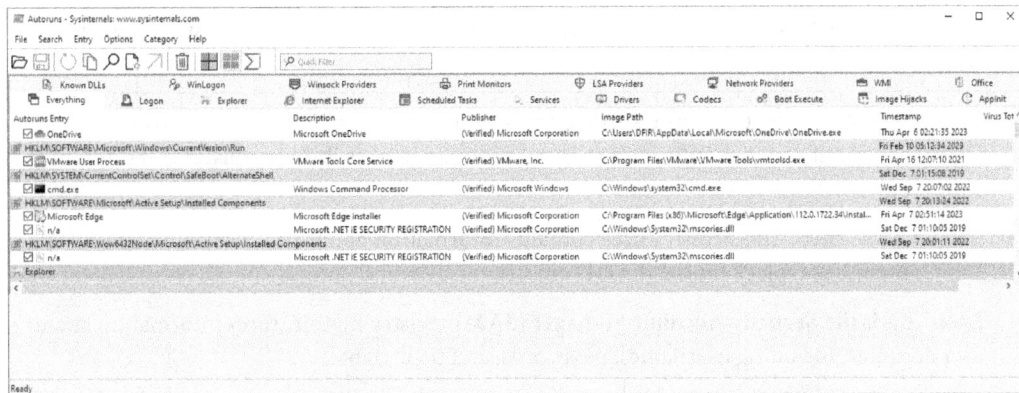

Figure 5.14 – The Autoruns tool: Sysinternals

Now, since we've learned about registry keys, let's profile user activity using what we've learned.

Profiling user activities

HKCU is a registry hive in the Windows Registry that stores user-specific settings and configurations for the currently logged-in user. It contains preferences, user environment variables, application settings, and other data related to the user's activities on the system.

During user profiling, analyzing the HKCU hive can provide insight into the user's behavior, habits, and preferences. By examining the hive, forensic analysts can determine the applications used by the user, the files accessed, the network connections established, and the system settings modified.

The HKCU hive contains subkeys for various software applications that have been installed or configured for the user. The subkeys store settings and preferences specific to each application, which can help forensic analysts determine the activities of the user. For example, the RecentDocs subkey stores a list of recently accessed files, while the Run subkey stores a list of applications that are launched at startup.

The HKCU hive can also provide information about the user's web browsing history, email activity, and instant messaging conversations. The Internet Settings subkey contains information about the user's web browsing habits, such as visited websites, cookies, and history. The Mail subkey contains information about the user's email accounts, including login credentials, email server settings, and message rules.

Also, profiling user activity using the Windows Registry involves analyzing the data present in the registry to gain insights into user behavior and activity. The Windows Registry is a central database where Windows stores all its configuration data and settings. It contains valuable information about user activity, such as user login and logoff times, applications used, websites visited, and files accessed or modified.

To profile user activities using the Windows Registry, a forensic analyst typically starts by analyzing the following keys:

- NTUSER.DAT: This is the user-specific registry hive file and stores all the settings for the logged-in user. It contains information about user preferences, browser history, and recently used files.

- UsrClass.dat: This registry hive contains information about the user's file associations and **Component Object Model (COM)** objects.

- SAM: This is the **Security Account Manager (SAM)** registry hive; it stores information about user accounts, including usernames, passwords, and their rights.

- Amcache.hve: This is a new registry hive introduced in Windows 10; it contains information about applications used by the user, including the time and date of their last use.

By analyzing the data present in these keys, a forensic analyst can identify user activity patterns, such as frequent application usage, suspicious login/logout times, and deleted or modified files. This information can be crucial in digital forensics investigations, where identifying user activity can help in reconstructing the sequence of events leading up to a security incident.

It is important to note that the process of profiling user activity using the Windows Registry requires a thorough understanding of the registry structure and its data. Therefore, it is recommended that forensic analysts have proper training and experience before attempting to analyze Windows Registry data. Additionally, it is essential to follow best practices and use forensic tools that do not alter the original data to avoid compromising the integrity of the investigation, so let's start the journey.

SAM registry hive

The SAM registry hive is one of the most important components of a Windows operating system from a forensic perspective. The SAM database stores all user account information, including usernames and hashed passwords. In order to investigate the SAM registry hive, you will need to access it using a tool that can read the registry hive.

Using Registry Explorer, do the following:

1. Open Registry Explorer and select **File** | **Load Hive** from the menu.
2. Navigate to the location of the SAM registry hive , which is typically located at `C:\Windows\ System32\config\SAM`.
3. Enter a name for the loaded hive, such as `SAM Hive`, and click **OK**.
4. The SAM hive will now be loaded under the name you specified, and you can explore its keys and values.
5. The `SAM\SAM\Domains\Account\Users` key contains information about the user accounts on the system. You can view the account names and other details by expanding this key.
6. To view the password hashes for the user accounts, navigate to the `SAM\SAM\Domains\ Account\Users[User SID]\V` key. V contains the encrypted password hash, which can be extracted and cracked using a password-cracking tool.

You can see an overview of the SAM hive here:

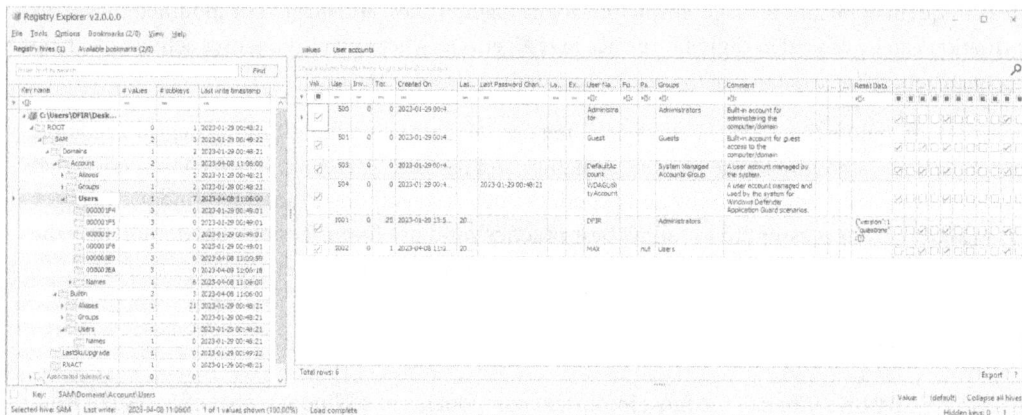

Figure 5.15 – The SAM registry hive

A **security ID (SID)** consists of a prefix and a UID, known as the **relative ID (RID)**. The prefix of a SID identifies the issuing authority that created the SID, such as a Windows domain controller or a local machine. The RID is assigned sequentially by the issuing authority for each new account that is created.

We will get the following forensic value from SAM:

- **User account information**: The SAM registry hive stores information about user accounts on the system, including the account name, SID, and password hashes. This information can be useful for identifying user activity on the system.

- **Last login information**: The SAM registry hive also stores information about the last time a user logged in to the system. This information can be useful for determining whether a user was active on the system at a particular time.

- **Account lockout information**: The SAM registry hive stores information about user account lockouts, including the number of failed login attempts and the time of the last lockout. This information can be useful for identifying attempts to gain unauthorized access to the system.

- **SID mapping**: The SAM registry hive includes information that maps SIDs to user accounts. This can be useful for identifying the owner of a file or other object on the system.

- **Password policy information**: The SAM registry hive includes information about the system's password policy, such as the minimum password length and the number of password attempts allowed before the user is locked out. This information can be useful for understanding the system's security configuration.

In the following screenshot, we can see information related to a user account, with details for creation and access:

Figure 5.16 – The SAM registry hive (2)

Domain and local user details

The `ProfileList` registry data is a subkey in the Windows Registry that contains information about user profiles on the system. Each user account on a Windows computer has a user profile that stores user-specific settings and data, such as desktop settings, program settings, documents, and user preferences.

The `ProfileList` subkey contains information about each user profile that has been created on the system, including the user's SID, profile path, and profile type. It is located in the HKLM registry hive under the `SOFTWARE\Microsoft\Windows NT\CurrentVersion\ProfileList` key, as shown here:

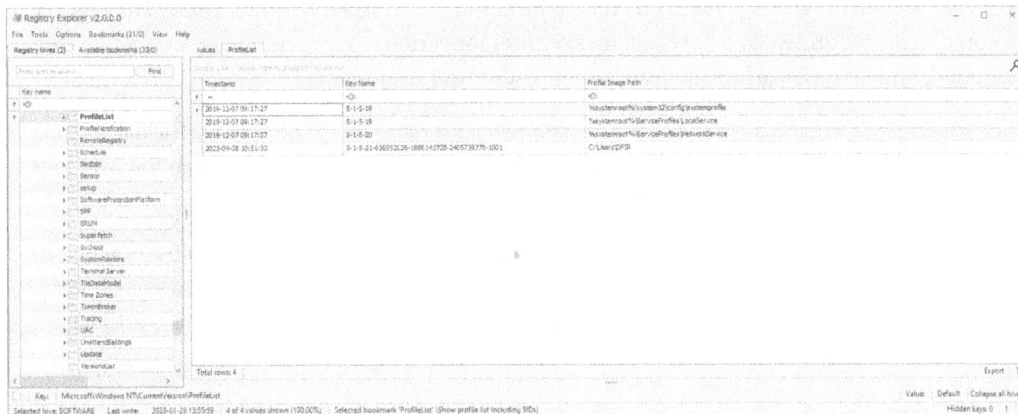

Figure 5.17 – The ProfileList subkey

As we can see in *Figure 5.18*, by exploring the `ProfileList` folder, we can list details regarding the image path and the SID:

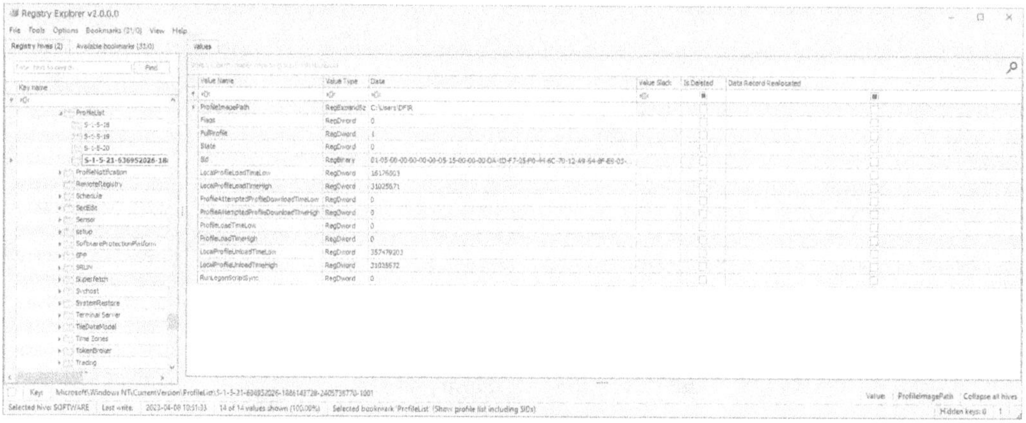

Figure 5.18 – The ProfileList subkey (2)

Forensic analysts can use `ProfileList` data to identify which user accounts exist on the system, determine when each user last logged in, and locate the profile folders associated with each user. This information can be useful for conducting user activity analysis and identifying potential evidence related to user actions on the system.

NTUSER.DAT

In Windows operating systems, the `NTUSER.DAT` hive is a file that contains user-specific registry data. It is located in the user's profile directory, typically at `C:\Users%username%`. The registry data stored in the `NTUSER.DAT` hive includes settings for various user preferences, such as desktop background, screensaver, startup applications, browser history, and more.

The `NTUSER.DAT` hive is loaded into the registry when a user logs on to the system. The data is then used to configure the user's environment and applications. The hive is unloaded when the user logs off, and any changes made to the hive during the session are saved to disk.

For forensic analysts, the `NTUSER.DAT` hive can provide valuable information about a user's activities on a system. The hive can be analyzed to determine the user's application usage, web browsing history, recent documents, and other user-specific settings. Additionally, the hive can contain artifacts of malicious activity, such as malware or unauthorized access.

The RecentDocs key

`RecentDocs` is a Windows feature that stores a list of recently accessed documents, files, and applications. This feature can be useful for users who want to quickly access frequently used files, but it can also be useful for forensic investigators who are looking for evidence of recent user activity. The `RecentDocs` feature is implemented in the Windows Registry, specifically in the `HKEY_CURRENT_USER\Software\Microsoft\Windows\CurrentVersion\Explorer\RecentDocs` key.

To investigate `RecentDocs` using the Windows Registry, an investigator can use a registry editor tool such as Registry Explorer or Registry Viewer to navigate to the `RecentDocs` registry key. Within this key, there are subkeys for different file types, such as `.doc`, `.txt`, `.pdf`, and so on. Each of these subkeys contains a list of the most recently accessed files of that type, as well as metadata about each file, such as the date and time it was last accessed.

You can see an overview of the `RecentDocs` key here:

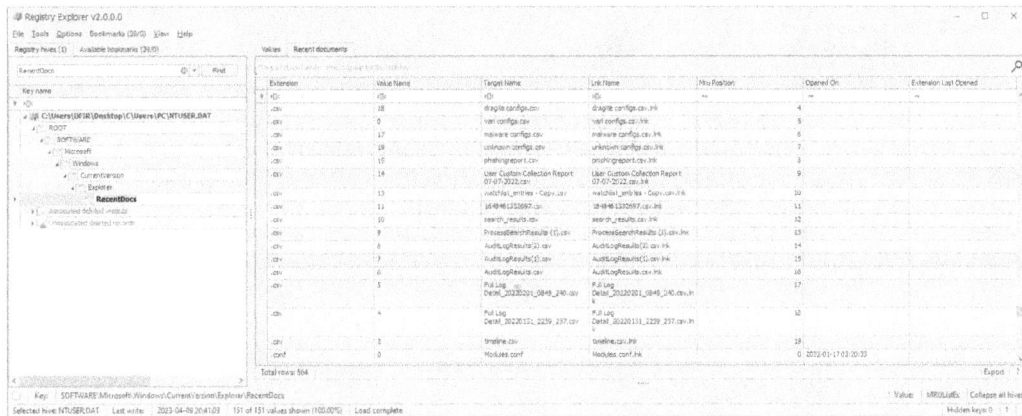

Figure 5.19 – The RecentDocs key

Or, we can explore by extension of the files shown; clicking on **RecentDocs** will show subkeys by extension. In the following screenshot, we are filtering for XLS sheets:

Figure 5.20 – RecentDocs showing XLS sheets accessed

The TypedPaths key

The `TypedPaths` registry key in Windows contains information about the paths of recently used files and folders accessed through File Explorer or the Run command. This information can be useful for forensic analysis as it can reveal the user's activities, interests, and potentially sensitive information:

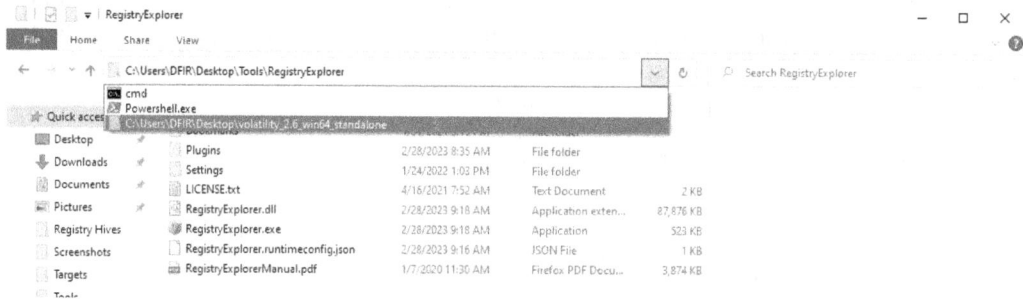

Figure 5.21 – The TypedPaths key in Windows Explorer

The `TypedPaths` key is located at the following registry path:

`HKCU\Software\Microsoft\Windows\CurrentVersion\Explorer\TypedPaths`

Under the `TypedPaths` key, there are several subkeys that contain recently used paths in a binary format. The subkeys are named with a letter. The binary data of each subkey contains the path of the recently used file or folder, as seen here:

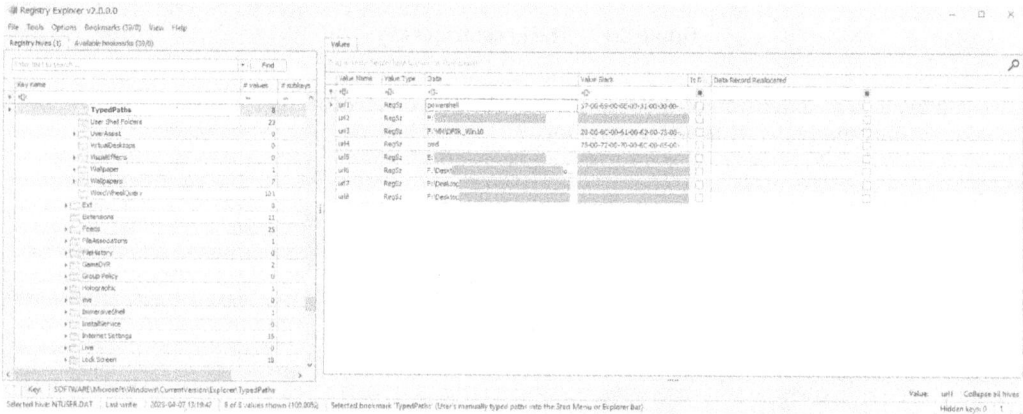

Figure 5.22 – TypedPaths shown in Registry Explorer

When analyzing `TypedPaths` data, the investigator can look for patterns of file and folder access that may be relevant to the case. For example, a user accessing sensitive company files or personal information may reveal a motive for the incident being investigated. Additionally, the analysis of `TypedPaths` data can be helpful in establishing a timeline of user activity and can assist in identifying potential sources of evidence for further examination.

The TypedURLs subkey

When a user enters a URL in their web browser, it is saved in the `TypedURLs` subkey of the Windows Registry. This subkey can be a valuable source of information during a digital forensic investigation as it can reveal the user's browsing history.

To investigate `TypedURLs` using Windows Registry keys, follow these steps:

1. Open Registry Explorer and navigate to `HKEY_CURRENT_USER\SOFTWARE\Microsoft\Internet Explorer\TypedURLs`.

2. In the right-hand pane, you will see a list of the most recently typed URLs. The `url1` value represents the most recent URL, `url2` represents the second-most recent, and so on.

3. You can double-click on any of these values to view the URL data in the **Edit String** dialog box. This will show you the actual URL that was typed.

4. You can also use the search function in Registry Explorer to find specific URLs or keywords. Click on the **Search** tab at the top of the window, enter your search term, and select **Keys and values** under **Search in**. Then, click **Start search** to begin the search.

5. Registry Explorer also allows you to export the `TypedURLs` subkey to a file for further analysis. Right-click on the `TypedURLs` subkey and select **Export** to save the key to a `.reg` file. You can then import this file into another instance of Registry Explorer or another registry editor for analysis.

You can see an overview of the `TypedURLs` subkey here:

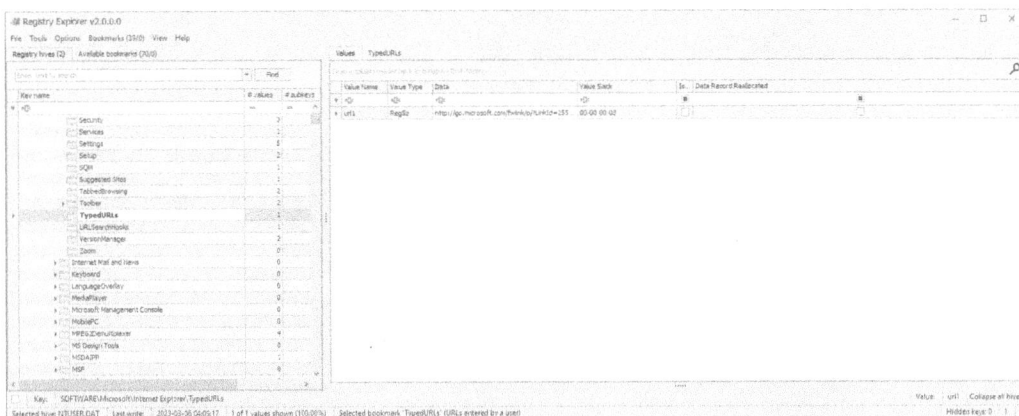

Figure 5.23 – The TypedURLs subkey

The Windows OS is a rich environment when it comes to artifacts. Once the core concepts are understood, a forensic analyst can follow their own path to research and explore more using multiple sources, including Microsoft's documentation.

User profiling using Windows Registry exercises

In this part, we will apply what we have learned so far. Try to work on the following exercises:

1. Perform an investigation on an MRU Office document for your own system.

2. Analyze the `RecentDocs` key for your own system.

3. Identify the command line executed using registry hives.

Summary

In this chapter, we explained the importance of profiling system details using the Windows Registry, such as identifying the Windows OS version, current control set, computer name, and time zone. We also covered investigating installed applications, network interfaces, historical network connections, user activities, shutdown information, and more.

We explored how to analyze Windows Registry data using tools such as Registry Explorer and how to extract information from specific registry keys, including `RecentDocs`, `TypedPaths`, and `TypedURLs`. By analyzing the Windows Registry, forensic analysts can determine system and user activity, identify potential security breaches, and create a timeline of events that can be used as evidence in legal proceedings.

In the next chapter, we will cover application execution artifacts, which is an important concept to understand for forensic analysts.

Part 2: Windows OS Additional Artifacts

In this part of the book, we will continue to deep dive into additional useful artifacts during a forensic examination. In this part, we will learn how to identify evidence of execution and move on to tracking USB usage. Also, we will explore the power of browser artifacts and how they can aid in drawing conclusions from an incident. In the last chapter, we will focus more on unique artifacts stored within the Windows OS.

This part contains the following chapters:

- *Chapter 6, Application Execution Artifacts*
- *Chapter 7, Forensic Analysis of USB Artifacts*
- *Chapter 8, Forensic Analysis of Browser Artifacts*
- *Chapter 9, Exploring Additional Artifacts*

Application Execution Artifacts

As technology continues to evolve and expand, the digital world is becoming increasingly complex and interconnected. Nowadays, a great deal of business and personal interaction happens online. Cloud computing and remote work have given rise to a new way of doing business, and many companies now rely on software applications to keep their operations running. Unfortunately, these applications can leave behind artifacts of interest to hackers, cybercriminals, and other malicious actors. To ensure the safety of their data and information, companies should invest in robust security protocols and be vigilant about monitoring their networks for suspicious activity. Additionally, they should make sure their software is updated regularly and that any artifacts that are left behind are properly secured and encrypted. By taking these measures, businesses can better protect their data and ensure the safety of their digital networks.

Application execution artifacts are traces of data left behind by software applications during their operation on a Windows operating system. These artifacts can provide valuable information to forensic investigators about how an application was used, who used it, and when it was used. Application execution artifacts are important because they can help forensic examiners reconstruct events that occurred on a system, including those that may have been intentionally or unintentionally deleted.

In this chapter, we will cover the following main concepts:

- Windows evidence of execution artifacts
- NTUSER.DAT, Amcache, and SYSTEM hives
- Windows Prefetch
- Application execution artifact exercises

Technical requirements

Windows registry analysis requires certain technical requirements to ensure that the process is executed efficiently and effectively. The following are the technical requirements that we have for this chapter:

- **Registry Explorer**: `https://ericzimmerman.github.io/#!index.md`
- **AppCompactCacheParser.exe**: `https://ericzimmerman.github.io/#!index.md`
- **PECmd.exe**: `https://github.com/EricZimmerman/PECmd`
- **WinPrefetchView**: `https://www.nirsoft.net/utils/win_prefetch_view.html`

Windows evidence of execution artifacts

Evidence of execution refers to the digital artifacts left behind on a system as a result of a program being run. This evidence can include Prefetch files, Shimcache entries, event logs, and link files, among others.

The identification of evidence of execution is important to forensic analysts because it can provide valuable insight into the activities that took place on a system. By analyzing this evidence, investigators can determine which programs were run, when they were run, and how often they were run. This information can be used to reconstruct a timeline of events and identify any malicious activity that may have occurred on the system.

Furthermore, evidence of execution can help forensic analysts identify malware and other types of malicious software that may have been used to compromise a system. Malware often leaves behind distinct patterns of execution, which can be identified by analyzing evidence of program execution. This information can be used to develop signatures and other detection mechanisms to help prevent future attacks.

Understanding evidence of execution artifacts in Windows forensics is crucial because it helps forensic analysts determine which programs were run on the system, when they were run, and how they were executed. This information is vital in identifying any malicious activity on the system, tracing the source of an attack, and determining the extent of the compromise.

Evidence of execution artifacts can be used to establish a timeline of events, which is essential in forensic investigations. By analyzing the timestamps of files, registry entries, and other system components modified during program execution, forensic analysts can reconstruct a sequence of events, identify any unusual or suspicious activities, and determine the impact of the attack.

Additionally, understanding evidence of execution artifacts allows forensic analysts to identify and isolate malware or other malicious code. Malware often leaves behind a unique set of artifacts, including modified registry entries, created files, and network connections. By analyzing these artifacts, forensic analysts can identify the type of malware, its capabilities, and its potential impact on the system.

Furthermore, evidence of execution artifacts can be used to identify potential sources of compromise. For example, if an unauthorized program was executed on the system, forensic analysts can trace its origin and determine how it was introduced into the system. This information can be used to prevent future attacks and improve the overall security posture of the organization.

Finally, evidence of execution artifacts can be used to provide valuable insights into the activities that occurred on the system. By analyzing which programs were run, how often they were run, and by whom, forensic analysts can identify patterns of behavior, potential security vulnerabilities, and areas for improvement.

There are many different types of artifacts, some of which we mentioned previously, that forensic examiners may analyze when conducting evidence of execution analysis, including the following:

- **Prefetch files** – Prefetch files are created by Windows to improve the startup time of frequently used applications. These files contain information about the programs that have been executed on the system, such as the last time they were run and how often they are run.

- **Shimcache** – Shimcache is a Windows mechanism that tracks the execution of programs on the system. It records information about when a program was last executed, as well as the location of the program on the system; it is stored in `HKLM\SYSTEM\CurrentControlSet\Control\SessionManager\AppCompatCache\AppCompatCache`.

- **Amcache** stores a record of applications that have been run on a Windows system; in other words, we can say all the software that was installed on the system can be seen in Amcache records. Details such as the file path for the executable, the date and time it was first run, the SHA-1 hash, and so on can be found in Amcache records and it is located in `C:\Windows\AppCompat\Programs\Amcache.hve`.

- **NTUSER.DAT and SYSTEM hives** – These registry hives contain valuable information about the programs that have been run on a Windows system, and can provide valuable insights into potential cyber-attacks.

- **Event logs** – Windows event logs record a variety of system events, including program execution. By analyzing event logs, forensic examiners can identify the programs that were run on a system and when they were run.

One scenario that highlights the importance of evidence of execution in Windows forensics is a ransomware attack on a corporate network. In this scenario, a ransomware infection has spread across the network, causing critical data to be encrypted and preventing users from accessing their files. The IT department of the organization suspects that the ransomware may have been introduced via a malicious email attachment, but they need to determine the scope of the attack and identify the source of the malware.

In this situation, evidence of execution artifacts can provide critical information to help forensic analysts identify the malware and determine how it was introduced into the system. By analyzing the prefetch files, Shimcache, and event logs, forensic analysts can identify the file path and timestamp of the malware, determine when it was executed, and which programs were run on the system leading up to the infection.

Forensic analysts can also use this evidence to identify any lateral movement of the malware across the network, helping them to isolate the affected systems and prevent the infection from spreading further. By analyzing the link files in the `Recent` directory, forensic analysts can determine which programs were executed on each system and when they were executed.

This evidence of execution can also be used to identify potential sources of compromise, such as a compromised user account or a vulnerability in the organization's security infrastructure. By analyzing the system components modified during program execution, forensic analysts can identify any unusual or suspicious activities that may have been missed by traditional security measures.

Ultimately, evidence of execution artifacts provides a critical piece of information in identifying and containing a ransomware attack. By using this evidence, forensic analysts can determine the extent of the compromise, identify the source of the infection, and provide recommendations for improving the organization's security posture. Without evidence of execution, the forensic investigation would be incomplete, leaving the organization vulnerable to future attacks.

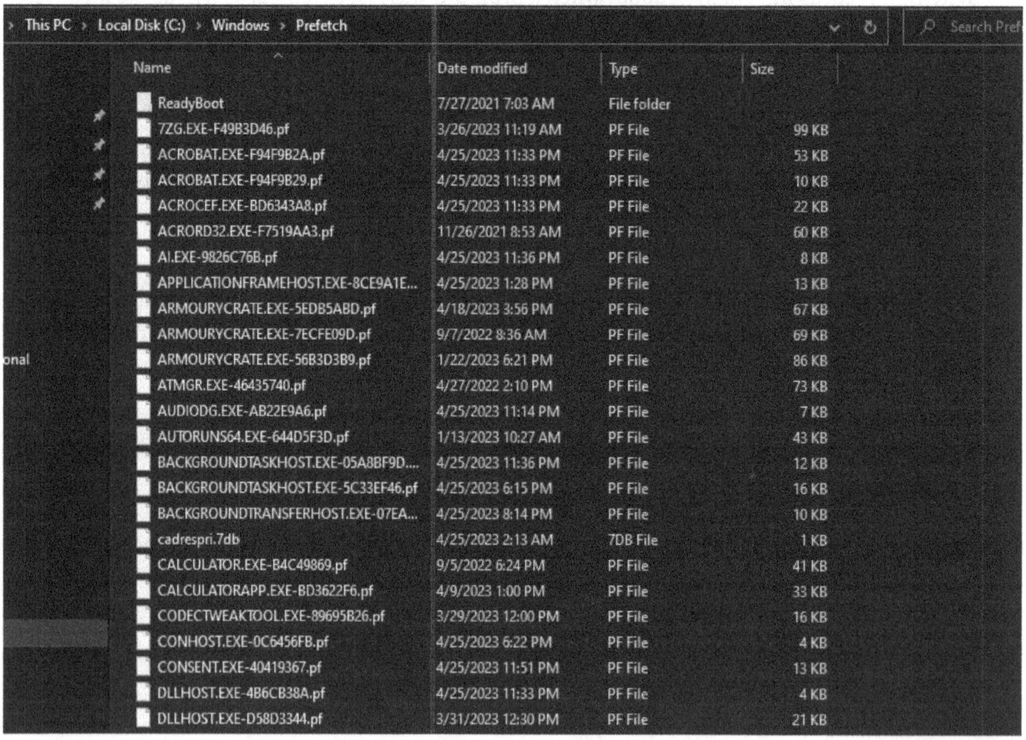

Figure 6.1 – Windows Prefetch

We have addressed a portion of the evidence of execution. Now, let's delve into the key components that make up the evidence of execution in more detail.

Looking at the NTUSER.DAT, Amcache, and SYSTEM hives

When investigating a Windows system for potential cyber-attacks, one of the most important pieces of information that a forensic examiner can gather is evidence of execution. As mentioned earlier, evidence of execution refers to artifacts left behind by programs that have been run on a system and can provide valuable insights into the activities that occurred on the system. Understanding how to analyze and interpret these artifacts is essential to conducting effective Windows forensics investigations.

Evidence of execution can take many different forms, including file metadata, registry entries, and log files.

The NTUSER.DAT file is another important artifact to consider when analyzing evidence of execution. The NTUSER.DAT file is a registry hive that contains configuration settings for the user account currently logged on to a Windows system. It contains information about the programs that have been run on the system, including recently opened files and applications, as well as the last time they were accessed. By analyzing the NTUSER.DAT file, forensic examiners can gain insights into the activities that occurred during the user's session.

The SYSTEM hive, on the other hand, is a registry hive that contains configuration settings for the Windows operating system. It includes information about the hardware and software installed on the system, as well as information about the services and drivers that are running. By analyzing the SYSTEM hive, forensic examiners can determine whether any unauthorized modifications have been made to the system and identify potential vulnerabilities that could be exploited by cyber-attackers.

When analyzing the NTUSER.DAT and SYSTEM hives, forensic examiners typically look for specific artifacts that can provide insights into potential cyber-attacks. For example, they may analyze the Run and RunOnce keys in the NTUSER.DAT file to identify programs that were run during a user's session. They may also analyze the LastWrite timestamps of registry keys in the SYSTEM hive to determine when modifications were made to the system.

We will start with the NTUSER.DAT registry and understand the relevant keys related to execution. From a forensic perspective, the NTUSER.DAT file can be a valuable source of evidence of execution. It contains information about the programs that have been executed by the user, as well as information about their usage patterns and preferences. This information can be used to identify potential cyber-attacks, track the activities of malicious actors, and provide evidence for legal proceedings.

Let's start with UserAssist.

Understanding and analyzing UserAssist

UserAssist is a Windows forensic artifact that contains information about the execution of programs on a Windows system. This artifact is located in the registry at NTUSER\Software\ Microsoft\Windows\CurrentVersion\Explorer\UserAssist. The UserAssist artifact is created by Windows to maintain a history of program execution, which is used to populate the jump lists in the **Start** menu and taskbar.

UserAssist contains a number of keys that are used to store execution information. The format of these keys includes a **globally unique identifier** (**GUID**) followed by a count. The GUID is used to identify the program that was executed, while the count indicates the number of times that the program has been executed. Each key contains a number of values that provide additional information about the program execution, including the time and date of execution, the number of times the program has been executed, and the focus time (that is, the amount of time for which the program was in the foreground).

Each subkey contains a number of values that provide information about program execution, including the following:

- Count: The number of times the program has been executed. This value is stored in an obfuscated format to prevent casual observers from easily reading the execution information.

- FocusTime: The amount of time the program was in the foreground (i.e., the active window) during each execution, measured in milliseconds.

- LastExecutionTime: The last time the program was executed, stored as a Windows FILETIME value.

One of the key values in the UserAssist artifact is the Count value, which indicates the number of times the program has been executed. This value is stored in an obfuscated format to prevent users from easily reading the execution information

Another important value in the UserAssist artifact is the Last Execution Time value, which indicates the last time the program was executed. This value is stored in a standard Windows FILETIME format, which represents the time as the number of 100-nanosecond intervals since January 1, 1601. Forensic examiners can use this value to determine when a program was last executed and potentially correlate it with other artifacts or events.

When examining this artifact's registry path, you will observe a {GUID} value. Within each UserAssist key, there are multiple subkeys, which are named using GUIDs. Each GUID denotes a different method through which the items can be executed. However, several of these GUIDs are rarely used on an average system, as most users do not execute software via unconventional methods. Although it is recommended to inspect each subkey for data, there are typically two GUIDs that hold the majority of information, which are CEBFF5CD (executable file execution) and F4E57C4B (shortcut file execution).

The `CEBFF5CD` subkey contains information about the execution of executable files on the system. Specifically, it maintains a list of system objects such as programs, applications, and other executable files that a user has accessed. This includes both built-in Windows programs (such as Notepad or Paint) and third-party applications (such as Microsoft Word or Adobe Acrobat).

The `F4E57C4B` subkey, on the other hand, maintains a list of shortcuts that the user has accessed. This includes shortcuts to files, folders, and applications that are stored on the system.

The `UserAssist` artifact can be a valuable source of evidence in Windows forensic investigations, particularly in cases where it is necessary to determine the programs that have been executed on a system. By analyzing the `UserAssist` artifact, forensic examiners can identify the programs that have been executed, the frequency of execution, and the last time the programs were executed. The data at hand has the potential to uncover potential threats, monitor malicious actors' activities, and serve as valuable evidence in legal proceedings.

We will start analyzing `UserAssist` by loading it into Registry Explorer:

1. Navigate to `NTUSER\ Software\Microsoft\Windows\CurrentVersion\ Explorer\UserAssist`:

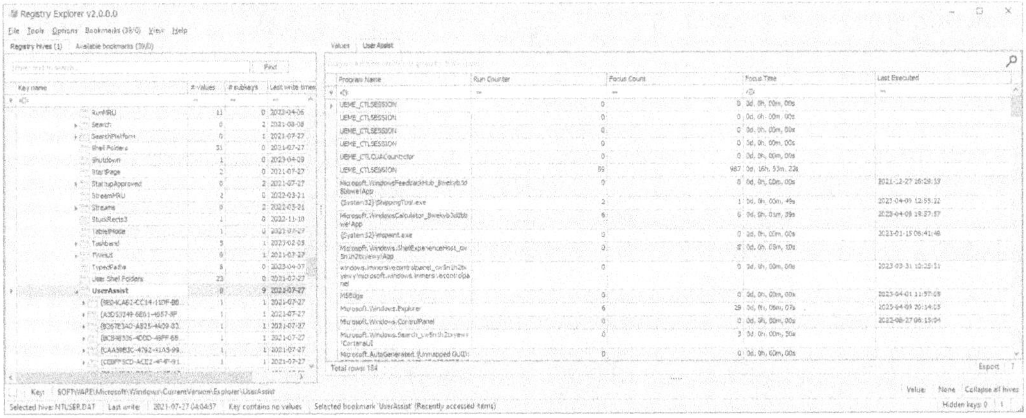

Figure 6.2 – UserAssist

2. **In the first step, locate the subkeys with GUIDs**: Under the `UserAssist` subkey, there will be several subkeys with long, alphanumeric GUIDs as their names. Each of these subkeys represents a different way the item within can be executed. What we notice here is that the **Values** tab holds data encoded in ROT-13. By clicking on the **UserAssist** tab, we can get the same details in human-readable format; you can also use decoding tools to decode the value as needed if that is required.

3. **Analyze the subkey values**: Click on one of the GUID subkeys to display the values associated with it in the right-hand pane of the Registry Explorer window. The values are stored in binary

format and are encrypted. However, many forensic tools, including Registry Explorer, can decode them to provide the relevant information.

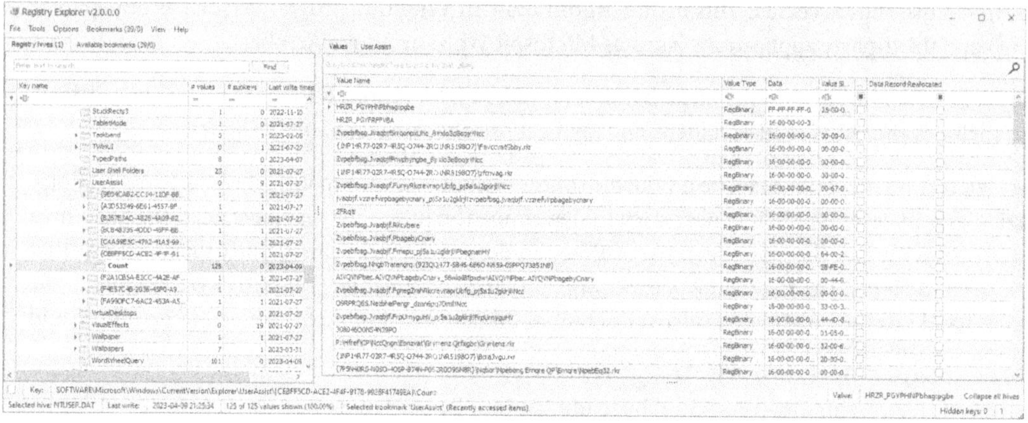

Figure 6.3 – The UserAssist subkey encoded in ROT-13

In the following figure, we can see multiple executables presented in the `UserAssist` registry key.

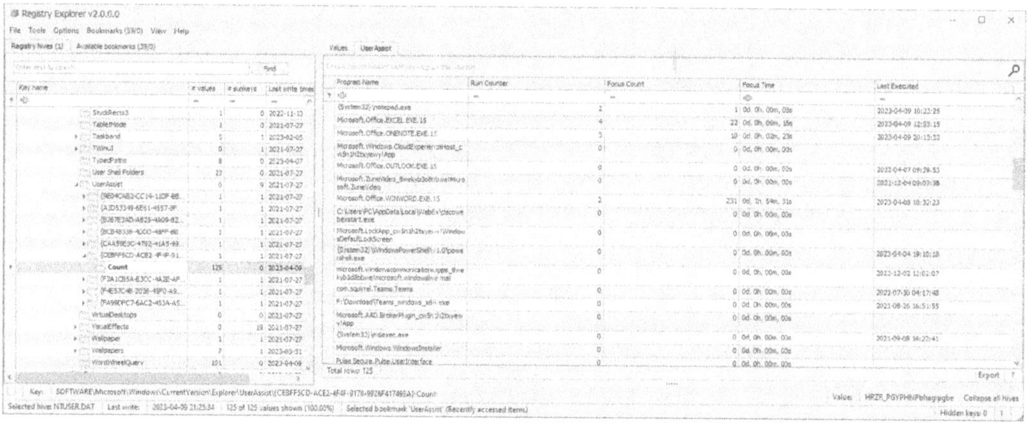

Figure 6.4 – The decoded values of the UserAssist subkey with a list of executable

`UserAssist` is extremely valuable in an investigation where an examiner wishes to see whether a particular application was run. As we move on, we will investigate more artifacts that are relevant to evidence of execution.

In the next section, we will cover Shimcache, Amcache, and multiple more artifacts, so let's dive into it.

Background Activity Moderator (BAM)

BAM is a service introduced in Windows 10 after the **Fall Creators Update** (version 1709) that controls and manages the activity of background applications. Its primary function is to conserve system resources and improve the overall system performance by monitoring the applications that run in the background. BAM maintains a list of all the applications that run in the background and records various details, such as the full path of the executable files that were run on the system, the last execution date and time of these files, and other relevant metadata.

For forensic investigators, BAM is a valuable source of evidence in determining the activity of background applications on a system. The data provided by BAM can be used to determine the behavior of a system, including the actions performed by various applications and the time of their execution. This information can be particularly useful in identifying potential malware and other malicious activities on the system.

We can look into the activities of BAM by navigating to the SYSTEM<CurrentControlSet>\ Services\bam\State\UserSettings{SID} registry key.

The **Security Identifier** (SID) refers to the unique identifier assigned to each user account on the system. Within this registry key, the BAM stores information related to the user's activities and the programs they have executed. This includes details such as the program name, the full path of the executable file, and the last time it was executed.

Each subkey within the UserSettings key is associated with a different user SID, allowing the forensic analyst to identify the activities of each individual user on the system. The subkeys contain a variety of values that provide information on the user's activities, such as the name of the program that was executed, the path to the executable file, and the last execution time.

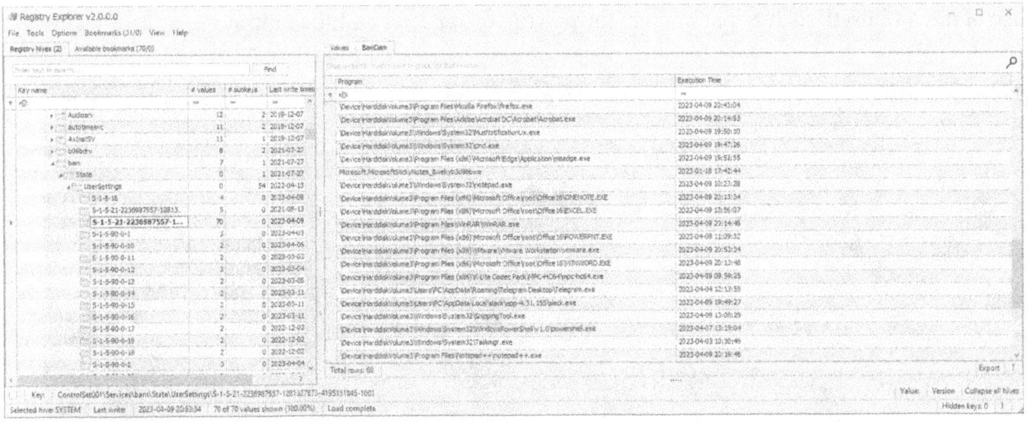

Figure 6.5 – BAM

Shimcache

`Shimcache` is an important Windows artifact that contains information about the execution of programs on a system. It is a Windows mechanism designed to improve application compatibility for programs that were developed for earlier versions of Windows. This is done by providing a compatibility layer for programs that rely on specific functions or behaviors that may have changed in newer versions of Windows.

`Shimcache` records information about the programs that were executed on a system, including the filename, file path, last modified date, and time of execution. This information is stored in a registry key called `AppCompatCache`, located at `System\CurrentControlSet\Control\Session Manager\AppCompatCache`.

`Shimcache` is a mechanism in Windows that logs the file path, the name of the executable file, and the date and time it was last modified. This information is valuable in determining whether or not an executable file has been executed on a system. In addition to storing data about executables on local drives, `Shimcache` also maintains records of executables on removable media and **Universal Naming Convention** (UNC) paths. Analyzing `Shimcache` can provide crucial insights to a forensic analyst investigating a system.

To analyze Shimcache, we will use a tool called **AppCompatCacheParser**, which is developed by *Eric Zimmerman*. You can download it from the link provided in the *Technical requirements* section of this chapter and run it using the command line like so:

```
C:\Users\DFIR\Desktop\Tools>AppCompatCacheParser.exe -f C:\Users\
DFIR\Desktop\C\Windows\System32\config\SYSTEM --csv C:\temp --csvf
Shimcache.csv
```

As we can see in the following figure, before running the tool for analysis, we need to understand the usage of the tool itself, such as parameters for passing the artifact and the output.

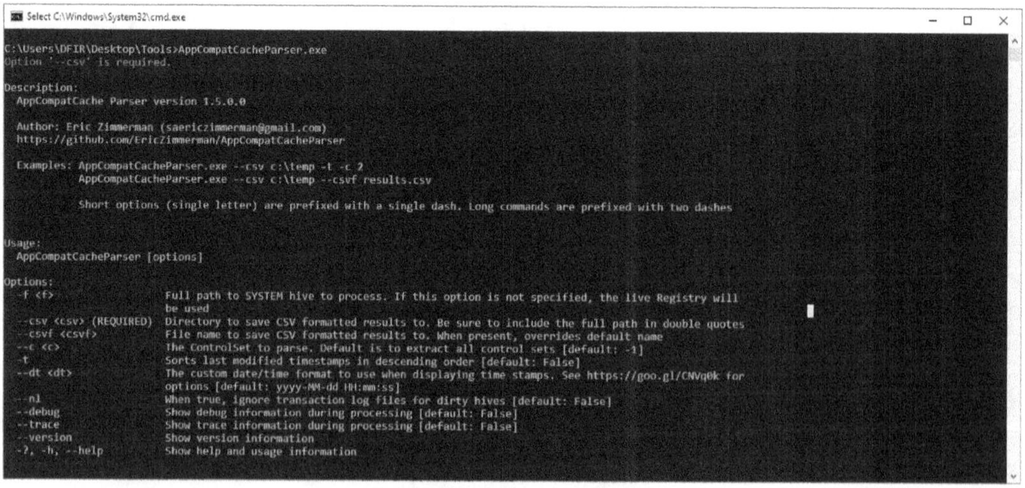

Figure 6.6 – AppCompactCacheParser.exe help

The cache stores various file metadata depending on the operating system, such as the following:

- The full path of the file

- The file size

- **$Standard_Information** (**SI**) last modified time

- Shimcache's last updated time

- The process execution flag

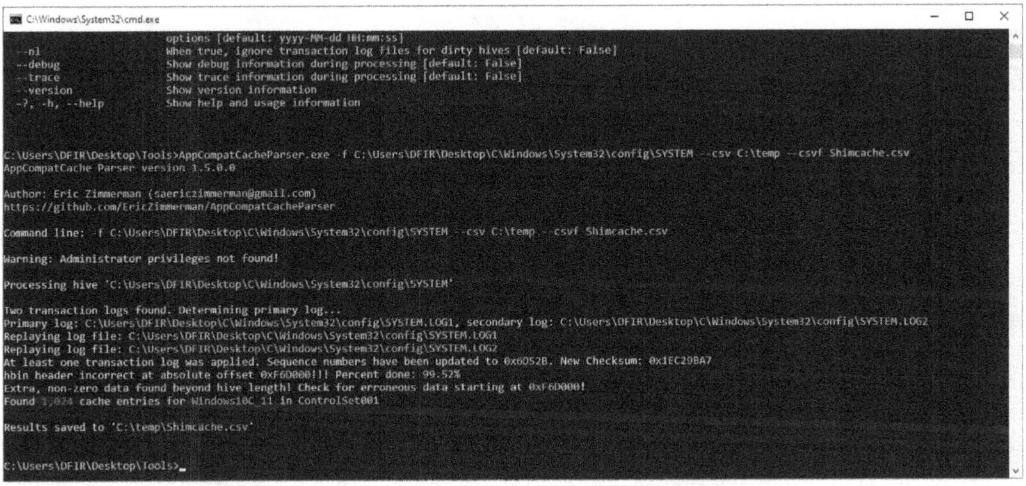

Figure 6.7 – AppCompactCacheParser 2

By using `TimeLineExplorer` in our example, we can navigate and investigate the result of the parsed `Shimcache`. We can use also a Microsoft Excel sheet to open the output.

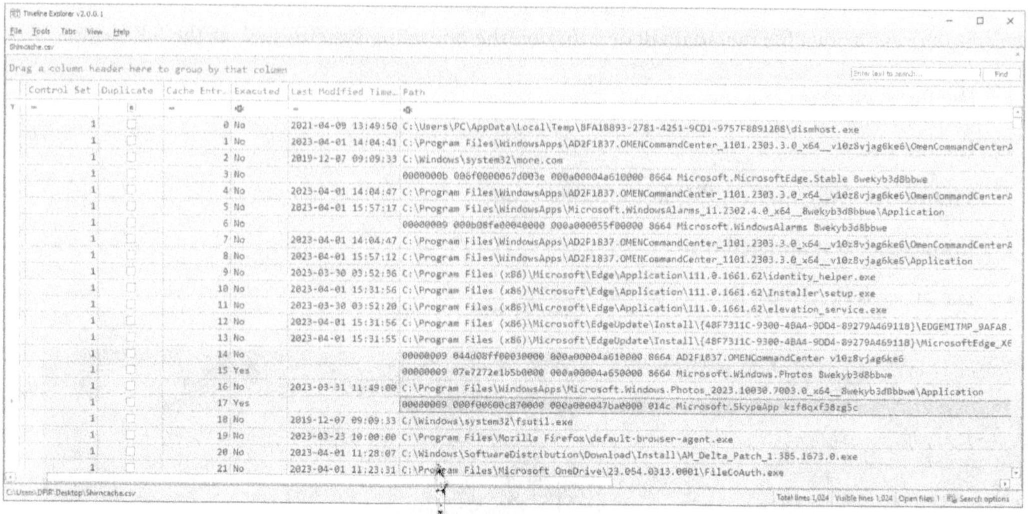

Figure 6.8 – AppCompactCacheParser output

Amcache.hve

Amcache.hve is a forensic artifact found on Windows operating systems. It is a database file that contains information about recently executed applications on the system. The Amcache.hve file was first introduced in Windows 7 and is available on Windows 7 and later versions of Windows. This file is created by the **Application Experience service (AeLookupSvc)**, which is responsible for collecting information about application compatibility and updating the compatibility database.

The Amcache.hve file is located in the %SystemRoot%\AppCompat\Programs\ Amcache. hve folder and it can only be accessed by users with administrative privileges. It is a binary file and can be parsed by various forensic tools such as FTK Imager. The Amcache.hve file contains information about the execution of applications and associated metadata.

The metadata stored in the Amcache.hve file includes the following:

- The filename and path of the application
- The file size and modification time
- A timestamp of the first and last execution of the application
- The SHA-1 hash of the application file
- The volume serial number and creation time of the volume where the application is located
- Application execution flags

By using Registry Explorer, we can open Amcache.hve and start the investigation process.

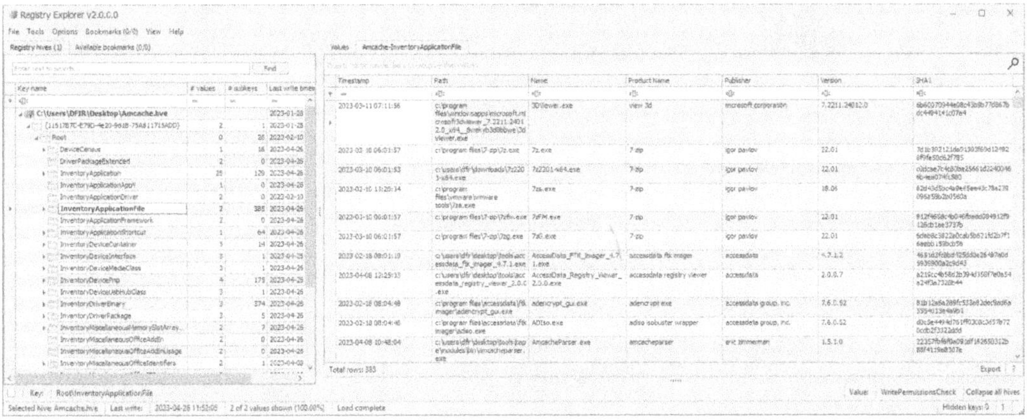

Figure 6.9 – Amcache Registry Hive

RunMRU

The `NTUSER\Software\Microsoft\Windows\CurrentVersion\Explorer\RunMRU` key is an artifact in the Windows registry that contains information related to the recently executed programs on a system. When a user runs a program, Windows logs this information in the `RunMRU` key as part of its functionality to maintain a list of recently executed programs.

The `RunMRU` key contains a subkey for each user who has logged into the system. Within each user's subkey, values correspond to the recently executed programs. Each value contains information about the program, such as its name, location, and the number of times it has been executed. As a forensic analyst, examining the `RunMRU` key can provide valuable information about the activities of a user on a system. By analyzing the key, an analyst can determine which programs have been recently executed, how often they have been executed, and the file paths in which they are stored.

Furthermore, the `RunMRU` key can provide insights into potentially malicious or unauthorized activity. For example, if an unfamiliar program is found in the `RunMRU` key of a user's account, it may be an indication of unauthorized access or malware.

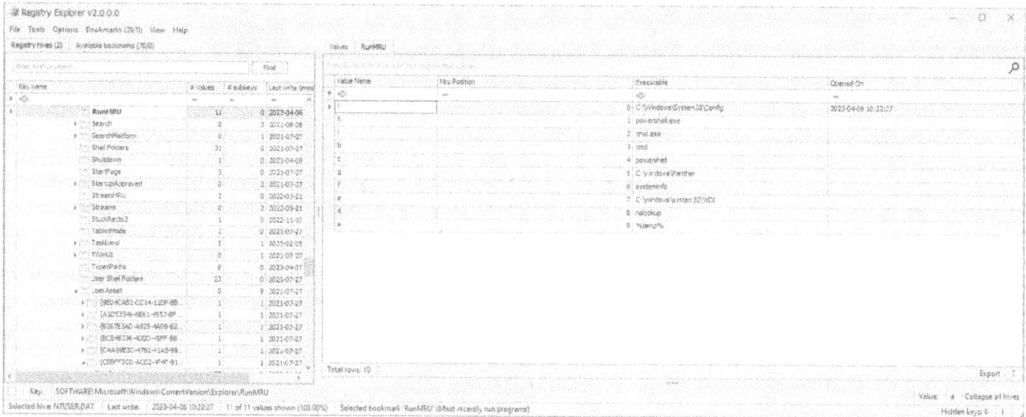

Figure 6.10 – Analyzing RunMRU

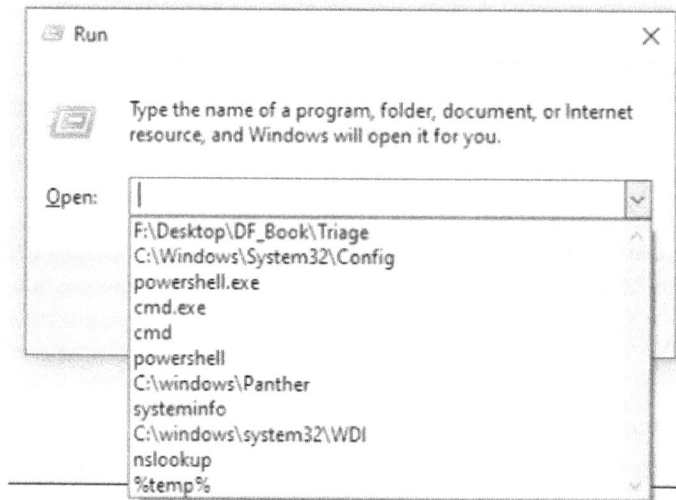

Figure 6.11 – RunMRU

LastVisitedPidlMRU

Common Dialog Keys refer to a set of Windows registry keys that store information about the file dialog boxes used by various applications in the Windows operating system. These keys can be useful to forensic analysts in understanding the applications used by a user and the files that were accessed or opened.

The Common Dialog Keys are located in the Windows registry under the following path: `NTUSER\Software\Microsoft\Windows\CurrentVersion\Explorer\ComDlg32\LastVisitedPidlMRU`.

This key contains a list of subkeys, each of which corresponds to a file dialog box used by an application.

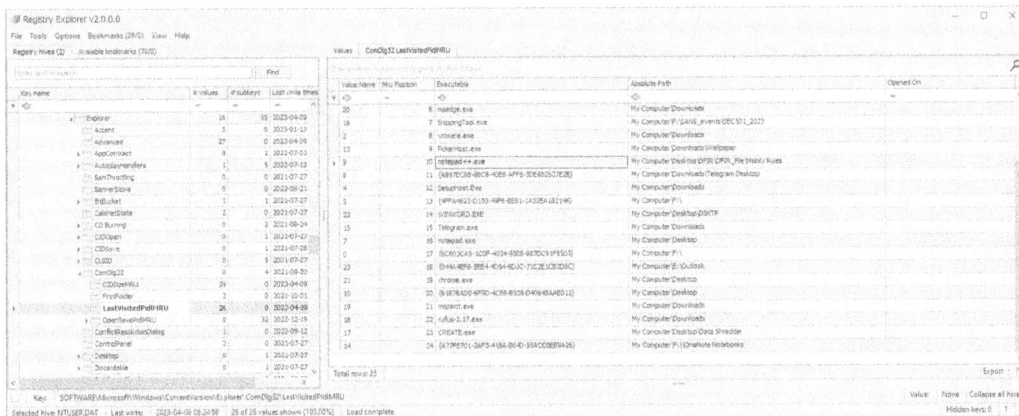

Figure 6.12 – LastVisitedPidlMRU

In the next section, we will explore the concept of prefetch and its significance in optimizing system performance, resource utilization, and forensic value.

Windows Prefetch

Windows Prefetch is a built-in performance optimization feature introduced in Windows XP that helps to reduce the startup time of frequently used applications by caching executable files and libraries into a preallocated space on the hard drive. The Prefetch feature is automatically enabled on modern versions of Windows, including Windows 7, 8, 8.1, and 10, and it's managed by the Task Scheduler service.

In addition to its primary function of speeding up the launch of applications, the Windows Prefetch feature also generates forensic artifacts, which can be useful in investigations. These artifacts are stored in the `%SystemRoot%\Prefetch` directory and have the `.pf` file extension.

Every time an application is launched, Windows Prefetch creates a new Prefetch file, which contains information about the application's execution. This information includes the application's name, its full path, its size, its last execution time, and a list of libraries and dependencies that were loaded during its execution.

To identify whether prefetch is enabled or not, we can check the `Computer\HKEY_LOCAL_MACHINE\ SYSTEM\CurrentControlSet\Control\Session Manager\Memory Management\ PrefetchParameters` registry key. By reading the `EnablePrefetcher` parameter, we can figure out whether it is enabled or not:

- **0**: Prefetching disabled
- **1**: Application prefetching enabled

- **2**: Boot prefetching enabled

- **3**: Application and boot both enabled

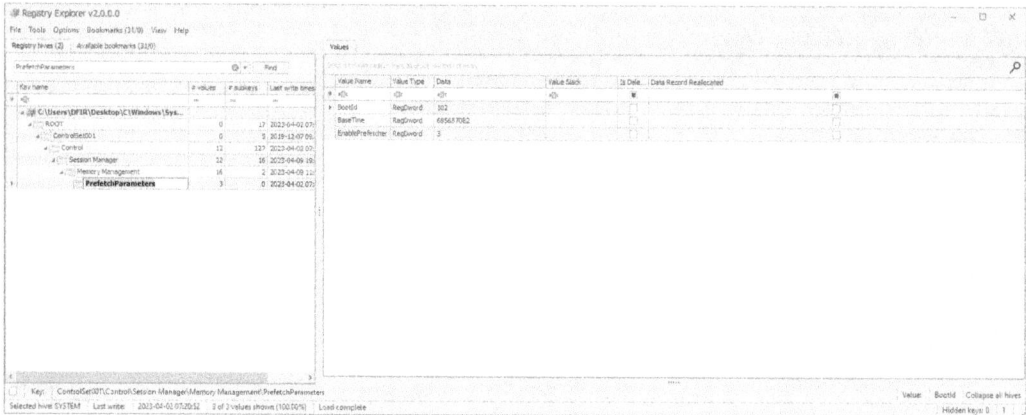

Figure 6.13 – The PrefetchParameters key

The following figure indicates the location of Prefetch in the `Windows` folder.

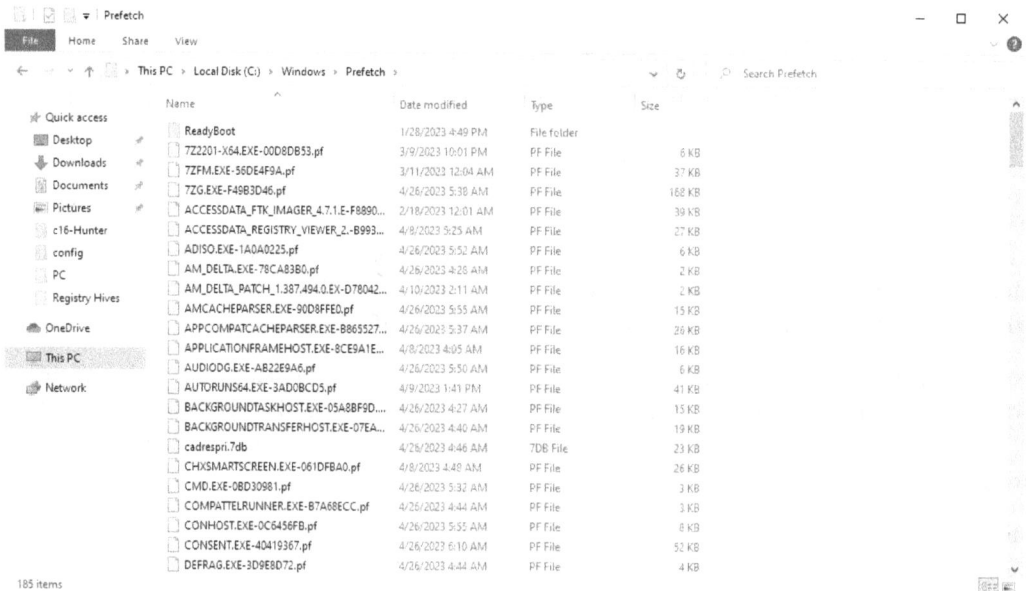

Figure 6.14 – Exploring the Prefetch folder

Prefetch can provide valuable information about the applications that have been run on a system, including when they were last accessed, how often they were used, and where they were located.

For example, if the analyst sees that a program called `Mimikatz` was run shortly before the attack was discovered, they might suspect that the attacker used this program to obtain credentials or escalate privileges. The Prefetch data can also show the location of the program, which can help the analyst identify whether it was downloaded from a suspicious website or transferred from a compromised system.

We can analyze Prefetch by using multiple tools. For the sake of demonstration, we will use the `PECmd` prefetch parser from *Eric Zimmerman* and `WinPrefetchView` from `NireSoft`.

Let's start with `PECmd.exe`. We can download `PECmd.exe` from the same repository shared in the *Technical requirements* section. By using the following on the command line, we can parse only one Prefetch file:

```
PECmd.exe -f C:\Windows\Prefetch\CMD.EXE-0BD30981.pf
```

By running the tool, we can see examples of using the tool. We will follow the same parameter depending on whether we want to parse a single artifact or a full folder.

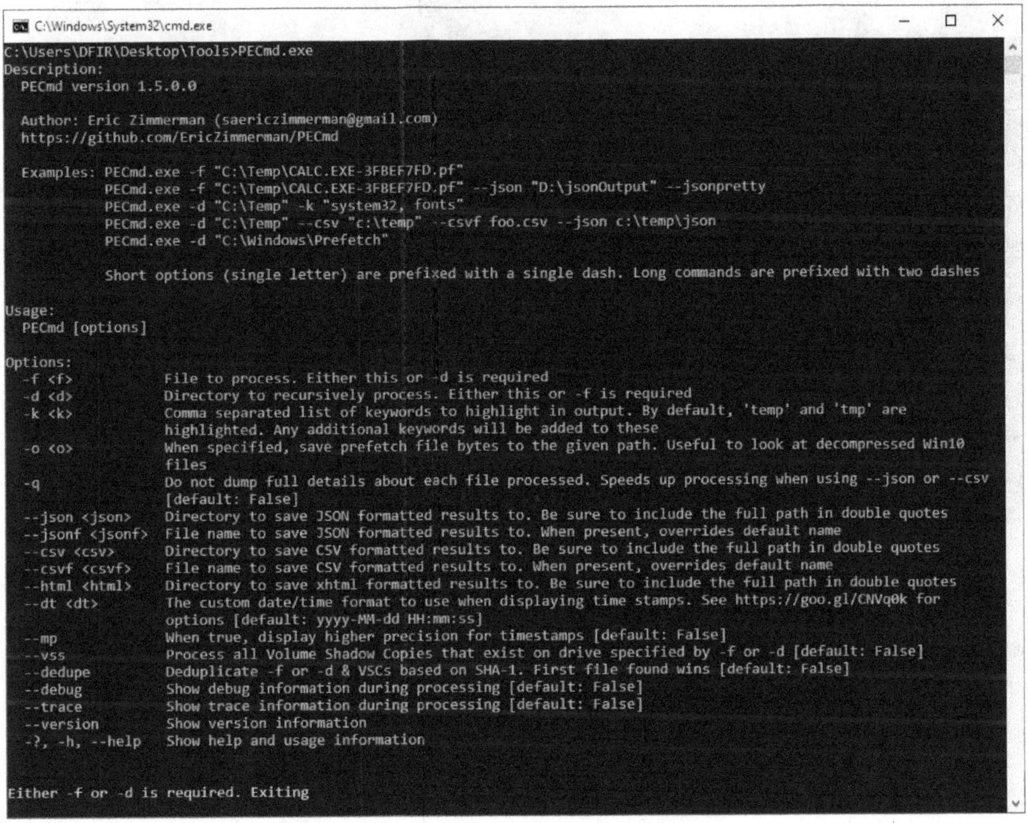

Figure 6.15 – PECmd.exe help menu

In the following figure, we can see the output of PEcmd.exe, which includes information on the filesystem time and executable information.

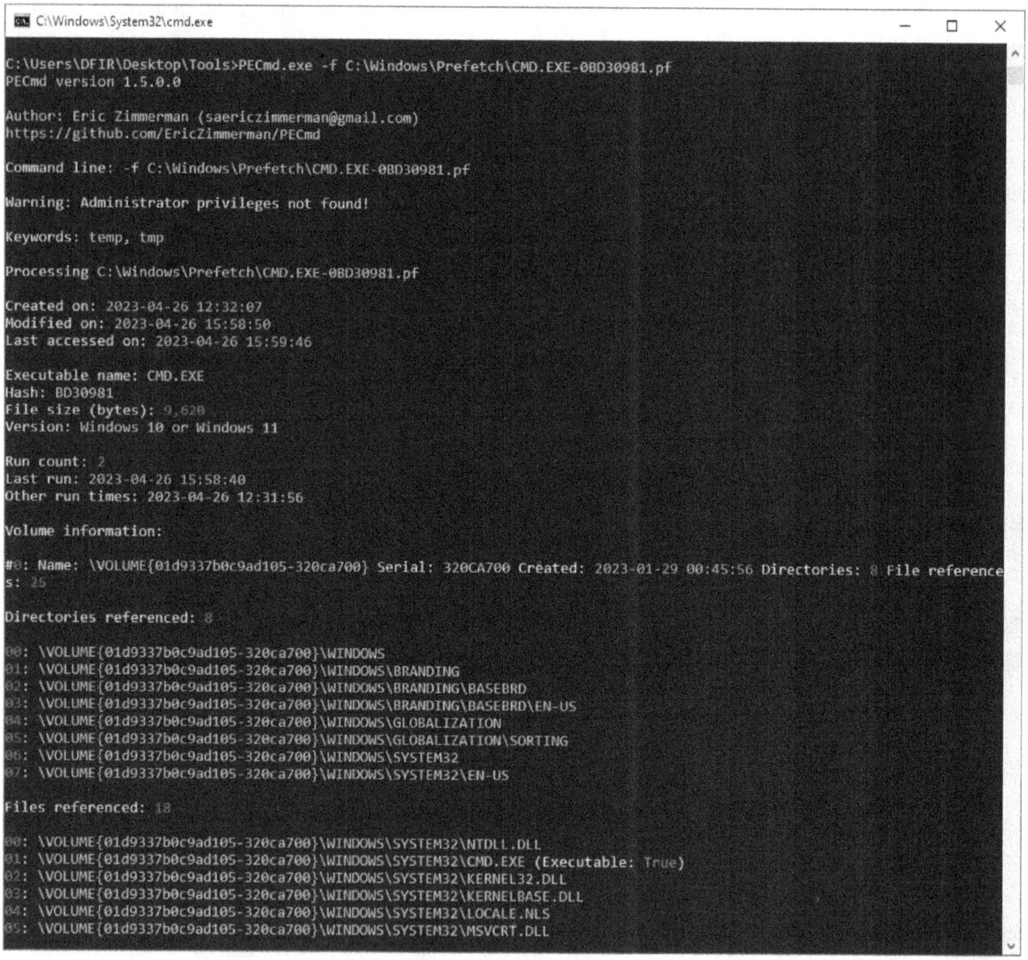

Figure 6.16 – PECmd.exe output

If we want to parse all prefetch files collected, we can use the following command and then load it into Timeline Explorer or Excel and start analyzing it:

```
PECmd.exe  -d C:\Windows\Prefetch --csv C:\temp --csvf Prefetch.csv
```

As we can see, we can load the output of the CSV file in Timeline Explorer or any preferred tool and start analyzing the findings from prefetch:

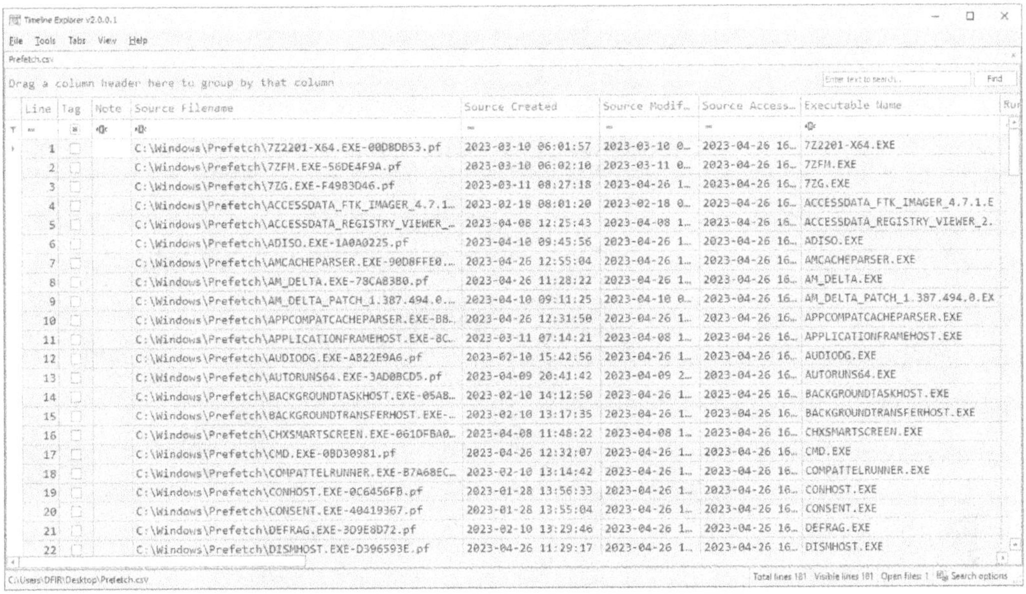

Figure 6.17 – PECmd.exe output for the Prefetch directory

Now we can use `NireSoftPrefetchView` to get the same result by loading the `Prefetch` folder into `NireSoftPrefetchView`. To load it, we need to select **Options** | **Advanced Options** and then select the `Prefetch` folder.

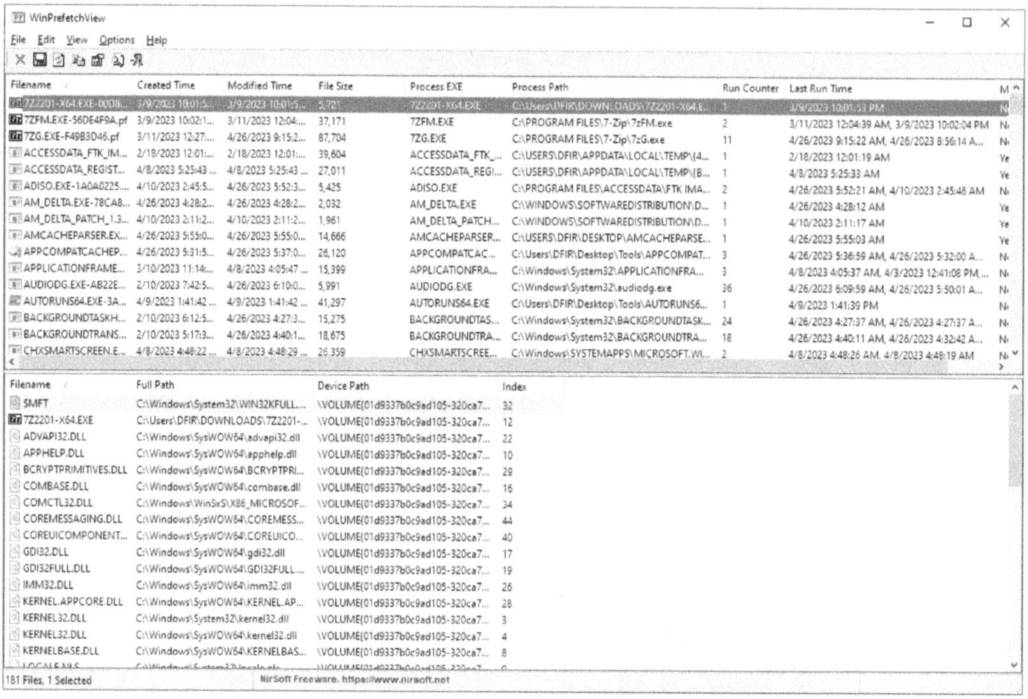

Figure 6.18 – WinPrefetchView v1.37

In conclusion, evidence of execution plays a critical role in cybersecurity investigations and incident response. By analyzing the traces left behind by executed processes and activities, cybersecurity professionals can gain valuable insights into potential threats and malicious actors' behaviors. This evidence serves as a powerful tool for identifying attack vectors, detecting unauthorized access, and understanding the scope and impact of security incidents. Furthermore, the data collected can be utilized to strengthen organizational defenses, refine security measures, and develop effective strategies to prevent future incidents. The comprehensive understanding of the evidence of execution empowers organizations to proactively protect their assets, enhance resilience, and respond swiftly to emerging cyber threats.

Application execution artifact exercises

In this part, we will apply what we have learned so far. Try to work on the following questions:

1. Using FTK Imager, export Prefetch from your local machine.

2. Identify whether CMD.exe executed on your machine by using Amcache.hve.

3. Validate how many times outlook.exe was run on your machine by using PECmd.exe.

4. Investigate the loaded files referenced for Calc.exe on your machine.

Summary

In this chapter, we learned about various artifacts that provide evidence of execution in Windows systems. We discussed NTUSER.DAT, which is a registry hive containing information about user activity, including the execution of programs and the use of various applications. We also examined the UserAssist key, which provides information about program execution, and the BAM service, which monitors the activity of background applications. Finally, we explored Shimcache, which contains metadata about executed files.

Each of these artifacts provides valuable evidence of program execution on a Windows system, and forensic analysts can use this evidence to reconstruct a timeline of activity and identify potentially malicious behavior. By analyzing these artifacts, analysts can determine what programs were executed, when they were executed, and by whom. This information can be used to investigate incidents, identify attackers, and support legal proceedings. Forensic analysts need to be familiar with these artifacts and how to analyze them effectively to support investigations.

In the upcoming chapter, our focus will shift to exploring USB artifacts. USB artifacts are crucial digital footprints left behind by USB devices connected to a system. By examining these artifacts, cybersecurity experts can uncover valuable information, including the history of USB connections, device details, and potentially malicious activities. Understanding USB artifacts aids in identifying unauthorized device usage, data exfiltration attempts, and potential introduction of malware through removable media. This knowledge empowers organizations to fortify their cybersecurity defenses, enforce strict access controls, and implement proactive measures to mitigate USB-related risks. By delving into USB artifacts, we will gain essential insights into enhancing overall security resilience and safeguarding critical data assets.

7

Forensic Analysis of USB Artifacts

Universal Serial Bus (**USB**) devices are ubiquitous in our daily lives and have become essential in transferring data between devices. With this convenience comes the potential for misuse, whether accidental or intentional. USB devices have been used in cyberattacks to deliver malware, steal sensitive information, and exfiltrate data from compromised systems. As digital forensic investigators, it's crucial to have a thorough understanding of USB devices and how to analyze them.

The analysis of removable devices, such as USB devices, has become increasingly important in digital forensics investigations. With the rise of remote work and the use of personal devices, USB devices have gained widespread popularity for seamless data transfer between devices. Nonetheless, this convenience brings along an inherent security risk, as USB devices can potentially serve as carriers for malware delivery or data exfiltration from compromised systems. Also, removable devices have been used in a variety of cybercrimes, such as data theft, intellectual property theft, and industrial espionage. In forensic investigations, analyzing USB devices can provide valuable evidence that can help identify the source of the attack, the extent of the damage, and the parties involved.

Moreover, the prevalence of USB devices in corporate and personal environments has made it a challenge for organizations to maintain control over the data leaving their networks. The analysis of USB devices can help organizations better understand their data flow and identify areas where they need to improve their security measures.

In this chapter, we will cover the following topics:

- Overview of USB devices and types
- Understanding stored evidence on USB devices
- Analyzing USB artifacts
- Exploring a real-world scenario of identifying the root cause
- USB analysis exercise

By the end of this chapter, you'll have a solid understanding of USB forensics and the techniques used in the analysis of USB devices. Let's dive in and explore the fascinating world of USB forensics!

Technical requirements

Windows registry analysis requires certain technical requirements to ensure that the process is executed efficiently and effectively. For this chapter, you need Registry Explorer, which can be downloaded from `https://ericzimmerman.github.io/#!index.md`.

Overview of USB devices and types

The **USB Mass Storage Class** (**USB MSC**) is a collection of communication protocols defined by the **USB Implementers Forum**. These protocols establish a standard for USB devices to be recognized and accessed by host computing devices, facilitating file transfer between the host and the USB device. When a USB device operates in MSC mode, it emulates the functionality of an external hard drive, allowing the host system to interact with it as if it were a traditional storage device. This protocol set enables compatibility with various storage devices, ensuring seamless data exchange between the host and the USB device.

Some common USB artifacts that can be analyzed in Windows include the following:

- **Registry keys**: When a USB device is plugged into a Windows system, it creates various registry keys that can be analyzed to determine information such as the device's serial number, its manufacturer, and timestamps indicating when the device was plugged in and removed.

- **Event logs**: Windows logs events related to USB devices, such as when a device is plugged in or removed. These logs can provide valuable information about the device and its activities.

- **Filesystem artifacts**: When a USB device is plugged into a Windows system, it creates various filesystem artifacts, such as file metadata and timestamps. These artifacts can provide valuable information about the files stored on the device, including when they were created, accessed, and modified.

Figure 7.1 – USB drive

In USB forensics, it's important to understand three different modes of operation for USB devices: **Media Transfer Protocol** (**MTP**), **Mass Storage Class** (**MSC**), and **Picture Transfer Protocol** (**PTP**).

These modes determine how the USB device interacts with the host system and impact the forensic analysis process:

- **MTP**: MTP is a protocol used for transferring media files between devices. It is commonly found on mobile devices such as smartphones and digital cameras. When a USB device is in MTP mode, it appears as a media device rather than a traditional storage device.

- **PTP**: PTP is a protocol that was developed by the International Imaging Industry Association specifically for transferring images from digital cameras to computers and peripheral devices. An advantage of PTP is that it eliminates the need for additional device drivers. However, it is important to note that PTP is limited to transferring images, videos, and their associated metadata. Other file types, such as documents, are not supported by this protocol. One distinctive feature of PTP is its one-way transfer capability. It allows users to download and copy files from the device to the computer, but it does not support the reverse process of copying files from the computer to the device. Additionally, when using PTP, it is not possible to view the underlying filesystem structure of the connected devices. This limitation restricts direct access to the filesystem, unlike protocols such as MSC, which provide a comprehensive view of the filesystem.

- **MSC**: MSC is a standard USB protocol used for connecting storage devices such as USB flash drives and external hard drives. In MSC mode, the USB device appears as a traditional storage device with a filesystem that can be accessed directly by the host system.

In the next section of this chapter, we will learn about evidence related to usage of USB devices and how to utilize it as forensic examiners.

Understanding stored evidence on USB devices

Let's dive into MTP and find out more about it. On personal computers, we often come across USB device classes known as MTP and PTP. These protocols are commonly utilized by a range of devices, including mobile phones, tablets, cameras, scanners, and music players. Unlike standard storage devices that fall under MSC, MTP and PTP offer a subset of capabilities. Consequently, the operating system treats them differently, recognizing their unique characteristics and functionalities. To identify a USB device we can check `SYSTEM\<CurrentControlSet>\Enum\USB` and `SOFTWARE\Microsoft\Windows Portable Devices\Devices`.

On the other hand, MSC is a transfer protocol that facilitates communication between a computer and a USB device. It enables the mounting of the USB device's storage area, granting direct access to these data areas for reading and writing. This allows users to conveniently view the internal filesystem structure of the USB device. MSC has been supported by Microsoft Windows since Windows 2000.

In Windows 10 and later versions, devices such as hard drives or USBs can be found in Windows Explorer under **Devices and Drives**. However, in old versions of Windows such as Windows 7 or XP, they may appear under **Devices** with the subcategory **Removable Storage**.

To get an idea of what forensic artifacts are left on Windows machines, we need to discuss and understand **USB Storage Port Driver (USBSTOR)**.

USBSTOR is a Windows component that plays a crucial role in USB storage device management and can be significant in forensic investigations involving USB devices. It serves as an interface between the operating system and connected USB storage devices, such as USB flash drives, external hard drives, and memory cards.

In Windows systems, USBSTOR manages the detection, installation, and interaction with USB storage devices. When a USB storage device is connected to a Windows computer, USBSTOR facilitates the identification and enumeration of the device, allowing the operating system to recognize it as a storage device and assign it a drive letter.

From a forensic perspective, USBSTOR leaves behind valuable artifacts that can provide insights into the history of connected USB storage devices. These artifacts include registry entries and related information stored in the Windows registry hive, specifically in the USBSTOR key.

The USBSTOR registry key maintains a record of USB storage devices that have been connected to the system. It stores information such as the device's unique identifier, the vendor ID, the product ID, and the device's serial number. Additionally, timestamps associated with device insertion and removal events may also be recorded.

Forensic examiners can leverage USBSTOR artifacts to determine which USB storage devices have been connected to a Windows system and the specific dates and times of device insertion and removal, and potentially gather information about the device itself, such as its manufacturer and model.

Furthermore, by analyzing USBSTOR artifacts in conjunction with other forensic evidence, it may be possible to establish a timeline of USB device usage, identify potential data exfiltration or unauthorized device usage, and link specific devices to user activity or events of interest in an investigation.

To retrieve USBSTOR artifacts during forensic analysis, examiners typically examine the windows registry, specifically the USBSTOR registry key, which is located at `SYSTEM\CurrentControlSet\Enum\USBSTOR` in the Windows registry hive.

As we delve further into this topic, the next section will explore the evidence by analyzing the artifacts.

Analyzing USB artifacts

Analyzing USB artifacts in Windows forensics involves examining the various traces and evidence left behind by USB devices and their interactions with the Windows operating system. USB artifacts can provide valuable insights into device connections, usage patterns, and potentially relevant information for forensic investigations. Here are some key aspects of analyzing USB artifacts in Windows forensics:

- **Registry analysis**: The Windows registry is a central database that stores configuration settings and information about connected hardware devices. In the context of USB artifacts, forensic analysts focus on specific registry keys such as `USBSTOR`, `Enum\USB`, and `MountedDevices`. These keys contain valuable information about connected USB devices, including their unique identifiers, vendor and product IDs, serial numbers, and timestamps of device connections and removals. Analyzing these registry keys can provide insights into the history of connected USB devices, device characteristics, and usage patterns.

- **System event logs**: Windows maintains event logs that record various system events, including USB device-related events. Examining the system event log can reveal timestamps, event descriptions, and details about device connections, removals, errors, and warnings. USB-related events logged in the event logs can help establish a timeline of device activities and identify any anomalies and suspicious events.

- **Volume shadow copies**: Windows may create volume shadow copies or system restore points, which capture the system's state at specific points in time. These shadow copies can be valuable for forensic analysis, as they can provide snapshots of the system, including USB device connections and their impact on the system during specific time periods. Analyzing these shadow copies can help reconstruct the history of USB device usage and gather additional evidence.

- **USB history artifacts**: Windows maintains a history of connected USB devices, which can be accessed through the `USBSTOR` and `Enum\USB` registry keys. This history includes information such as device names, timestamps of device connections and removals, device properties, and sometimes even user information. By analyzing these artifacts, forensic examiners can reconstruct the timeline of USB device usage, identify specific devices used during a particular timeframe, and potentially link device usage to user accounts or events of interest.

- **Filesystem metadata**: When USB storage devices are connected to a Windows system, filesystem metadata such as timestamps (creation, modification, and access) and file access logs may be updated. Analyzing this metadata can provide insights into the files accessed or modified on the USB device, which can be valuable in understanding the types of data transferred, potential indicators of malicious activity, or the presence of sensitive information.

- **Link analysis**: USB artifacts can be linked with other digital evidence to establish associations and correlations. For example, correlating USB device connections with user account information, file access logs, or network logs can help identify the individuals responsible for specific USB device activities. Link analysis can provide a more comprehensive understanding of the context and potential motives behind USB device usage.

- **File and filesystem analysis**: Examining files stored on USB devices can yield further insights into the nature of data transferred or stored on the device. Analyzing file metadata, file content, file types, and filesystem artifacts can help identify potential evidence, such as confidential documents, proprietary files, or malicious executables, that may be relevant to the investigation.

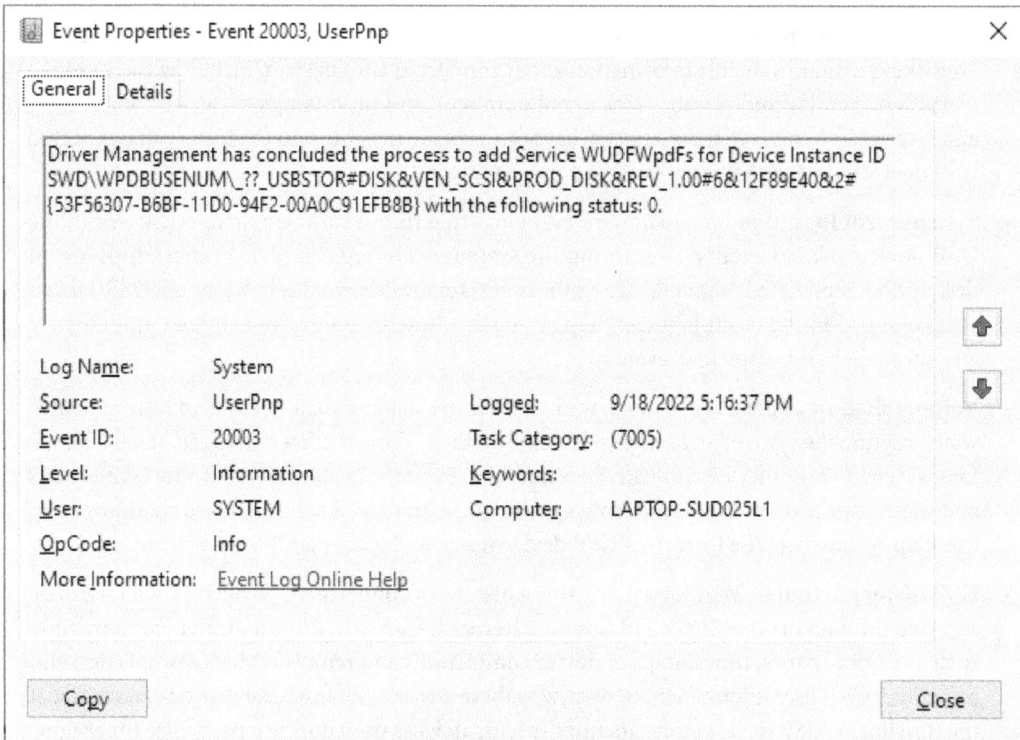

Figure 7.2 – Windows event 20003

To perform a proper investigation on USB type, we will gather some useful information related to connected USB devices on the Windows host, such as the following:

- Identifying the product, vendor ID, and type of USB

- Identifying the volume serial number

- Identifying the volume name

- Investigating user activity

- Collecting information using the USBDeview tool

Identifying the USB device type, product, and vendor ID

To identify the type of USB device, we will analyze the `SYSTEM` hive. If we go to `SYSTEM\CurrentControlSet\Enum\USB`, we can see USB device classes, such as MSC or MTP, as mentioned earlier.

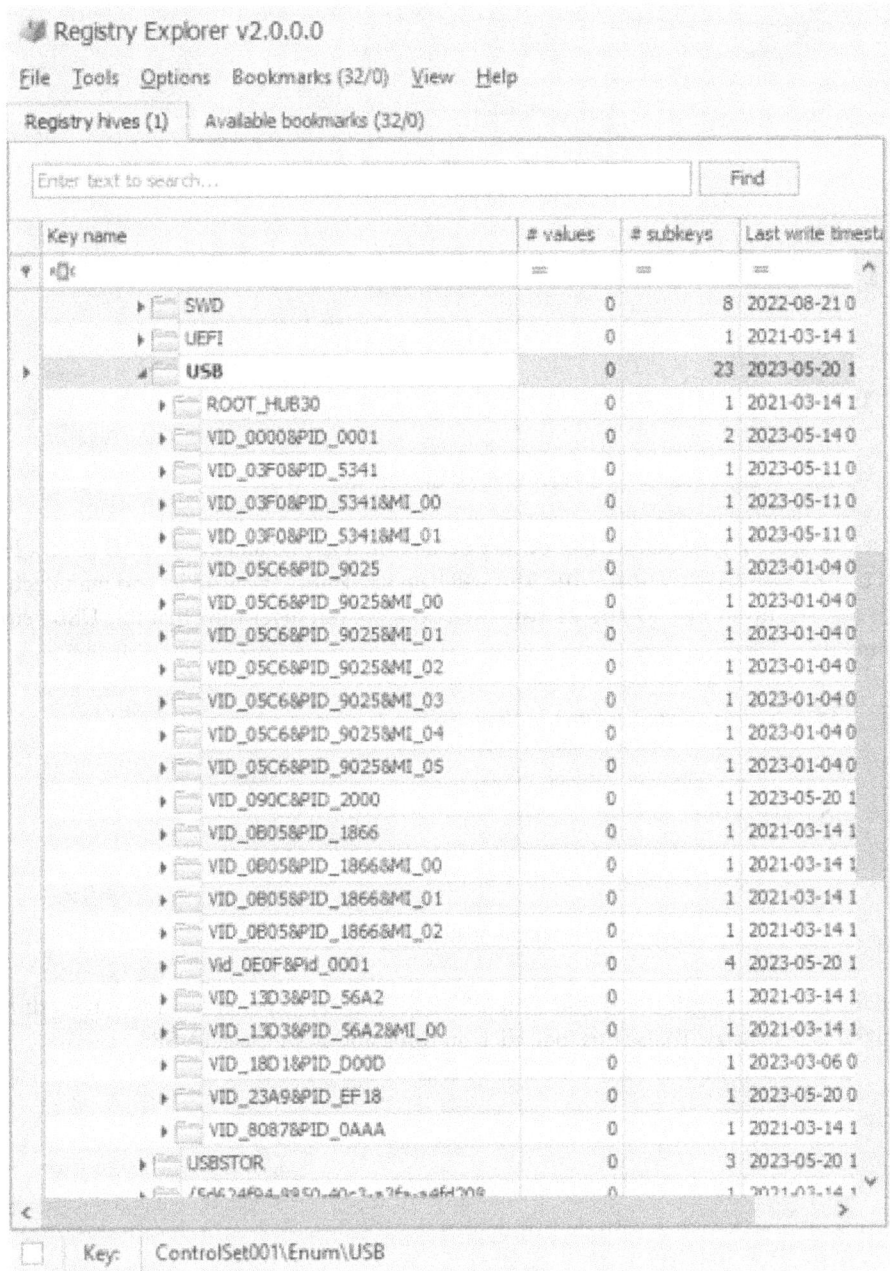

Figure 7.3 – The SYSTEM registry

In the following figure, we can see **vendor ID** (**VID**) and USB information:

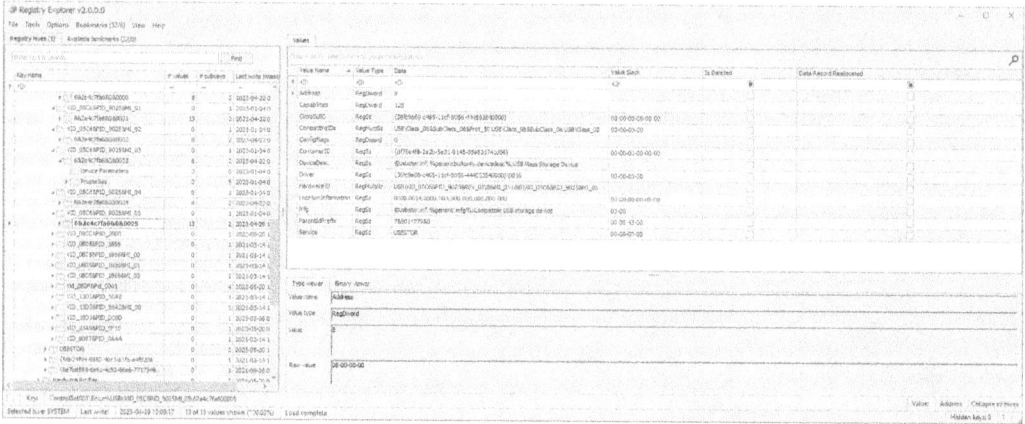

Figure 7.4 – USB type

As we can see in *Figure 7.4*, we can see that the key name contains VID and **product ID** (PID). Here, we have VID_05C6&PID_9025&MI_05. This will help us identify the product and manufacturer. If we check the VID on https://devicehunt.com, we can determine that this USB belongs to *Qualcomm, Inc.*

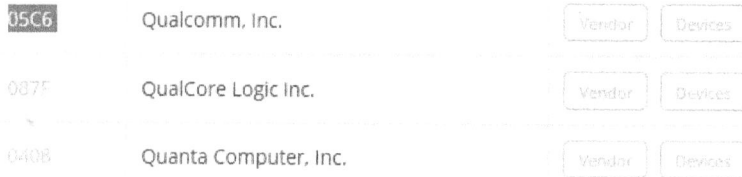

Figure 7.5 – Vendor name mapped using the VID

Apart from the manual navigation to explore the USB key, Registry Explorer has a plugin for directly jumping to the USB registry. To use this tool, click on **Bookmarks** and select **USB**.

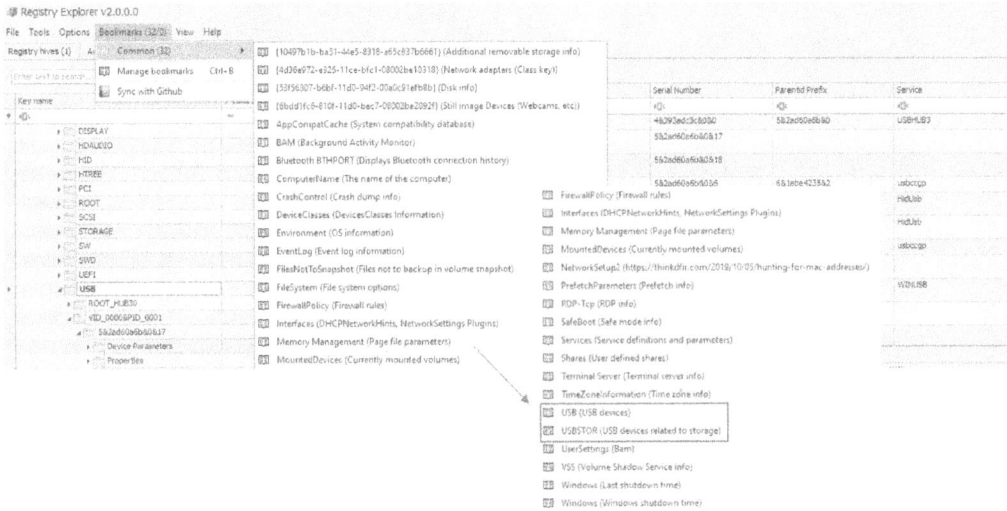

Figure 7.6 – Registry Explorer bookmark for USB

Identifying the volume serial number

Within the realm of USB devices, two distinct serial number identifiers are typically present: the device serial number and the volume serial number. The device serial number is an intrinsic component that's integrated into the device's firmware and can solely be observed by inspecting the physical device. On the other hand, the volume serial number pertains to the time and date of the **File Allocation Table (FAT)** or **New Technology File System (NTFS)** systems employed for formatting, and it can be accessed from a physical forensic image.

To extract the device serial number, we investigate two specific locations within the Windows operating system. Firstly, we explore the `\CurrentControlSet\Enum\USB` path within the `SYSTEM` file, which resides in the `\Windows\System32\Config\` directory. Secondly, we examine the EMDMgmt entry located at `\Microsoft\WindowsNT\CurrentVersion\` within the `SOFTWARE` system file, also found in the same directory. By exploring these locations, you can retrieve the necessary information regarding the device's serial number.

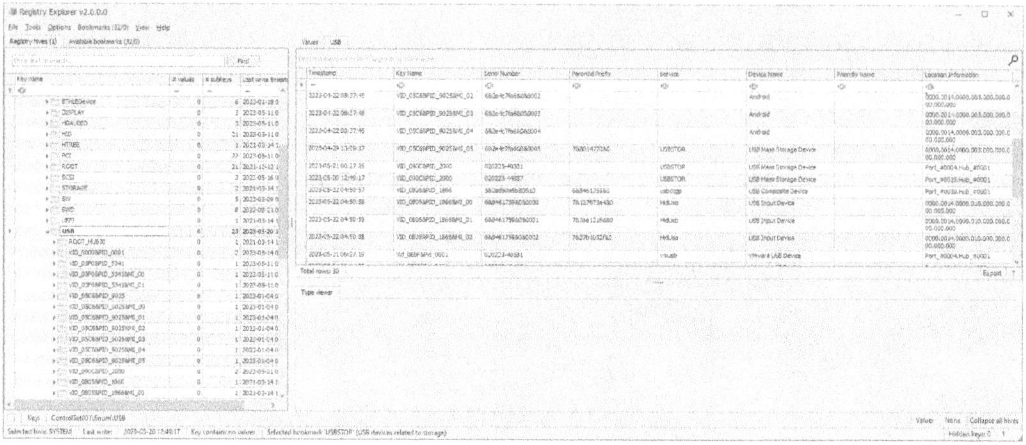

Figure 7.7 – USB serial number

Identifying the volume name and letter

To identify the USB volume name, we can examine the registry key path, `SOFTWARE\Microsoft\Windows Portable Devices\Devices`. Within this location, specific entries hold information about connected portable devices, including USB devices. By analyzing the relevant entries, such as the device's unique identifier or other associated values, the USB volume name can be determined. This volume name is typically assigned to the USB device and serves as an identifier for the storage volume within the Windows operating system. Once we get the device ID, we can check the `ENUM\USB` registry key to map it to a specific USB device.

For example, if we take the serial number `6&253473AF&3` and search on the `SYSTEM` hive using the previously mentioned registry key, when we check the volume serial number, we can map it to the `E:\` drive, as shown here:

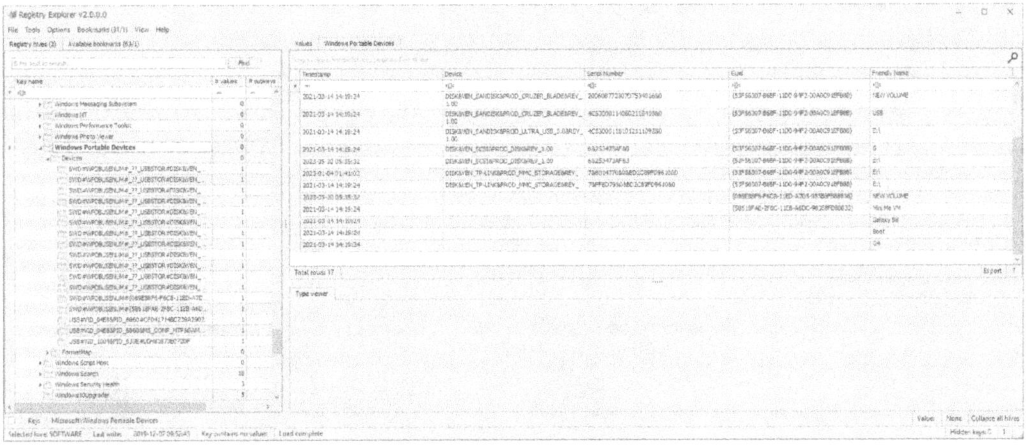

Figure 7.8 – USB driver letter

Using the USBDeview tool

USBDeview is a software utility developed by **NirSoft** that enables users to view and manage USB devices connected to their Windows system. It provides a comprehensive and user-friendly interface for analyzing USB devices, their properties, and associated information.

Upon launching USBDeview, it presents a list of all USB devices currently connected to the system. The list includes details such as device name, description, device type, device instance ID, manufacturer, PID, serial number, and more. This overview allows users to quickly identify and locate specific USB devices of interest.

Selecting a USB device from the list provides detailed information about that particular device. This includes information about the device's interfaces, endpoints, driver details, and other relevant attributes. Users can access specific properties, view related events, and examine various device-specific parameters.

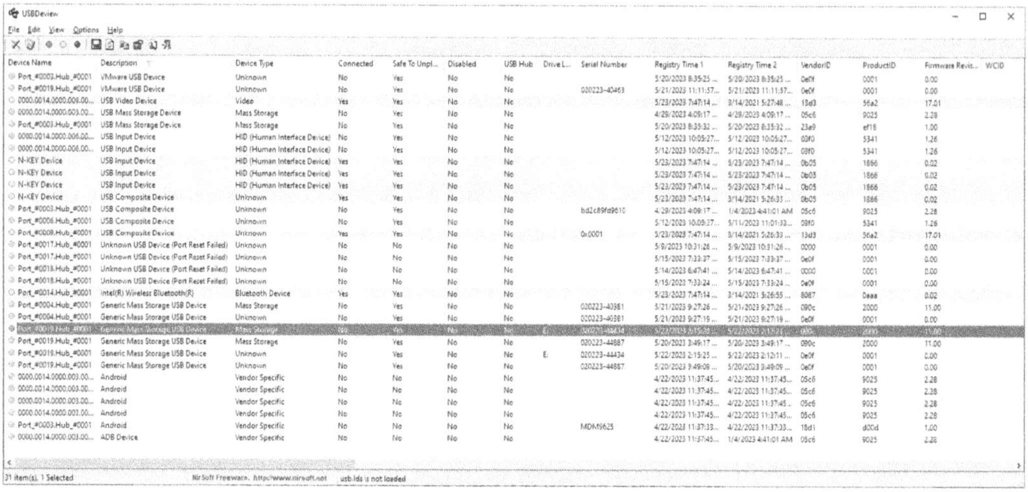

Figure 7.9 – USBDeview

In the preceding figure, we can see all USB devices plugged in with detailed information.

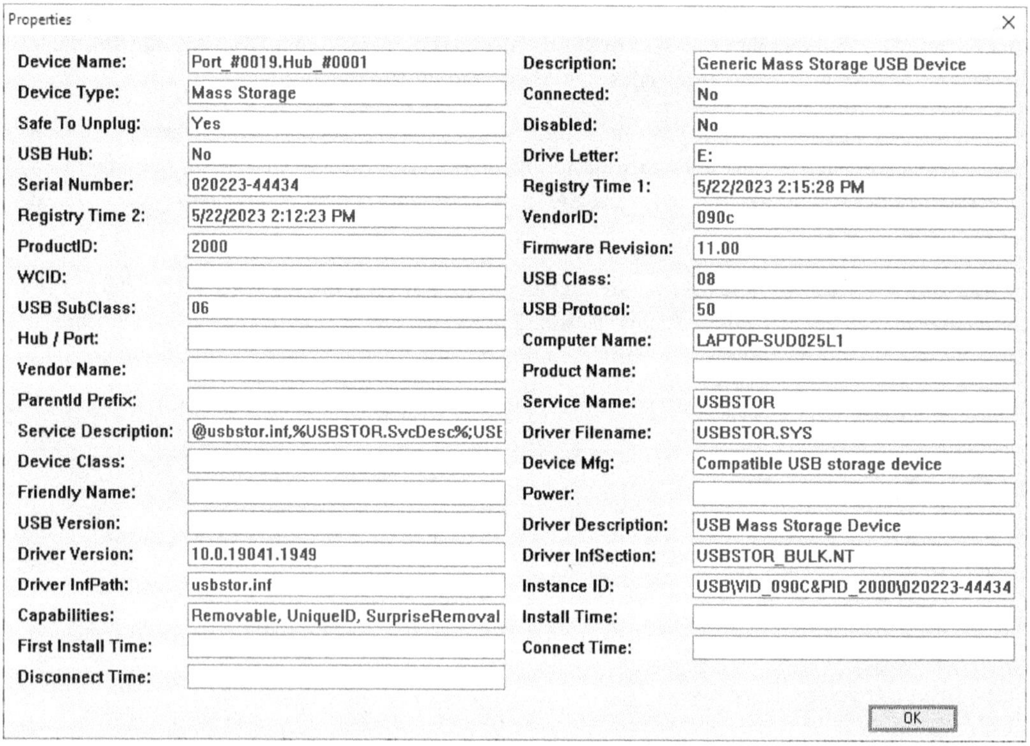

Figure 7.10 – USBDeview USB details

We now know that USB investigation has provided critical information for identifying potential security threats and improving the overall security posture of the Windows system.

In the next section, let's demonstrate what we learned by using a real-world scenario in which we identify the root cause.

Exploring a real-world scenario of identifying the root cause

The cybersecurity team reported an alert triggered on hostname (DESKTOP-T7HCR2I) for a malicious hacking tool, and during the investigation, the team could not identify the root cause. As digital forensic examiners, we are now tasked with identifying the source of the malicious binary and reporting back to the cybersecurity team.

One of the things we check during such an incident is what log source types we have and how we can find our evidence to map it for the current incident. Since we are focusing on Windows artifacts, we need a way to pull the triage image over the network or we can perform that locally. In the real world, usually, we use tools such as endpoint detection and response to access the endpoint directly and collect the desired artifacts. However, in our lab scenario, we will perform manual collection using KAPE, as we covered it in *Chapter 2*.

By running the following KAPE script, we will collect our triage from which we can filter artifacts later needed for analysis:

```
kape.exe --tsource C:\ --tdest C:\ KAPE\output\ --target
!BasicCollection,Symantec_AV_Logs,Chrome,ChromeExtensions,Edge,
Firefox,InternetExplorer,WebBrowsers,ApacheAccessLog,$Boot,$J,
$LogFile,$MFT,Amcache,ApplicationEvents,EventLogs,EventLogs-RDP,
EventTraceLogs,EvidenceOfExecution,FileSystem,MOF,Prefetch,
RDPCache,RDPLogs,RecentFileCache,Recycle,RecycleBin,
RecycleBinContent,RecycleBinMetadata,RegistryHives,
RegistryHivesSystem,RegistryHivesUser,ScheduledTasks,SRUM
```

In the preceding script, we are collecting browser artifacts, evidence of execution, and registry hives along with some really interesting artifacts, which we will cover during our last chapter.

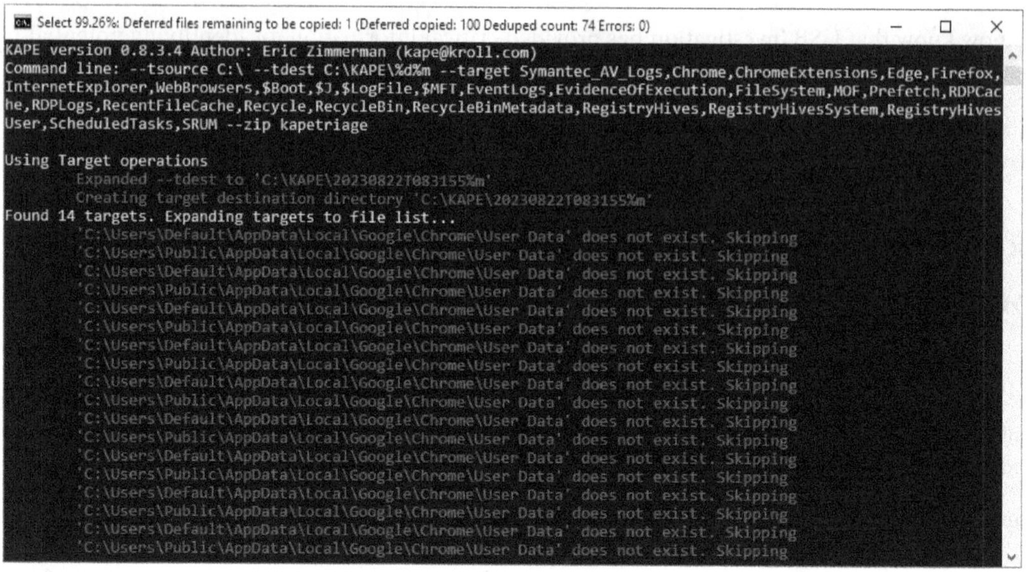

Figure 7.11 – KAPE collection script running

As we see in the screenshot above, we are processing multiple targets such as `RegsitryHive` and more, also note that we can see 99.26% of the process is completed, this can be useful to determine the progress collection.

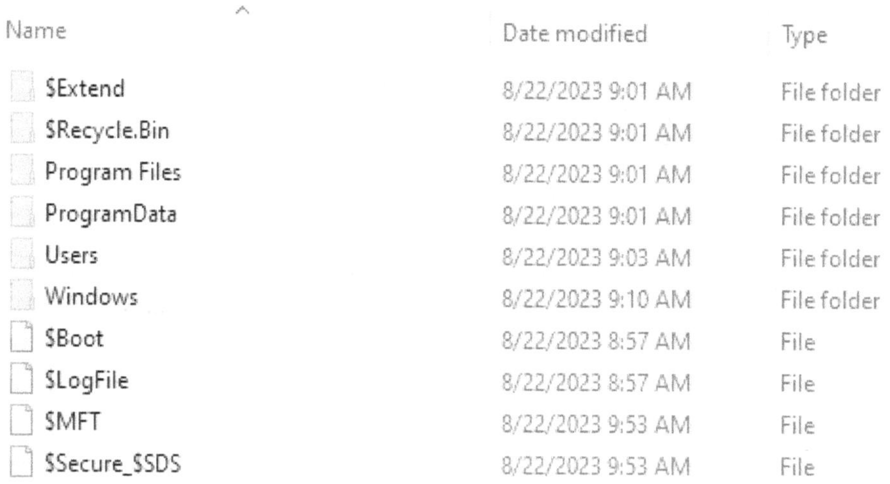

Name	Date modified	Type
$Extend	8/22/2023 9:01 AM	File folder
$Recycle.Bin	8/22/2023 9:01 AM	File folder
Program Files	8/22/2023 9:01 AM	File folder
ProgramData	8/22/2023 9:01 AM	File folder
Users	8/22/2023 9:03 AM	File folder
Windows	8/22/2023 9:10 AM	File folder
$Boot	8/22/2023 8:57 AM	File
$LogFile	8/22/2023 8:57 AM	File
$MFT	8/22/2023 9:53 AM	File
$Secure_$SDS	8/22/2023 9:53 AM	File

Figure 7.12 – KAPE collection output folder

Now we have the artifacts ready to work with, we start first with Windows event logs for Windows Defender to baseline the activity that was observed. We will provide a more in-depth analysis of Windows event logs in *Chapter 9*, but for now, we will focus on our investigation and what forensic value we get from the events we collected.

By navigating to `C:\Windows\System32\winevt\logs` within collected triage, open the `Microsoft-Windows-Windows Defender%4Operational.evtx` logs using **Event Log Explorer**.

As we can see in the following figure, we can identify the binary that triggered the alert on Windows Defender along with the path, which, in this case, is the `E:` drive.

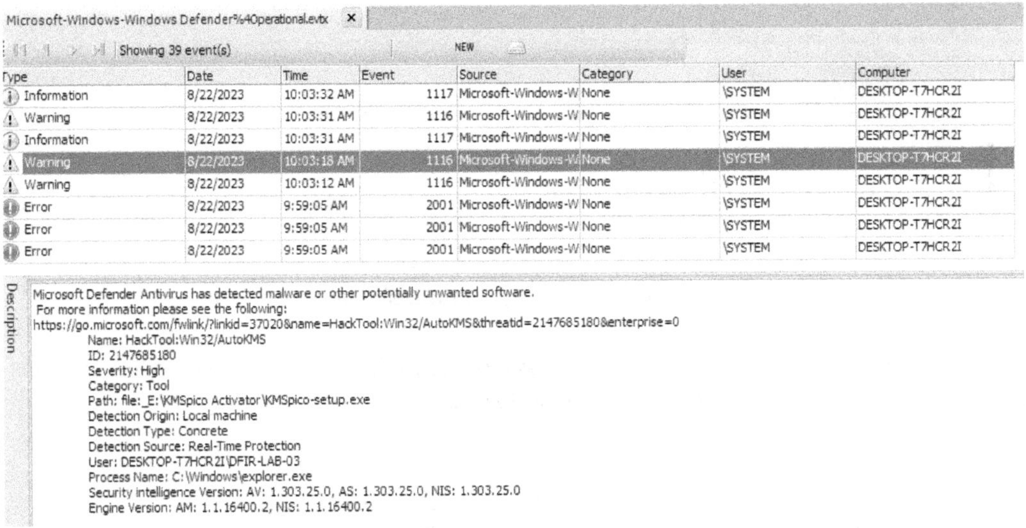

Type	Date	Time	Event	Source	Category	User	Computer
Information	8/22/2023	10:03:32 AM	1117	Microsoft-Windows-W	None	\SYSTEM	DESKTOP-T7HCR2I
Warning	8/22/2023	10:03:31 AM	1116	Microsoft-Windows-W	None	\SYSTEM	DESKTOP-T7HCR2I
Information	8/22/2023	10:03:31 AM	1117	Microsoft-Windows-W	None	\SYSTEM	DESKTOP-T7HCR2I
Warning	8/22/2023	10:03:18 AM	1116	Microsoft-Windows-W	None	\SYSTEM	DESKTOP-T7HCR2I
Warning	8/22/2023	10:03:12 AM	1116	Microsoft-Windows-W	None	\SYSTEM	DESKTOP-T7HCR2I
Error	8/22/2023	9:59:05 AM	2001	Microsoft-Windows-W	None	\SYSTEM	DESKTOP-T7HCR2I
Error	8/22/2023	9:59:05 AM	2001	Microsoft-Windows-W	None	\SYSTEM	DESKTOP-T7HCR2I
Error	8/22/2023	9:59:05 AM	2001	Microsoft-Windows-W	None	\SYSTEM	DESKTOP-T7HCR2I

Microsoft Defender Antivirus has detected malware or other potentially unwanted software.
For more information please see the following:
https://go.microsoft.com/fwlink/?linkid=37020&name=HackTool:Win32/AutoKMS&threatid=2147685180&enterprise=0
    Name: HackTool:Win32/AutoKMS
    ID: 2147685180
    Severity: High
    Category: Tool
    Path: file:_E:\KMSpico Activator\KMSpico-setup.exe
    Detection Origin: Local machine
    Detection Type: Concrete
    Detection Source: Real-Time Protection
    User: DESKTOP-T7HCR2I\DFIR-LAB-03
    Process Name: C:\Windows\explorer.exe
    Security intelligence Version: AV: 1.303.25.0, AS: 1.303.25.0, NIS: 1.303.25.0
    Engine Version: AM: 1.1.16400.2, NIS: 1.1.16400.2

Figure 7.13 – Windows Defender event logs

We can check the logs and see that Defender already deleted the binary. Now we have confirmed that we have a malicious binary that resides in this particular host, we can move to the next step and identify the actual location of this file.

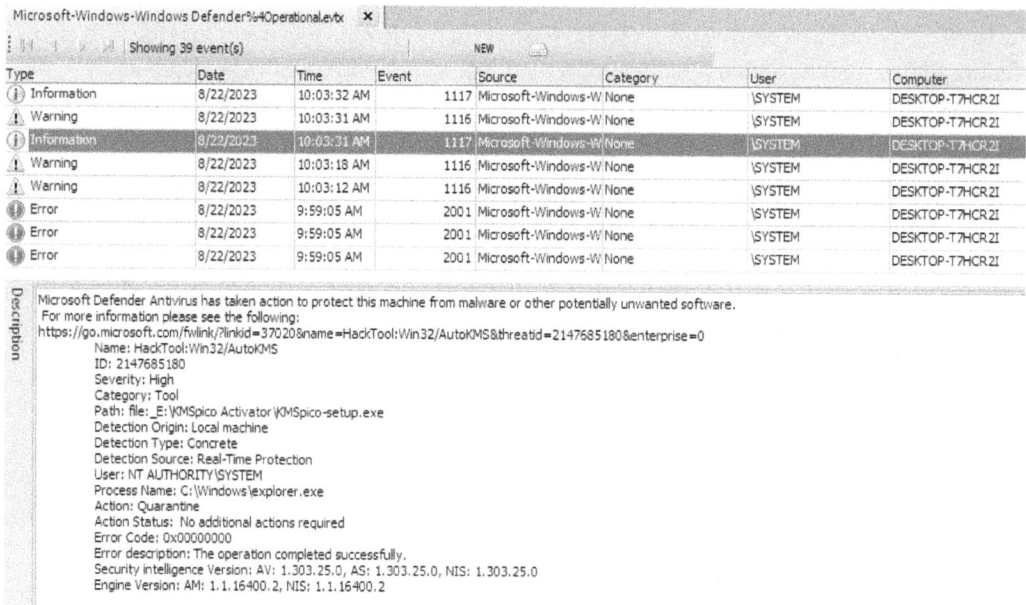

Figure 7.14 – Windows event logs for the Defender action

From the registry, we can verify whether a USB was inserted in this system or not by validating the driver letter following **MountedDevices** within the SYSTEM hive.

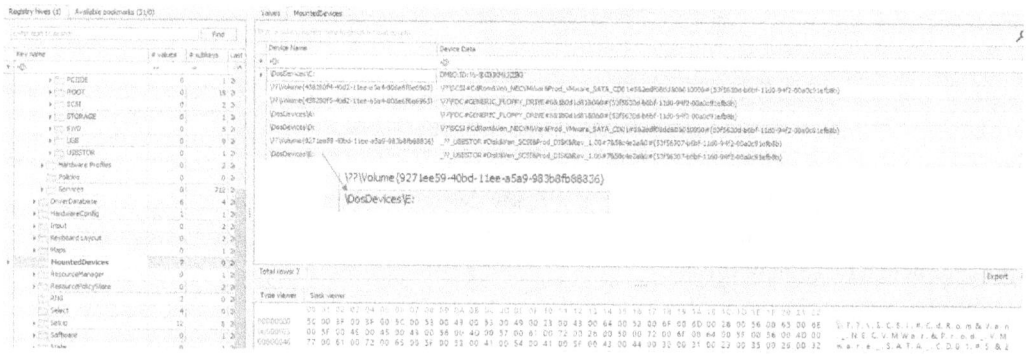

Figure 7.15 – The SYSTEM hive displaying MountedDevices

To conclude, USB forensic analysis is a vital part of digital investigations. It can help us uncover valuable evidence and gain insights into potentially malicious activities. This chapter introduced the key techniques and tools used in USB forensic analysis, from the initial acquisition of USB device data to the in-depth examination of its contents.

As technology advances and USB devices become more common, the need for robust and effective USB forensic analysis methodologies will only grow. Digital forensic professionals must stay up to date on the latest developments in this field and regularly practice these techniques.

USB artifacts analysis exercises

In this section, we will apply what we have learned so far:

1. Using the Windows registry, identify the letter assigned to a recently plugged-in USB device on your home computer.

2. Validate the serial number and vendor ID of the USB device.

3. By using the USBDeview tool, explore the installed and plugged-in USB devices on your local machine.

Summary

In conclusion, USB forensic analysis plays a crucial role in modern digital investigations. The examination of USB artifacts provides valuable insights into the usage, history, and interactions of USB devices within a system. By leveraging forensic techniques and tools, investigators can uncover critical evidence related to data breaches, intellectual property theft, and other malicious activities involving USB devices.

Throughout this chapter, we have explored various aspects of USB forensic analysis. We discussed the significance of USB artifacts as a rich source of evidence, including device information, timestamps, and file transfer activities. We examined the importance of understanding different USB protocols, such as MTP and MSC, which enable the transfer of data between USB devices and host systems.

Moreover, we delved into the analysis of USB artifacts in Windows, exploring key registry locations and files that store valuable information about connected USB devices, including device types, serial numbers, volume names, and more. We also discussed the role of USBSTOR, a significant registry key, in tracking device insertion and removal events.

By effectively applying USB forensic techniques, investigators can reconstruct events, establish timelines, and identify potential sources of data leakage or unauthorized access. This knowledge aids in the attribution of actions, the identification of responsible individuals, and the overall strengthening of digital security.

In the next chapter, we will dive into another interesting artifact (browser artifacts) that holds important evidence for browsing activity and user access to the internet.

8

Forensic Analysis of Browser Artifacts

In today's digital age, web browsers have become an integral part of our daily lives. From browsing websites to accessing online services, browsers store a wealth of valuable information that can aid in forensic investigations. This article explores the significance of browser artifacts in forensic analysis of the Windows operating system, shedding light on the valuable digital footprints left behind by users.

When users interact with web browsers, a variety of artifacts are generated and stored on their Windows systems. These artifacts include browsing history, cookies, cache files, bookmarks, downloads, form data, and session information. Each of these artifacts provides a unique glimpse into the user's online activities and can serve as critical evidence in forensic investigations.

In this chapter, we will cover the following topics:

- Overview of browsers
- Internet Explorer and Edge
- Google Chrome
- Firefox
- Browser analysis exercises

By the end of this chapter, you'll have a solid understanding of browser forensics and the techniques used in the analysis of each browser. Let's dive in and explore the fascinating world of digital forensics!

Technical requirements

Browser forensic analysis requires multiple tools to parse the evidence. The tools utilized in this chapter are as follows:

- DB Browser: `https://ericzimmerman.github.io/#!index.md`

- Nirsoft Web Browsers Tools: `https://www.nirsoft.net/web_browser_tools.html`

- BrowsingHistoryView: `https://www.nirsoft.net/utils/browsing_history_view.html`

Overview of browsers

The usage of web browsers on Windows operating systems has become ubiquitous in today's digital landscape. With a wide array of browser options available, it is crucial to understand the various browsers utilized by Windows users. This section provides an in-depth overview of the most commonly used browsers on Windows, offering technical insights into their features and security aspects.

In the realm of digital forensics, the examination of web browsers on Windows operating systems holds significant importance. Web browsers serve as a gateway to users' online activities and can contain a wealth of valuable forensic artifacts. Understanding the most commonly used browsers on Windows and their technical aspects is crucial for digital forensic investigators. This article provides a comprehensive overview of these browsers, focusing on their relevance to digital forensic investigations.

During a digital forensic investigation, analyzing web browsers can yield a plethora of valuable evidence. As mentioned before, browsers store various artifacts, including browsing history, cookies, cached files, downloads, and bookmarks. These artifacts can provide critical insights into a user's online behavior, visited websites, login credentials, and even potential involvement in illicit activities.

By delving into the technical details of commonly used browsers on Windows, digital forensic investigators can better comprehend the structure and storage mechanisms of browser artifacts. This knowledge aids in locating and extracting relevant information during forensic examinations, ensuring a thorough and accurate analysis. Moreover, understanding the security aspects of web browsers is paramount in digital forensic investigations. Browser vulnerabilities, privacy settings, and encryption protocols can impact the integrity and reliability of the collected evidence. Investigative techniques and tools must take into account browser security features and potential anti-forensic measures employed by malicious actors.

Let's look at the most widely used browsers:

- **Internet Explorer** (**IE**): IE has been the default browser on Windows for many years. Although its usage has significantly declined, it remains relevant due to legacy systems and specific enterprise requirements. The next section delves into the technical details of IE, including its **Trident** rendering engine, supported versions, and notable security considerations. It also discusses compatibility modes and **ActiveX** controls, which have been associated with potential security vulnerabilities.

- **Microsoft Edge**: Microsoft Edge, introduced with Windows 10, replaced IE as the default browser. It offers enhanced performance, improved security, and compatibility with modern web standards. We will explore the technical features of Edge, such as its **Chromium**-based engine, unique security enhancements such as **Windows Defender Application Guard**, and integration with **Windows Defender SmartScreen**. We will also cover features such as **Collections**, **Web Capture**, and **vertical tabs** that enhance productivity and user experience.

- **Google Chrome**: Google Chrome is one of the most widely used web browsers on Windows operating systems, making it a significant focus in digital forensic investigations. As a forensic analyst, understanding the intricacies of Chrome and its forensic artifacts is crucial for conducting thorough examinations and extracting valuable evidence. Chrome stores a vast number of forensic artifacts that can provide valuable insights into a user's online activities. These artifacts include browsing history, download history, cookies, bookmarks, autofill data, and cached files. Analyzing these artifacts can reveal visited websites, search queries, login credentials, online communication, and even evidence of malicious activities such as phishing attempts or unauthorized access.

- **Mozilla Firefox**: Mozilla Firefox is a popular web browser used by millions of users worldwide, making it a significant area of focus in digital forensic investigations. Forensic analysis of Firefox can provide valuable insights into a user's online activities, preferences, and potential evidence of malicious activities. This chapter explores the key aspects of Mozilla Firefox forensic analysis, including its storage mechanisms and forensic artifacts, and the challenges faced by investigators. One of the primary storage mechanisms used by Firefox is the **SQLite** database. Firefox maintains several databases, including `places.sqlite` (containing browsing history and bookmarks), `cookies.sqlite` (storing cookie data), and `formhistory.sqlite` (retaining form input data). Analyzing these databases can reveal the websites a user has visited, bookmarked URLs, form input history, and authentication-related information.

Internet Explorer

IE is a web browser developed by Microsoft that has been through several versions from IE6 to IE11. Let's explore the key features and changes introduced in each version:

- **Internet Explorer 6** (**IE6**) was a popular browser released in 2001. It introduced tabbed browsing, allowing users to open multiple websites in a single window. However, it faced criticism for security vulnerabilities and limited support for web standards.

- **Internet Explorer 7** (**IE7**) was released in 2006, addressing the security concerns of its predecessor. It provided enhanced security features, including protection against phishing attacks. IE7 also improved support for web standards, making websites look and function better.

- **Internet Explorer 8 (IE8)**, launched in 2009, focused on compatibility and security. It introduced features such as accelerators, enabling quick access to web services, and web slices, which allowed users to monitor specific parts of a web page. IE8 also enhanced developer tools for troubleshooting and debugging websites.

- **Internet Explorer 9 (IE9)**, released in 2011, prioritized speed and performance. It utilized hardware acceleration to render graphics faster and introduced support for HTML5, enabling more interactive web content. IE9 also featured a simplified user interface.

- **Internet Explorer 10 (IE10)** arrived in 2012, optimized for touch-enabled devices. It had a streamlined interface and improved support for web standards such as CSS3 and HTML5. IE10 provided a smoother browsing experience on tablets and touch-enabled computers.

- **Internet Explorer 11 (IE11)**, introduced in 2013, focused on performance improvements and security enhancements. It boasted faster page load times, better JavaScript execution, and advanced security features. IE11 also included updated developer tools for easier website development and debugging.

Throughout the IE6 to IE11 releases, Microsoft aimed to enhance the browsing experience by improving security, compatibility with web standards, and overall performance. However, with the introduction of Microsoft Edge, Microsoft transitioned to a new browser that further improved speed, security, and compatibility with modern web technologies.

We will just focus on a couple of artifacts of IE11 since it is no longer actively used in modern Windows systems. Let's dive into analyzing history and the cache:

IE11 history location
`%USERPROFILE%\AppData\Local\Microsoft\Windows\WebCache\`
`WebCacheV#.dat`
IE11 cache
`%USERPROFILE%\AppData\Local\Microsoft\Windows\`
`INetCache\IE`
`%USERPROFILE%\AppData\Local\Microsoft\Windows\`
`INetCache\Low\IE`

The `%USERPROFILE%\AppData\Local\Microsoft\Windows\WebCache` directory and the `WebCacheV*.dat` files within it are related to the IE11 browser cache known as `WebCache`. Here's an explanation of this directory and its significance:

- **Directory location**: `%USERPROFILE%\AppData\Local\Microsoft\Windows\WebCache` refers to the file path where IE11 stores its WebCache files. The `%USERPROFILE%` variable represents the user's profile folder, which varies depending on the logged-in user.

In most cases, it would be something like `C:\Users<Username>\AppData\Local\Microsoft\Windows\WebCache`.

- **WebCache and WebCacheV*.dat files**: The WebCache is a component of IE11 that stores cached copies of web pages, images, scripts, and other resources for faster loading and improved browsing performance. The `WebCacheV*.dat` files within the WebCache directory represent the cache database files.

Each `WebCacheV*.dat` file contains a subset of the cached data, with the asterisk (`*`) representing a version number. IE11 creates new versions of the WebCache database as it evolves or when it reaches a certain size limit. The most recent version will have the highest version number.

As we mentioned, since IE is no longer used, we will skip it and move on to Microsoft Edge's useful artifacts.

Microsoft Edge

Microsoft Edge is a web browser developed by Microsoft as a successor to IE. Here's a brief history of Microsoft Edge:

- **Microsoft Edge** (2015): Microsoft Edge was first introduced in 2015 with the release of Windows 10, replacing IE as the default browser. It was built from scratch using a new rendering engine called **EdgeHTML**, which aimed to improve performance, security, and compatibility with modern web standards.

- **EdgeHTML** and **Legacy Edge** (2015-2019): In its early years, Microsoft Edge relied on the EdgeHTML rendering engine, which offered faster page rendering and better standards compliance than IE. The browser featured a minimalist design, with a focus on speed, simplicity, and integration with Microsoft services such as **Cortana** and **OneDrive**. However, despite its improvements, the adoption rate of Edge was relatively low compared to other browsers, such as Google Chrome and Mozilla Firefox.

- **Transition to Chromium** (2019): In December 2018, Microsoft announced a major shift for Edge by adopting the open source Chromium project as its new rendering engine. Chromium is the same engine that powers Google Chrome, and the move aimed to improve compatibility, performance, and support for web standards. The transition to Chromium allowed Microsoft Edge to leverage the extensive **Chrome Web Store** for extensions and offered a more familiar browsing experience to users.

- **Microsoft Edge (Chromium)** (2020-present): In January 2020, Microsoft officially released the new version of Microsoft Edge based on Chromium. The revamped browser retained the name Microsoft Edge but featured a redesigned user interface and enhanced features, including improved performance, better compatibility, and increased support for extensions. Microsoft Edge also integrated several unique features, such as Collections for organizing and saving web content, built-in support for PDF annotation, and deep integration with Microsoft services and platforms.

Since its transition to Chromium, Microsoft Edge has seen increased popularity and adoption among users. It has become a competitive browser option, offering a balance between performance, compatibility, and integration with Microsoft's ecosystem. Microsoft continues to update and enhance Edge with new features, security improvements, and regular updates to provide a robust browsing experience for users.

Now, we will dive into each artifact and start analyzing them. First, we will focus on browser history. The following table contains the location of forensically valued evidence that is stored in the `%AppData%\Local\Microsoft\Edge\User Data\Default\` folder:

Artifact Name	File
History	History and top sites
Bookmarks	Bookmarks.bak
Download History	History
Auto Complete	Web data, history
Extensions	Extension folder
Synchronization	Sync data

After exploring the artifacst to perform forensic analysis of Edge and IE, it's time to shift our focus to another widely used web browser: Chrome. As we proceed, we will uncover the essential file locations and artifacts associated with Chrome, shedding light on potential digital evidence and user activities within the browser. Let's take a closer look at Chrome's browser.

Google Chrome

Google Chrome was first announced by Google in September 2008 with the goal of creating a fast, secure, and user-friendly web browser. The browser's development was based on the open source Chromium project, which uses the **Blink** rendering engine.

Google Chrome emphasized speed and simplicity as its key features. It introduced a minimalist user interface, with a focus on efficient performance and a streamlined browsing experience. Chrome introduced the concept of each tab running in a separate process, enhancing stability and isolating potential crashes to individual tabs.

Google Chrome adopted a rapid release cycle, with frequent updates that brought new features, security patches, and performance improvements. The regular updates ensured that users had access to the latest browser advancements and security enhancements.

Google Chrome, being a widely used web browser, generates various forensic artifacts that can be valuable for digital forensic investigations. These artifacts can provide insights into a user's browsing activities, stored data, and interactions within the browser. The following are some key forensic artifacts associated with Google Chrome:

- **History** and **Downloads**: Google Chrome maintains a detailed browsing history, which includes a record of visited websites and the timestamps of those visits. The **History** database contains information such as URLs, page titles, visit frequencies, and timestamps. Additionally, the **Downloads** database keeps track of files downloaded through the browser, including the source URLs, download locations, and timestamps.

- **Cache**: The cache stores temporary copies of web page elements, such as images, scripts, and other resources, to enhance browsing performance. The cache can provide valuable artifacts, including remnants of visited websites, images, and other downloaded content.

- **Cookies**: Google Chrome stores cookies, which are small text files containing data that websites use for various purposes, such as user authentication and session management. The **Cookies** database contains information such as website names, cookie names, expiration dates, and encrypted cookie values. Analyzing cookies can reveal user preferences, visited websites, and online activities.

- **Autofill** and **Passwords**: Google Chrome provides autofill functionality for forms and saves user passwords for automatic sign-in on websites. The **Autofill** and **Passwords** databases store information such as website URLs, form field names, usernames, and hashed passwords. These artifacts can provide insights into the user's online accounts, credentials, and potentially compromised or vulnerable accounts.

- **Bookmarks** and **Preferences**: Google Chrome allows users to bookmark web pages for easy access. The **Bookmarks** database contains information about bookmarked URLs, folder structures, and timestamps. The **Preferences** database stores various browser settings, including startup URLs, search engine preferences, and extension configurations.

- **Extensions** and **web applications**: Google Chrome supports extensions and web applications that enhance its functionality. The **Extensions** database contains information about installed extensions, including their names, IDs, and permissions. Additionally, web applications accessed through Chrome generate artifacts too.

Chrome artifacts

Investigating the history of Google Chrome can provide valuable insights into a user's browsing activities and visited websites, and potential evidence in a digital forensic investigation. Chrome stores data in the SQLite database format, and we can identify visited websites, URLs, titles of pages that have been browsed, and more.

The **Profile Path** holds the majority of the user's profile data and forensic artifacts.

The Chrome browser's artifact locations are as follows:

- `C:\Users\USER_NAME\AppData\Local\Google\Chrome\User Data\Default`
- `C:\Users\USER_NAME\AppData\Local\Google\Chrome\User Data\ChromeDefault\Data`

Figure 8.1 shows the default profile for Chrome, listing databases such as `History` and `Cookies`:

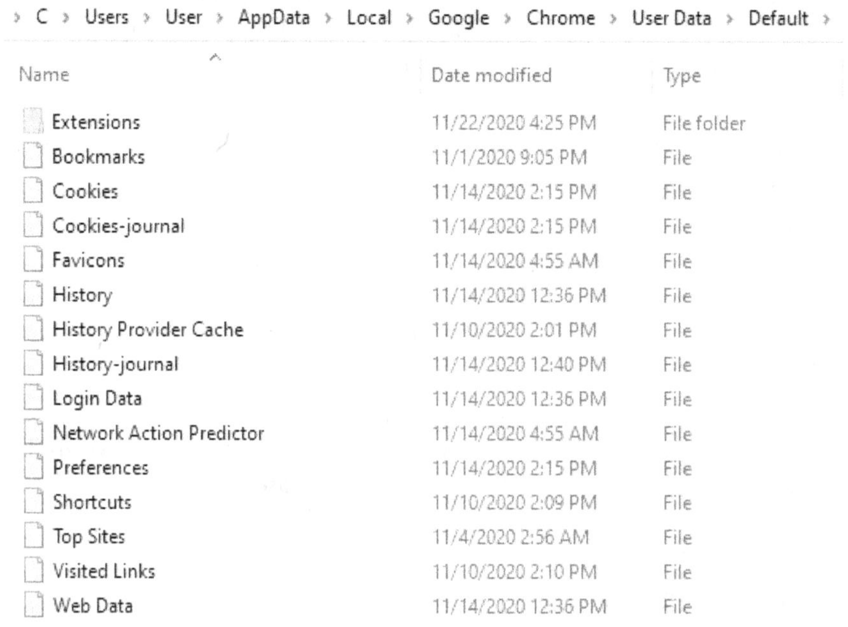

> C > Users > User > AppData > Local > Google > Chrome > User Data > Default >
Name
Date modified
Type
Extensions 11/22/2020 4:25 PM File folder
Bookmarks 11/1/2020 9:05 PM File
Cookies 11/14/2020 2:15 PM File
Cookies-journal 11/14/2020 2:15 PM File
Favicons 11/14/2020 4:55 AM File
History 11/14/2020 12:36 PM File
History Provider Cache 11/10/2020 2:01 PM File
History-journal 11/14/2020 12:40 PM File
Login Data 11/14/2020 12:36 PM File
Network Action Predictor 11/14/2020 4:55 AM File
Preferences 11/14/2020 2:15 PM File
Shortcuts 11/10/2020 2:09 PM File
Top Sites 11/4/2020 2:56 AM File
Visited Links 11/10/2020 2:10 PM File
Web Data 11/14/2020 12:36 PM File

Figure 8.1 – Google Chrome user's Profile Path

The *downloads* and *search history* in Google Chrome are stored in the form of `SQLite` databases.

The search history locations are as follows:

- `C:\Users\USER_NAME\AppData\Local\Google\Chrome\User Data\Default\History`
- `C:\Users\USER_NAME\AppData\Local\Google\Chrome\User Data\ChromeDefault\Data\History`

When analyzing Chrome's History database, we will use a tool called DB Browser for SQLite:

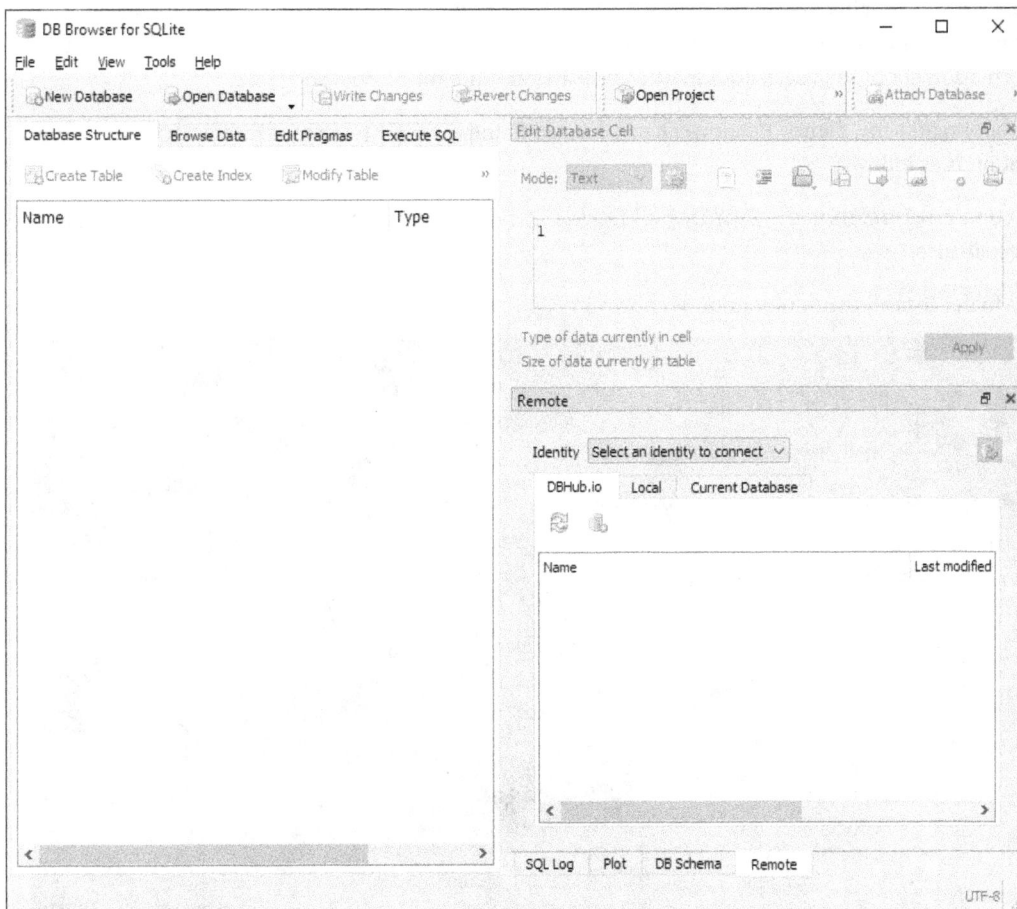

Figure 8.2 – SQLite parsing tool GUI

Another artifact we look at while investigating is the **Chrome cache**. The cache serves as a temporary storage location for various web page elements such as images, scripts, and other resources, which are downloaded and stored locally to enhance browsing performance. Investigating the Chrome cache can provide valuable forensic artifacts and insights into a user's online activities.

The Chrome cache locations are as follows:

- `C:\Users\USER_NAME\AppData\Local\Google\Chrome\User Data\Default\Cache`

- `C:\Users\USER_NAME\AppData\Local\Google\Chrome\User Data\ChromeDefault\Data\Cache`

In Google Chrome, *bookmarks* are stored in a file format called **JavaScript Object Notation (JSON)**. JSON is a lightweight data-interchange format that is easy for computers to parse and humans to read. For forensic analysts, investigating Chrome bookmarks involves analyzing the JSON file to gather information about the user's bookmarked websites and organizational structure.

The bookmarks file, named `Bookmarks`, is located in the user's Chrome profile directory. The default location is as follows:

```
C:\Users<Username>\AppData\Local\Google\Chrome\User Data\Default\
Bookmarks
```

This folder lists all the bookmarks, as shown in *Figure 8.3*:

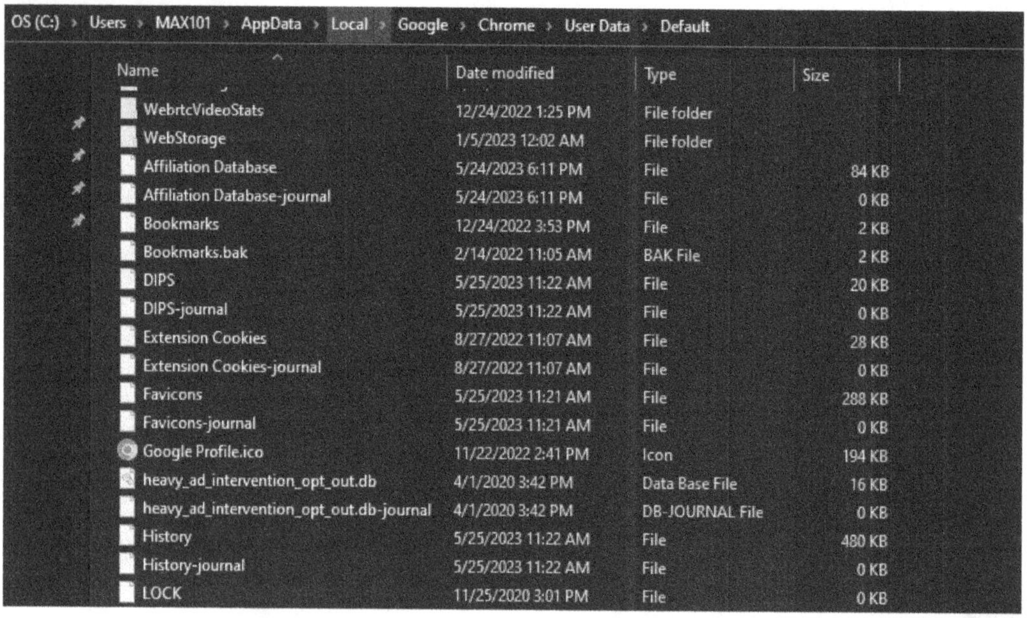

Figure 8.3 – Chrome bookmarks

The last thing we will discuss is **Chrome extensions**. Extensions in Google Chrome are additional software components that users can install to enhance functionality and customize their browsing experience. For forensic analysts, investigating Chrome extensions involves examining these components to understand their impact on the user's browser and potentially uncover valuable evidence of illicit activity, such as cybercriminals using it for crypto mining activities or the use of a VPN.

The add-ons and extensions in Google Chrome are stored in the following directory:

```
C:\Users\USER_NAME\AppData\Local\Google\Chrome\User Data\Default\
Extensions
```

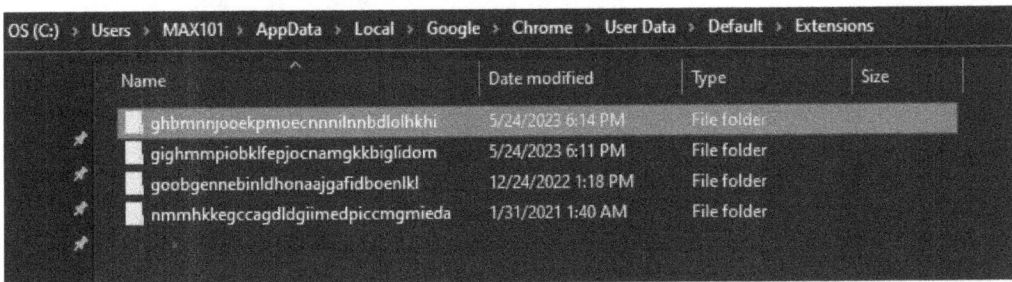

Figure 8.4 – Chrome extensions folder

Here's a tip for investigation: we can copy the folder name and check it on the Chrome store to validate the extension.

Now, let's explore Firefox.

Firefox

Firefox is a popular open source web browser developed by Mozilla Corporation. Since its initial release in 2004, Firefox has become one of the world's leading browsers, gaining a substantial user base worldwide. This summary provides an overview of the browser, its key features, and its impact on the web browsing landscape.

Firefox is known for its commitment to user privacy and security. It offers a range of privacy-oriented features, such as enhanced tracking protection, which blocks third-party trackers, preventing advertisers from monitoring users' online activities. Additionally, it has a robust set of security features, including regular updates to address vulnerabilities and protect against potential threats.

One of Firefox's distinctive features is its customizability. Users can extend and personalize their browsing experience through a vast library of add-ons and extensions. These add-ons enable users to tailor the browser to suit their preferences, adding functionality and improving productivity.

For forensic analysts, having a comprehensive understanding of the file locations and artifacts related to the Firefox web browser is essential in uncovering potential digital evidence. Firefox stores a wide range of user-related data, including browsing activities, preferences, and extensions, in specific locations within the filesystem. Here, we present a detailed explanation of some significant Firefox file locations with which forensic analysts should be well-acquainted:

- **Profile folder**, **cookies**, and **history**: Firefox stores user-specific data, including bookmarks, browsing history, saved passwords, cookies, extensions, and other settings, in a folder called `profile folder`. The location of the profile folder varies based on the operating system. In Windows, the location is as follows: `C:\Users<Username>\AppData\Roaming\Mozilla\Firefox\Profiles<ProfileID>.default`

Each user may have multiple profiles, and each profile has a unique alphanumeric identifier (`ProfileID`). The `places.sqlite` file within the profile folder is particularly relevant to forensic analysis as it contains the browser's history and bookmark data. Firefox stores cookies, which are small text files that websites use to store user information, in a `cookies.sqlite` file within the profile folder. These cookies can provide valuable information about a user's browsing habits and interactions with websites. User-entered form data, such as search queries and form submissions, are stored in the `formhistory.sqlite` file within the profile folder. This file can provide insights into a user's recent activities and interests:

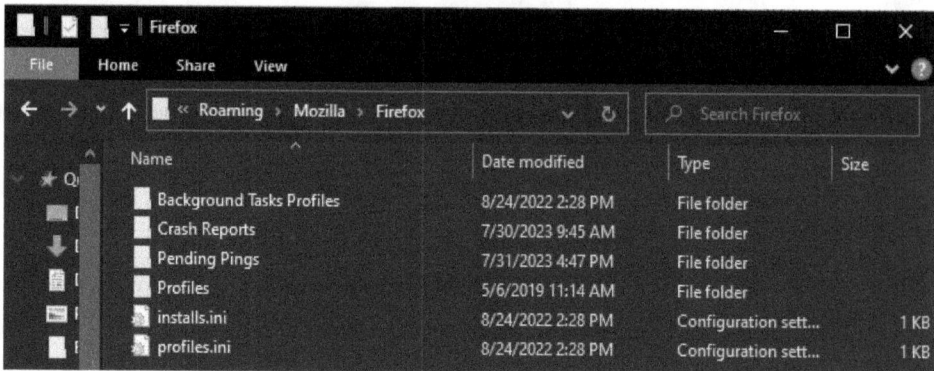

Figure 8.5 – Firefox profile folder

By clicking on **Profiles** and then navigating to any profile within the folder, we can see a list of files that we can analyze, such as `places.sqlite`, as shown in *Figure 8.6*.

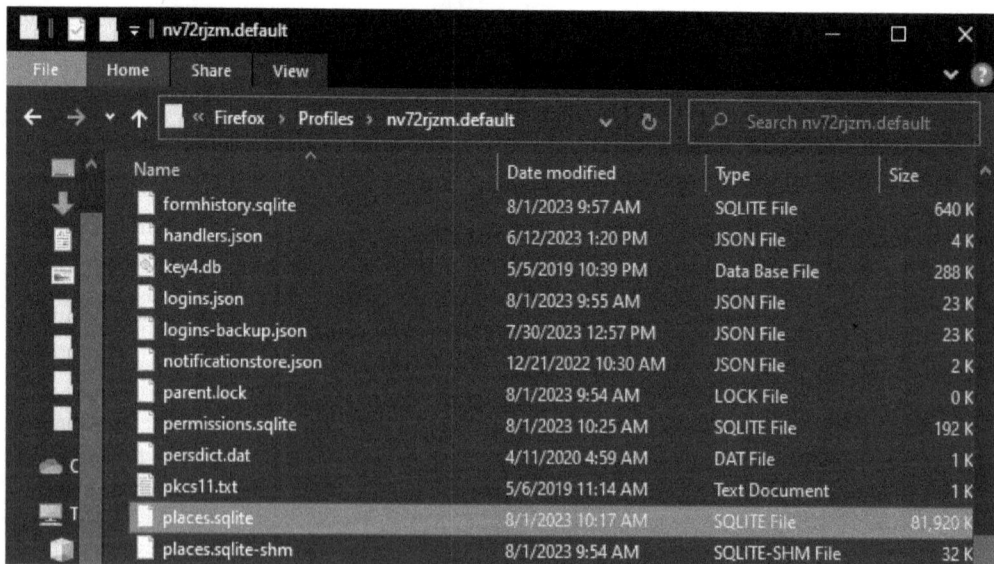

Figure 8.6 – places.sqlite profile in Firefox

Since we want to focus on valuable information that will help forensic examinations, we will focuse on the following:

- **Cache**: The browser's cache, which stores temporary copies of web pages and media, is saved in the `cache2` folder within the profile folder. The cached files can be useful for understanding a user's online activities but may also contain remnants of previously visited websites.

- **Bookmark**: Bookmarks and navigation history are stored in an SQLite database, providing an organized and efficient way to manage this data. The SQLite database used for this purpose is named `places.sqlite`.

- **Extensions and add-ons**: Add-ons and extensions in Firefox are stored in the form of folders. The Firefox browser utilizes two separate SQLite databases to manage these files.

- **Preference setting**: Firefox stores various user-specific configurations, options, and preferences in a configuration file named `prefs.js`. This file contains a collection of key-value pairs representing different settings that users have customized within the browser, located at `C:\Users\USER_NAME\AppData\Roaming\Mozilla\Firefox\Profiles[profileID].default\prefs.js`.

In *Figure 8.7*, we can see a list of extensions within the `Extensions` folder.

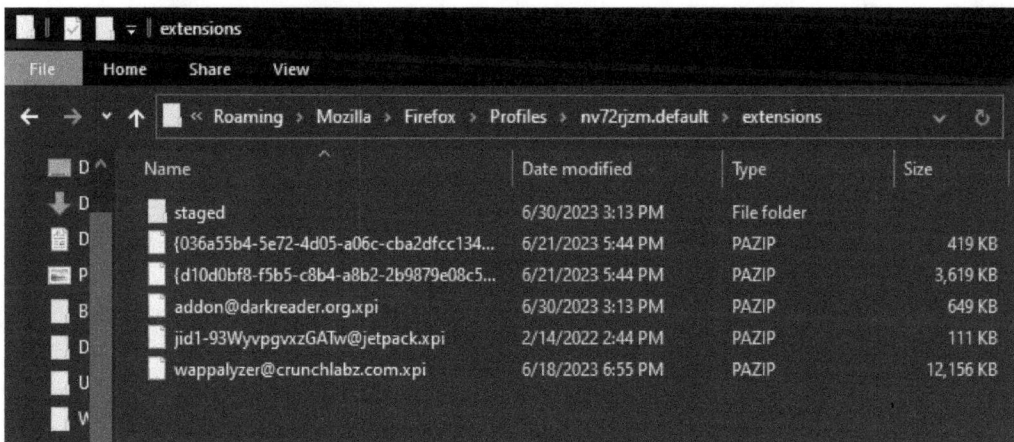

Figure 8.7 – Firefox add-ons extensions folder

Since Firefox 3, there has been a significant shift in how the browser stores its critical information. Firefox developers opted for the SQLite format, which has remained consistently used in subsequent versions. SQLite is favored for applications requiring lightweight database capabilities without the complexities of a full database solution.

SQLite is an efficient, self-contained, open source database engine known for its simplicity. Its standardized format makes it an excellent fit for handling various user-related information within

Firefox, including history, bookmarks, cookies, and form entries. This choice enables Firefox to efficiently organize and manage data in a structured manner.

By adopting SQLite, Firefox significantly improved its data storage and retrieval processes, leading to enhanced performance and reduced overhead compared to traditional database solutions. The lightweight nature of SQLite aligns perfectly with Firefox's aim to deliver a fast and responsive browsing experience for its users.

In the context of Firefox, SQLite is used to handle critical data, and several important databases are maintained within the browser's profile folder. Some of the key databases used by Firefox include the following:

- `places.sqlite`: This database is one of the most crucial ones in Firefox. It stores the browser's history, bookmarks, and tags. The `moz_places` table within `places.sqlite` contains the URLs visited by the user, along with timestamps, visit count, and other related information. The `moz_bookmarks` table stores the user's bookmarked URLs and their folder structure.

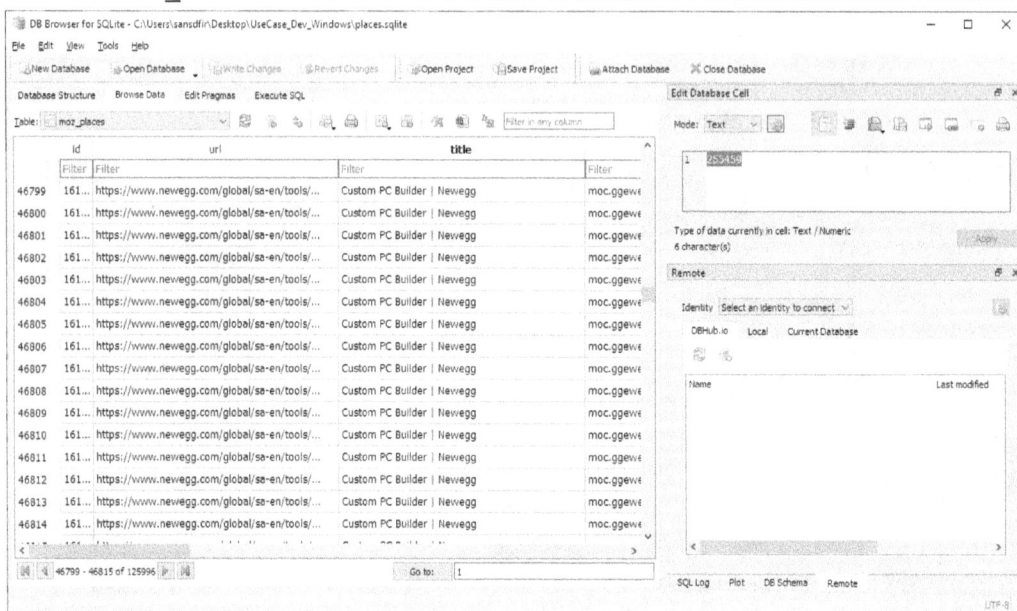

Figure 8.8 – moz_places in Firefox

- `cookies.sqlite`: This database stores cookies from websites visited by the user. Cookies are small pieces of data that websites use to remember users and their preferences, such as login information and session data.

- `formhistory.sqlite`: This database maintains form history data, storing user-entered information in web forms, such as search queries and form submissions, as we can see in the following PowerShell search result from Google:

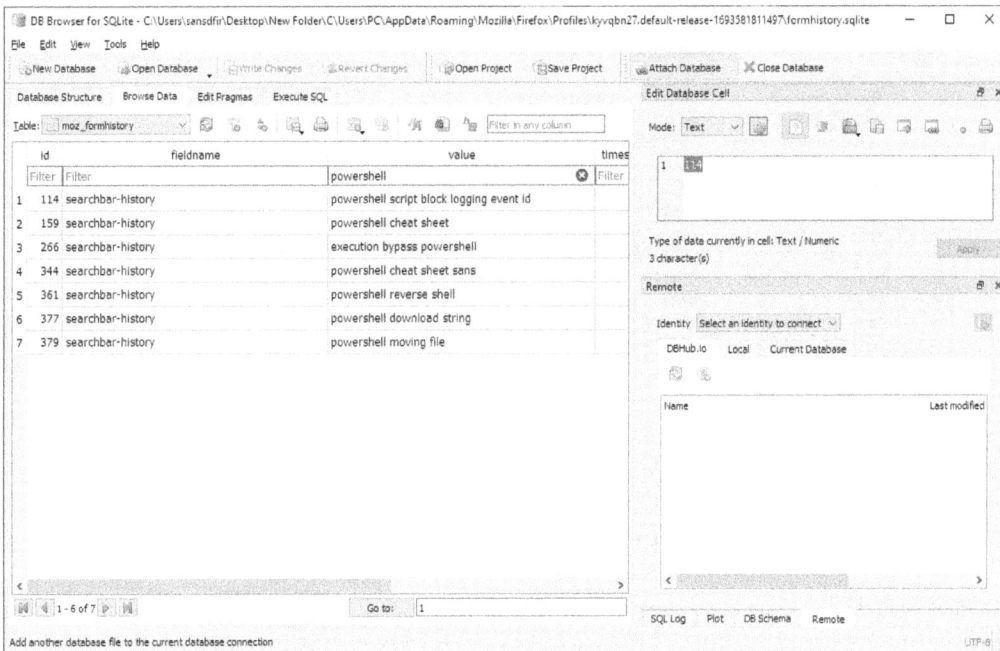

Figure 8.9 – formhistory.sqlite result in Firefox

- `downloads.sqlite`: This database keeps track of downloaded files, recording details such as the download URL, destination folder, start and end times, and downloaded file size
- `webappsstore.sqlite`: This database stores web application data, including data from web applications that implement the **Web Storage** API, such as `localStorage` and `sessionStorage`

The `moz_places` table contains information about each website that the user has visited, including the URL, as shown in *Figure 8.10*.

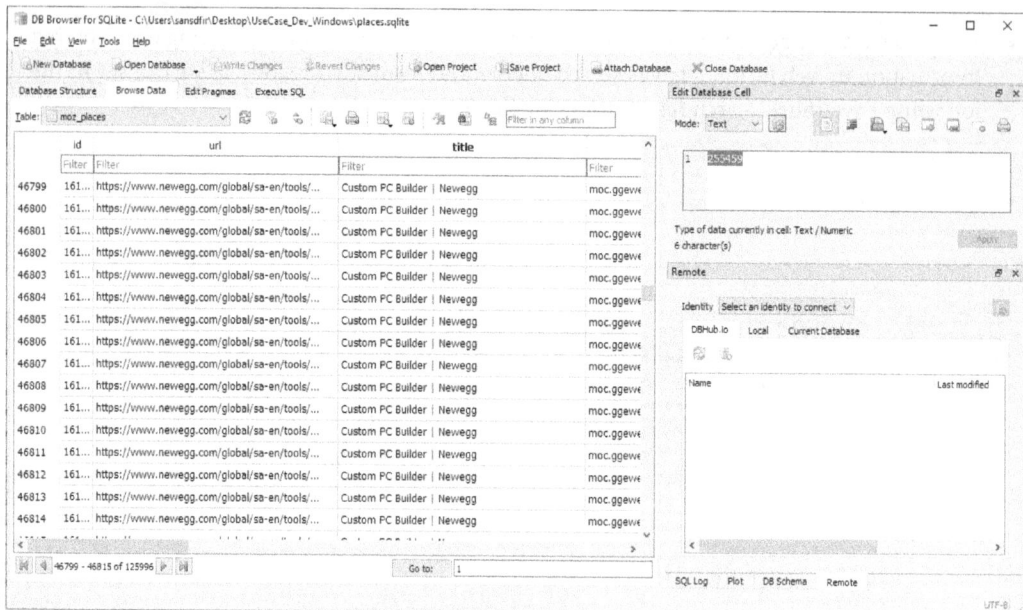

Figure 8.10 – moz_places table in places.sqlite

As we have seen, browser artifacts contain valued evidence in digital forensics. As web technologies continue to evolve, the field of web browser forensic analysis will also advance, presenting new challenges and opportunities. Staying up to date with the latest browser versions, techniques, and tools is essential for digital forensic practitioners.

Browser forensics exercises

Let's apply what we have learned so far. Try to complete these exercises:

1. Check the 24-hour history for Google Chrome using the DB for SQLite tool.

2. Validate the downloaded files from Google Chrome.

3. Explore Firefox's `places.sqlite` file and extract evidence of file downloads.

Summary

In conclusion, the field of browser forensics encompasses the investigation and analysis of various web browsers to extract valuable evidence related to a user's online activities. Throughout this chapter, we have explored the forensic artifacts and techniques associated with popular web browsers, such as IE, Microsoft Edge, and Google Chrome.

We learned about the different versions of IE, from IE6 to IE11, and the evolving features and improvements of each iteration. We discussed the location of important data, including the history and the cache, and how forensic analysts can extract and analyze this data to gain insights into a user's browsing habits.

Moving on to Microsoft Edge, we explored its transition from the legacy EdgeHTML engine to the Chromium-based Edge. We discussed the databases used by Edge to store browsing history, cookies, and other artifacts, and how they can be examined to uncover evidence.

Google Chrome, one of the most popular web browsers, provides us with a wealth of forensic artifacts. We examined its history, cache, bookmarks, extensions, and downloads, and discovered the locations of these files and the significance of their contents in forensic investigations.

Throughout the chapter, we emphasized the importance of proper forensic techniques, tools, and methodologies for extracting, parsing, and analyzing browser artifacts. The ability to reconstruct a user's browsing history, identify visited websites, retrieve deleted files, and uncover potential evidence is crucial in digital investigations.

Browser forensics requires a deep understanding of the underlying data structures, storage locations, and encryption mechanisms employed by different browsers. It also necessitates staying up-to-date with the latest browser versions and their evolving features.

By using the knowledge and techniques discussed in this chapter, forensic analysts can effectively navigate the complexities of browser forensics, aid in the investigation of various cybercrimes and digital incidents, and uncover valuable evidence for legal proceedings.

In the next chapter, we will be diving into additional important artifacts for Windows.

Exploring Additional Artifacts

In today's interconnected world, where digital technologies permeate every aspect of our lives, email communication and cloud storage services have become indispensable tools for individuals and organizations alike. The reliance on these platforms for communication, data storage, and collaboration has elevated their importance in forensic investigation as rich sources of digital evidence.

Email forensics focuses on the examination and analysis of email communications to uncover valuable insights. It involves techniques for retrieving, preserving, and analyzing email metadata, message content, attachments, and associated artifacts. In legal proceedings, email forensics can help establish timelines, identify key individuals involved, authenticate messages, and provide crucial evidence for cases ranging from cybercrime to intellectual property disputes.

Event logs serve the important purpose of recording actions taken by the operating system, applications on a server or device, or the user. Understanding how to analyze and investigate them is one of the essential skills a forensic analyst needs.

In this chapter, we will cover the following topics:

- Email analysis
- Event log analysis
- $MFT forensic analysis
- LNK files
- Recycle Bin
- ShellBags
- SRUM forensics
- Case study – malware infection

By the end of this chapter, you'll have a solid understanding of email forensics, event logs, and the techniques used in analyses.

Technical requirements

There are certain technical requirements for additional Windows artifacts analysis to ensure that the process is executed efficiently and effectively. The following are the technical requirements of this chapter:

- **Kernel OST viewer:** `https://www.nucleustechnologies.com/ost-viewer.html`

- **Kernel PST viewer:** `https://www.nucleustechnologies.com/pst-viewer.html`

- **Eric Zimmerman's tools:** `https://ericzimmerman.github.io/#!index.md`

Email forensic analysis

In a modern digital environment, email threats present a substantial risk, and among them, phishing emails stand out as highly pervasive and successful tactics employed by malicious actors. It is of utmost importance for individuals and organizations to grasp the nature of email threats and gain knowledge about the diverse forms of phishing emails in order to strengthen their cybersecurity measures.

Email threats encompass a wide range of malicious activities conducted through email communication. These threats aim to exploit vulnerabilities, manipulate users, and compromise systems. Common email threats include the following:

- **Phishing emails:** Phishing emails are fraudulent messages that mimic legitimate entities, such as banks, social media platforms, or trusted organizations. They aim to deceive recipients into revealing sensitive information, such as login credentials, financial data, or personal details. Phishing emails often use social engineering techniques to create a sense of urgency or fear, enticing users to click on malicious links or download infected attachments.

- **Malware distribution:** Emails can serve as carriers for malware, including viruses, ransomware, or trojans. Attackers disguise malicious software as harmless attachments or links within emails. When users interact with these attachments or links, the malware is executed, compromising the user's device and potentially spreading to connected systems.

- **Business Email Compromise (BEC):** BEC attacks target organizations by impersonating high-level executives or trusted partners. Attackers use sophisticated social engineering tactics to trick employees into performing unauthorized actions, such as transferring funds, disclosing sensitive information, or initiating fraudulent transactions. BEC attacks can result in significant financial losses and reputational damage.

- **Spam and unsolicited emails:** Spam emails are unsolicited, bulk messages sent indiscriminately to a large number of recipients. They often promote counterfeit products, scams, or malicious websites. Spam emails can clog inboxes, waste resources, and occasionally carry malware or phishing attempts.

Types of phishing emails

Phishing emails exhibit a wide range of variations, each characterized by distinct techniques and objectives. Acquiring a comprehensive understanding of the different types of phishing emails empowers individuals and organizations to effectively recognize and counter these threats. By familiarizing themselves with the common variations, they can implement proactive measures to identify and mitigate the risks posed by phishing attacks:

- **Deceptive phishing**: Deceptive phishing involves impersonating legitimate entities to trick recipients into divulging sensitive information. Attackers may create fake login pages or emails that appear to be from trusted organizations, aiming to collect usernames, passwords, or financial details.

- **Spear phishing**: Spear phishing targets specific individuals or groups, often using personalized information to gain the target's trust. Attackers conduct extensive research to craft tailored emails that appear legitimate, increasing the chances of success.

- **Whaling attacks**: Whaling attacks focus on high-profile individuals, such as executives or high-ranking officials, who possess valuable information or authority within an organization. These attacks leverage social engineering techniques to exploit the target's position and manipulate them into performing specific actions.

- **Clone phishing**: Clone phishing involves creating a replica of a legitimate email, replacing the original link or attachment with a malicious version. Attackers capitalize on the familiarity of the original email to deceive recipients into interacting with the malicious content.

- **Voice Phishing (vishing) and SMS Phishing (smishing)**: Vishing and smishing are variations of phishing that utilize voice calls or text messages instead of traditional emails. Attackers use social engineering tactics to extract sensitive information or manipulate users into taking specific actions through these channels.

Email header analysis

In cybercrime investigations involving the use of emails as a means of communication, digital forensic professionals play a critical role in examining relevant email evidence. Since criminals often employ tactics to disguise their activities, email forensics experts must employ techniques such as email header analysis to uncover crucial evidence.

Email headers contain vital information regarding the trajectory of a message from its origin to its destination. This information encompasses details such as the names of recipients and senders, timestamps indicating the times at which a message was received or sent, the email client utilized, the **Internet Service Provider** (**ISP**) involved, and the IP address of the sender. By scrutinizing these header fields and other pertinent information, forensic analysts can assess the authenticity and integrity of suspicious or malicious emails, aiding in the determination of their legitimacy and potential evidentiary value. But before jumping to header analysis, let's understand email authenticity with **Sender Policy Framework** (**SPF**), **DomainKeys Identified Mail** (**DKIM**), and **Domain-based Message Authentication, Reporting and Conformance** (**DMARC**).

When **Simple Mail Transfer Protocol (SMTP)** was initially introduced in 1982 for email transmission, email security was not a primary concern. It was anticipated that security measures would be addressed through alternative means. Over time, the need for secure email communication became evident, leading to the development of protocols that provide authentication and validation.

SMTP traffic between email servers can now be secured using the **Transport Layer Security (TLS)** protocol, which encrypts and authenticates communication. However, the original SMTP protocol did not include provisions for email authentication. As email has become a major target for various cybersecurity threats, such as spam, phishing, and email spoofing, the development of authentication and validation protocols has become crucial.

Three main email authentication and validation protocols have been created to combat these threats:

- **SPF**: SPF allows domain owners to specify authorized mail servers in DNS records. When an email is received, the recipient's mail server can check whether the sending server's IP address matches the authorized servers specified in the SPF record. This helps verify the authenticity of the sender's domain and reduces the risk of email spoofing.

- **DKIM**: DKIM uses digital signatures to authenticate the source and integrity of an email message. The sender's domain signs the email using cryptographic techniques, and the recipient's mail server can verify the signature by checking the DKIM record published in the DNS. This ensures that the email has not been modified during transit and helps detect forged or tampered messages.

- **DMARC**: DMARC combines SPF and DKIM to provide a comprehensive email authentication framework. It allows domain owners to set policies on how to handle emails that fail authentication checks. DMARC also enables reporting mechanisms that provide insight into email delivery and potential abuse, helping organizations monitor and protect their email domains.

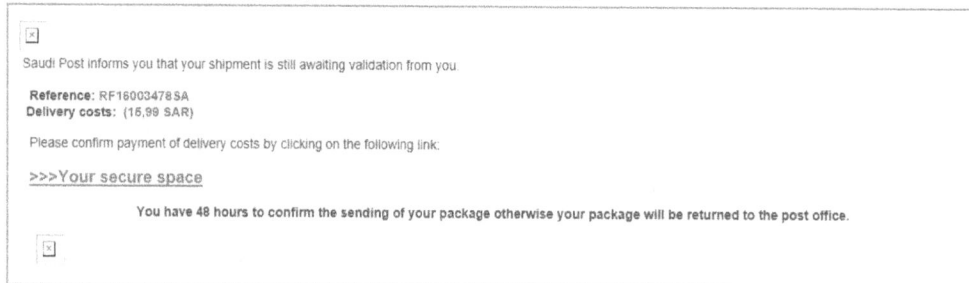

On Sun, 28 Feb at 8:56 AM , Saudi Post <support@newaccount1614437244036.freshdesk.com> wrote:

Saudi Post informs you that your shipment is still awaiting validation from you.

Reference: RF16003478SA
Delivery costs: (16,99 SAR)

Please confirm payment of delivery costs by clicking on the following link:

>>>Your secure space

You have 48 hours to confirm the sending of your package otherwise your package will be returned to the post office.

Figure 9.1: Phishing email sample

The email header is an essential element found in every email, serving as the informational "envelope" that ensures the message reaches its intended destination. It can be likened to a transit ticket that provides vital details about the email's journey. The header reveals key information, such as the sender (who made the booking), the recipient (the destination), the timestamp at which it was sent (the departure date and time), the path taken by the message (servers traversed), and the final receipt timestamp (the arrival date and time at the last server).

Considered the backbone of email communication, the header encapsulates crucial metadata that facilitates the proper routing and delivery of messages across the internet. By analyzing the email header, investigators and email administrators can gain insights into the origin, path, and timing of email transmissions. This information is invaluable in various scenarios, such as tracking the source of malicious emails, diagnosing delivery issues, investigating email-based incidents, or simply understanding the flow of communication between parties.

The key fields in email headers

The following are important fields in an email header:

Header Field	Description	Context
From	Specifies the sender of the email	The "From" field typically contains the sender's name and email address. It indicates who initiated the email communication.
To	Indicates the recipient(s) of the email	The "To" field lists the primary recipient(s) of the email. It shows who the message is intended for and who should take action or respond to the email.
Cc	Stands for "carbon copy" and includes additional recipients who receive a copy	The "Cc" field is used to include secondary recipients who receive a copy of the email. It is visible to all recipients, allowing them to see who else has been copied into the message.
Bcc	Stands for "blind carbon copy" and hides the additional recipients from others	The "Bcc" field is similar to "Cc," but it hides the secondary recipients from other recipients. This field is useful when you want to keep the list of additional recipients confidential.
Date	Specifies the date and time the email was sent	The "Date" field indicates when the email was originally sent by the sender. It helps establish a timeline for email communication and can be valuable in investigations or when tracking the sequence of events.

Header Field	Description	Context
Subject	Contains a brief description or details on the topic of the email	The "Subject" field provides a summary or description of the content or purpose of the email. It gives recipients a quick overview of the email's main subject and helps them prioritize or categorize their messages.
Message-ID	Provides a unique identifier for the email message	The "Message-ID" field is a unique identifier assigned to each email message. It helps ensure that each email can be distinguished and referenced uniquely, especially in situations where email threads or conversations are involved.
MIME-Version	Indicates the version of **Multipurpose Internet Mail Extensions (MIME)** used	The "MIME-Version" field specifies the version of the MIME protocol used for encoding email messages. MIME allows for the inclusion of various content types, such as plain text, HTML, attachments, or embedded images, in a single email message. The version number helps ensure the compatibility and proper interpretation of the message.
Content-Type	Describes the type and format of the message content	The "Content-Type" field specifies the type of content within the email, such as plain text, HTML, or multimedia attachments. It helps the recipient's email client interpret and display the message correctly. The field may also include character encoding information, allowing the recipient's email client to render the content accurately.
Return-Path	Specifies the email address to which bounce notifications should be sent	The "Return-Path" field identifies the email address where **Delivery Status Notifications (DSNs)** or bounce messages should be sent if the email encounters any delivery issues. This allows for proper error handling and enables the sender to receive notifications about undeliverable messages.
Received	Shows a history of the email's journey through different servers	The "Received" field contains a series of headers that provide a trace or record of the email's path as it traverses through various email servers. Each server that handles the message adds its own "Received" header, creating a chronological trail that can be analyzed to track the route and the sequence of servers involved in delivering the email.

Header Field	Description	Context
X-Mailer	Specifies the software or program used to send the email	The "X-Mailer" field indicates the email client or software used by the sender to compose and send the email. It provides information about the platform or application that generated the message and can be useful in diagnosing compatibility issues or identifying specific email client behaviors.
DKIM-Signature	A digital signature added by the sender to verify the integrity of the email	The "DKIM-Signature" field contains a cryptographic signature generated by the sender's domain using the DKIM protocol. This signature helps verify the authenticity and integrity of the email message, ensuring that it has not been altered or tampered with during transit. It aids in detecting forged or modified messages.
SPF-Record	Indicates the sender's specified SPF record	The "SPF-Record" field indicates the SPF record published by the sender's domain. SPF is a DNS-based email authentication protocol that specifies which mail servers are authorized to send emails on behalf of a domain. The "SPF-Record" field helps recipients verify whether the sending server is authorized, reducing the risk of email spoofing or impersonation.
X-Originating-IP	Provides the IP address of the device that originated the email	The "X-Originating-IP" field reveals the IP address of the device from which the email originated. It can provide insights into the geographic location or network from which the email was sent. This information can be valuable in identifying the source of suspicious or malicious emails, aiding forensic investigation in determining the authenticity of the email's origin.

Table 9.1: The key elements of email headers

Analyzing an email header sample from the phishing_pot project

Here, we will present an email header sample from the `phishing_pot` project, which is hosted on `https://github.com/rf-peixoto/phishing_pot`.

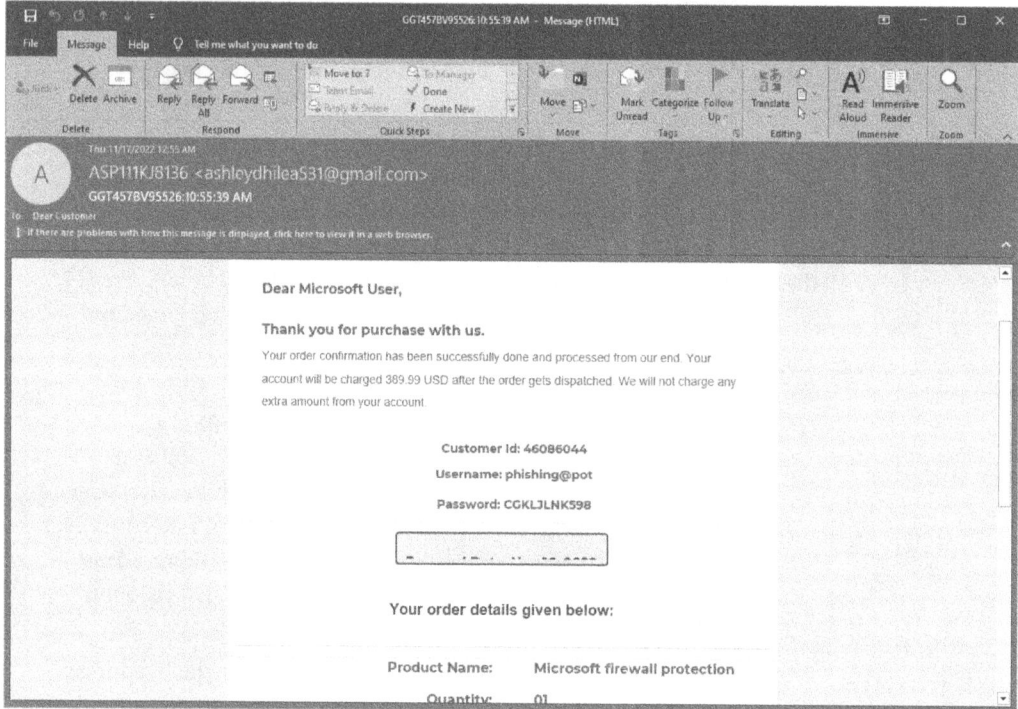

Figure 9.2: Phishing email sample 2

Since we have learned about the multiple fields found in email headers, let's examine an email header and try to incorporate what we have learned into our initial investigation of a potentially suspicious email.

In order to get the email header, we need to get it mostly on an enterprise level from email gateway security control; alternatively, if we have a sample of the email, we can get it using Outlook by clicking on **File | Properties**, which will show us the email header.

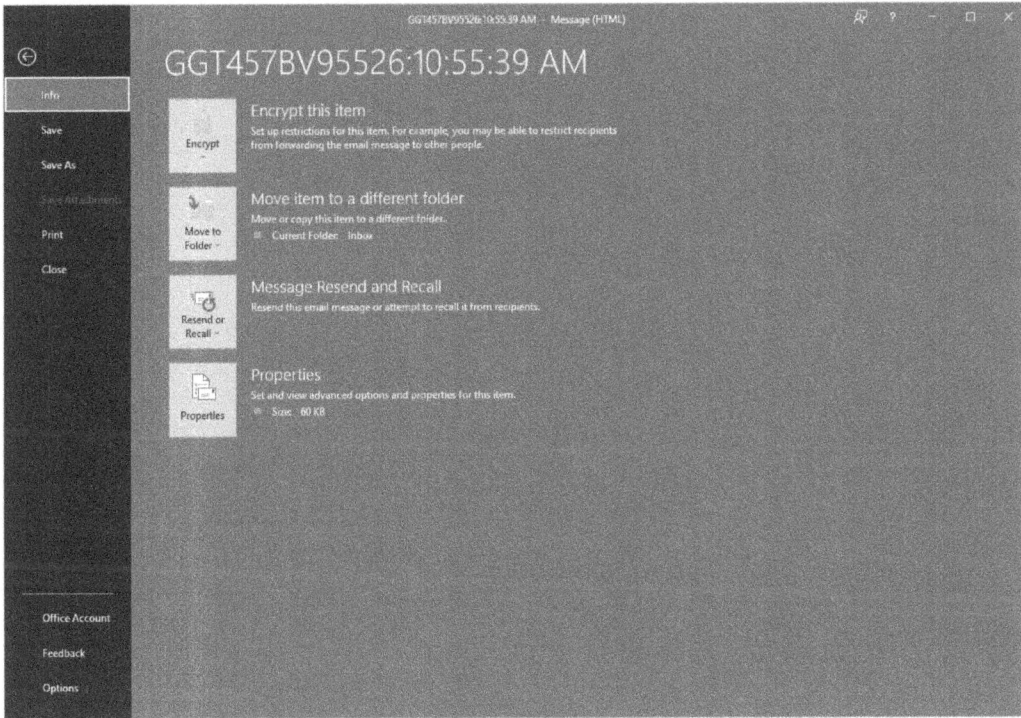

Figure 9.3: Option to display the email header using Outlook

The sample can then be copied and pasted into Notepad for analysis:

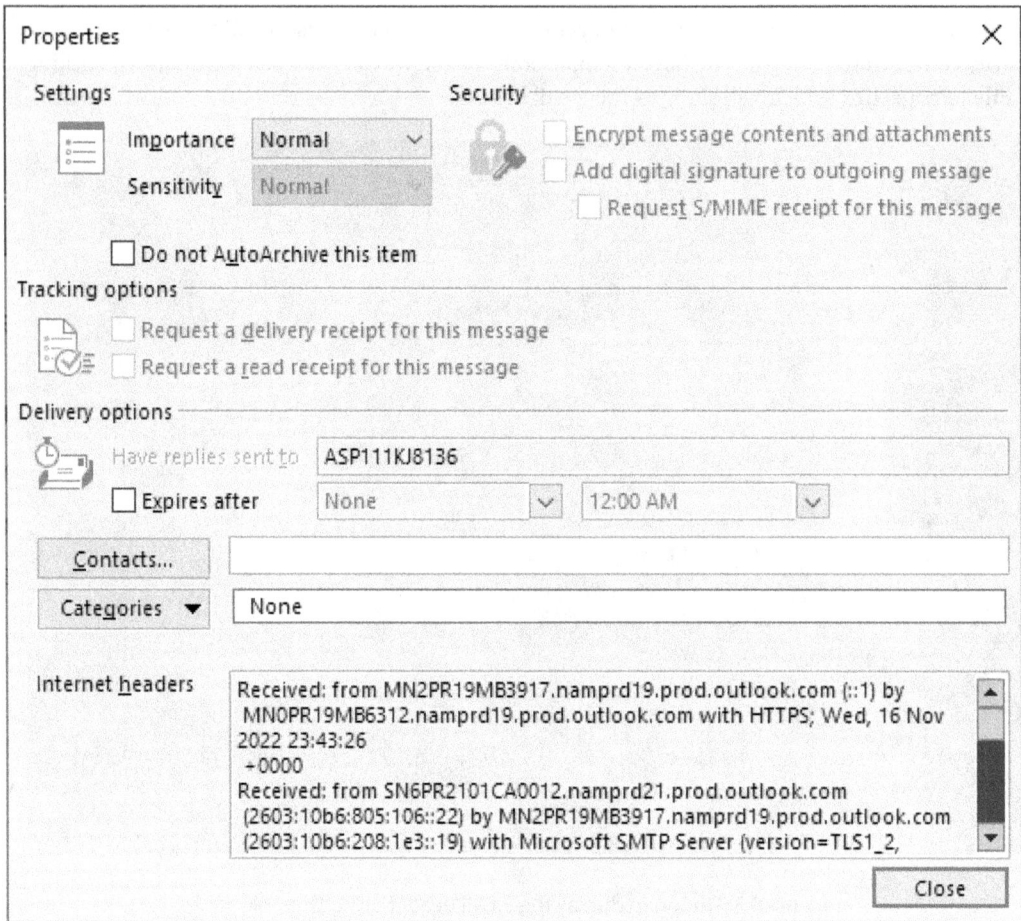

Figure 9.4: Exploring the email header using Outlook

The following screenshot shows some samples of Email headers with some important field highlighted:

```
Received-SPF Pass (protection.outl  •   +
File   Edit   View

Received-SPF: Pass (protection.outlook.com: domain of gmail.com designates
 209.85.218.68 as permitted sender) receiver-protection.outlook.com;
 client-ip=209.85.218.68; helo=mail-ej1-f68.google.com; pr=C
Received: from mail-ej1-f68.google.com (209.85.218.68) by
 SN1NAM02FT0062.mail.protection.outlook.com (10.97.4.69) with Microsoft SMTP
 Server (version=TLS1_2, cipher-TLS_ECDHE_RSA_WITH_AES_256_GCM_SHA384) id
 15.20.5813.12 via Frontend Transport; Wed, 16 Nov 2022 23:43:25 +0000
X-Incoming TopHeaderMarker:
OriginalChecksum:58AF42866522C312266BB570F1819A9821D3CD0D268CFBB47DC753DFEBEFC7F0;UpperCasedChecksum:A7223D6C0EFB8B4B70AA4C9991933A98955CA3135037651E23
83A39CA32E4D99;SizeAsReceived:2714;Count:18
Received: by mail-ej1-f68.google.com with SMTP id n21s0978775ejb.9
    for <phishing@pot>; Wed, 16 Nov 2022 15:43:25 -0800 (PST)
DKIM-Signature: v=1; a=rsa-sha256; c=relaxed/relaxed;
    d=gmail.com; s=20210112;
    h-content-transfer-encoding:mime-version:date:subject:to:from
    :reply-to:message-id:from:to:cc:subject:date:message-id:reply-to; bh=SMJ90oCQwkRk8anwke3ltgoFxXfCi+EnU3IP2tP3sUc=;
    rklg==
X-Google-DKIM-Signature: v=1; a=rsa-sha256; c=relaxed/relaxed;
    d-1e100.net; s=20210112;
    h-content-transfer-encoding:mime-version:date:subject:to:from
    :reply-to:message-id:x-gm-message-state:from:to:cc:subject:date
    :message-id:reply-to;
    bh-SMJ900CQwkRk8anwke3ltgoFxXfCi+EnU3IP2tP3sUc=;
    XH9w==
X-Gm-Message-State: ANo85pnXncGhduTazPRPLSVXLJErijxHQ+19EJUuLXuoPeE/VRn05dc+ CH9SwcFkBde2hxgEuXkuTKZ7hje1iUb+Og==
X-Google-Smtp-Source: AA0mqf4BZgrG98lUk05GqzcF2r1tzRFVjRc/yQDCTAOqAgRtew30ac5cZBL3jEurkzcK+pdH7H6/gg==
X-Received: by 2002:aa7:c74c:0:b0:44e:bee5:4242 with SMTP id c12-20020aa7c74c000000b0044ebee54242mr20823401eds.128.1668635742644;
    Wed, 16 Nov 2022 13:55:42-0800 (PST)
Return-Path: ashleydhilea531@gmail.com
Received: from admin0006 ([92.223.89.133])
    by smtp.gmail.com with ESMTPSA id 23-20020a170906329700b007821f4bc328sm7381778ejw.178.2022.11.16.13.55.41
    for <phishing@pot>
    (version=TLS1 cipher-DES-CBC3-SHA bits=112/168);
    Wed, 16 Nov 2022 13:55:42 -0800 (PST)
Message-ID: <028bb749-44882-06f94553209954@admin0006>
Reply-To: "ASP111KJ8136" <ashleydhilea531@gmail.com>
From: "ASP111KJ8136" <ashleydhilea531@gmail.com>
To: "Dear Customer" <phishing@pot>
Subject: GGT457BV95526:10:55:39 AM
Date: Thu, 17 Nov 2022 10:54:41 +1300
Content-Type: text/html
Content-Transfer-Encoding: 8bit
X-IncomingHeaderCount: 18
X-MS-Exchange-Organization-ExpirationStartTime: 16 Nov 2022 23:43:25.7793(UTC)
Ln 44, Col 74                                                        100%
```

Figure 9.5: Email header sample with fields highlighted

Analyzing Outlook emails

Our focus in this book will be on Microsoft Outlook for investigation. However, we can apply the same concept when it comes to email header analysis to any other mail application.

Since Outlook is dominant at the enterprise level and is the most used email client software, it helps us in terms of knowing where we can locate the repository that holds the emails. Outlook saves files under the `%UserProfile%\AppData\Local\Microsoft\Outlook` folder; or, in `%UserProfile%\Documents\Outlook`, we can see **Offline Storage** (**OST**) and PST files. OST files are offline storage table data files. An OST file is created when Outlook is configured to work in Cached Exchange Mode, which allows users to access their mailbox data even when offline. PST files are commonly used for POP3, IMAP, or web-based email accounts where messages are downloaded to the user's computer.

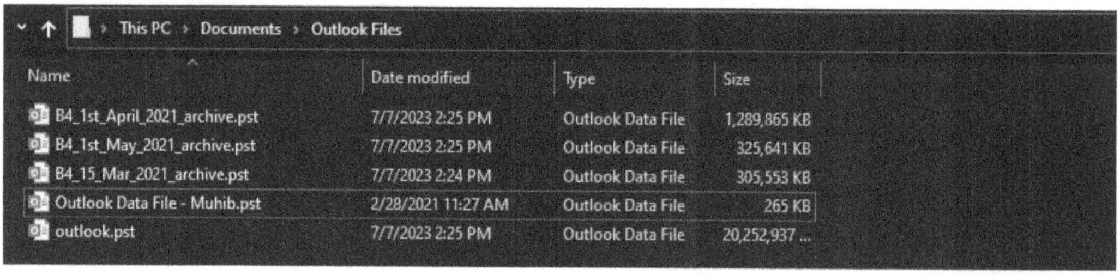

Figure 9.6: PST files in the Documents folder

To analyze such a file, we will use **Kernel OST viewer** and **Kernel PST viewer**; these can be downloaded by visiting `https://www.nucleustechnologies.com/ost-viewer.html` for Kernel OST viewer and `https://www.nucleustechnologies.com/pst-viewer.html` for Kernel PST viewer.

Kernel OST viewer is a powerful software tool designed specifically for forensic examiners and investigators who deal with Microsoft Outlook OST files. OST files are local copies of mailbox data that allow users to access their Outlook emails, contacts, calendars, and other items even when they are not connected to the Exchange server.

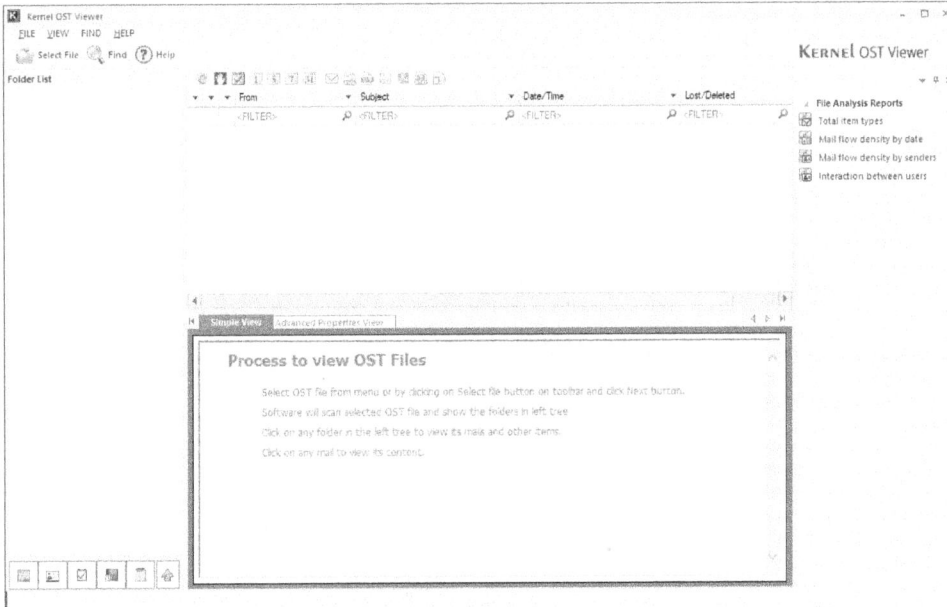

Figure 9.7: The Kernel OST viewer GUI

To open an OST file, we can click on **Select File**, as highlighted in the preceding figure, and select the path in which we stored or collected the OST file to start loading it. Similar to Kernel OST viewer, we can use Kernel PST viewer to load a PST file, as shown here.

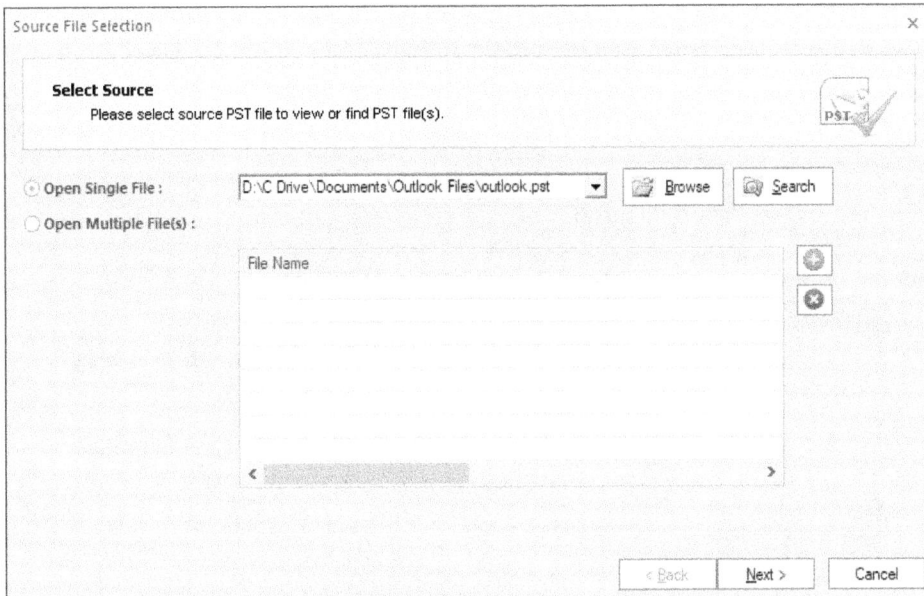

Figure 9.8: Loading a PST file using Kernel PST viewer

Once we click on **Next >**, it will start loading it; the time taken will be based on the size of the PST file.

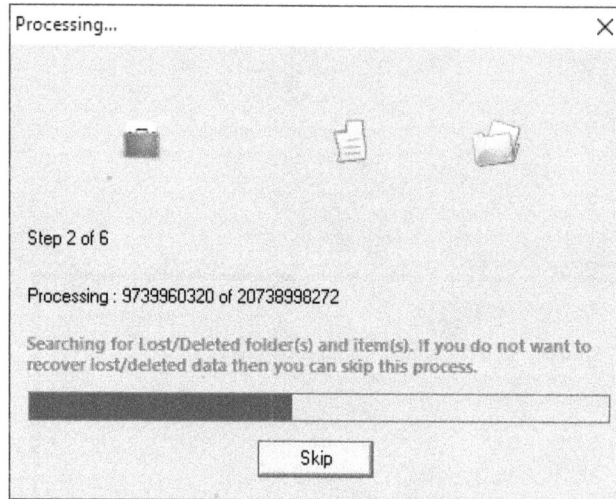

Figure 9.9: PST viewer processing a PST file

Another great feature is that we can use the application to load multiple PST files to explore. After loading the content of the PST file, in the following screenshot, I've blurred the section that contains sensitive information.

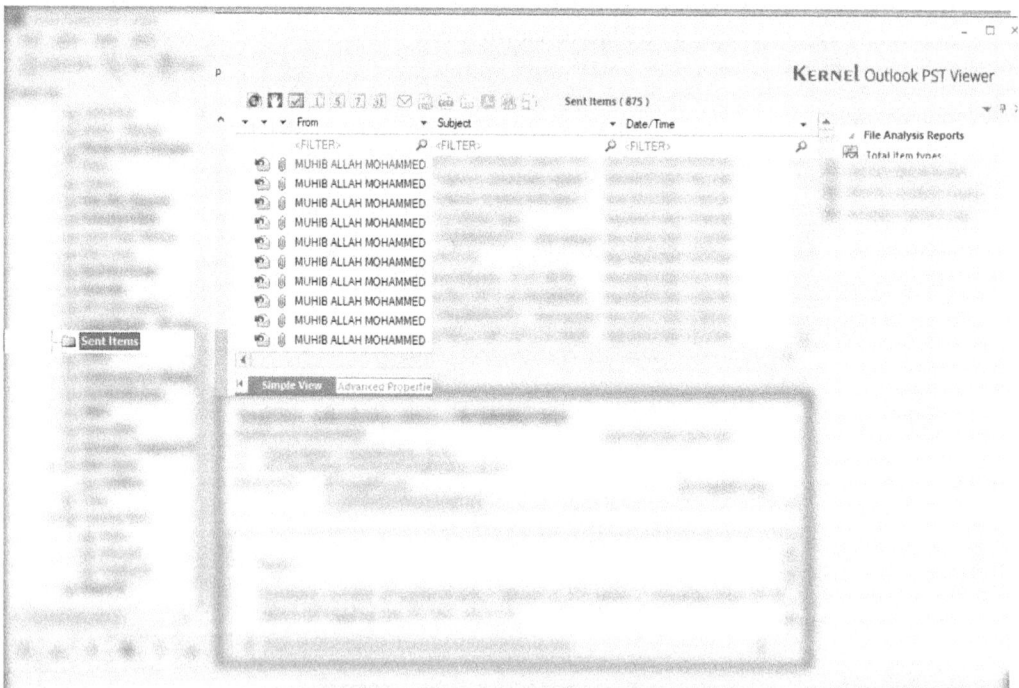

Figure 9.10: Kernel PST viewer after loading the PST file

Now we can explore the content of the collected PST file and analyze it. Some of the scenarios in which it might be useful to use such a tool include insider threats and phishing investigations to check whether an email exists or not.

Now we have covered email analysis and understood which tools to use, let's move on to event log analysis.

Event log analysis

Windows event logs serve as a valuable source of digital evidence for forensic analysts investigating security incidents, system anomalies, or suspicious activities on Windows operating systems. These logs record a variety of events and activities that occur within the operating system, providing a detailed trail of information that can aid in understanding the timeline of events, identifying potential threats, and reconstructing the sequence of actions taken by users or attackers.

Windows event logs serve as a crucial resource for forensic analysts for the following reasons:

- **Event collection**: Windows event logs encompass a broad spectrum of events, including system events, security events, and application events. These logs capture essential information regarding user logins, system startup and shutdown, file access, network connections, software installations, and other significant activities. Through the collection and examination of these logs, forensic analysts gain valuable insights into the actions executed on the system.

- **Timelines and correlation**: Event logs play a pivotal role in establishing timelines and correlating activities across various events. By scrutinizing the timestamps of events, investigators can decipher the chronological order, detect patterns, and comprehend the progression of an incident. This comprehensive perspective on the transpired activities assists in constructing a cohesive narrative during forensic investigations.

- **User activity analysis**: Event logs offer visibility into user activities, including logins, logouts, account creations, and modifications. Forensic analysts scrutinize these logs to identify unauthorized access attempts, suspicious user behaviors, or any indications of compromised accounts. Such insights are crucial for attributing specific actions to individuals, establishing associations between user accounts, and detecting potential insider threats.

- **System and application monitoring**: Event logs capture system and application events that can provide insights into system health, errors, and anomalies. Forensic analysts analyze these logs to identify system misconfigurations, software crashes, or indications of malware infections. By examining error codes and descriptions, analysts can pinpoint potential issues or vulnerabilities that may have contributed to a security incident.

- **Security incident response**: Windows event logs play a vital role in security incident response efforts. In the event of a security breach, forensic analysts utilize event logs to identify the initial point of compromise, track lateral movement within the network, and determine the scope of the incident. Furthermore, event logs can provide valuable **indicators of compromise** (**IOCs**), which aid in identifying malicious activities, such as unauthorized access attempts, malware execution, or suspicious network connections.

Main event logs are a fundamental component of Windows event logging and record a wide range of system and application events occurring on a Windows operating system. These logs play a critical role in system monitoring, troubleshooting, and forensic investigations. There are several main event logs in Windows, each serving a specific purpose:

- **Application logs**: An application log captures events related to applications installed on the system. This log records information such as application crashes, errors, warnings, and other events generated by applications running on the system. It helps in identifying issues with specific applications and provides insights into their performance and behavior.

- **Security logs**: A security log is crucial for monitoring security-related events. It records events such as successful or failed login attempts, changes to user accounts and security policies, system access permissions, and other security-related activities. The security log is a valuable resource for detecting unauthorized access attempts, identifying potential security breaches, and investigating security incidents.

- **System logs**: A system log captures events related to the Windows operating system itself. It records information about system startup and shutdown, hardware and driver failures, system service events, and other system-level events. The system logs help in diagnosing system issues, identifying hardware or software failures, and tracking changes to system configurations.

Event logs are stored in .evt files for versions of Windows before Vista, such as Windows XP and Server 2003, under `%systemroot%\system32\config\security.evt`. Newer versions of Windows store it in .evtx format in `%systemroot%\system32\winevt\logs\security.evtx`.

Here are the most utlized logs within Windows events:

Log Name	Location
Application log	`%SystemRoot%\System32\Winevt\Logs\Application.evtx`
Security log	`%SystemRoot%\System32\Winevt\Logs\Security.evtx`
System log	`%SystemRoot%\System32\Winevt\Logs\System.evtx`

Table 9.2: Windows event logs location

Security event logs

Security logs are important in any forensic investigation when it comes to user authentication, user action, and security setting changes. A security log is a critical component of auditing and recording events based on the specified criteria defined by the audit policy. It offers valuable insights into a wide range of system and user actions, including user authentication procedures such as logons, RunAs commands, and remote access. Furthermore, the security logs track user activities after authentication, enabling administrators to effectively monitor and analyze user interactions within a system.

An important aspect of a security log is its ability to capture events related to privilege use and object auditing. For example, if a protected file or folder is accessed, the security log generates an event that provides details such as the user account responsible for the access and the precise date and time it occurred. This information serves as a vital resource for tracking and investigating potential security breaches or instances of unauthorized access.

Additionally, the security log allows you to audit security settings themselves, creating a comprehensive record of any modifications made to the existing security policies on the system. This feature ensures that changes to security configurations are accurately documented and can be reviewed to ensure compliance and strengthen overall security measures.

In the following table, we have listed some of the important event IDs that are considered during an investigation:

Event ID	Description
4624	An account was successfully logged on
4625	An account failed to log on
4634	An account was logged off
4647	The user-initiated logoff
4656	A handle for an object was requested
4658	The handle for an object was closed
4663	An attempt was made to access an object
4672	Special privileges were assigned to a new logon
4688	A new process has been created
4698	A scheduled task was created
4700	A scheduled task was enabled
4719	A system audit policy was changed
4720	A user account was created

Event ID	Description
4726	A user account was deleted
4728	A member was added to a security-enabled global group
4729	A member was removed from a security-enabled global group
4732	A member was added to a security-enabled local group
4733	A member was removed from a security-enabled local group
4740	A user account was locked out
4741	A computer account was created
4742	A computer account was changed
4743	A computer account was deleted
4756	A member was added to a security-enabled universal group
4757	A member was removed from a security-enabled universal group
4776	The domain controller attempted to validate the credentials for an account
4778	A session was reconnected to a Windows station
4779	A session was disconnected from a Windows station
4781	The name of an account was changed
4798	A user's local group membership was enumerated
4799	Security-enabled local group membership was enumerated
4800	The workstation was locked
4801	The workstation was unlocked
4802	The screen saver was invoked
4803	The screen saver was dismissed
4964	Special groups have been assigned to a new logon
5024	The Windows Firewall service was started successfully
5025	The Windows Firewall service has been stopped
5032	Windows Firewall was unable to notify the user that it blocked an application from accepting incoming connections on the network

Table 9.3: List of important Windows event IDs

To analyze `evtx` files, we can use PowerShell if we are using live response, or we can use `LogParser`, `evtwalk`, or `EvtxECmd`, which are command-line tools used to parse and export `evtx` files into multiple formats, such as CSV format.

Application event logs

Application event logs in Windows play a crucial role in tracking and recording events related to applications and software running on the system. These logs provide valuable information about application errors, installations, updates, and other critical events. Here is an overview of the application events:

Event ID	Description
1000	An application error occurred, indicating a crash or unexpected termination of an application
1001	**Windows Error Reporting (WER)** – an application crash occurred, providing additional information about the application error and potential solutions
1002	An application hang event, indicating an application became unresponsive or stopped responding
1003	WER – an application hang event, providing detailed information about the application hang and suggestions for resolving the issue
1004	An application information event, providing general details about an application launch or start
1005	WER – application launch failure event, indicating that an application failed to start or launch
1006	An application performance event, providing information about the performance of an application
1007	An application error occurred due to a faulty module or component
1008	WER – an application error reporting event, indicating the application's response to a WER request for additional data or debugging information
1010	An application information event, providing details about the application being updated or patched
1011	WER – application check event, indicating that the application is performing a check for a specific condition or state

Table 9.4: Application event IDs

Windows event analysis is a critical practice for maintaining the security, stability, and performance of Windows systems along with the evidence it provides for forensic examination. By understanding the significance of event logs and being familiar with key event IDs, organizations can effectively detect, protect, and respond to potential threats, ensure optimal system performance, and safeguard their digital ecosystems.

This interactive journey into the world of Windows event analysis has equipped us with the knowledge and tools to become digital detectives and uncover hidden insights in event logs.

Analyzing $MFT

Within the realm of computer forensics, the **Master File Table (MFT)** assumes a pivotal role within the Windows operating system. Functioning as a repository, the MFT houses vital details pertaining to every file and directory stored on a computer's hard drive.

The $MFT is one of the most important files within NTFS. This artifact keeps a record of all files in the volume, as well as the file location and metadata, and an entry for dates relating to creation, modification, and access. The information stored within this artifact is called MFT entries.

Each file has its own entry in $MFT, starting from 0 being the $MFT entry.

The structure of the MFT in NTFS is complex and consists of multiple records, each of which represents a file or directory on the NTFS volume. Each MFT record is 1,024 bytes, making the MFT very simple to parse. An MFT record has the following general structure:

- **File record header**: This section contains information about the record itself, including the size of the record, the offset of the update sequence, and the flags that indicate the state of the file or directory.

- **File attribute list**: This section contains a list of attributes that describe the file or directory, including its name, timestamps, size, and data. Each attribute is stored as a separate structure with its format.

- **Data runs**: This section describes the location of the file or directory's data on the disk. The data runs are stored as a series of extents describing the starting cluster and the length of each contiguous data block.

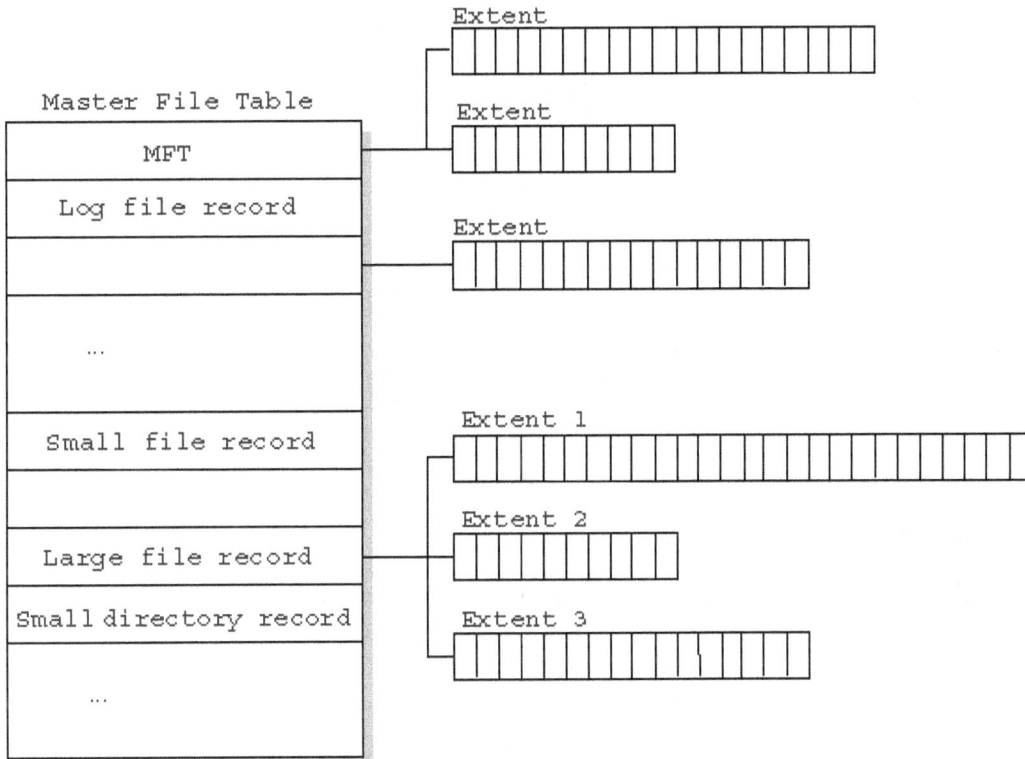

Figure 9.11: MFT structure

When a file's attributes can fit within the MFT file record, they are called resident attributes. For example, information such as filename and timestamp are always included in the MFT file record.

When all of the information for a file is too large to fit in the MFT file record, some of its attributes are nonresident. The nonresident attributes are allocated one or more clusters of disk space elsewhere in the volume.

When all attributes cannot be accommodated within a single MFT record, NTFS generates additional MFT records. It then includes an Attribute List attribute within the first file's MFT record to outline the whereabouts of all the attribute records.

The following table lists all of the file attributes currently defined by NTFS. This list is extensible, meaning that other file attributes can be defined in the future:

Attribute Type	Description
Standard Information	Includes information such as timestamp and link count.
Attribute List	Lists the location of all attribute records that do not fit in the MFT record.
File Name	A repeatable attribute for both long and short filenames. The long name of the file can be up to 255 Unicode characters. Additional names, or hard links, required by POSIX can be included as additional filename attributes.
Security Descriptor	Describes who owns the file and who can access it.
Data	Contains file data. NTFS allows multiple data attributes per file. Each file typically has one unnamed data attribute. A file can also have one or more named data attributes, each using a particular syntax.
Object ID	A volume-unique file identifier. Used by the distributed link tracking service. Not all files have object identifiers.
Logged Utility Stream	Similar to a data stream, but operations are logged to the NTFS log file just like NTFS metadata changes. This is used by EFS.
Reparse Point	Used for volume mount points. They are also used by **Installable File System (IFS)** filter drivers to mark certain files as special to that driver.
Index Root	Used to implement folders and other indexes.
Index Allocation	Used to implement folders and other indexes.
Bitmap	Used to implement folders and other indexes. It's a special file within the NTFS filesystem. This file keeps track of all of the used and unused clusters on an NTFS volume.
Volume Information	Used only in the $Volume system file. Contains the volume version.
Volume Name	Used only in the $Volume system file. Contains the volume label.

Table 9.5: NTFS attributes

NTFS comprises multiple system files, all of which remain concealed from sight and hidden within the NTFS volume. A system file serves as a repository for a filesystem's metadata and functions as an enabler for the filesystem's operation. The placement of these system files onto the volume is carried out by the format utility:

System File	Filename	MFT Record	Purpose of the File
Master file table	$MFT	0	Contains one base file record for each file and folder on an NTFS volume. If the allocation information for a file or folder is too large to fit within a single record, other file records are allocated as well.
Master file table 2	$MftMirr	1	A duplicate image of the first four records of the MFT. This file guarantees access to the MFT in case of a single-sector failure.
Log file	$LogFile	2	Contains a list of transaction steps used for NTFS recoverability. The log file size depends on the volume size and can be as large as 4 MB. It is used by Windows NT/2000 to restore consistency to NTFS after a system failure.
Volume	$Volume	3	Contains information about the volume, such as the volume label and the volume version.
Attribute definitions	$AttrDef	4	A table of attribute names, numbers, and descriptions.
Root filename index	$	5	The root folder.
Cluster bitmap	$Bitmap	6	A representation of the volume showing which clusters are in use.
Boot sector	$Boot	7	Includes the BPB used to mount the volume and additional bootstrap loader code used if the volume is bootable.
Bad cluster file	$BadClus	8	Contains bad clusters for the volume.
Security file	$Secure	9	Contains unique security descriptors for all files within a volume.
Upcase table	$Upcase	10	Converts lowercase characters into matching Unicode uppercase characters.
NTFS extension file	$Extend	11	Used for various optional extensions, such as quotas, reparse point data, and object identifiers.

System File	Filename	MFT Record	Purpose of the File
Quota management file	$Quota	24	Contains user-assigned quota limits on the volume space.
Object Id file	$ObjId	25	Contains file object IDs.
Reparse point file	$Reparse	26	This file contains information about files and folders on the volume including reparse point data.

Table 9.6: NTFS system files

When we consider analyzing $MFT, we have multiple tools that can help us parse this amazing artifact. For the purposes of demonstration, we will use MFTEcmd.exe, a tool developed by Eric Zimmerman.

Let's get started with MFTEcmd.exe.

MFTEcmd.exe

MFTEcmd.exe is a tool developed by Eric Zimmerman to facilitate the understanding of the metadata files on a Windows system. It is capable of processing the $MFT file, $J file, $Boot file, $SDS file, and, in the future, $LogFile file. When parsing the MFT, the user will be able to view not only the Standard_Information (x10) timestamp that is visible when using Windows File Explorer or an alternative but also the File_Name attribute (x30). The File_Name attribute can contain both long and short attributes, and additional timestamps can be added to the filename to aid in the identification of antiepileptic artifacts.

```
E:\C>mftecmd.exe -h
Description:
  MFTECmd version 1.2.2.1

  Author: Eric Zimmerman (saericzimmerman@gmail.com)
  https://github.com/EricZimmerman/MFTECmd

Examples: MFTECmd.exe -f "C:\Temp\SomeMFT" --csv "c:\temp\out" --csvf MyOutputFile.csv
          MFTECmd.exe -f "C:\Temp\SomeMFT" --csv "c:\temp\out"
          MFTECmd.exe -f "C:\Temp\SomeMFT" --json "c:\temp\jsonout"
          MFTECmd.exe -f "C:\Temp\SomeMFT" --body "c:\temp\bout" --bdl c
          MFTECmd.exe -f "C:\Temp\SomeMFT" --de 5-5
          MFTECmd.exe -f "C:\temp\SomeJ" --csv c:\temp
          MFTECmd.exe -f "C:\temp\SomeBoot"
          MFTECmd.exe -f "c:\temp\SomeSecure_SDS" --csv c:\temp
          MFTECmd.exe -f "c:\temp\SomeI30" --csv c:\temp
          Short options (single letter) are prefixed with a single dash. Long commands are prefixed with two dashes
```

Figure 9.12: MFTecmd.exe usage

By running the following command, we can start parsing $MFT:

```
MFTEcmd.exe -f $MFT --csv C:\Users\Muhib\Desktop --csvf MFT_Output.csv
-f <f>          File to process ($MFT | $J | $Boot | $SDS | $I30).
Required

--csv <csv>     Directory to save CSV formatted results to.

--csvf <csvf> File name to save CSV formatted results to. When
present, overrides default name
```

Once the process is completed, we can open the CSV file using either Microsoft Excel or, as preferred by most digital forensic examiners, Timeline Explorer. The following is what it looks like if you open the file using Timeline Explorer.

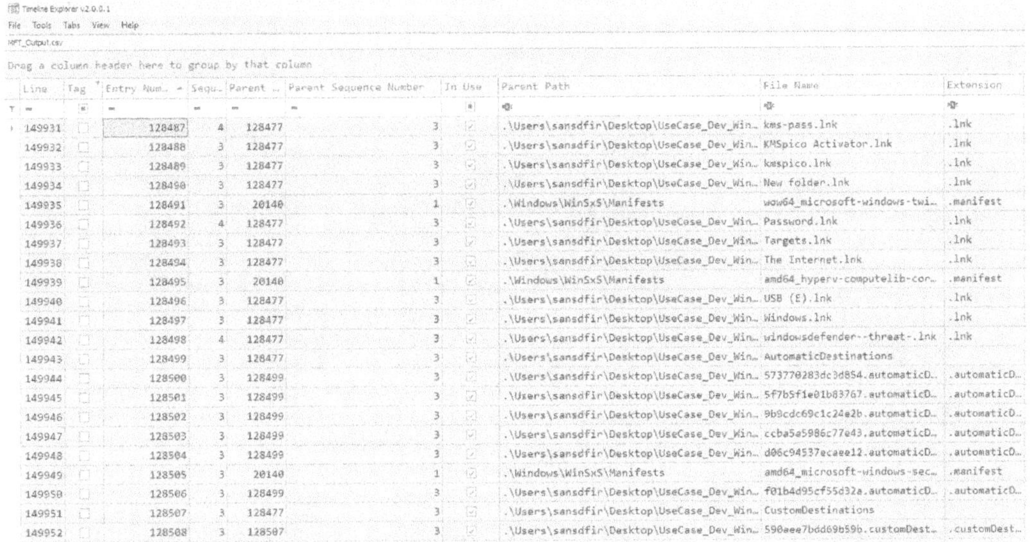

Figure 9.13: Timeline Explorer output

As we can see in the preceding screenshot, we can get useful evidence from $MFT, such as the entry number and parent entry number along with additional details on the filename and path. The most important field that we will focus on is the timestamp for each record.

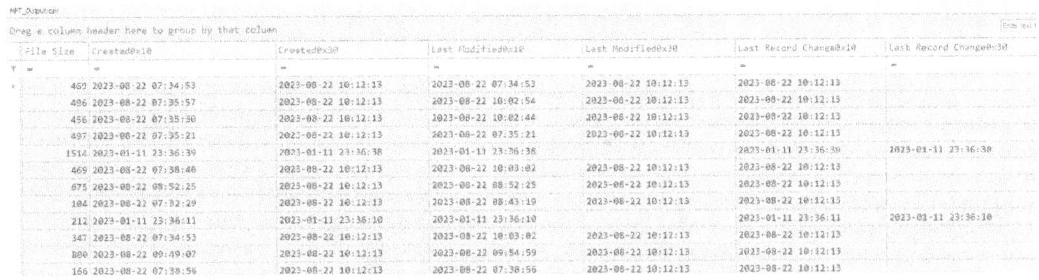

Figure 9.14: Timestamp for each entry of $MFT

Another great tool is MFT Explorer, which helps us visually explore $MFT. However, if you are considering using large $MFT files, it will take longer to process the artifact:

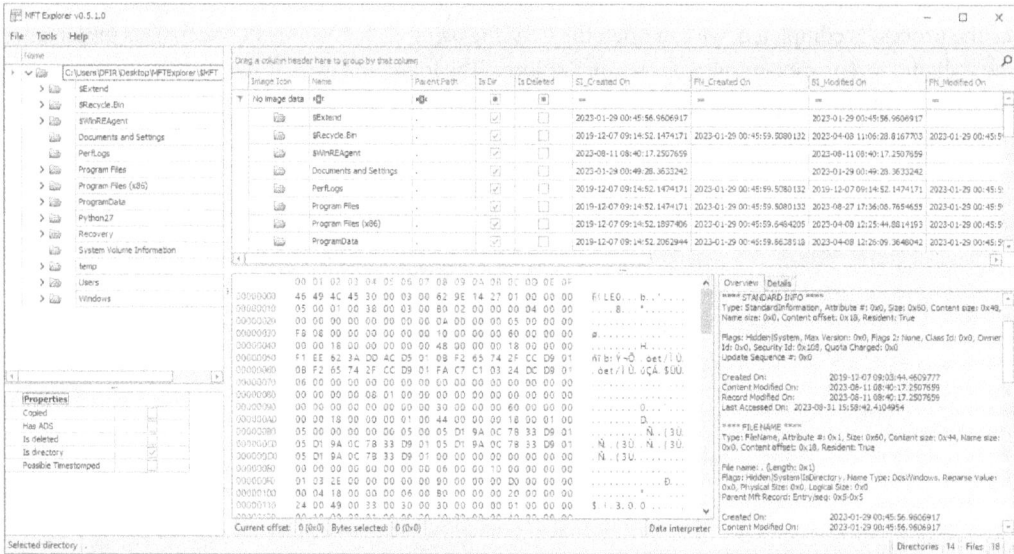

Figure 9.15: MFT Explorer GUI

As highlighted in *Figure 9.15*, we can see entries structured as a folder tree and an associated timestamp presented under **Overview**.

Moreover, as we can see in *Figure 9.16* , we can observe multiple fields presented with timestamps. This is useful if we are going to focus on anti-forensic techniques such as timestamping.

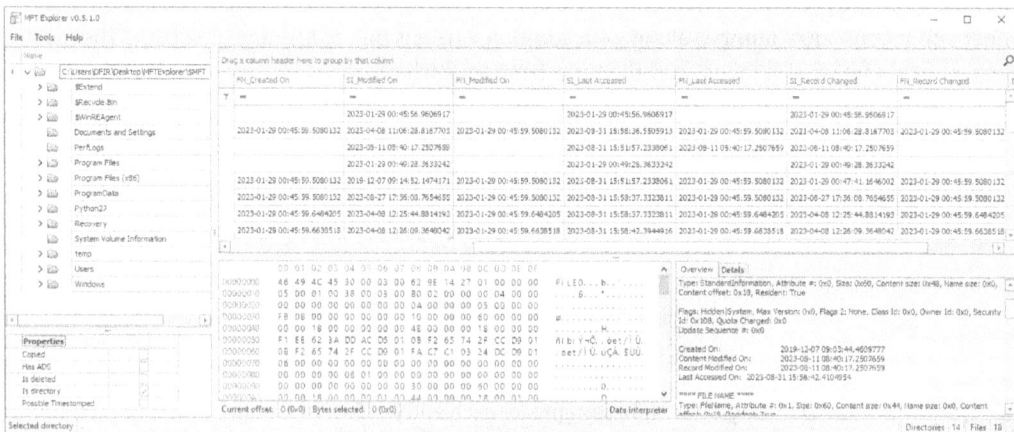

Figure 9.16: MFT Explorer timestamp columns

Another great aspect of MFT explorer is listing contents of the directories and loading it as it's presented In *Figure 9.17,* we can see the Download folder with all its contents:

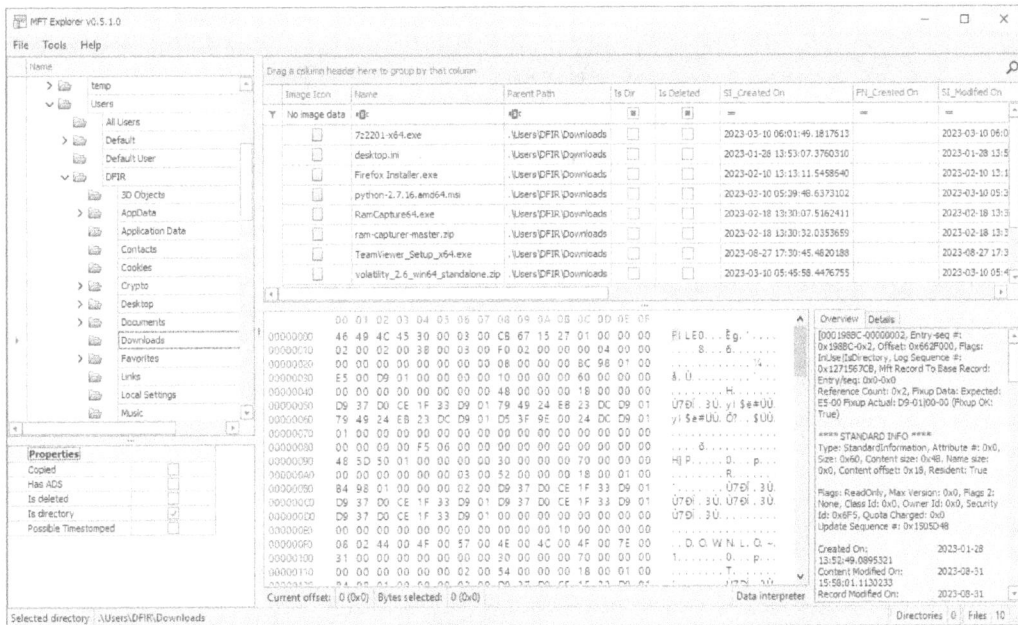

Figure 9.17: MFT Explorer presenting the Downloads folder

MFT Explorer is an invaluable tool for anayzing and visualizing a suspect's filesystem. It allows you to browse through the filesystem as if you were on the computer itself, making it much easier to understand the data and identify potential evidence.

LNK file analysis

LNK files, or shortcut files, are a valuable source of evidence for digital forensic investigators. They are created by the user or automatically by the Windows operating system when a file or document is opened. LNK files can contain a wealth of information, including the filename, path, size, timestamps, and even the user who created or opened the file. LNK files are valuable artifacts for digital forensic investigators because they can reveal information about files that may no longer exist on the system. Even if a file has been deleted or moved to a different location, the LNK file may still be present. The LNK file can provide information about the file's original name, path, and size, as well as the time and date it was created or last accessed. This information can be used to track down deleted files, identify malicious files, and reconstruct a suspect's activity. For example, if an investigator is trying to find a file that has been deleted, they can search for the LNK file associated with that file. The LNK file will contain the file's original name and path, which can be used to recover the file from a backup or an other location.

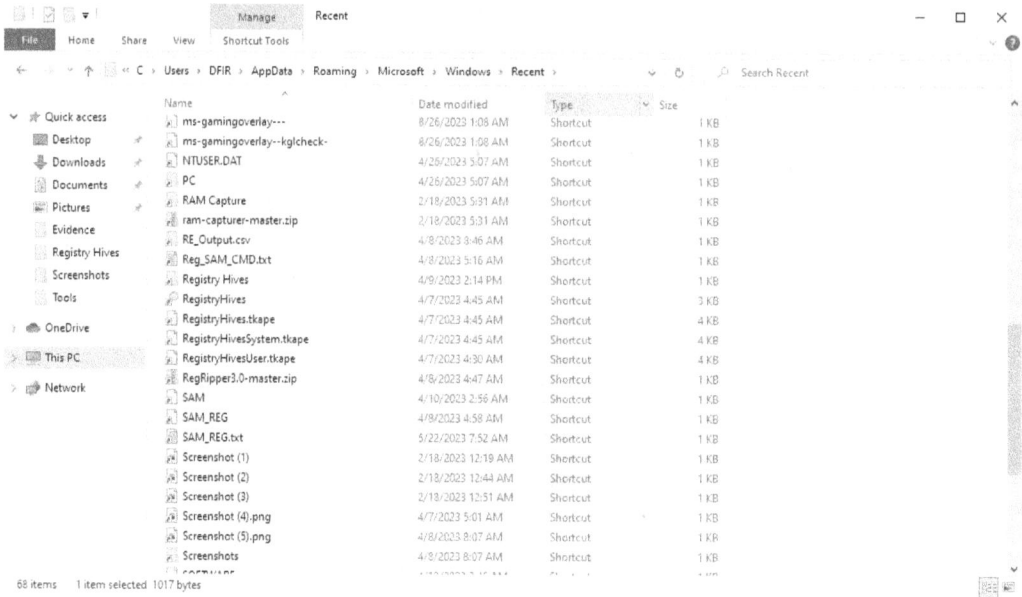

Figure 9.18: LNK files in the Recent folder

As a forensic value, we can get the original path of the file, MAC times associated with the original file, information about the volume that is stored, the file size, and network details if it is stored on a network.

LNK files are stored at the following paths:

- **Windows 7+**: `C:\Users\%USERNAME%\AppData\Roaming\Microsoft\Windows\Recent`

- **Windows XP**: `C:\Documents and Settings\%USERNAME%\Recent`

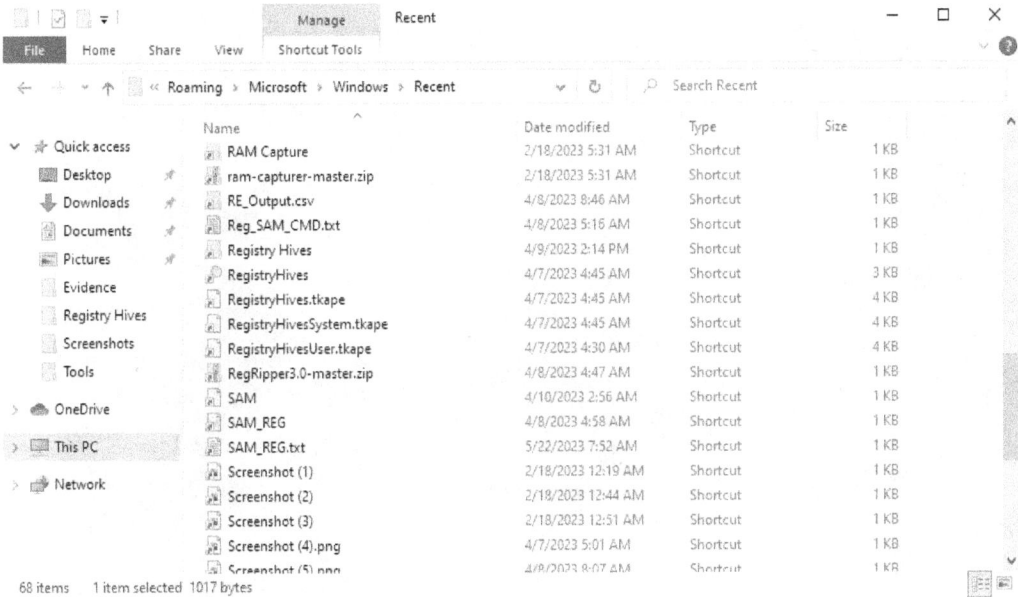

Figure 9.19: Modification represents last opened timestamp

As shown in *Figure 9.19*, we can see the **Date modified** column, which tells us the last time the file was opened.

To analyze LNK files, we will use multiple tools to parse. One of the tools is LECmd.exe (the LNK Explorer command line). We can parse a single LNK file or a full directory and save it as a CSV file.

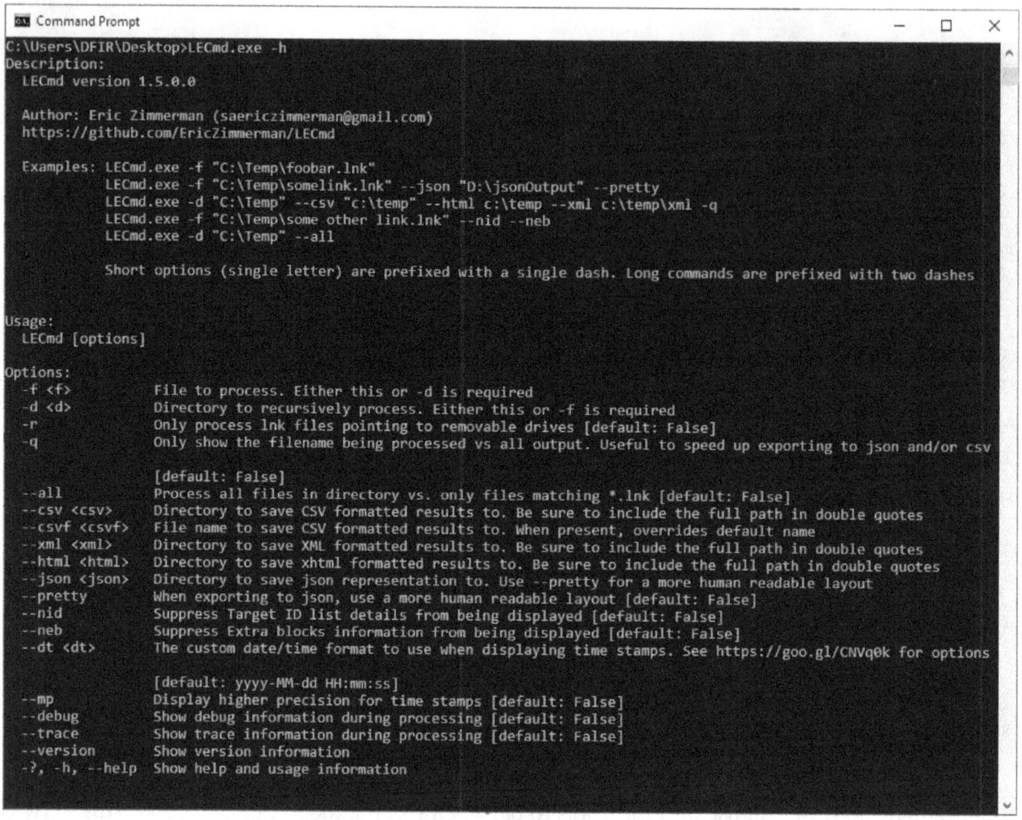

Figure 9.20: LECmd.exe help menu

To parse a single file, we will be using the following command:

```
LECmd.exe -f "E:\C\Users\DFIR\AppData\Roaming\Microsoft\Windows\
Recent\FTK Imager.lnk"
```

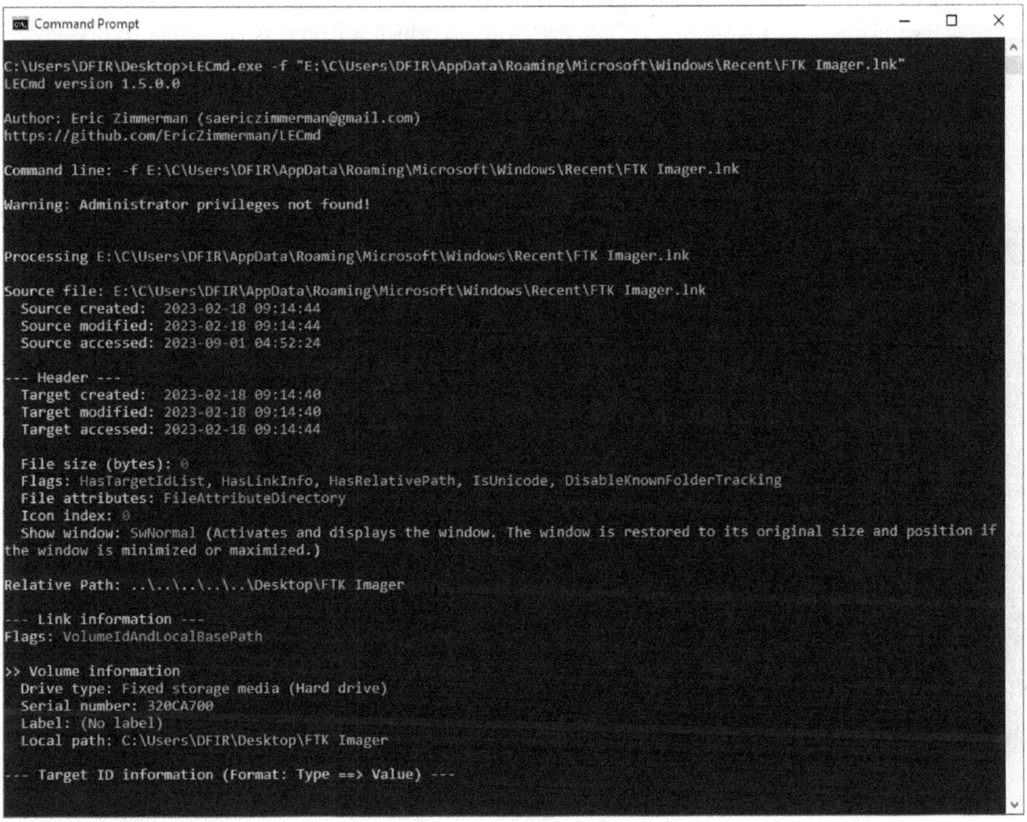

Figure 9.21: LECmd.exe output for a single LNK file

In *Figure 9.17*, LNK files contain up to six different timestamps, which an investigator may find useful. The LNK file itself contains timestamps for file creation, file access, and file modification. Similarly, the file contains information regarding the target file's creation, access, and modification dates. The modification timestamp for the LNK file will provide insight into when the file was last accessed on the system in question, and the LNK file creation timestamp will tell you when the file was first accessed on the system.

To analyze the full directory, we can run LECmd.exe with -d, which will process a directory recursively:

```
LECmd.exe -d "E:\C\Users\DFIR\AppData\Roaming\Microsoft\Windows\
Recent" --csv "C:\Users\DFIR\Desktop\Evidence" --csvf LNK_Output.csv
-q
```

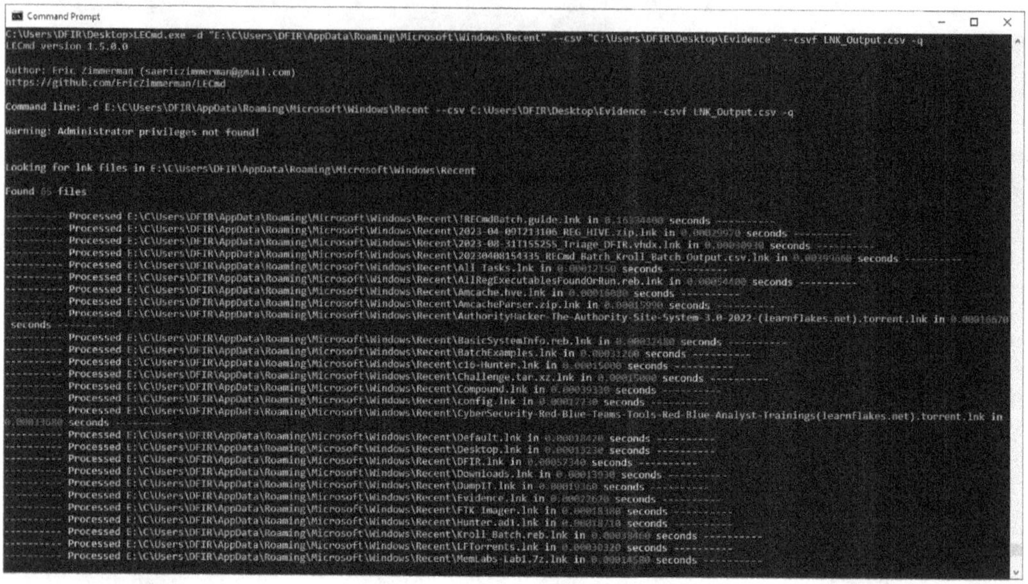

Figure 9.22: LEcmd.exe output for directory

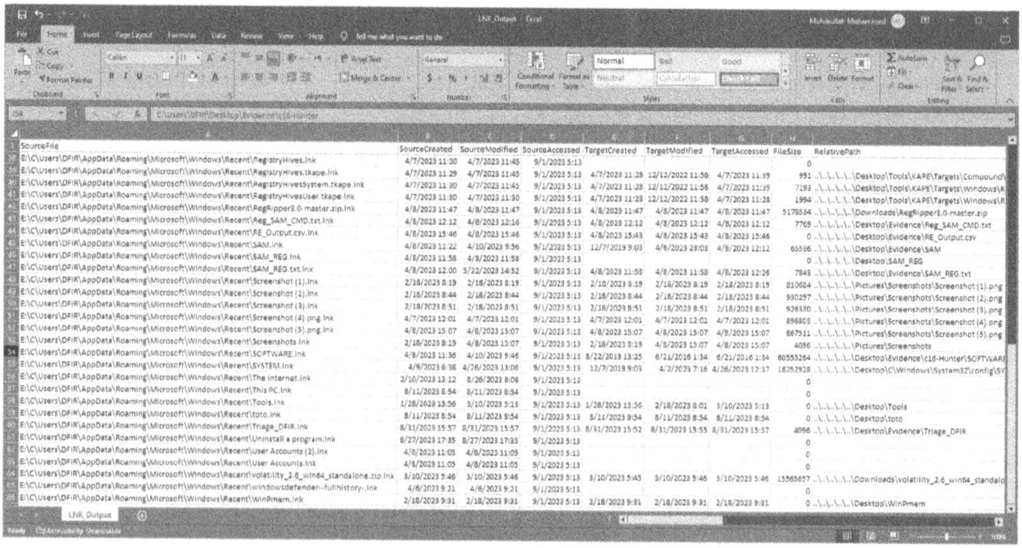

Figure 9.23: LEcmd.exe output

Now that we have learned how to analyze LNK files, let's cover another valuable tool for forensic evidence, which is Recycle Bin.

Recycle Bin analysis

Microsoft first introduced Recycle Bin in 1995 with the Windows 95 operating system. However, there were significant changes in the implementation of the Recycle Bin technology with the release of Windows Vista in 2007 and Windows 7 in 2009. These changes are important for modern forensic computer examiners to understand, as they can affect the ability to recover deleted files.

The Windows Recycle Bin is a valuable source of evidence in digital forensics investigations. Any file that is deleted using File Explorer is initially placed in Recycle Bin. Recycle Bin artifacts can contain valuable information about the deleted file, such as its name, original location, size, and date and time of deletion.

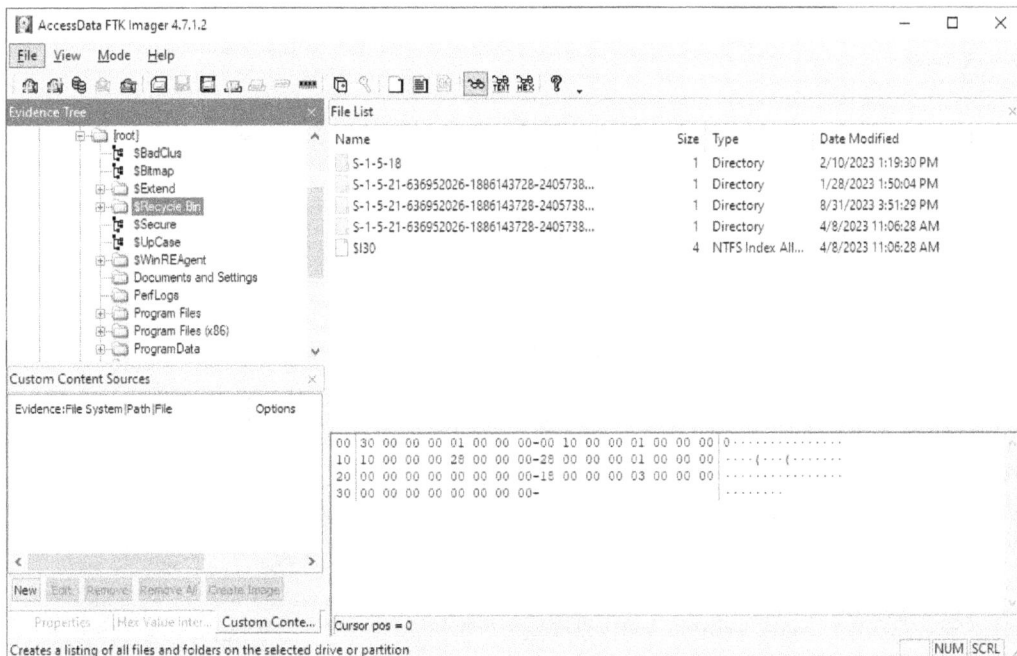

Figure 9.24: Recycle Bin folder explored using FTK Imager

Windows Recycle Bin artifacts are stored in a hidden system folder called `Recycle.Bin`. On Windows 2000, NT, XP, and 2003, Recycle Bin artifacts are stored in an INFO2 file within the user's SID subfolder at `C:\RECYCLER{SID}\INFO2`, and on Windows Vista +, it's stored in `$Recycle. bin"`. `C:\$Recycle.Bin\{SID}\$I######`.

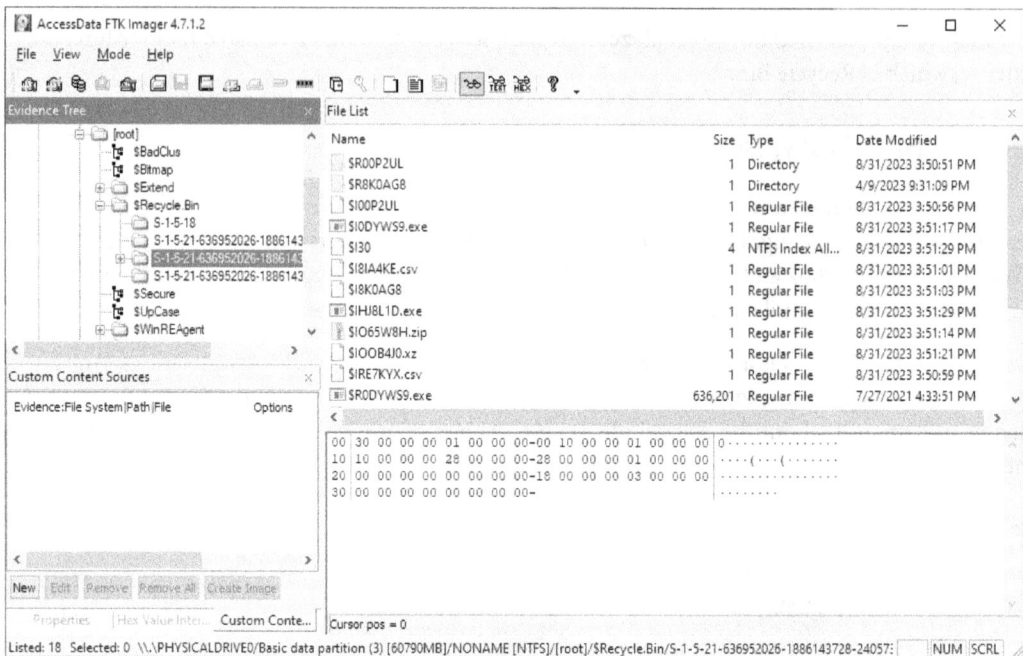

Figure 9.25: Deleted file for user

For every deleted file, two files are generated within the designated path, as we see in *Figure 9.25*. The initial file, denoted as $I, contains metadata pertaining to the deleted file. This metadata includes the original filename, the file's former path before deletion, its size, and the timestamp of its deletion. Subsequently, the file's actual contents are stored in another file, named $R. Both these files undergo a renaming process, receiving random six-character identifiers. Following this renaming, $I and $R are, respectively, added as prefixes to create an eight-character filename for each.

Most commercial tools, such as EnCase, have developed their own plugins for parsing Recycle Bin. However, for the sake of demonstration, we will be using two tools, Rifiuti2 and another amazing tool developed by Eric Zimmerman, RBCmd.exe.

Rifiuti2 is used to analyze Windows Recycle Bin INFO2 files. Analysis of Windows Recycle Bin is usually carried out during Windows computer forensics. Rifiuti2 can extract the file deletion time, the original path and size of deleted files, and whether the trashed files have been permanently removed.

Rifiuti2 is designed to be portable and runs on a command-line environment. Depending on the Windows Recycle Bin format, there are two binaries to choose from (most users would want to use the first one):

- Rifiuti-vista: Used for Windows Vista +. It scans the \$Recycle.bin folder.

- Rifiuti: Used for Windows 95 to XP. It reads INFO2 files within the \RECYCLED folder.

We can download this tool from https://github.com/abelcheung/rifiuti2:

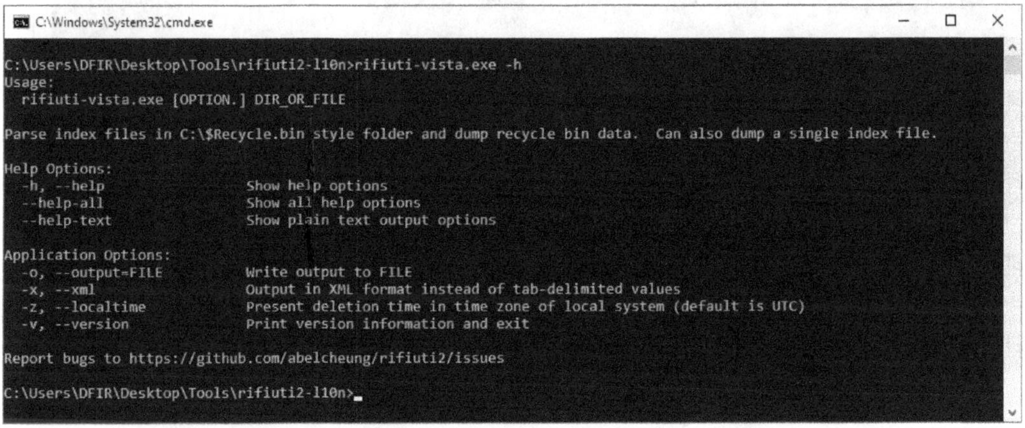

Figure 9.26: Rifiuti2 help menu

In *Figure 9.26*, we initiated the Rifiuti2 tool to parse collected Recycle Bin files. As we can see from the output, it presents in clear text names of files that have been deleted.

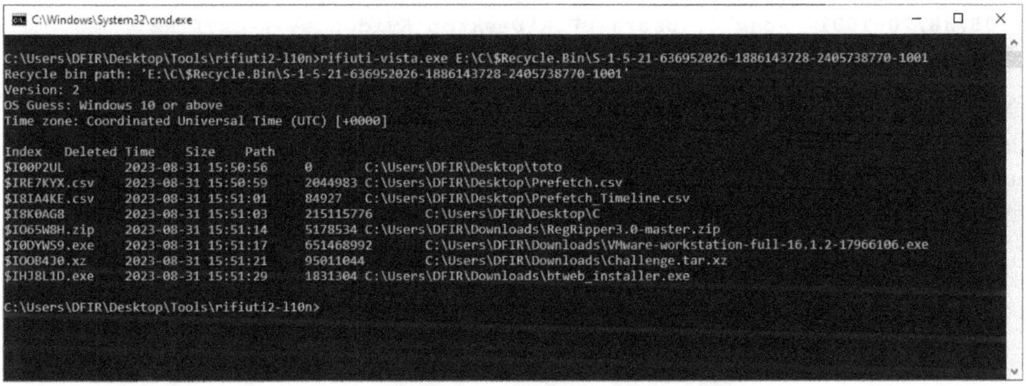

Figure 9.27: Rifiuti2 output for $I files

As we can see in *Figure 9.27*, once we add the file path for Recycle Bin, it will show us the $I content clearly.

Another useful tool here is RBCmd.exe. This tool will parse $I and INFO2.

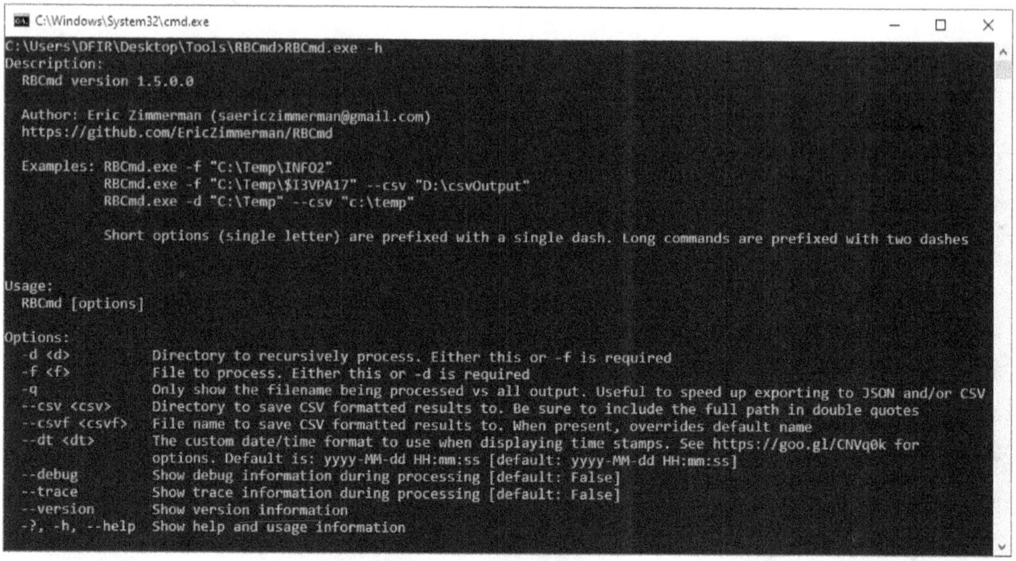

Figure 9.28: RBCmd.exe help menu

Typically, in a forensics investigation, when we are conducting analysis on large data, we parse the whole directory and save the output as a CSV file. By using the following command, we will parse the full directory recursively:

```
RBCmd.exe -d E:\C\$Recycle.Bin\S-1-5-21-636952026-1886143728-
2405738770-1001 --csv C:\Users\DFIR\Desktop\Evidence\ --csvf RB_
Output.csv
```

In the previous command, we specified using -d. This option allows us to process a directory recursively. Either this or -f is required if we need to parse a single file, and we select the output in CSV format by using –csv and direct the output to the directory. The last option is for naming the output file using --csvf:, which is RB_Output.csv.

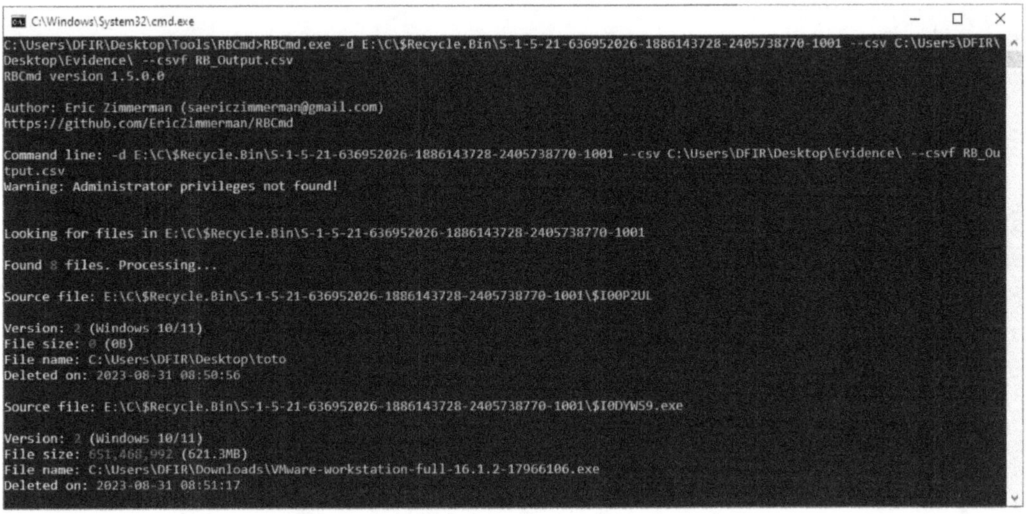

Figure 9.29: RBCmd.exe output

In conclusion, Recycle Bin is a powerful forensics tool for uncovering deleted files and can transform investigations.

ShellBags and jump lists

ShellBags, introduced in Microsoft's Windows 7 operating system and persisting across later Windows platforms, are registry keys designed to enhance the user experience by preserving user preferences. These preferences are recalled as needed, based on the user's interactions. Shellbags are a valuable tool in the field of digital forensics. They can be used to track the folders that a user has accessed, as well as the existence or creation of folders. Shellbags can also be used to identify whether external directories on external devices were accessed. They are primarily designed to store data about a user's interactions with the Windows operating system. For example, if a user changes the size of icons, the change will be reflected in the corresponding Shellbag entry. If a folder is opened or closed or its viewing options are changed, whether in Windows Explorer, on the desktop, by right-clicking, or by renaming, a corresponding Shellbag record is created or updated.

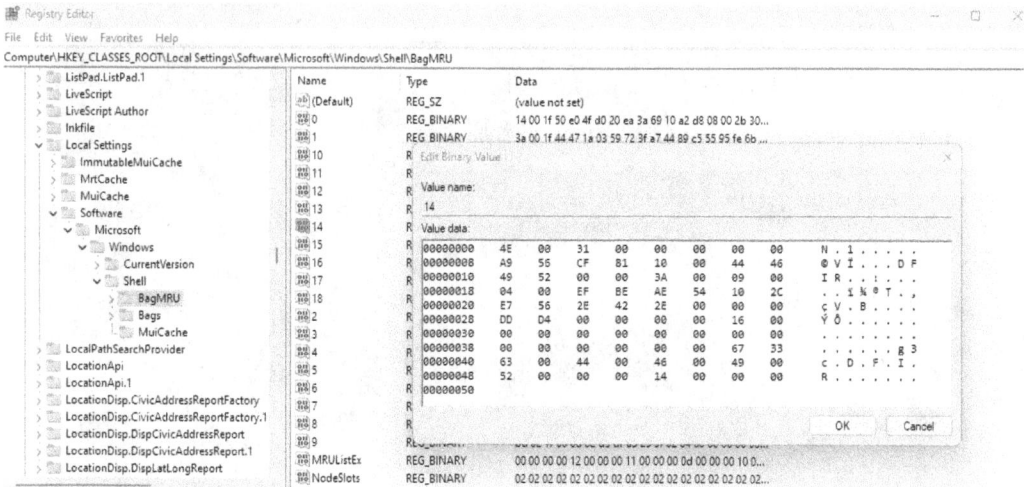

Figure 9.30: Registry editor BagMRU

The shellbags held in BagMRU follow a similar structure and hierarchy as found within the File Explorer, with the numbered folders representing parent/child folders, as shown in *Figure 9.30*.

ShellBags are stored in Windows 7+ in the following directories:

- USRCLASS.DAT\Local Settings\Software\Microsoft\Windows\Shell\BagMRU

- USRCLASS.DAT\Local Settings\Software\Microsoft\Windows\Shell\Bags

- NTUSER.DAT\Software\Microsoft\Windows\Shell\Bags

- NTUSER.DAT\Software\Microsoft\Windows\Shell\BagMRU

As we can see in *Figure 9.31*, we have the last write timestamp, which is updated each time a key is modified. Also, we can see the folder name which is relevant to this shell item in right corner of the screenshot.

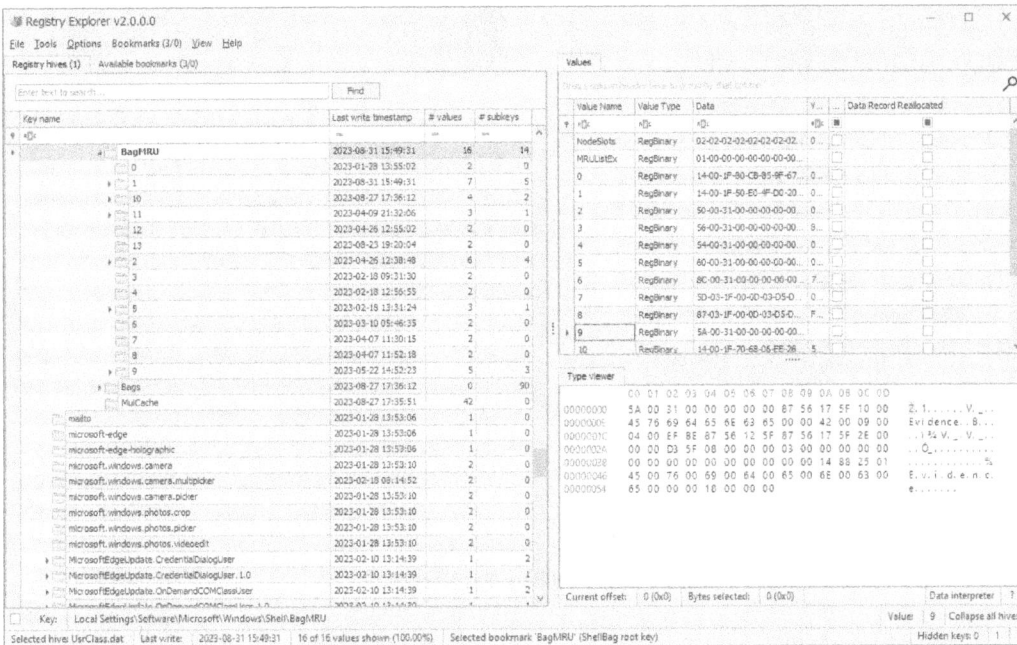

Figure 9.31: Registry Explorer showing the Evidence folder

Within these shellbags, we can see a set of keys, which provides valuable information. MRUListEx presents the order in which the child folder in BagMRU was accessed. NodeSlot contains view preferences and settings for the shellbag. This value is only located in the BagMRU key and it is updated upon new Shellbag creation.

To analyze shellbags, we will utilize ShellBags Explorer. You can download it from the following link:

```
https://ericzimmerman.github.io/#!index.md
```

This tool is easy for an examiner to use. Load the shellbags by following file option then selecting Load offline hive option, these options will be present within the GUI, as shown in *Figure 9.32*. We have a section for folder metadata, which shows us the timestamps of creation, modification and interaction, and on the left, the tool present BagMRU list. As forensic examiners, we focus on the first interacted timestamp as this represents the first time the user opened the folder using the GUI:

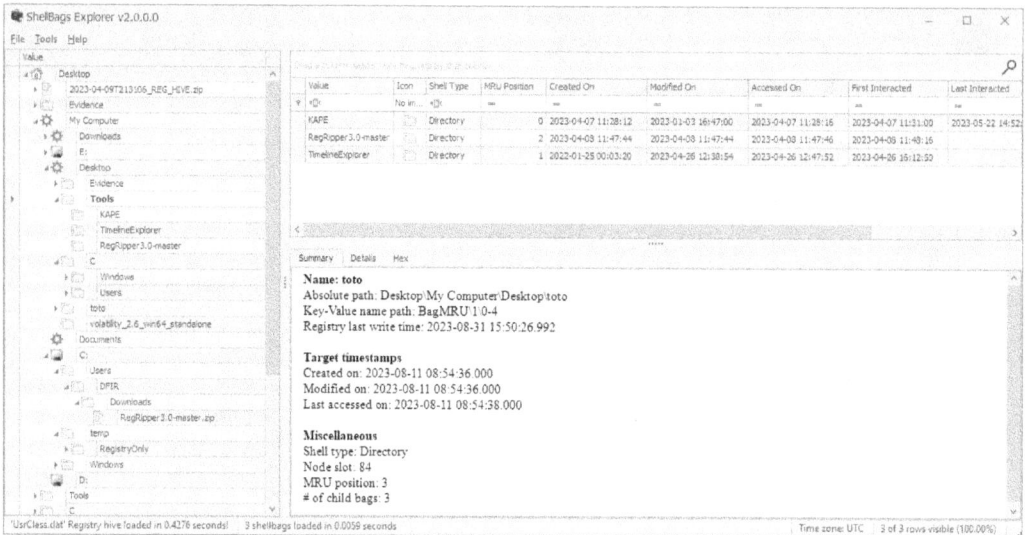

Figure 9.32: ShellBags Explorer GUI

When investigating shellbags, we focus mostly on filtering folder names, which is relevant to our working case. Also, we check the timestamps to correlate and identify the baseline of the activity and look for access to cloud storage and removable devices.

Alternatively, we can use the ShellBags Explorer command-line version, as we can see in *Figure 9.33*.

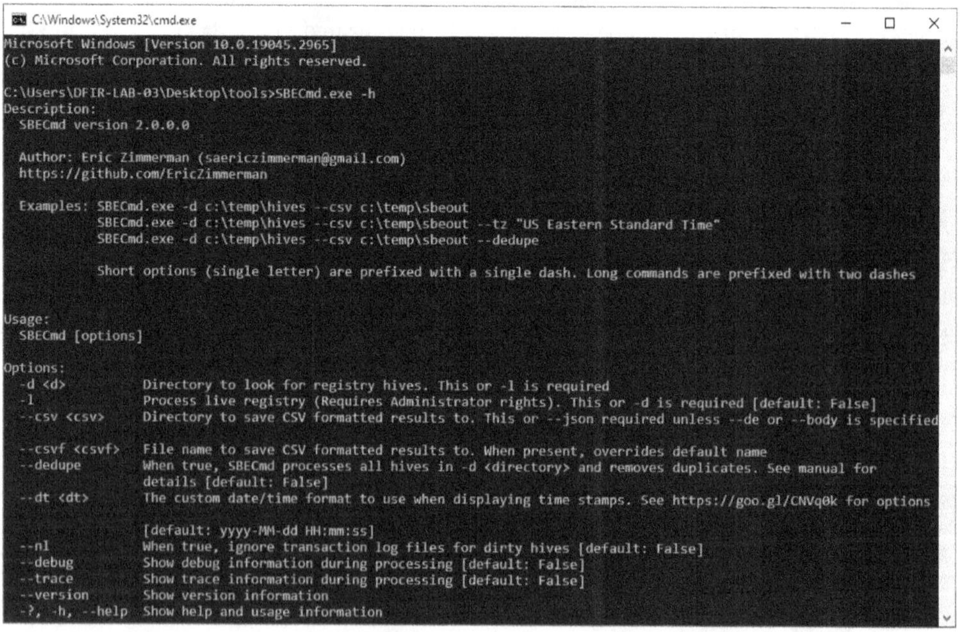

Figure 9.33: ShellBags Explorer command-line version

In the following figure, we are using `SBECmd.exe` to parse shellbags stored in the DFIR-LAB-03 triage image. By using `-d`, we are specifying the directory from which we will parse the shellbags. To output the file in CSV format, we will use `-csv` and direct it to the destination path to save the output.

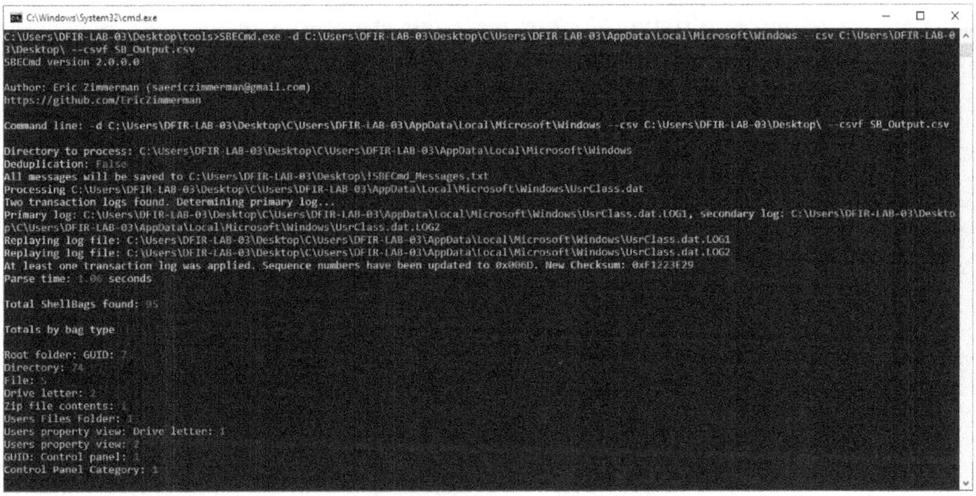

Figure 9.34: SBECmd.exe processing shellbags

In *Figure 9.35*, we can see important fields that have been parsed, such as MFTEntry, and the last write time. By analyzing this evidence, we can confirm whether this evidence is relevant to our incident or not.

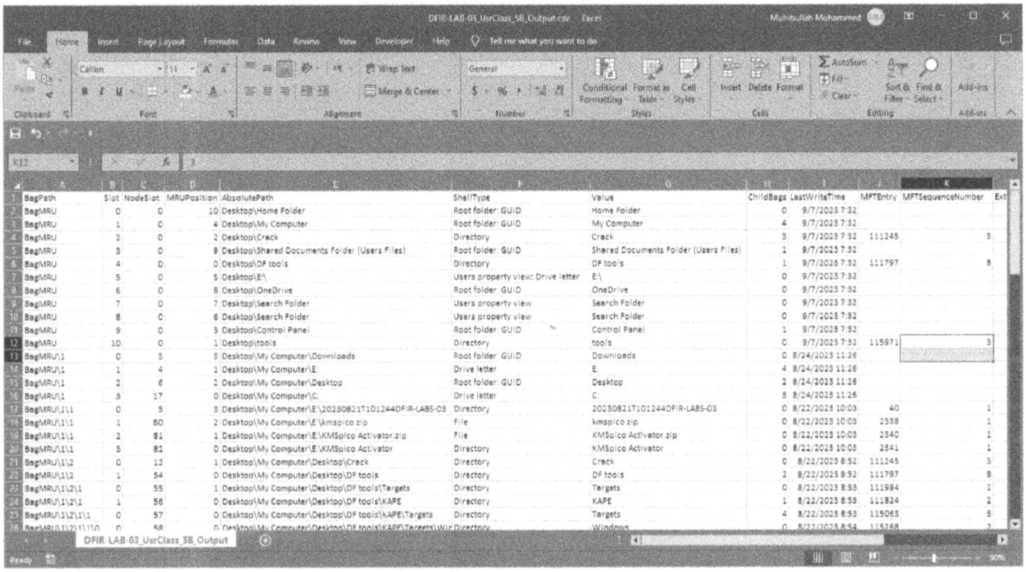

Figure 9.35: SBECmd.exe processing Shellbags

Now that we have learned about Shellbags and how it is important, let's move on to another artifact: SRUM.

System Resource Utilization Monitor (SRUM)

SRUM, or **System Resource Utilization Monitor**, is a feature of modern Windows systems intended to track the application usage, network utilization, and system energy state.

It is a feature of Windows 8 and later versions that tracks system resource usage, including application resource usage and energy usage, Windows push notifications and network connectivity, and data usage. The data is collected for 30 to 60 days and is stored in a database.

The SRUM database is not visible to the end user, but some of the data is available through the **App history** tab in Task Manager. This data can be used to track application usage, identify energy hogs, and troubleshoot performance problems.

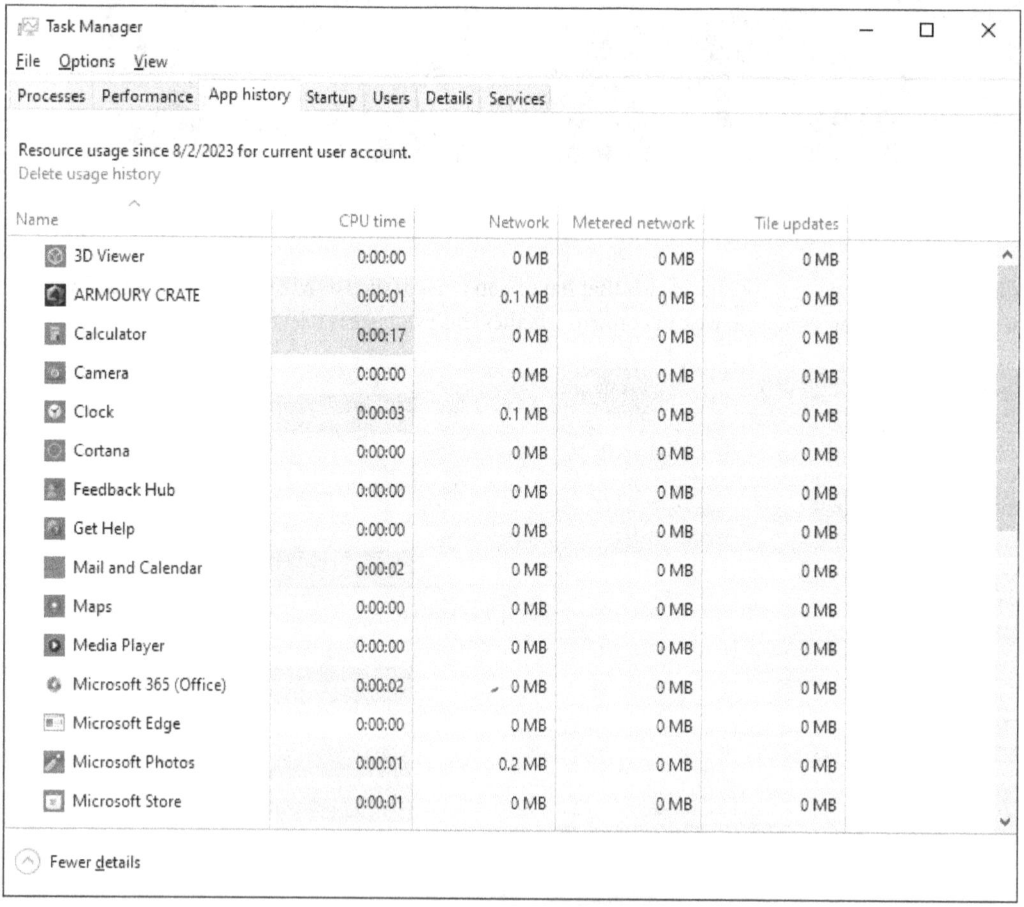

Figure 9.36: Task Manager App history

The SRUM database can also be used by forensic investigators to reconstruct events that occurred on a system. For example, an investigator could use the SRUM database to identify applications that were running at the time of a malware infection. This type of information enables the examiner to gain insights into the previous activities and events on a system. SRUM databases are stored in `C:\Windows\System32\SRU\SRUDB.dat`.

By using the ESEDatabaseView tool, we can review the tables stored within `SRUDB.dat`.

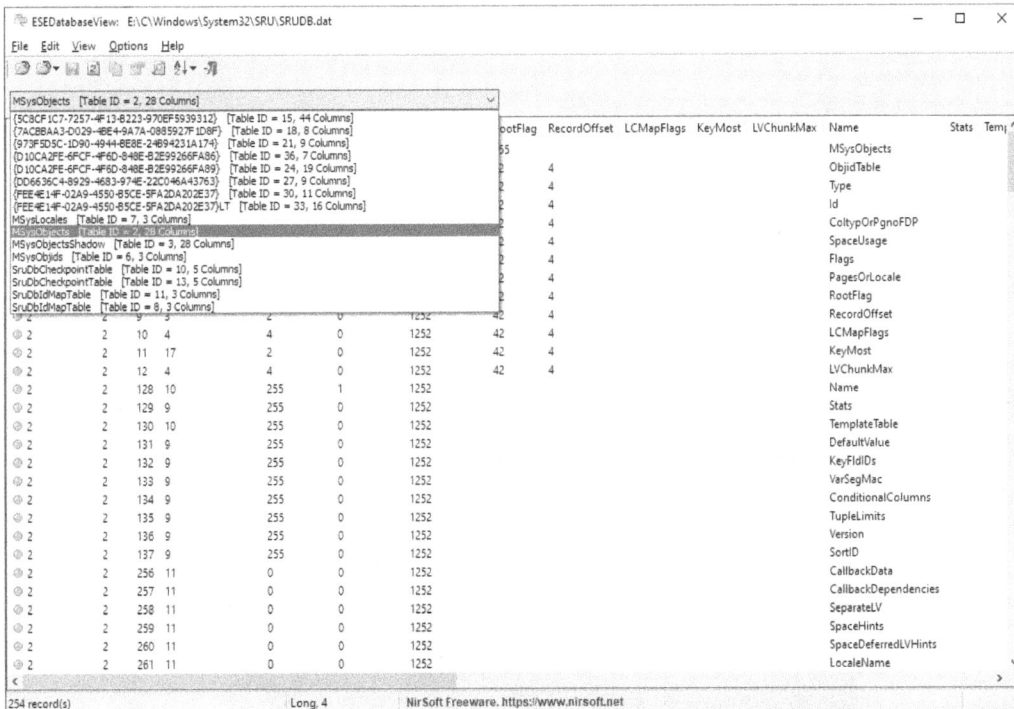

Figure 9.37: ESEDatabaseView GUI

To better understand this, each presented value in highlighted part of figure 9.27 is associated with registry key stored in SRUM at `Microsoft\Windows NT\CurrentVersion\SRUM\extensions`.

For example, as we can see in *Figure 9.38*, `{d10ca2fe-6fcf-4f6d-848e-b2e99266fa89}` is associated with Application Resource Usage Provider.

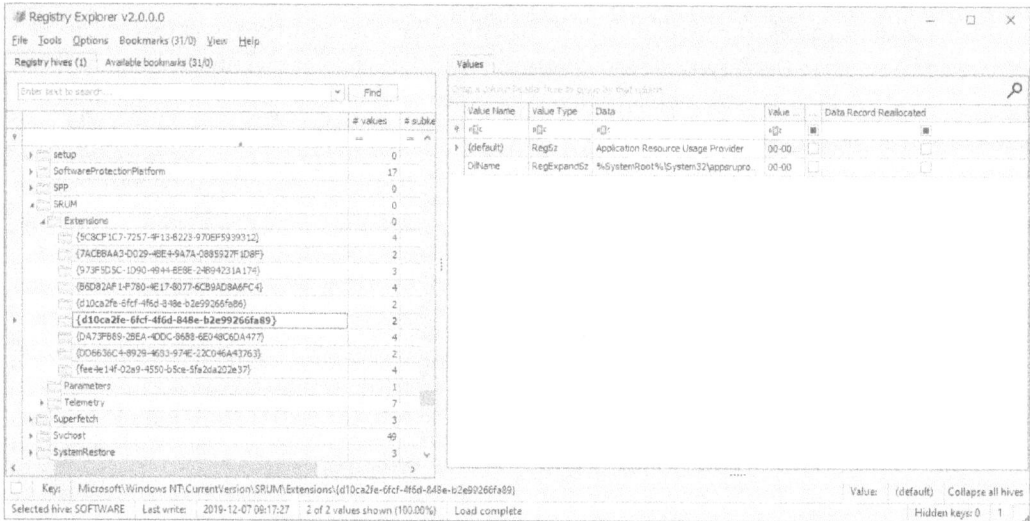

Figure 9.38: Registry Explorer SRUM extensions

To parse `SRUMDB.dat`, we can use multiple tools. We will focus on the `SRUM_DUMP` tool for parsing.

`SRUM_DUMP` extracts information from the SRUM database and creates an Excel spreadsheet. We can download this tool with its Excel template from `https://github.com/MarkBaggett/srum-dump/releases/tag/2.5`.

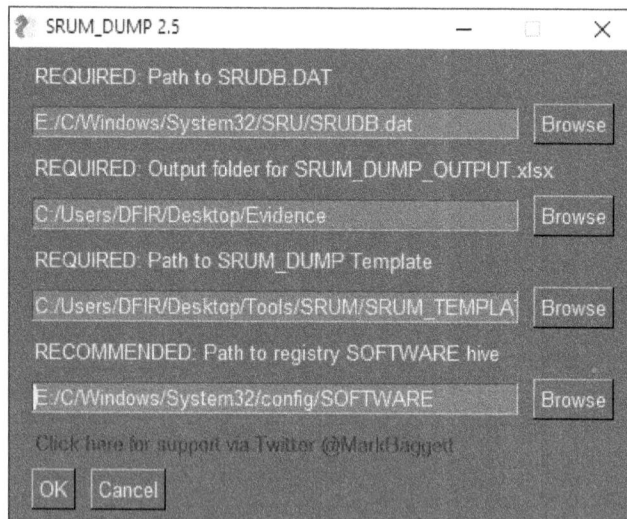

Figure 9.39: SRUM_DUMP GUI

Once the parsing is done, we can proceed and open the output file in Microsoft Excel. What we notice is that we have multiple sheets for different system resource usage. Most of the time, we will focus on network data usage and application resources.

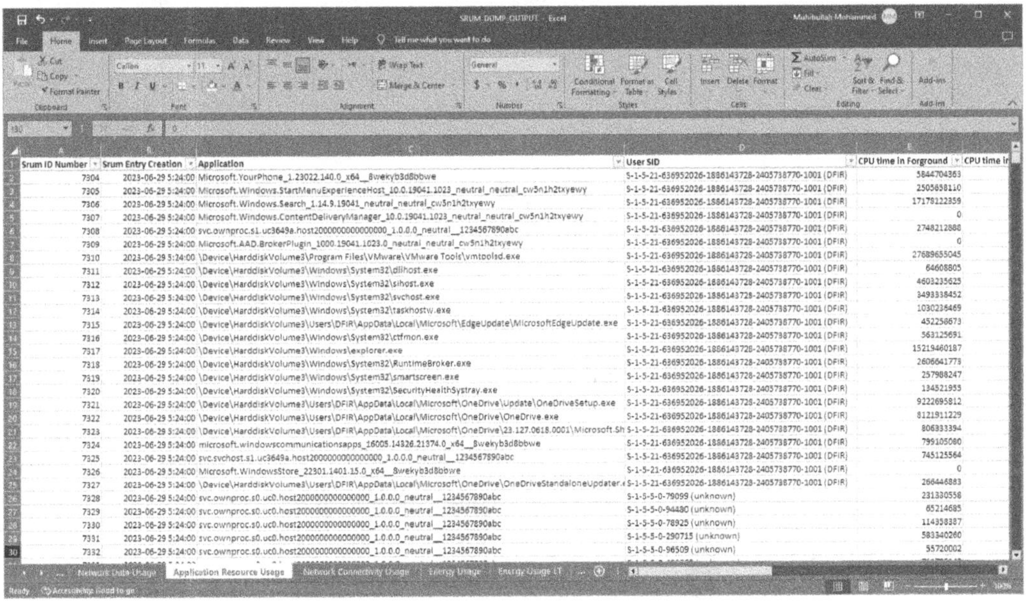

Figure 9.40: SRUM_DUMP output app resource usage

Application resource usage tracks every executable that is executed on the system and stores the full path of the application executed along with additional important information, such as the application ID, background bytes read, created date, and user SID.

Network data usage tracks wired and wireless connection and its SSID. It also captures the bandwidth usage for both sent and received bytes. It also includes the full path of the application.

We can use SRUM to identify the user who executed a process, the amount of data that was transmitted or exfiltrated, and a record of all binaries that were executed, including files that were previously deleted. We can also estimate the time window during which the process was executed, with an accuracy of up to an hour.

Whether these artifacts are enough to prove our case or simply add to the evidence, SRUM can provide us with valuable clues about what happened and who was responsible.

As we learned, SRUM provides valuable insight into system resource usage. Now, let's dive into a scenario in which we apply what we have learned so far.

Case study – analyzing malware infections

It's a regular Monday morning. Sarah, a financial analyst at your company, is going through her emails. Among the emails in her inbox, she notices one that appears to be sharing memes of cats, which she loves. However, she notifies the security team about sudden popups and abnormal activities on her system after she clicked on the link.

Analysis

Since this was handed over to the DFIR team, what we do is initiate a triage image and memory dump, as we covered in *Chapter 2* and *3* of this book. Using Belksoft Live RAM Capture, we will collect volatile data and KAPE to collect relevant artifacts to identify the root cause of this behavior on her system. For the sake of demonstration, we are assuming that we have direct access to Sarah's system using the GUI and we will invoke all the utilities and tools we have learned. In reality, in the majority of cases, we depend on EDR or tools such as Velociraptor to collect artifacts.

Belksoft Live RAM Capturer

In *Figure 9.41*, we are running Belkasoft Live RAM to collect memory images.

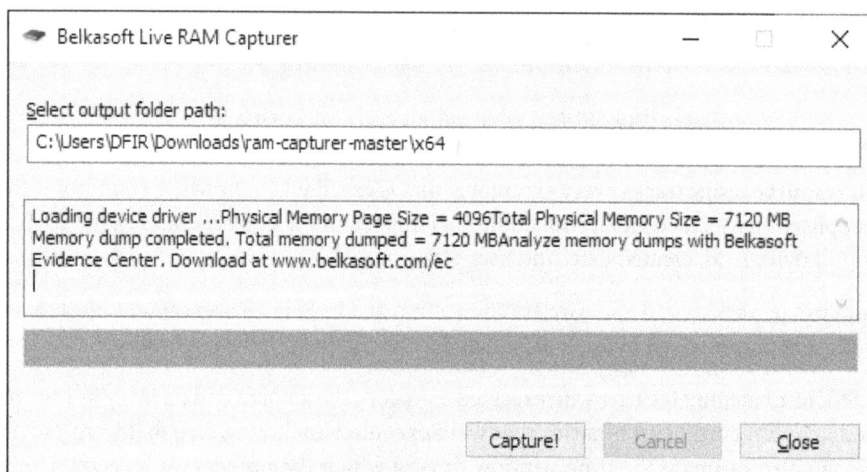

Figure 9.41: RAM Capturer memory collection

KAPE

Now we have collected the memory image, the next step for us will be collecting the triage image using KAPE. As we learned in *Chapter 2*, we will utilize SANS Triage Collection target to collect the most relevant artifacts to our case.

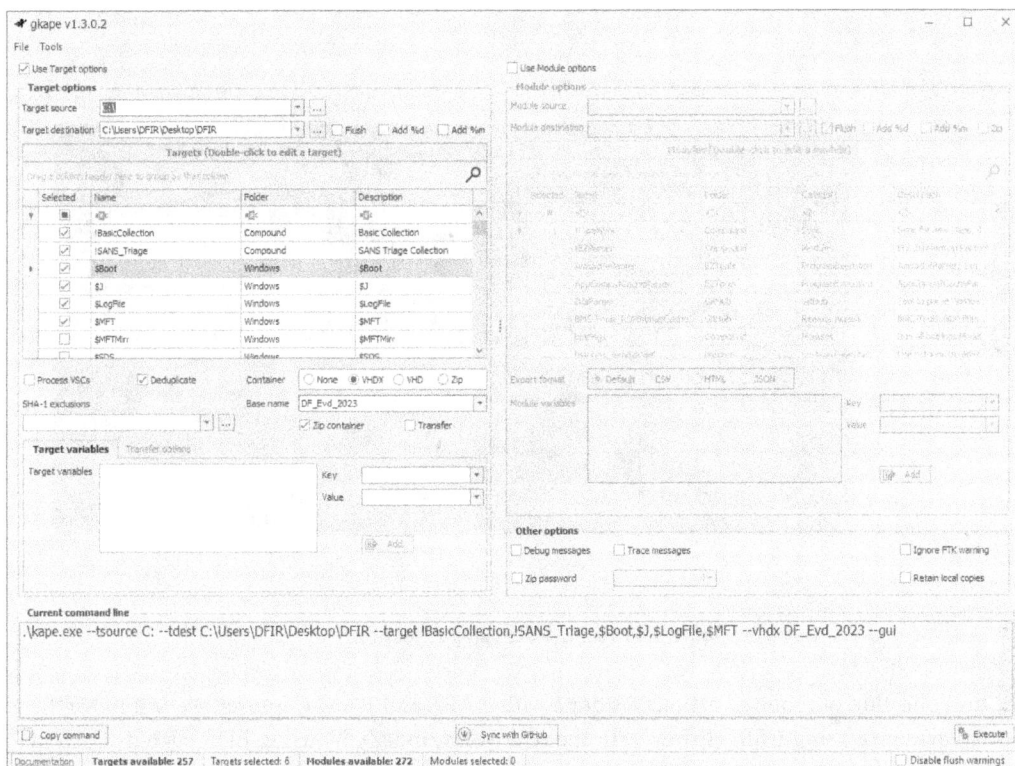

Figure 9.42: KAPE GUI collecting triage data

In the following figure, we can see KAPE starting the collection of triage data.

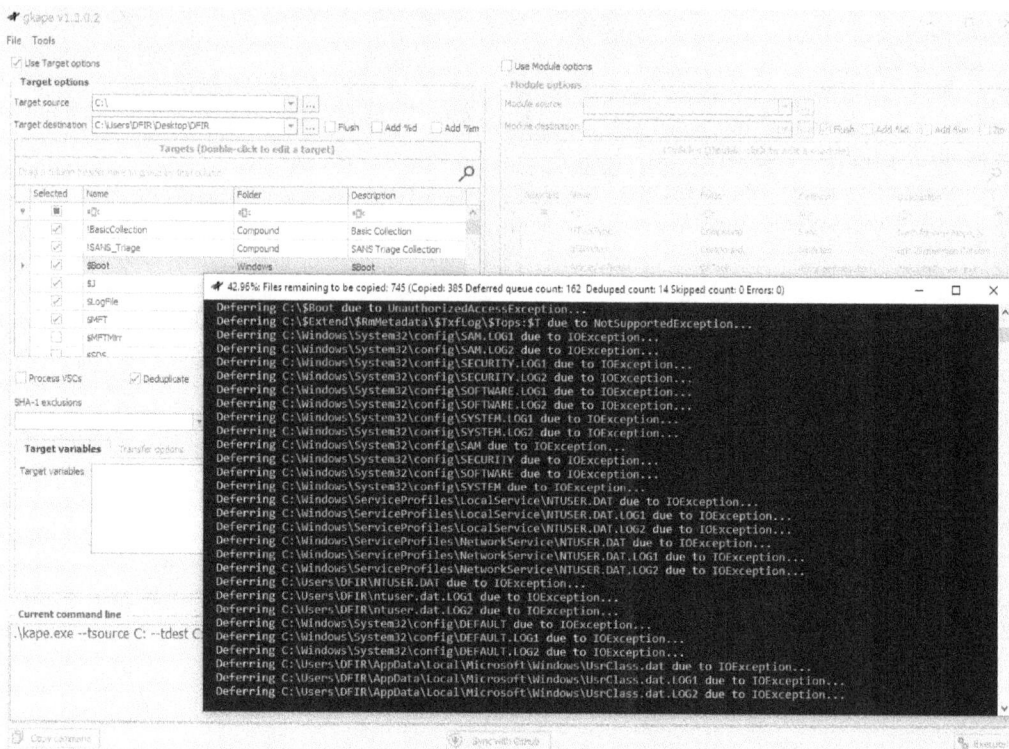

Figure 9.43: KAPE processing collection

Once the collection of required artifacts is done with KAPE and RAM Capturer, we will move the collected evidence using USB. However, in the real world, mostly by using EDR such as Carbon Black, we connect over a network and initiate the KAPE command line to collect and push the data to an internally hosted server for evidence collection (DFIR server) and start parsing and analyzing.

Now, for our demo, we collected everything we needed by using Basic Collection (`!BasicCollection`).

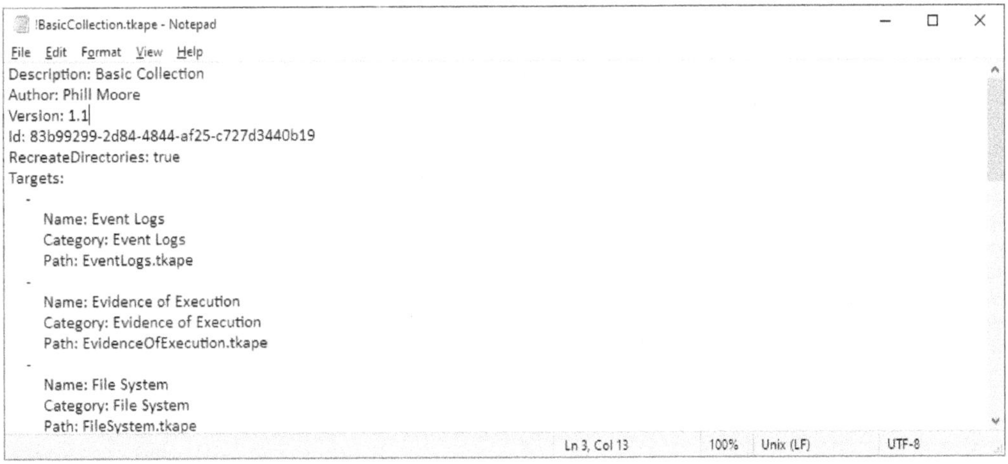

Figure 9.44: !BasicCollection target for KAPE

Now, let's start analyzing the evidence:

1. First, what we need to do is understand the whole picture of the escalation. Why were the security team concerned about a possible infection? If we remember, the security team confirmed with Sarah that after interacting with the link provided in the email, she started noticing abnormal activity in her system.

    For the sake of demonstration, let's consider `DFIRlabSIC@gmail` as Sarah's email. As we can see in the browser artifacts using the Chrome History view, there were multiple searches made by Sarah related to cat memes. In the following figure, we can see her search keywords.

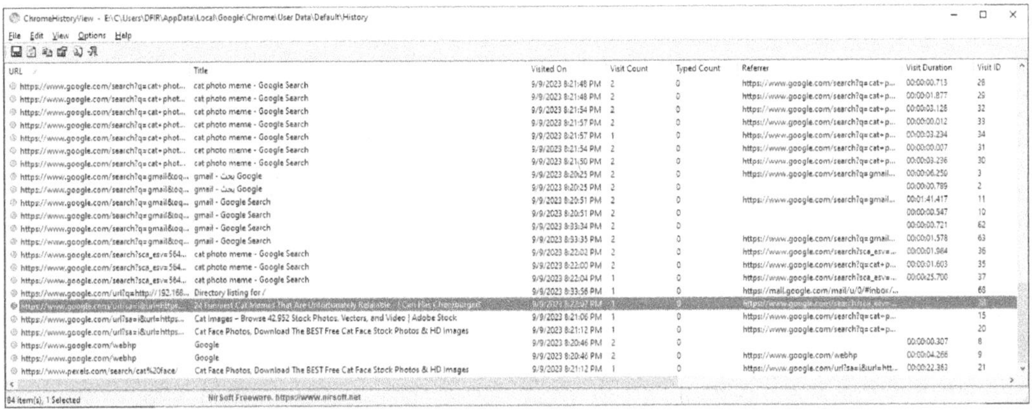

Figure 9.45: BrowserHistoryView output

We know that Sarah used to access her email using the browser. By using DB Browser for SQLite, we can see a binary was downloaded and stored on her system.

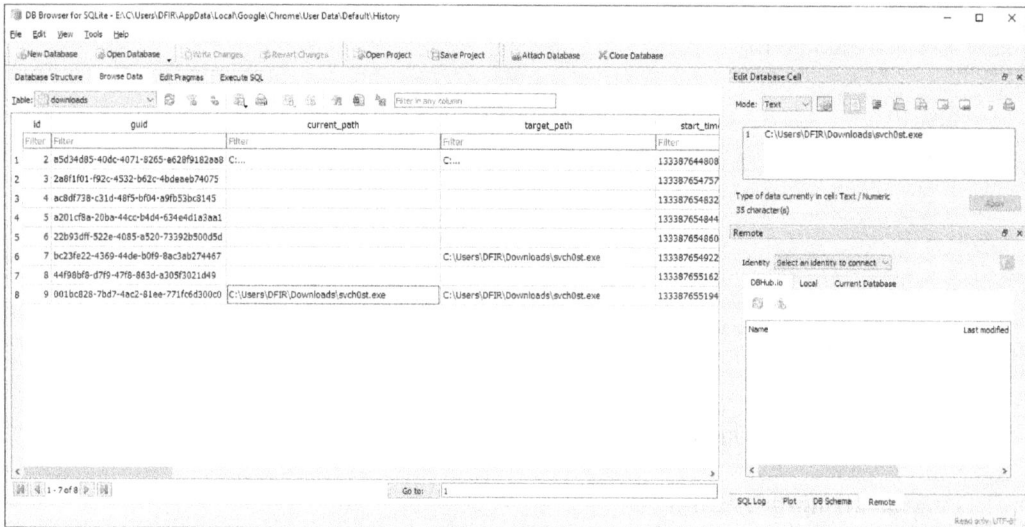

Figure 9.46: Suspicious binary showing as svch0st.exe

2. Now, since we have a suspicious binary, we need to verify whether the user executed it after download or not. Based on the evidence of execution, by examining the collected `prefetch` folder, we can see an entry for the `svch0st.exe` binary. Examining it using `pecmd.exe`, we confirm the execution of this binary.

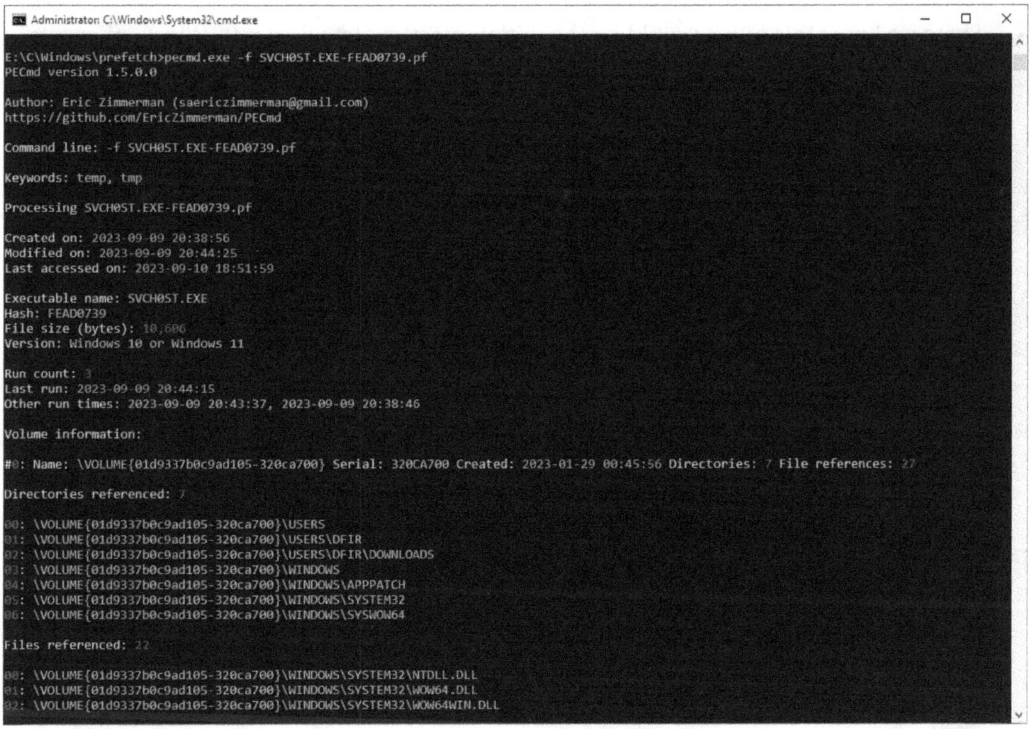

Figure 9.47: Parsing svch0st.exe prefetch

3. By moving on and examining the `UserAssist` key, we can verify that the user interacted with and executed this binary.

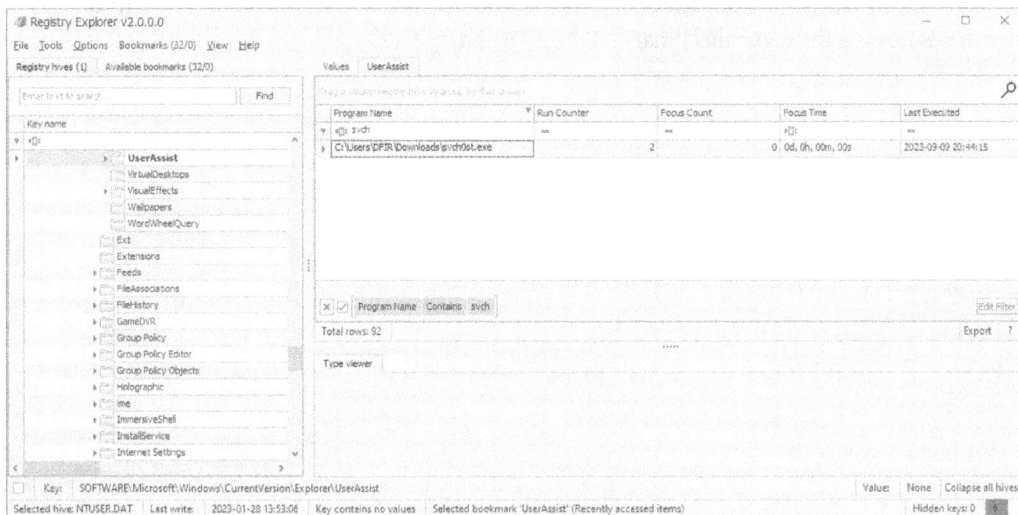

Figure 9.48: UserAssist key showing execution of svch0st.exe

4. Since we know this binary could be the initial infection, let's dive into Windows events related to Windows Defender by checking event ID 1116. svch0st.exe was detected by Windows Defender.

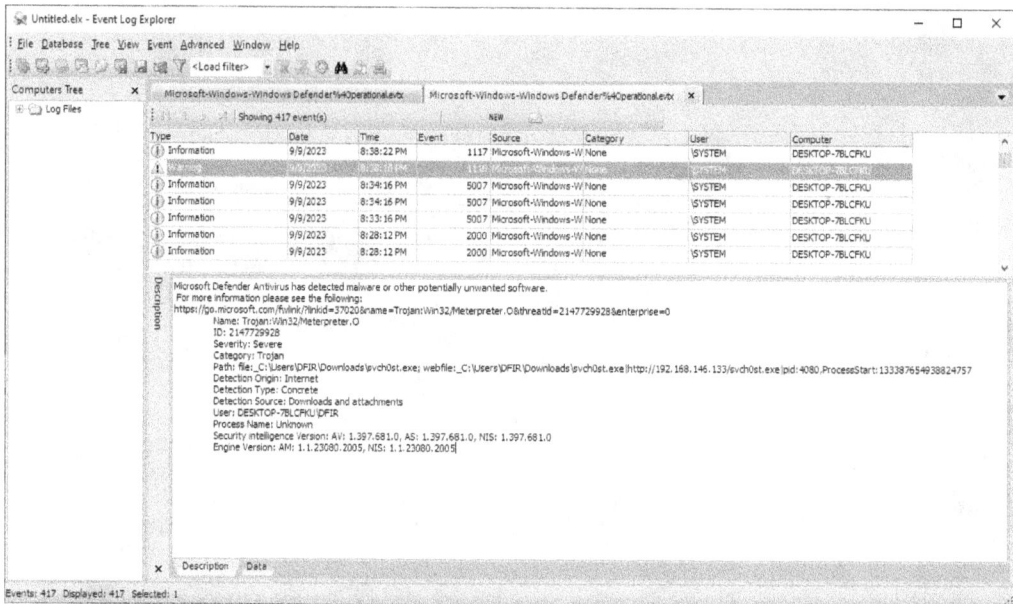

Figure 9.49: Windows Defender log

5. Based on the triggered signature, this was a binary that was mostly crafted by msfvenom and uses Meterpreter for reverse shell connection. Another IOC we identified here is the IP address that is hosting the malicious binary, 192.168.146.133.

Now, we have multiple pieces of evidence showing a malicious binary delivered by phishing email. Another interesting finding within the Windows Defender logs is Mimikatz. This tool is utilized by multiple threat actors for post-exploitation activities such as dumping processes and extracting hashes or clear text passwords.

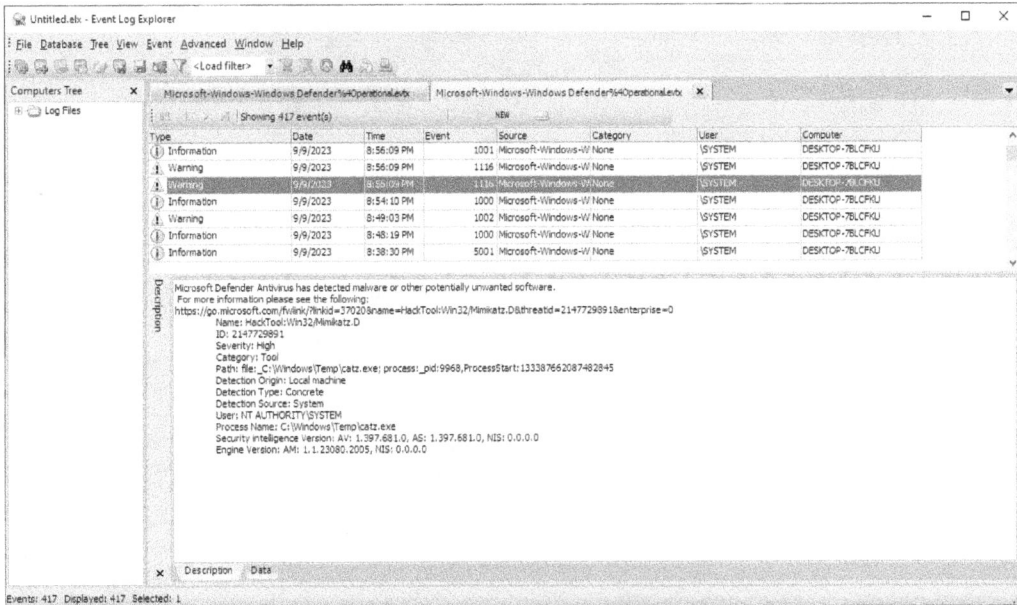

Figure 9.50: Mimikatz detected by Windows Defender

6. Moreover, moving to the 4688 event which shows us process creation, we can list the malicious binary spawning from the chrome.exe process, as shown in the following figure.

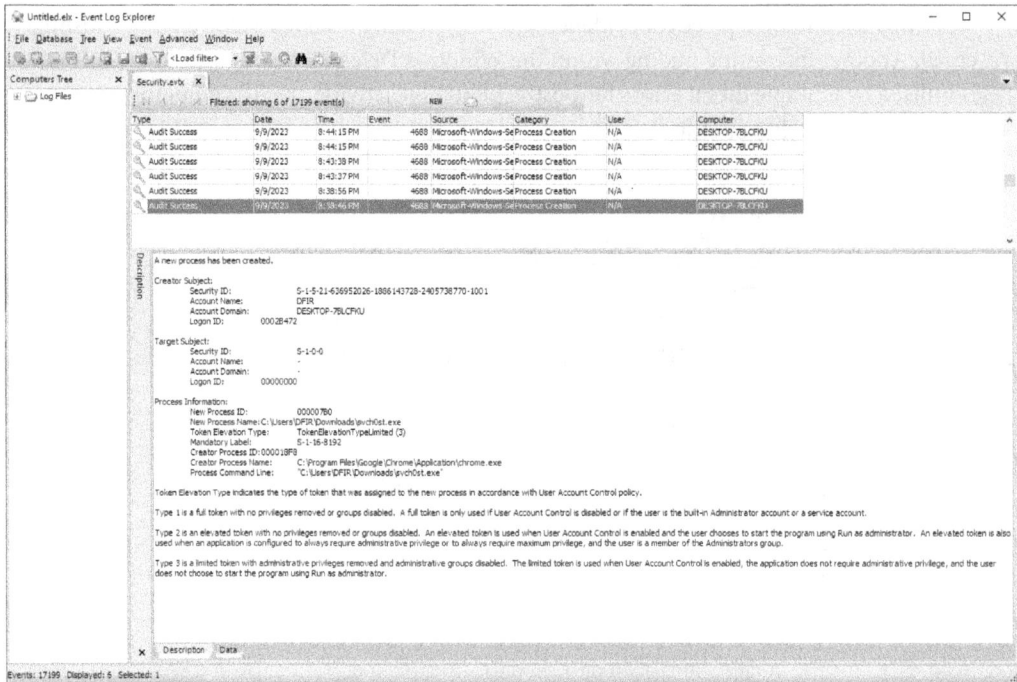

Figure 9.51: Execution of svch0st.exe

7. Once svch0st.exe is executed, we can see multiple enumeration commands run on the system, such as whoami /all and net users.

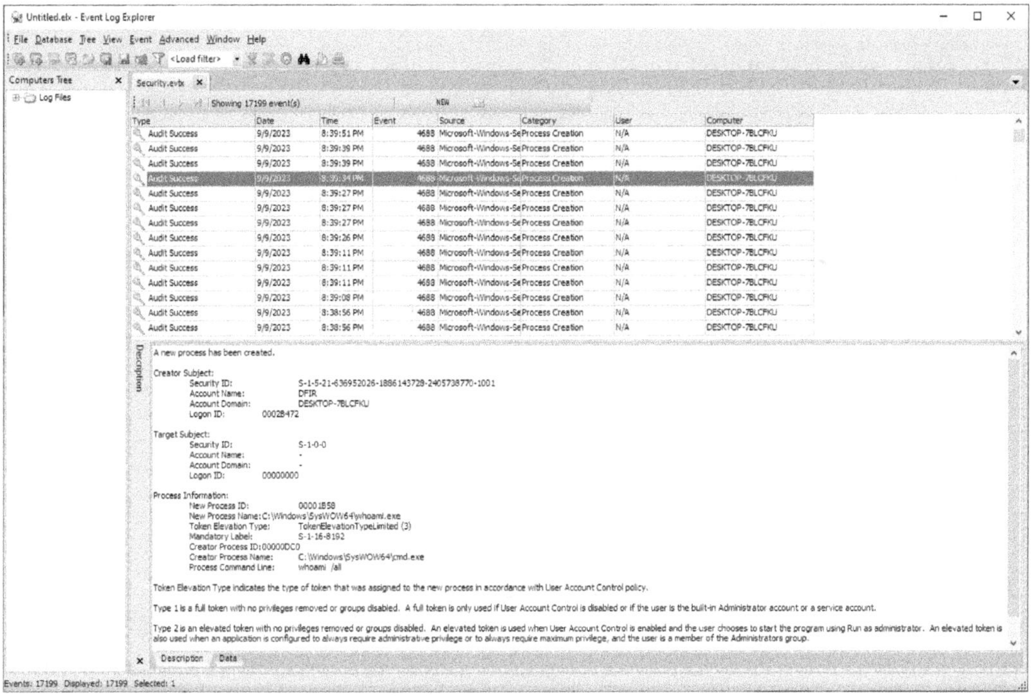

Figure 9.52: whoami execution

Then, we can see the execution of `Mimikatz` by `powershll.exe`.

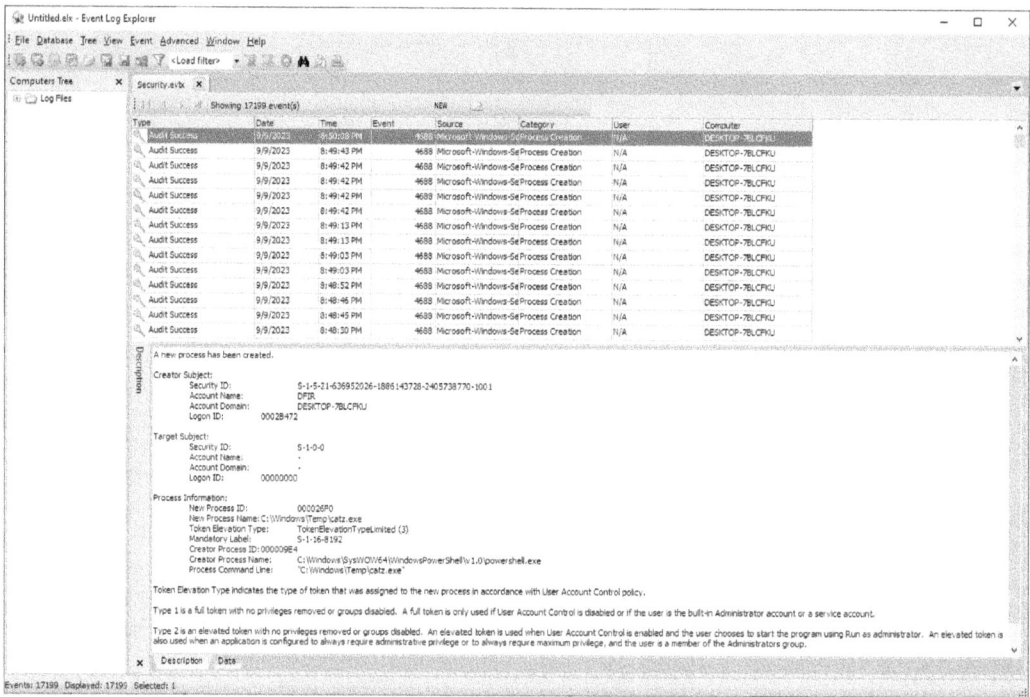

Figure 9.53: catz.exe execution

Another interesting finding is that `certutil.exe` was used to download the binary called `cat.exe`, which is the renamed version of `nc.exe`.

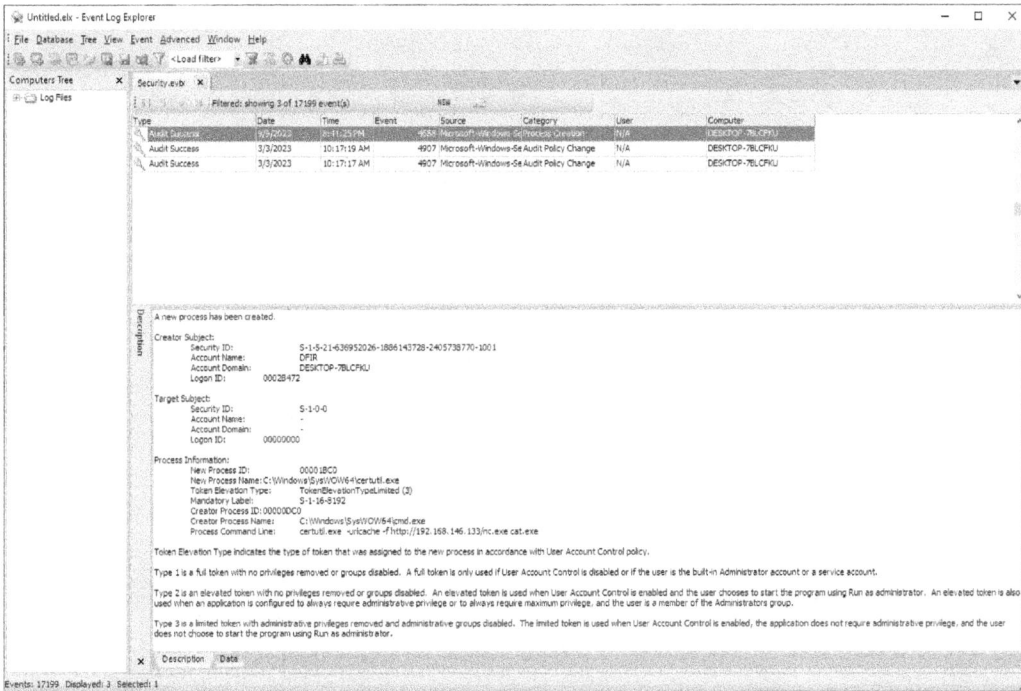

Figure 9.54: nc.exe present within security events

8. By filtering `cat.exe`, we can see an outbound connection toward the same IP address
    (`192.168.146.133`) over port `4455` as a reverse shell.

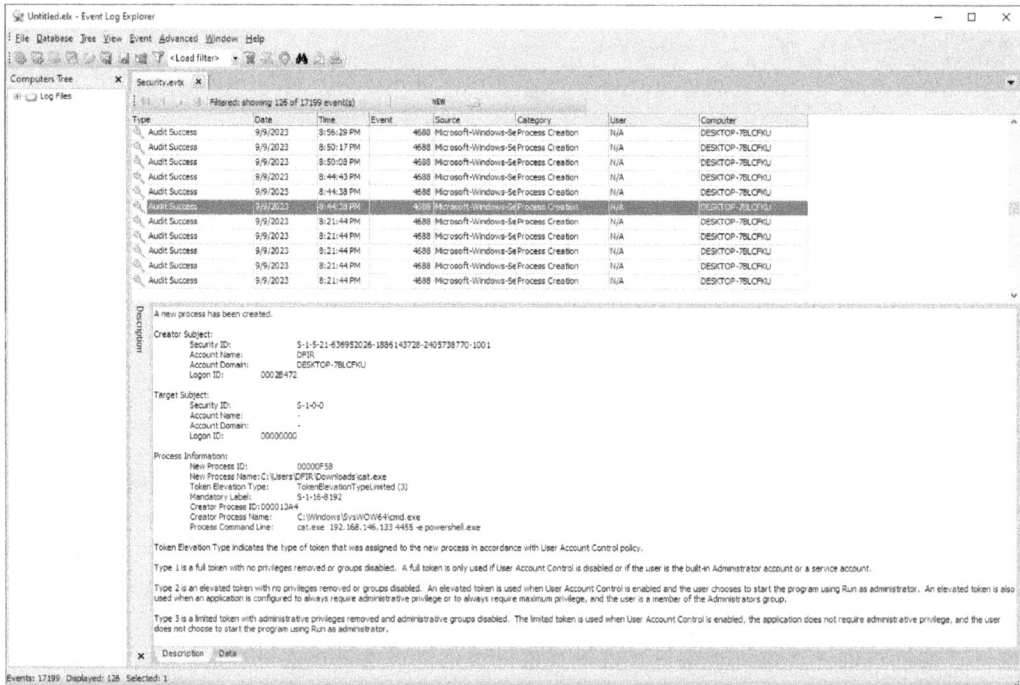

Figure 9.55: Usage of cat.exe for reverse shell

After gathering all of the evidence using Windows artifacts, we can conclude that this incident had two stages. The first is delivering `svch0st.exe` to the endpoint and gaining initial access. Afterward, the threat actor used `certutil.exe` to download multiple binaries to gain admin rights.

This was a simple demonstration of how to utilize Windows artifacts to correlate evidence and build up your theory to provide a proper investigation. In reality, when we are dealing with cyber criminals or cases related to human rights, we need to make sure that our presented evidence is accurate as someone's life might depend on our analysis. Always double-check with multiple tools to verify and validate the results.

Additional forensic artifacts exercises

In this part, we will apply what we have learned so far. Try to work on the following exercises:

1. Load your PST file into Kernel PST viewer.

2. Using `Security.evtx`, explore and track user activity using event IDs 4624 and 4625.

3. Track an application crash using `application.evtx`.

4. Parse `system.evtx` using `Evtxcmd.exe` and save the output into a CSV file.

5. Parse `SRUMDB.dat` for your local machine using `SRUM_DUMP` and map network activity using Windows Registry by identifying the profile ID.

Summary

In this chapter, we explored two crucial areas of digital forensics: email forensics and Windows event log forensics.

Email forensics involves the analysis of email communications to uncover valuable evidence in legal, corporate, and law enforcement investigations. We learned about the significance of email headers, which provide crucial information such as sender and recipient details, timestamps, and routing information. By analyzing email headers, forensic analysts can determine the legitimacy of messages and identify potential threats, such as phishing attacks.

Windows event log forensics focuses on extracting and analyzing events recorded in Windows event logs to reconstruct activities and detect security incidents. We examined different types of Windows event logs, such as security, application, and system logs, and their importance in tracking user activities, system events, application errors, and security-related incidents.

Both email forensics and Windows event log forensics play integral roles in digital investigations, providing investigators with valuable insights and evidence. By leveraging these forensic techniques, analysts can enhance their understanding of digital interactions, uncover malicious activities, and contribute to the successful resolution of cases.

In this final chapter of the book, we've dived deep into the world of digital forensics and covered the vast landscape of Windows system and user activities.

As we draw the curtains on this comprehensive journey, we extend our gratitude to you, the reader, for embarking exploration of digital forensics with us in this book.

This book was crafted with the intention of teaching and equipping you with the knowledge and tools needed to become a digital forensic examiner. This journey includes everything from the initial acquisition of digital evidence to the intricate analysis conducted within the digital domain.

As a reminder, it is not only the technical skills that help you to be a better forensic examiner but also the analytical mindset, which peels away layers of complexity to reveal the truth. It is about understanding each artifact and constructing your conclusion based on it.

As you continue your journey beyond this book, remember that the field of digital forensics is ever-evolving; technology changes, attackers adapt, and new challenges will arise. Embrace the journey and hold onto the spirit of continuous learning and curiosity that has brought you this far in this book. Also, stay attuned to the latest tools and technology.

As a forensic examiner leaves no stone unturned, always approach your work with thought and commitment, whether you are working in digital forensics for law enforcement, cybersecurity, or any realm in which digital evidence plays a major role.

Index

‹packt›

Packtpub.com

Subscribe to our online digital library for full access to over 7,000 books and videos, as well as industry leading tools to help you plan your personal development and advance your career. For more information, please visit our website.

Why subscribe?

- Spend less time learning and more time coding with practical eBooks and Videos from over 4,000 industry professionals

- Improve your learning with Skill Plans built especially for you

- Get a free eBook or video every month

- Fully searchable for easy access to vital information

- Copy and paste, print, and bookmark content

Did you know that Packt offers eBook versions of every book published, with PDF and ePub files available? You can upgrade to the eBook version at packtpub.com and as a print book customer, you are entitled to a discount on the eBook copy. Get in touch with us at customercare@packtpub.com for more details.

At www.packtpub.com, you can also read a collection of free technical articles, sign up for a range of free newsletters, and receive exclusive discounts and offers on Packt books and eBooks.

Other Books You May Enjoy

If you enjoyed this book, you may be interested in these other books by Packt:

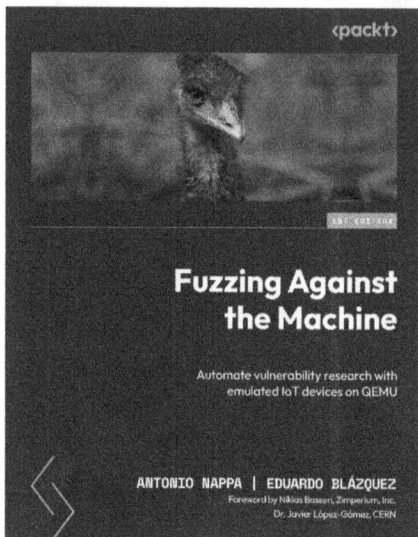

Fuzzing Against the Machine

Antonio Nappa, Eduardo Blázquez

ISBN: 978-1-80461-497-6

- Understand the difference between emulation and virtualization
- Discover the importance of emulation and fuzzing in cybersecurity
- Get to grips with fuzzing an entire operating system
- Discover how to inject a fuzzer into proprietary firmware
- Know the difference between static and dynamic fuzzing
- Look into combining QEMU with AFL and AFL++
- Explore Fuzz peripherals such as modems
- Find out how to identify vulnerabilities in OpenWrt

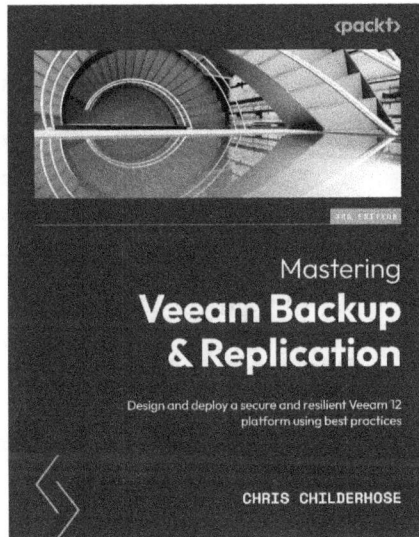

Mastering Veeam Backup Replication - Third Edition

Chris Childerhose

ISBN: 978-1-83763-009-7

- Understand installing and upgrading Veeam to v12
- Master the ability to use PostgreSQL for databases
- Explore SOBR – Direct to Object storage in performance tier
- Explore enhanced security, including MFA and Auto-Logoff
- Understand NAS Backup with Immutability Support
- Discover how GDP to vCD works for Cloud Connect
- Learn how to get instant VM Recovery on VCC

Packt is searching for authors like you

If you're interested in becoming an author for Packt, please visit `authors.packtpub.com` and apply today. We have worked with thousands of developers and tech professionals, just like you, to help them share their insight with the global tech community. You can make a general application, apply for a specific hot topic that we are recruiting an author for, or submit your own idea.

Share Your Thoughts

Now you've finished *Windows Forensics Analyst Field Guide*, we'd love to hear your thoughts! Scan the QR code below to go straight to the Amazon review page for this book and share your feedback or leave a review on the site that you purchased it from.

`https://packt.link/r/1803248475`

Your review is important to us and the tech community and will help us make sure we're delivering excellent quality content.

Download a free PDF copy of this book

Thanks for purchasing this book!

Do you like to read on the go but are unable to carry your print books everywhere?

Is your eBook purchase not compatible with the device of your choice?

Don't worry, now with every Packt book you get a DRM-free PDF version of that book at no cost.

Read anywhere, any place, on any device. Search, copy, and paste code from your favorite technical books directly into your application.

The perks don't stop there, you can get exclusive access to discounts, newsletters, and great free content in your inbox daily

Follow these simple steps to get the benefits:

1. Scan the QR code or visit the link below

https://packt.link/free-ebook/9781803248479

2. Submit your proof of purchase
3. That's it! We'll send your free PDF and other benefits to your email directly